TRANSFORMING ADDICTION

"*Transforming Addiction: Gender, Trauma, Transdisciplinarity* is a much-welcomed contribution, showing us quite clearly that transdisciplinarity is the future in the addiction field. Its approach is transformative, compelling, and of great use to addiction researchers, educators, and mental health professionals."

—**Elizabeth Ettorre**, PhD, Professor of Sociology, University of Liverpool

"*Transforming Addiction* is a significant contribution to the literature on women and addictive disorders. It challenges us to integrate research from numerous disciplines in order to improve treatment services. This edited volume is a useful text for both researchers and clinical practitioners. It moves us out of the historical, single-focused approach to addiction and applies a wider lens to enable us to view the multifaceted complexity of women's addiction."

—**Stephanie S. Covington**, PhD, LCSW, Author, *Helping Women Recover: A Program for Treating Addiction, Beyond Trauma: A Healing Journey for Women*, and *A Woman's Way Through the Twelve Steps*

"This book weaves together the threads of trauma, addiction, mental health and gender in original and exciting ways. Different professional groups, each with their own unique skills and expertise, can together develop ways of working that are more effective than the sum of the individual parts, yet, in many countries this still does not happen. This book provides innovative and practical approaches to making it happen."

—**Moira Plant**, Emerita Professor of Alcohol Studies, University of the West of England

Addiction is a complex problem that requires more nuanced responses. *Transforming Addiction* advances addictions research and treatment by promoting transdisciplinary collaboration, the integration of sex and gender, and issues of trauma and mental health. The authors demonstrate these shifts and offer a range of tools, methods, and strategies for responding to the complex factors and forces that produce and shape addiction. In addition to providing practical examples of innovation from a range of perspectives, the contributors demonstrate how addiction spans biological, social, environmental, and economic realms. *Transforming Addiction* is a call to action, and represents some of the most provocative ways of thinking about addiction research, treatment, and policy in the contemporary era.

Lorraine Greaves, PhD, is a medical sociologist, Senior Investigator at the British Columbia Centre of Excellence for Women's Health in Vancouver, Canada, and its former executive director from 1997–2009.

Nancy Poole, PhD, is Director of Research and Knowledge Translation at the British Columbia Centre of Excellence for Women's Health in Vancouver, Canada.

Ellexis Boyle, PhD, is Director of the Intersections of Mental Health Perspectives in Addictions Research Training program at the British Columbia Centre of Excellence for Women's Health in Vancouver, Canada.

TRANSFORMING ADDICTION

Gender, Trauma, Transdisciplinarity

Edited by
Lorraine Greaves
Nancy Poole
Ellexis Boyle

First published 2015
by Routledge
711 Third Avenue, New York, NY 10017

and by Routledge
27 Church Road, Hove, East Sussex BN3 2FA

Routledge is an imprint of the Taylor & Francis Group, an informa business

© 2015 Taylor & Francis

The right of the editors to be identified as the authors of the editorial material, and of the authors for their individual chapters, has been asserted in accordance with sections 77 and 78 of the Copyright, Designs and Patents Act 1988.

All rights reserved. No part of this book may be reprinted or reproduced or utilized in any form or by any electronic, mechanical, or other means, now known or hereafter invented, including photocopying and recording, or in any information storage or retrieval system, without permission in writing from the publishers.

Trademark notice: Product or corporate names may be trademarks or registered trademarks, and are used only for identification and explanation without intent to infringe.

Library of Congress Cataloging-in-Publication Data
Greaves, Lorraine. Transforming addiction : gender, trauma, transdisciplinarity / Lorraine Greaves, Nancy Poole, Ellexis Boyle. — 1 Edition.
 pages cm
 Includes bibliographical references and index.
 1. Substance abuse. 2. Substance abuse—Treatment. 3. Drug addiction. 4. Drug addiction—Treatment. I. Poole, Nancy. II. Boyle, Ellexis. III. Title.
 HV4998.G74
 2015616.86'06—dc23   2014043155

ISBN: 978-1-138-82878-0 (hbk)
ISBN: 978-1-138-82879-7 (pbk)
ISBN: 978-1-315-73808-6 (ebk)

Typeset in Bembo
by Apex CoVantage, LLC

Printed and bound in the United States of America by Publishers Graphics, LLC on sustainably sourced paper.

CONTENTS

Preface ix
Acknowledgements xv
List of Contributors xvii

PART 1
What Is the Promise of Transdisciplinarity? 1

1 Cracking the Problem of Addiction with a
  Transformative Approach 3
  Lorraine Greaves, Nancy Poole and Ellexis Boyle

2 Fostering Transdisciplinarity in Addictions Research Training 20
  Ellexis Boyle, Mary Elizabeth Snow and Nicole Vittoz

3 Integrating Trauma with Addiction Research and Treatment 36
  Nancy Poole

4 Of Mice and Wo/Men: Transdisciplinarity in the Laboratory 50
  *Travis E. Baker, Vivian Lam, Ni Lan, Kristina Andrea Uban
  and Joanne Weinberg*

5 Two-Eyed Seeing in Indigenous Addiction
  Research and Treatment 69
  Laura Hall

PART 2
How Does Transdisciplinarity Work?   77

6   Linking Addiction, Gender and Trauma in the Neonatal
Intensive Care Unit   79
Lenora Marcellus

7   Bridging the Biological and the Social in Neuroscience   97
Gillian Einstein

8   Moving towards Transdisciplinarity in Research
with Marginalized Populations   107
Iris Torchalla, Verena Strehlau, Erika Neilson and Michael Krausz

9   Using Reflexivity to Achieve Transdisciplinarity
in Nursing and Social Work   120
Nancy Clark, Ingrid Handlovsky and Deborah Sinclair

10   Trauma and Transdisciplinarity in Women's
Addiction Treatment   137
Denise Bradshaw

11   Expanding Systematic Reviews Using Transdisciplinarity   143
Natalie Hemsing, Lorraine Greaves and Nancy Poole

PART 3
What is the Future of Transdisciplinarity?   159

12   Migrating toward Transdisciplinarity in Addiction Treatment   161
Peter Selby

13   Building a Theoretical Bridge for Transdisciplinary Exchange   167
*Alina Sotskova, Cecilia Benoit, Lauren Casey, Bernadette Pauly
and Barna Konkolÿ Thege*

14   The Challenge of Trans-sectoral Policy in Pregnancy
and Addiction   184
Lorraine Greaves

15	Enlarging Knowledge Translation to Reflect Transdisciplinarity *Nancy Poole and Lorraine Greaves*	203
16	The Future of Transdisciplinarity in Addiction *Lorraine Greaves, Nancy Poole and Ellexis Boyle*	216

Index *225*

PREFACE

Transforming Addiction: Gender, Trauma and Transdisciplinarity is about altering our approach to studying and treating addiction. It recognizes that addiction is a complex problem, and one that requires multiple and more nuanced perspectives than it usually receives. Addiction is often seen through one particular disciplinary lens or viewpoint, which works to favor some understandings above others. Worse, a singular approach can create divisions that do not ultimately serve the individuals or societies dealing with addiction. We think that fostering transdisciplinarity in order to transform research, practice and training will assist in broadening our knowledge and action on addiction and ultimately, lead to better treatment.

The origins for this book emerge from a twelve-year research and education group IMPART (this first stood for Integrated Mentor Program in Addictions Research Training, and later, Intersections of Mental Health Perspectives in Addictions Research Training). The program began in 2003 and was funded by the Canadian Institutes of Health Research. Its intent was to train more researchers in Canada in gender, women and addiction. Our approach was to create a transdisciplinary research training program and a community of scholars and practitioners who focused on the development of methods and frameworks integrating sex, gender, mental health and trauma in addictions research. While there was an initial emphasis on women's health, this broadened to a gender and health perspective over time.

The IMPART program brought together over 100 mentors and trainees, from across North America and from a wide range of disciplines, research pillars and sectors, towards the development of transdisciplinary and transformative approaches that could better address the problem of addiction. This book is part of the legacy of IMPART, and includes many contributions from members of the IMPART program.

In this book, we highlight a transformative approach to addiction research, education and treatment by showing the value of bringing multiple disciplines and sectors to bear on addiction issues. We also demonstrate the inclusion of sex and gender in all aspects of research and treatment, and the value of an integrated response that recognizes the many issues often linked with addiction such as trauma, violence and mental health. There are varied contributions from a range of players and sectors: from lab researchers to clinicians, from social policy critics to knowledge translation experts.

One theme is dominant: transdisciplinarity. Each of the chapters in this book considers and provides insight into how transdisciplinarity can be successfully achieved in different research areas, contexts, issues, and at various levels. *Transforming Addiction* brings together authors and interviewees who have been researching, practicing, teaching, treating or thinking about transdisciplinary principles in a range of settings and confronting a range of addiction-related issues.

We recommend that transdisciplinarity be adopted as an overarching framework in addiction for bridging conversations among multiple disciplines, sectors, stakeholders and perspectives. The challenge of creating shared theories, methods, language, themes or perspectives with which to approach addiction problems is still a frontier, but one important to explore and cross. Accurately and appropriately, including sex and gender represents the crux of blending biology and sociology and is a critical dimension of creating better science and, ultimately, more nuanced and tailored treatment. Acknowledging the many issues that are related to addiction, such as trauma, violence and mental health is also crucial, but often overlooked, as these factors often play a role in the problem and persistence of addiction.

This book is organized into 3 main sections: (1) What is the promise of transdisciplinarity? (2) How does transdisciplinarity work? and (3) What is "the future of transdisciplinarity" in addiction? Taken together, the chapters in each section explore the various challenges and outcomes of using transdisciplinarity in addictions research, treatment, training and policy. Each section contains chapters by collaborative teams of researchers and clinical experts who span diverse research pillars, from cell to society, and multiple health sectors, from research to services and policy.

In Part 1, authors address the promise of transdisciplinarity, by first noting some historical approaches to addiction, the challenges in identifying its causation and how transdisciplinarity is long overdue in research, training and practice. In Chapter 1, the editors open the conversation by discussing a range of approaches to addiction and make the argument that we must collectively think differently in order to truly crack the problem of addiction. In addition to summarizing key works and frameworks that have offered ways to consider the problem, they argue that three key elements—sex and gender, integrated responses and transdisciplinarity—are the keys to moving the addiction field forward. In

Chapter 2, Boyle and colleagues describe research training approaches that build transdisciplinary communities and utilize innovative pedagogy and knowledge translation strategies to support communication and practice. They suggest that among the key benefits of transdisciplinary research training is enhanced ability to respond to the complexity of addiction.

In Chapter 3, Poole demonstrates how the concept of trauma is defined and considered very differently by each discipline. She uses two examples of addressing trauma in research and practice to illustrate the need for fusing understandings of trauma to reach transdisciplinary understanding in the context of addiction. In Chapter 4, Weinberg and colleagues explain how a laboratory focused on research with animal models to investigate fetal alcohol spectrum disorder consciously reaches towards a more transdisciplinary model. The team integrates insights about trauma and mental health in human research into animal model laboratory research, recognizing sex differences along the way. In Chapter 5, Laura Hall discusses the logistics and potential of "Two-Eyed Seeing" bringing Indigenous perspectives together with Western discipline-based approaches to better understand addiction, gender and trauma. This approach broadens the view of responding to and researching addictions and consciously merges Indigenous approaches with "mainstream" understandings.

In Part 2, authors address the logistics of how to do transdisciplinary work. They present several examples of grappling with transdisciplinarity in a range of settings and issues, but all focusing on the challenges of merging thoughts, methods and disciplines. In Chapter 6, Marcellus, a nurse and researcher, takes us to the NICU (neonatal intensive care unit) to artfully critique prevailing approaches to treating neonates born to mothers with addiction issues. She reframes NICU practices by applying gender considerations and linking the multiple factors that shape women's addiction as a platform for challenging currently accepted family-centered and developmental approaches in NICU care that are sex and gender blind. Chapter 7 recounts an interview with Gillian Einstein, a neuroscientist, who explains that integrating sex and gender is essential to transdisciplinarity as it fuses biological and social understandings. She describes crossing this bridge by creating a transdisciplinary team and methods for her research on the links between the brain and body, illustrated by her study on female genital cutting. The application of this research to addiction, plus Einstein's thoughts on how doing transdisciplinary work has changed her, are both inspirational and pragmatic.

This theme of reaching for and integrating methods, issues and disciplinary perspectives is continued in Chapter 8, where Torchalla and colleagues discuss their research on mental health, trauma, gender and homelessness. They share their experiences in three projects and how they needed to recognize and reach out to cross-disciplinary and cross-sectoral colleagues who could help them integrate and better grapple with the complexities related to gender, trauma, homelessness and mental health. In Chapter 9, Clark and colleagues focus on the importance of reflexivity as a technique for dual identified researcher–practitioners as nurses and social workers. They illustrate how critical reflexivity and understanding intersectionality are key strategies for both researchers and practitioners engaged in interdisciplinary and transdisciplinary work.

In Chapter 10, Denise Bradshaw, a social worker and director of a women's addiction treatment center, reflects on her practice in an interview with the editors, and explains how trauma-informed care and gender concerns lie at the heart of implementing inter- and transdisciplinary approaches in treatment contexts. In Chapter 11, Hemsing, Greaves and Poole demonstrate the value of applying transdisciplinarity to evidence reviews, drawing on two reviews of interventions to address smoking and alcohol use during pregnancy. They describe how they extended standard systematic review methodology by expanding the breadth of evidence, inviting perspectives from different sectors and integrating evidence from contextual factors that enhanced resulting recommendations.

In Part 3, we consider the future of transdisciplinarity. Contributors meditate on the future of transdisciplinarity and key strategies for moving forward. In Chapter 12, Peter Selby discusses his work in the area of tobacco cessation, pregnancy and gender in relation to the concept of transdisciplinarity. He shares his own journey to adopting transdisciplinarity shaped by experiences of migration and belonging and suggests that transdisciplinarity is a Renaissance concept that may be fully embraced by future generations of researchers and clinicians. In Chapter 13, Sotskova and colleagues illustrate how collectively adopting a theory, such as meaning management theory, can be a bridge for connecting the perspectives of multiple practitioners and researchers. They identify some 'givens' that emerge from this theory that assist in understanding and responding to addiction.

In Chapter 14, Greaves takes up the possibility of applying transdisciplinarity and intersectoral approaches to developing programs and policy. She uses the example of responding to substance use during pregnancy, a typically contentious area, and argues that trans-sectoral policy development is the policy version of transdisciplinarity and could work to enhance our response. In Chapter 15, Poole and Greaves argue that transdisciplinarity not only fulfills a key need in addictions research and treatment but also demands advanced approaches to knowledge translation. They suggest that a fine balance of multiple forms of evidence, capacity to meaningfully factor in multiple contexts for application to practice, and policy and skilled facilitation of wide, multisector engagement is necessary for effective knowledge translation of transdisciplinary content in addiction. Finally, in Chapter 16, the editors consider the challenges and facilitators for including transdisciplinary, sex and gender and a more integrated approach to addiction can offer hope for a more integrated field, improving future treatment and policy responses to the problem of addiction. Along with practical insights into the benefits and challenges of bridging gaps between disciplines, fields and sectors, all the authors provide further resources for discussion and further readings after each chapter.

As *Transforming Addiction* suggests, this book offers concepts, methods, material and thinking to *challenge* prevailing unidisciplinary approaches to addiction that stand to advance knowledge and practice. This book provides a cutting edge and contemporary look at addictions research and training from a transdisciplinary collaborative perspective that reflects addiction in its complexity. By providing practical frameworks, theories, methods, and examples, *Transforming Addiction* advances the field of addictions research and training beyond unidisciplinary, uni-problem, and sex and/or gender-blind efforts. In doing so, it is hoped that this book inspires researchers, practitioners, clinicians, policy makers and students alike to reconsider their approaches to addiction, and ultimately to shift their work to better benefit the overall health and well-being of women and men, boys and girls.

Lorraine Greaves, Nancy Poole and Ellexis Boyle
September 2014
Vancouver, Canada

ACKNOWLEDGEMENTS

We thank the Canadian Institutes of Health Research, especially the Institute of Gender and Health, for their funding support in establishing the training program that forms the bedrock for this book. This book reflects a twelve-year program of research and research education aimed at shifting addictions research, education, practice and policy to account for women and girls. The program, Intersections of Mental Health Perspectives and Addictions Research Training (IMPART), supported numerous trainees over the years, and was funded by the Canadian Institutes of Health Research, Strategic Training Initiative in Health Research (STIHR), a national training program for health researchers.

We also thank the trainees and mentors involved in IMPART over the years representing numerous disciplines, sectors, clinical areas, universities, hospitals and communities for their engagement and contributions to the IMPART community. IMPART brought together over 100 mentors and trainees from across Canada with expertise in the areas of addiction, mental health, sex, gender, trauma and violence. We also thank the directors and coordinators of the IMPART program, particularly, Barbara Berry, Beth Snow, Nicole Vittoz and Ellexis Boyle, who offered singular insights to the program and helped develop its pedagogy, resources and profile. Together with staff and colleagues at our home base, the British Columbia Centre of Excellence for Women's Health, and our key partners, the British Columbia Women's Hospital and Health Centre, and the University of British Columbia, this community of experts has greatly contributed to the evolution of this book; its key frameworks and insights.

Finally, we also wish to thank our publisher, Routledge International, especially Marta Moldvai, for her administrative and editorial support.

Lorraine Greaves, Nancy Poole, Ellexis Boyle
Vancouver, Canada. September, 2014

CONTRIBUTORS

The Editors

Lorraine Greaves, PhD, is a medical sociologist, senior investigator at the British Columbia Centre of Excellence for Women's Health and its former executive director from 1997–2009. She is a clinical professor in the School of Population and Public Health at the University of British Columbia, and research associate with the Centre for Addiction and Mental Health in Toronto, Canada. Greaves is an international expert in tobacco use, addictions, women and gender, and violence and trauma issues.

Nancy Poole, PhD, is the director of the British Columbia Centre of Excellence for Women's Health in Vancouver. She is known for her work related to women and alcohol and tobacco use, Aboriginal women's health, prevention of fetal alcohol spectrum disorder (FASD), trauma-informed practice and knowledge generation and exchange within virtual networks and communities of inquiry.

Ellexis Boyle, PhD, is director of the Intersections of Mental Health Perspectives in Addictions Research Training program and a research associate at the British Columbia Centre of Excellence for Women's Health. Her research examines the socio-historical construction of the body and power with a particular focus on gender, race and class.

Contributors

Travis E. Baker, PhD, is a postdoctoral fellow at CHE Sainte-Justine Children's Hospital Research Center, University of Montreal. He uses a variety of neuroimaging techniques to investigate neurobiological mechanisms underlying cognitive control and decision making in humans, and how these functions are disrupted in clinical populations' substance use disorders.

Cecilia Benoit, PhD, is a professor in the Department of Sociology and Scientist at the Centre for Addictions Research of BC. She investigates the health of different vulnerable groups, including Aboriginal women, young people confronting health stigmas linked to obesity and asthma, street-involved youth, workers in lower-prestige service occupations and pregnant and parenting women dealing with addiction issues.

Denise Bradshaw, MSW, is a social worker and program director of Heartwood Centre for Women, a program of BC Mental Health & Substance Use Services (BCMHSUS), located at the British Columbia Women's Hospital in Vancouver.

Lauren Casey, MA, is a PhD candidate in the University of Victoria's Social Dimensions of Health program. She is an advocate for the health and well-being of vulnerable populations, especially relating to substance abuse, sex work and women's health. She has developed and delivered successful government-funded harm reduction programs and has been interviewed by radio, print and television media about these issues.

Nancy Clark, PhD, RN, is a community mental health nurse in Vancouver inner city. She has a special interest in the intersections of gender, migration and mental health. Her work examines the community capacity to support Karen refugee women's mental health and well-being in the context of resettlement.

Gillian Einstein, PhD, is a professor in the Department of Psychology and the Dalla Lana School of Public Health at the University of Toronto. She is founder and director of the Collaborative Graduate Program in Women's Health. Her current research spans memory, pain, sex/gender representations in the nervous system, cultural practices, and understanding the nervous system and identity, self and feminism.

Laura Hall, MA, is of Haudenosaunee/English-Canadian descent and is working toward completion of a PhD in environmental studies on the importance of Indigenous gendered and temporal understandings within movements and studies of sustainable community development.

Ingrid Handlovsky, MSc, RN, is a PhD candidate in the School of Nursing at the University of British Columbia. Her research focuses on structural factors affecting health care practices and experiences and the influence of sexual identity and gender on the health management practices and health care experiences of men who identify as gay.

Natalie Hemsing, MA, is a research associate at the British Columbia Centre of Excellence for Women's Health. She specializes in research on sex- and gender-based analysis, smoking prevention, cessation and tobacco policy among diverse populations, and systematic reviews and knowledge syntheses.

Michael Krausz, MD, PhD, FRCPC, is professor of psychiatry, epidemiology and public health at the University of British Columbia and program director for addiction psychiatry. His clinical and academic focus is on innovative health-care solutions for the most vulnerable urban populations.

Vivian Lam, BSc, is a PhD candidate in neuroscience at the University of British Columbia. She uses a rat model of fetal alcohol spectrum disorder to investigate the impact of prenatal exposure to alcohol on stress responsivity and mental health in adulthood, with a particular interest in sex differences in brain and behavior.

Ni Lan, PhD, is a research associate at the University of British Columbia. Her expertise lies in the areas of stress, fetal programming and neuroendocrine function, with a particular focus on sex differences in offspring outcomes and roles of sex steroids on brain function.

Lenora Marcellus, PhD, is an associate professor in the School of Nursing at the University of Victoria and a member of the Canada FASD Partnership Network Action Team on Prevention from a Women's Health Determinants Perspective. Her research interests include substance use during pregnancy, neonatal withdrawal and infants in foster care.

Erika Neilson, MPH, has a master of public health degree from the University of British Columbia and a BAH in international development from the University of Guelph. She is currently a research coordinator for the Addictions and Concurrent Disorders team at the Centre for Health Evaluation and Outcome Sciences.

Bernadette Pauly, RN, PhD, is an associate professor in the School of Nursing and a Scientist at the Centre for Addictions Research of BC at the University of Victoria. Her work focuses on the conduct of community–university research that addresses health equity, substance use, harm reduction and homelessness.

Peter Selby, MD, MBBS, CCFP, MHSc, FASAM, is a professor in the departments of Family and Community Medicine and Psychiatry and the Dalla Lana School of Public Health, and the chief and clinician scientist of the Addictions Division at the Centre for Addiction and Mental Health (CAMH). His research and clinical work includes smoking cessation in pregnant women, people with co-morbid conditions and web-based interventions.

Deborah Sinclair, MSW, RSW, is a PhD candidate at the Factor-Inwentash Faculty of Social Work at the University of Toronto. Her involvement in the social justice and feminist movements has been as a social work activist, clinician, writer, public speaker, trainer, researcher, community organizer and expert witness on the prevention of and recovery from domestic violence.

Mary Elizabeth Snow, PhD, is the program evaluation lead at the Centre for Health Evaluation and Outcome Sciences (CHÉOS) and an adjunct professor in the Faculty of Health Sciences at Simon Fraser University. She was a former director of the IMPART program between 2007–2009.

Alina Sotskova, MA, PhD (c), is a doctoral student in clinical psychology at the University of Victoria. Her research and clinical interests span the intersections of substance misuse, aggression, trauma, post-traumatic stress and existential psychology and philosophy.

Verena Strehlau, PhD, is Psychiatry resident at the University of British Columbia in Vancouver, Canada. Prior to her residency, she completed a postdoctoral research fellowship working with homeless populations, including homeless women who are living with psychiatric illness and are using substances.

Barna Konkolÿ Thege, PhD, is a postdoctoral fellow at the Addictive Behaviours Laboratory, University of Calgary, Canada. His research interests focus on psychometrics, epidemiology of addictions and the role of existential concerns in the development, maintenance and quitting of substance-related and behavioural addictions.

Iris Torchalla, PhD, FRAC, is a clinical psychologist with the Resilience over Psychological Trauma (RoPT) program at the OrionHealth Vancouver Pain Clinic, and a scientist with the Centre for Health Evaluation and Outcome Sciences (CHÉOS) in Vancouver. Her research is on women's mental health and substance use behaviors, trauma and integrated trauma-informed interventions.

Kristina Andrea Uban, PhD, is a postdoctoral trainee at Children's Hospital Los Angeles. Her research and expertise in developmental neuroscience is focused on substance use disorders, stress and the effects of prenatal alcohol exposure on the developing brain.

Nicole Vittoz, PhD, is a faculty member in the Psychology Department at Douglas College, New Westminster, BC. She is a researcher and educator trained in neuroscience and psychology, with long-standing interests in the areas of drug addiction and decision making. She was a former director of IMPART program, between 2009–2011.

Joanne Weinberg, PhD, is a professor and distinguished university scholar in the Department of Cellular and Physiological Sciences at the University of British Columbia. She is also a member of the Brain Research Center, and an associate member of the Department of Psychology and of the Child and Family Research Institute at Children's Hospital. Her laboratory utilizes a rat model to examine the effects of prenatal exposure to alcohol on offspring neurobehavioral development.

PART 1
What is the Promise of Transdisciplinarity?

This section addresses some key questions affecting transformation in addictions research and treatment. Why do we need a new approach? Why are transdisciplinarity, the integration of issues such as trauma and mental health, and the inclusion of sex and gender in research and treatment, necessary? How will including these ideas assist in elevating our understanding of addiction and substance use and improve our responses? What does transdisciplinarity promise?

The introductory chapter covers the general approaches that have been proffered over the years to explain addiction and to frame societal responses to addiction. These vary widely, from punitive, legalistic approaches to public health and, harm-reduction approaches, and drawing on medicine, psychology, law, users' views and lots in between. This variance is emblematic of the wide set of opinions, voices of dissent and the mix of rational and emotional positioning on this vexing and volatile issue.

The rest of this section demonstrates the value and promise of improving our approach. Boyle and colleagues reflect on creating and managing a training program aimed at fostering a community of scholars and clinicians in taking a transdisciplinary approach. Such organized attempts to bring very different disciplines and research projects together may be the route to encouraging transdisciplinarity in education and training. As a key example of current thinking, Poole reflects on various discipline-based interpretations of the concept of trauma, noting their vast differences. She then offers two examples, one on women's service provision and one on Indigenous approaches to trauma, that offer insight into how trauma can be integrated into practice, indicating a way forward.

Weinberg and colleagues reveal how introducing sex (and gender) into rat-based laboratory work on fetal alcohol syndrome disorder contributes brand new knowledge to the field and uncovers huge gaps in biomedical science.

The idea of introducing a range of disciplines and a sex-based framework in animal research is long overdue, but this chapter shows its huge promise for improving science. Finally, in an interview with the editors, Hall discusses Two-Eyed Seeing, the idea of weaving together the insights of Indigenous and Western ways of knowing. She marks its potential for widening the understanding of addictions and contributing to transdisciplinarity in research, training and treatment.

Taken together, these seemingly disparate chapters reveal a range of attempts to make sense of, and improve upon, the current state of addiction research and treatment. They all add to the argument that transdisciplinarity matters—that it requires training and skill development, an open mind and the courage to innovate—even in discipline-based environments and varied cultural contexts. Most of all, they show the promise of transdisciplinarity in a range of contexts, from various points of view.

1
CRACKING THE PROBLEM OF ADDICTION WITH A TRANSFORMATIVE APPROACH

Lorraine Greaves, Nancy Poole and Ellexis Boyle

Addiction is a complicated, expensive, painful and sometimes tragic social problem. In the interests of seeking pleasure, altering consciousness or submersing pain, people can develop addictions to a range of substances and behaviors, often, but not always, to the point of interference with daily life, long-term aspirations and social, family and work relationships. Societies pay the burden in lost lives, productivity, crime, social and health costs.

Over the centuries, many explanations have been offered to make sense of addiction. Varied responses have been made to people with addiction, in societal reactions to addiction and in regulating the sources of various addictive substances. These have included medical, moral, legal, social, economic, cultural and religious perspectives, theories and frameworks. More contemporary responses include public-health and harm-reduction approaches, reducing the blame and shame historically applied to those with addictions, and rethinking policy, legal and justice responses to the sale and distribution of substances. But even these more contemporary approaches remain built on an historical bedrock of legal, medical and moral perspectives that are often hard to ignore.

This book is about addiction: Its vexing complexity and its hard-to-solve and hard-to-remediate effects. It is also about failure: failure of any one type of response to treating addiction or controlling addictive substances; failure to bring scientific evidence to practice in a timely fashion; failure to think about addiction and act on addiction in a consistently humane manner, free of stigma and blame; and failure to think broadly and to listen to all sectors and perspectives. This book addresses those failures with a view to transformation. In addressing failure of any kind, options can be reduced and choices narrowed, but the process can open up our thinking to more intriguing insights and higher level solutions. While this book will not solve the problem of addiction, it explores the viability of transforming our approach to addiction in research and treatment and policy, by unambiguously and consciously doing things differently.

Specifically, we advocate for taking a transdisciplinary approach in addiction treatment, research and policy. This means that all disciplinary perspectives are actively sought, welcomed and valued and a there is a conscious and shared decision to transcend, or rise above any one perspective or discipline. The effect of taking a transdisciplinary approach is not merely a melding of perspectives but the encouragement of a conscious aspiration among researchers and treatment providers to contribute to the growth of a new, transformed perspective that reflects a range of different knowledge and contributions, experiences and successes. For example, responding to alcohol overuse with knowledge derived from biomedical or clinical research alone is important, but melding such with social, cultural, psychological and legal perspectives is essential. This approach will foster the growing of a more informed and broader understanding. Indeed, all forms of scientific research are critical, but melding those with the voices of those affected, their helpers and families and program and policy developers expands the discourse to a more meaningful level.

Second, we advocate for an integrated response to addiction. This means that we pay heed to the linked issues often underlying or co-occurring with addiction, such as trauma and violence, mental health and multi-substance use. Many individuals with addiction are experiencing one or more of these issues, either in their past or present. These are some of the key reasons that addiction is so vexing, as the short-term pleasures, gratifications or escapes associated with addiction are often interwoven and knotted up with a range of other serious issues, making singular treatment or policy responses insufficient, and in some cases irrelevant. These links between adverse child experiences, addiction and trauma, violence and mental health issues are not just correlative curiosities, but rather they indicate systemic interactions that either underlie or manifest in peoples' bodies and brains, and make addiction such a tenacious phenomenon. The preponderance of these linkages, mixed with short-term rewards, often make addiction an ongoing and sticky social problem as well, defying neat solutions, prescriptions or treatments. It also means that an integrated approach to treatment and policy is crucial, one that engages multiple voices and sectors, to bring forward action on addiction.

Finally, we advocate taking sex and gender into account. Integrating sex and gender into research, programming or policy means better science, practice and public policy. This is a simple concept, and one that is finally gaining critical acceptance in several areas of health research and practice. Both of these factors are important to addiction research and treatment. Key changes in research practices, analysis, writing and reporting could illuminate the effects of sex (biological) related factors on addictive processes, and on treatment options and trajectories. Equally important, assessing gender-related factors (social and cultural), taking into account gender identity, gender relations, power structures and their concomitant limitations and expectations could illuminate the effects of gender on addiction onset and treatment. Together, these approaches take into account the biology of addiction, and the powerful forces affecting becoming and remaining addicted, as well as the gendered social aspects of addiction that are as important in becoming and remaining addicted, or seeking treatment.

These three components, transdisciplinarity, integration and taking sex and gender into account, form the backbone of this book. All of the chapters address these issues somehow, and delve into different substances, populations, issues, problems or approaches. However, shifting from unidisciplinary, gender-blind, non-integrated responses to addiction to these more complex approaches does not come easy. There is little structural support for broad transdisciplinarity in research training, or indeed in higher education or in health care systems. Some multi-and interdisciplinary approaches have been encouraged, but actively seeking to reach a new, common understanding of addiction is rarely aspired to. Further, seeking integrated solutions make sense from an individual client's perspective, and often can lead to increased interagency or interdepartmental or ministry policy development. However, creating the space for integrated solutions is typically avoided. And while integrating sex and gender into research, treatment and policy is increasingly required by funders, much addictions research and treatment still ignores these factors.

This book will demonstrate a range of efforts to try to bring these threads together. It explicitly describes training and knowledge transfer, along with research, policy and practice, in order to bring the meaning of transdisciplinarity, gender and integration to life. In discovering the essence of transdisciplinarity in relation to addiction, and explicitly recognizing real-life factors such as trauma and violence and the crucial contributions of sex and gender to better science, it is hoped that our collective understanding and response to addiction and those who experience addiction is improved, and our motivation to work across sectors and disciplines increased.

What Does Addiction Mean?

Addiction has been variously defined over the years, and the word is used in different ways by different players (Alexander 2008). These differences often reflect position, location or discipline, but also evolve in cultural contexts over time. Often, uses of the word *addiction* reflect prior beliefs, training or value positions. While often focused on the overuse of alcohol, tobacco and drugs to the point of dependence, there are increasing numbers of behaviors that get labeled as addictive such as sex, eating and gambling, stretching the boundaries of meaning of the term. Schaef (1987, p.19) usefully distinguishes between substance addictions (where ingestion occurs) and process addictions (such as accumulating money, workaholism, worry). But, according to Alexander (Alexander 2008, pp. 41–42), the use of the term *addiction* can be exploited, taking away from the essential meaning of addiction as a practice or phenomenon that is destructive to individuals and societies.

What Understandings of Addiction Have Been Proffered?

There are some entrenched explanatory views of addiction that present themselves as threads in our social discourse and shape our collective and individual understandings (Schaef and Fassel 1988). Historically, addiction has been viewed through a moral lens, invoking issues of weakness or depravity, or in other cases a religious lens, invoking issues of evil, sin or sloth. In these frameworks, people with addiction and mental health issues have suffered through the imposition of stigma, isolation and in some cases, punishment, incarceration or sterilization. Both addiction and mental illnesses have been associated with weak characters and moral depravity, and often associated violence and poverty have exacerbated these views. These perspectives rarely led to humane and treatment-oriented responses.

These historical attitudes have supported a legal framework surrounding the issue of addiction that has often largely focused on demand for, and control of, addictive substances. It highlights damage done to society and individuals but also aims to control addiction, by curtailing or limiting access to drugs, alcohol, tobacco or other substances and opportunities, such as gambling. In addition, there have been evolving legal and judicial responses to those who use addictive substances and exhibit negative behaviors such as violence, drunk driving, public intoxication, illegal sales or selling to minors. Such regimes have varied in their punitiveness or liberalness, and are, like any norms, subject to change over time. Depending on social values and cultural context, responses, legal or otherwise, vary in their coerciveness and severity.

A more recent framework is the disease model, first proposed by Jellinek (1960) rendering addiction as an illness, requiring treatment, or, in some cases, a medical response. From this perspective, addiction is commonly perceived as a disease that overtakes an individual: a viewpoint put forth by organizations such as Alcoholics Anonymous and its various offshoots. Many addictions professionals also use this approach and see the disease of addiction as chronic and persistent, rendering an individual 'sick' and in need of continuing care in hospitals, clinics, treatment centers and doctor's offices. This view of addiction is not benign, having significant effects on health systems, social perceptions of addictions and on people with substance use issues. It places addiction firmly in the category of illnesses, albeit one still very stigmatized. More fundamentally, it suggests that addiction controls individuals' behaviors and actions, often requiring a blend of treatment, containment and sometimes separation or seclusion. The disease model of addiction engages medicine, psychiatry, psychology, nursing, and social work. It places addiction as an inhabitant of the person's genes, brains or body. It implies that addiction needs to be controlled, often by controlling the individual, especially when the disease is out of control and behaviors appear to be dysfunctional.

There are those who reject these approaches, preferring to suggest that the disease model is ultimately disempowering (Peele 1987), as it ignores the impact of social and cultural values and influences and the impact of values on individual choices. This perspective also references those who are not addicted, despite having similar circumstances, or those (some say the majority) of people with addiction problems who successfully recover without intervention, or "on their own." Peele suggests that processes of addiction and the myriad of circumstances, value positions and choices that go into the development of addiction can also be key to recovery, in that individuals can reflect on these elements in self directed recovery processes, preferably in a context of harm reduction and empowerment (The Fix 2011). In this way, his position implicates individual, cultural and social differences in values as critically important in making decisions about substance use and recovery, among other addictive behaviors.

Though perspectives inevitably shift and change, threads of these approaches persist in assumptions and stereotypes about addiction and those challenged by it. It is not unusual for individuals with addiction to be met with anger, frustration, stigma and shunning, with assumptions about strength of "will," and weakness of personality still prevalent in general discourse and social response. While these attitudes are being addressed and challenged in contemporary society, and direct attempts being made to destigmatize addiction (and mental illness) residuals of these attitudes still emerge in casual conversation and media coverage.

Contemporary Thinking on Addiction

There are numerous contemporary approaches to explaining addiction that build on these general approaches, illustrating the complexities and contradictions of addiction and, in some cases, our responses to addiction. For example, Bickel and Potenza (2006) suggest that addiction is a multicomponent phenomenon that has its roots in evolutionary principles. They suggest that evolutionary-old portions of the brain are implicated in addiction: areas that reinforce food, sex, drink and social interaction (2006, p. 10) and that more recently evolved areas of the brain, such as the frontal cortical regions, are less implicated. In this sense, addiction can be understood as adaptive and survival-oriented. This perspective is a useful addition to our understanding, in that it identifies deep roots to current behavior, and signals some adaptive qualities to addiction. The notion of adaptation is pertinent, as substance use or other forms of addictive behavior can be seen as antidotes, in many cases to negative experiences or circumstances. The capacity of humans to seek stasis and resolve or balance stressors with rewards in the form of food, drugs or alcohol may have long and deep roots.

In synch with this, ethnographers remind us that the use of psychoactive drugs, such as alcohol or hallucinogens has a long cross-cultural history (Carlson 2006). The impetus to alter consciousness, to generate links to the spiritual world, to mark life transitions or to simply feel good has examples across many cultures (Tupper 2008). When such use becomes devalued is when participants lose control over their use, isolating users from others. Carlson (2006) reminds us that the neurobiological reinforcing properties of some drugs makes them targets for commodification and profiteering, leading to states of addiction. This shift from positive social function to less so leads to a divergence where addicted users develop a structure and social system of their own, and non-addicted users develop stigmatized attitudes about them. Globalization has increased the nature and scope of categories of drugs and their distribution, as well as highlighting inequalities across groups, all of which contribute to more use of drugs to alter realities and deal with oppressive conditions (Carlson 2006, pp. 215–216).

Addiction may also have other systemic homes. Anne Wilson Schaef (1987) considers the concept of addiction in organizational values, structures, processes and systems. She distinguishes between substance addictions (alcohol, drugs, tobacco, etc.), process addictions (gambling, worry, sex, work, etc.) and relationship addictions. She suggests that process addictions are ultimately more damaging in a wide ranging way, serving to distort moral and social perspectives, while ingesting substances is damaging on individual levels (Schaef 1987, p. 147). Her writing inspires thinking about the "addictive system" as one in which choices are limited for individuals, supported by closed and tight rules and expectations around human relationships, marriage and family, the church, work and patriarchal power (Schaef 1987). The limits of such a closed system create a malaise that sets the stage for the development of individual addictive behaviors, according to Schaef.

Bruce Alexander, a Canadian psychologist, consciously taps history, philosophy and economics to understand contemporary responses to addiction and offers a welcome fusion of thinking (Alexander 2008). He rejects the entrenched focus on understanding the location of addiction as in the individual, as opposed to the society. He also refutes the notion that mere exposure to some addictive substances such as heroin is enough to cause addiction. He rejects both the moral and disease models of addiction as insufficient, singly or together (Alexander 2008, p. 63). Alexander illustrates these viewpoints by using Vancouver, Canada, a prosperous city with an entrenched addiction problem, as a structural case study, describing addiction as part of a social structure that responds to global economics, historical influences and a range of social and economic determinants.

Alexander considers current approaches to addiction as failures, and offers some innovative alternative explanations and solutions. He suggests that 'dislocation' is the key firmament for addiction. This refers to the lack of integration between self and society, and a resulting lack of connection. This concept has many historical contributors from both a range of disciplines—such as anthropology, philosophy, sociology and psychology—and a range of perspectives from existentialism to neo-Freudianism (see, for example, Durkheim 1951; Frankl 1985; Erikson 1959). Dislocation refers to feeling of marginalization, alienation or anomie and the effects of not finding meaning in relation to self and others. While the most obvious manifestation appears in disadvantaged individuals who are homeless, destitute, physically violated or abandoned, Alexander suggests that it can also be present in those who are addicted to work, consumerism or acquisition (Alexander 2008, pp. 60–64). Alexander suggests that dislocation and hence, addiction, is a side product of free market capitalism, enhanced by globalization's effects and pressures.

Gabor Maté is another important contemporary thinker on addiction. His perspective is derived from years of work with patients who have a range of addictions, as well as his self-disclosure of his own workaholic and collecting behaviors. He describes a void that addiction is meant to fill:

> (This is) the domain of addiction, where we constantly seek something outside ourselves to curb an insatiable yearning for relief or fulfillment. The aching emptiness is perpetual because the substances, objects or pursuits we hope will soothe it are not what we really need. (Maté 2010, p. 1)

As Maté describes, addiction on a physiological level is "brain chemistry gone askew under the influence of a substance"(Maté 2010, p. 29). But this narrow definition, reflecting a medical or disease model, is not enough to describe the compulsions that encourage self-destructing abuses of drugs or alcohol. Rather, Maté describes this as "drug as emotional anesthetic; as an antidote to a frightful feeling of emptiness; as a tonic against fatigue, boredom, alienation and a sense of personal inadequacy; as stress reliever and social lubricant" (Maté 2010, pp. 31–32). In Maté's view, addiction is a response to internal pain, and can be seen as self-medication. Not surprisingly, when it comes to defining addiction, Mate takes a very broad view, asserting that "addiction has biological, chemical, neurological, psychological, medical, emotional, social, political, economic and spiritual underpinnings—and perhaps others I haven't thought about" (Maté 2010, p. 130). Such a broad definition, based on years of firsthand clinical work in Vancouver's Downtown Eastside, is a clear indication of the need for transdisciplinarity.

As Gabor Maté reasserts, the voices of some who have experienced addiction are critically important to our understanding. There have been many memoirs, accounts and participatory research reports depicting the experiences of alcoholism and recovery (see, for example, Johnston 2013), drug use and misuse (see, for example, Gadsby 2000), tobacco dependence and gendered trauma and violence (see, for example, Greaves 1996) or recovery processes (see, for example, Hall and Cohn 1987). Addiction has been linked to despair, trauma and despondency, as well as to creativity, thrill seeking and being an outsider. One collection by Crozier and Lane brings together this range of experiences and articulates reflections on addiction by a range of Canadian writers (Crozier and Lane 2006).

One of these, Evelyn Lau, reflecting on a history of food, cigarettes, alcohol, sex and drug misuse, says:

> Is this behavior something that can be changed by force of will? The feelings behind that scenario: what are they? Are they symptoms of some other hunger, emotional lack or some faulty wiring in the brain? I don't know, but

> I have lived with those feelings, those uncontrollable impulses, all my life. (Crozier and Lane 2006, p. 82)

A poet, Sheri-D Wilson, reflects on her 17-year old self and the impetus for her life of excessive drinking and drug taking, wrapped up in her desire to be a creative, rebellious type:

> I wasn't going to be the goody-goody bunhead from Calgary, Alberta, who married, had kids and dreamed of the things she might have seen and done. Oh, no, ... I would be the one who smoked and drank and swore and did drugs and had wild sex and wrote poetry and made jazz till dawn like the women I had read about. My behavior would not be limited by my gender. (Crozier and Lane 2006, p. 126)

Stephen Reid, a writer who gained fame after writing his memoirs in prison, reflected on a life of drug addiction, early sexual abuse and crime.

> Prisoners are about addictions. Most prisoners are casualties of their habits. They have all created victims—some in cruel and callous ways—but almost to a man they have first practiced that cruelty on themselves. Prison provide the loneliness that fuels addiction. (Crozier and Lane 2006, p. 180)

Why Take an Integrated Approach?

Given these varied historical and contemporary perspectives, it is easy to see how diverse and at times inconsistent these approaches and philosophies are in explaining addiction. Reconciling these approaches has not really occurred in decades of legal, medical and social responses. One framework that has been proposed that aims to bridge some of these perspectives in both mental health and addiction treatment is the biopsychosocial model. This approach does not advance a theory of causation for addiction but does highlight the interactions and mutually reinforcing forces and elements in creating and treating addiction (Bethea 2009). It draws on biology, sociology and psychology, recognizes cultural factors and incorporates a systems perspective for framing addiction self-help, care and treatment. It also leaves room for including influences such as culture and spirituality, often ignored in many scientific approaches to addiction, but a component in many self-help and treatment approaches.

Despite this effort to create a holistic response, we continue to see various legalistic and criminalizing approaches to addiction and substance use, ranging from prohibition to regulation of sale, growing, manufacturing, advertising and control of a range of substances such as alcohol, tobacco and various drugs. Substances are deemed legal or illegal, but these categories shift over time, dependent upon social forces and attitudes that get reflected in law and regulatory schemes. Often, governments are ambivalent about substances, offering assistance with treatment on one hand, and garnering taxes from legal drugs on the other. In other cases, ambivalence is reflected in regulations not being enforced, or simply ignored, as norms change before legislation. In many cases, these systems remain divorced, with correctional or judicial responses ignoring addiction and leaving it untreated in correctional settings.

All of these discrepant patterns affect the user, whether he or she is interested in treatment or not. Criminalization of substance use or behaviors creates secondary effects and unintended consequences for those with addiction issues, such as incarceration, unemployment, discrimination or lifelong stigma. State ambivalence about some substances (e.g., marijuana) or behaviors (e.g., gambling) creates uncertainty and mixed messages or inconsistent and inequitable application of regulations or laws. In other circumstances, residual moral messages create guilt or stigma and shame for those with addiction issues. Clashes between a view of addiction as a health issue, with either a moral or legalistic view, can serve to create vacuums of treatment for those with addiction issues. Clearly, these clashes affect individuals and their families directly, but also sow dissonance and disjointedness between sectors interested in responding to addiction either in individuals with issues, their families and communities or societally.

Bringing sectors and disciplines together in generating new approaches or responses to health issues is difficult, due to differences in mandates, language, goals and rules that act as barriers to integration (Greaves et al. 2001). Sectoral interests and rules may mean that certain territory is the purview of certain departments of ministries by legislation. Attempts have been made to erode some of the divisions between substance use and mental health services in Canada, for example, by instituting more melded approaches, integrating initiatives into a more unified view, often by restructuring policy departments, health care organizations or government mandates. These initiatives are not without issues and concerns about subsuming some interests under others (Greaves 2006). Typically, such attempts can be met with defensiveness and territoriality, as groups opt to maintain boundaries in the interests of maintaining control over areas of work.

Why Include Sex and Gender in Addiction?

A gendered understanding of addiction is underdeveloped. In 2003 the National Institutes of Health (NIH) in the United States summarized the evidence on gender differences in drug abuse by stating there are sex-specific biological mechanisms, origins (risk factors, pathways and contexts of use) and gendered courses, consequences and impacts of substance use as well as different access to and responses to treatment for girls and women (NIDA 2013). In Canada, Poole and Greaves, in the book *Highs and Lows: Canadian Perspectives on Women and Substance Use* (Poole and Greaves 2007) brought attention to sex- and gender-based influences on women's substance use by integrating a range of research as well as testimony from women, service providers and policy actors regarding their experiences in and with the addictions field. In the UK, Ettorre has addressed the gap in development of a gendered understanding of addiction by proposing a critical feminist view of drug use, based on an understanding of the complexities of gender as a social and regulatory process (Ettorre 2007). Gender affects patterns of addiction, substance use and the responses to users. However, Ettorre also illustrates that gender permeates researchers' analyses of such phenomena by providing templates for understanding behavior, and additionally gender affects users' self-analyses of their use as well (Ettorre 2007, p. 21). These examples illustrate the pervasive nature and impact of gender in understanding addiction and substance use.

Taking sex and gender into account in research, policy and programming is long overdue, but it is the way of the future (Oliffe and Greaves 2011; Clow et al. 2009; Health Canada 2003; Wizemann and Pardue 2001). These approaches are supported and mandated by increasing numbers of research funding agencies, particularly in North America, and the information they produce is increasingly demanded by treatment providers and the public. Requirements from the National Institutes of Health in the USA mandate inclusion of women and minorities in biomedical and behavioral research and in clinical trials, and reporting requirements are strengthened regularly (National Institutes of Health 2011, 2013). These moves build on decades of activity, culminating in the 1993 Public Health Revitalization Act (National Institutes of Health 1993), and follow several accountability assessments of that Act which indicated that compliance was often present, but analysis of data collected was often overlooked (General Accounting Office 2000). In Canada, early reports affected the Canadian Institutes of Health Research (CIHR) creation of the Institute of Gender and Health (IGH). These initiatives rested on increasing awareness and education about the critical importance of sex in general to human health, and health research in general (Greaves et al. 1999; Grant and Ballem 2000).

It is known that sex-based factors (biological) affect responses to substances (Greenfield and O'Leary 2002; Bangasser et al. 2010; Fox and Sinha 2009), and gender-based factors (social and cultural) generate limits or opportunities for substance use, addictive behaviors and social responses to them (Grella 2003; Leibschutz et al. 2002; Lemke et al. 2008). Gender is composed of several elements, each of which affect addiction and our collective responses to addictive behavior: gender relations, identity and institutional gender (Johnson, Greaves, and Repta 2007). These different elements of gender all matter in considering how sex and gender operate to affect addiction, its uptake, treatment, relapse and social responses. However, incorporating sex and gender into addictions thinking is slow in being adopted, reflecting a general reluctance to understanding the effects of sex and gender on any health matter, resistance to change entrenched disciplinary approaches and a lack of training in many disciplines and fields.

Efforts are being made in North America by both the CIHR and the NIH to incorporate knowledge about sex and gender into health research, and to generate more effective compliance among researchers for including sex and gender into their research. The advent of the IGH at the CIHR was the result of much lobbying (Greaves 2009) that was initially focused on developing an institute for women's health research. Since the inception of the IGH in 2000, measures have been taken to educate and expand knowledge and research on health in Canada via a series of actions, including training, funding and rule setting.

Similarly, in the USA, numerous regulatory approaches have been taken since 1993 to advance sex and gender in health research, not only in clinical trials but also in other enterprises (Food and Drug Administration 1993). These efforts strengthen the rights of women, children and minorities to be represented in health research, as well as generate much needed evidence that is sex- and gender-sensitive and specific. With this history, it is evident that even though including sex and gender creates better science (Johnson, Greaves, and Repta 2009), it has been necessary to pressure scientists to both adopt these inclusions and to do so in effective ways. It has also been essential to provide illustrations, theory and training materials (Oliffe and Greaves 2011). Our proposition in this book is that taking a transdisciplinary approach that *includes* sex and gender is an essential next step for the addictions field.

Why Take a Transdisciplinary Approach?

Transdisciplinarity has been heralded for some decades as a positive way to improve health research. Rosenfield, a former economist with the Tropical Disease Research program at the World Health Organization (WHO), is credited with proffering transdisciplinarity as a solution to the shortcomings of research programs and collaborations at WHO during the 1990s. She felt that post-war ideals of her predecessors aimed at integrating social and biological perspectives were not being fully honored (Kessel and Rosenfield 2008), particularly as review processes were dominated by medical doctors, leading to the marginalization of social perspectives. Kessel and Rosenfield (2008) reflect:

> What was called multidisciplinary or even interdisciplinary research involved primarily separate input of different disciplines, but not creative ways to blend those to yield deeper understanding of the problem or integrative solutions that would be both more acceptable to the population at risk and more cost-effective in the long run. (p. S226)

Similar critiques of institutional and organizational resistance to change have been leveled at universities. For example, Poole et al. (2009), point out that knowledge production in universities is typically structured in discipline-segregated "silos" that "foster competitiveness and individualism . . . more than cooperation and consensus-building" (Poole, Egan, and Iqbal 2009, p. 148–149). While over the past few decades we have witnessed greater utilization of collaborative research frameworks such as interdisciplinarity, multidisciplinarity and to a lesser extent transdisciplinarity, unidisciplinarity remains the typical training approach for many researchers and practitioners. Yet, it is clear that complex health problems such as addictions require more integrated and innovative approaches. While transdisciplinarity is the most nascent of the collaborative frameworks, we argue that it is also the most promising approach for tackling complex health issues, such as addiction, as the aim of transdisciplinarity is to transcend disciplinary boundaries and traditional methods of knowledge production. Hall et al. (2008) offer the following definitions:

> A unidisciplinary research orientation is characterized by the use of theories and methods drawn from a single field, whereas cross-disciplinary (i.e., multidisciplinary, interdisciplinary, transdisciplinary) research orientations entail the combined use of concepts and methods drawn from two or more distinct disciplines. Multidisciplinary collaborations involve researchers who share their own disciplinary insights and perspectives with colleagues who are trained and work in fields different from their own. Interdisciplinary collaborations involve a higher level of integration among the different disciplinary perspectives of team members than is evident in multidisciplinary collaborations. Transdisciplinary collaborations, like interdisciplinary ones, strive toward the integration of two or more disciplinary perspectives, but are uniquely characterized by the creation of novel conceptualizations and methodological approaches that transcend or move beyond the individual disciplines represented among team members (p. 164).

Transdisciplinarity is fundamentally distinct from other types of collaborative research because the goals of inter- and multidisciplinary research ultimately stay within a framework of disciplinarity, the aim of transdisciplinarity is to transcend such boundaries. Importantly, the concept of transdisciplinarity is applicable beyond research and contains a particular worldview. According to Nicolescu (1998), transdisciplinarity is a transcendental philosophy; an ontology for viewing multiple levels of reality at once. For Nicolescu, transdisciplinarity offers transformation beyond scientific research and "entails a new vision and a lived experience. . . a way of self-transformation . . . a new art of living in society" (p. 3). Certainly, the concept of transdisciplinarity holds promise for shifting and reorienting thinking and action in ways that has the potential to produce major change at various levels of society and in this book, we probe the meaning of transdisciplinarity in practice, policy and training and knowledge exchange.

There are numerous goals in reaching for transdisciplinarity. Snow et al. (2010) point out that one effect is a "blurring of boundaries" between disciplines and areas of research that aims to produce a novel and shared epistemology, and theoretical and methodological frameworks, with the goal of creating more nuanced understandings of a problem. From the "blurring of boundaries" emerge new and transformed research products that are different to those of traditional disciplinary research (e.g., academic publications and presentations in discipline-specific journals and conferences). Indeed, transformation is a leitmotif in transdisciplinary work because it has the potential to "fundamentally transform the disciplinary identities of the collaborating researchers" (Derry and Fischer 2005, p. 4). Orozco and Cole (2008) argue that this type of identity transformation contains "growing commitments to social and even political action among students, as future innovators able to create alternatives for sustainability" (p. 493).

Transdisciplinarity has the potential to offer significant contributions to the field of addiction. But it requires change and nurturing on several fronts, ranging from university reward systems, to disciplinary education, to developing individual questioning and holistic thinking in individuals. As those involved in transdisciplinary training and work point out, collaborative research, let alone transdisciplinary research, is complicated and often requires skills that are beyond those typically taught in graduate training, and beyond their university mentors for whom transdisciplinarity is by and large a foreign and/or new concept (Nash 2008; Hall et al. 2008; Snow et al. 2010). Transdisciplinarity, while not a new concept, is still an emerging area. There remains only a small number journal articles on the topic and few books, including the newly published *Transdisciplinary Public Health: Research, Education, and Practice* (Haire-Joshu and McBride 2013). While these provide some promise of a potential growing interest in this framework, the dearth of writing and training tools also suggest that transdisciplinarity remains not well understood and at present only marginally utilized in health research and practice. Transdisciplinary partnerships have the ability not only to generate new approaches to research and treatment but can have a key impact on the translation and dissemination of knowledge, given their ability to integrate players and generate broader evidence (Dankwa-Mullan et al. 2010; Godemann 2008). Like others who promote transdisciplinarity for moving health issues forward, we argue that addiction research and treatment demands transformation and this book is a catalyst to this call.

Doing transdisciplinary work is not easy. Being prepared to travel outside the typical boundaries of discipline, scope of practice, department, ministry or sector is the underpinning of transdisciplinarity. Being able to do this requires imagination, risk, and some courage, as well as an openness and respect for others' experiences and viewpoints. It requires the ability to integrate such perspectives, not just by summing, but by extending this knowledge into a transformed understanding. Transdisciplinarity is not usually encouraged or understood, nor is such blurring of the lines easily supported by rules, funders, regulatory bodies or institutions. Issues of control and territory also come into play, defining the "best" way to approach addiction. Hence, a transdisciplinary approach requires support, leadership and training.

Similarly, producing integrated evidence and direction on the complex problem of addiction requires a willingness to blur the boundaries of typical research methods, analysis and categories of thinking. Most importantly, it needs to link evidence and action to the real needs of people and communities, especially those struggling with addiction. This requires innovative knowledge translation that is able to bridge evidence, boundaries and policy and program development. From the point of view of individuals and communities who are dealing directly with addiction, this is a welcome possibility. Dealing with practitioners, policy makers and researchers who are already listening to each other and moving beyond lip service to each other's specialties is bound to be reassuring.

As for integrating sex and gender into all work on addiction, be it research, policy or programming, the time has long since come. Doing so creates better science, and better science leads to better treatment. Resistance to incorporating such concepts will inevitably reduce, as funders and regulators weigh in with increased pressures to change the way health research is done and to demand approaches that that are relevant to women and men, girls and boys, and minorities, not just generic humans, and not just males, as is still the case with some laboratory-based preclinical research and with many human clinical trials. This shift will take a generation at least to complete, but scientists, program and policy developers are well on their way, with better training, and more pressure and demands from journals, funders and the public to respond to. The essence of understanding how to use sex and gender in research and treatment is also the essence of transdisciplinarity—involving the integration of both biological and sociological thinking, and marrying these two sides of human life in understanding addiction and defining action.

Whose business is addiction, anyway? Over the centuries, various perspectives have persisted as offering explanations for addiction, and each of these has their own implications for how to respond, and who might best do that responding. But this book is suggesting that to move forward, we look between those entrenched disciplines, perspectives and views, to occupy the liminal space between rigidities and boundaries in order to make progress on a complex issue such as addiction. Doing so requires sharing ownership, innovation, pioneering and transformative thinking.

References

Alexander, Bruce K. 2008. *The globalisation of addiction: A study in poverty of the spirit.* Oxford, UK: Oxford University Press.

Bangasser, D.A., A. Curtis, B.A.S. Reyes, T.T. Bethea, I. Parastatidis, H. Ischiropoulos, E.J. Van Bockstaele, and R.J. Valentino. 2010. Sex differences in corticotropin-releasing factor receptor signaling and trafficking: Potential role in female vulnerability to stress-related psychopathology. *Molecular Psychiatry* 15 (9):877, 896–904.

Bethea, J. 2009. Biopsychosocial model of addiction. In *Encyclopedia of Substance Abuse Prevention, Treatment, & Recovery*, edited by G. Fisher and N. Roget, 129–131. Thousand Oaks, CA: SAGE.

Bickel, Warren K., and Mark N. Potenza. 2006. The forest and the trees: Addiction as a complex self-organizing system. In *Rethinking Substance Abuse: What the Science Shows, and What We Should Do About It*, edited by William R. Miller and Kathleen M. Carroll, 8–21. New York: Guilford Press.

Carlson, Robert G. 2006. Ethnography and applied substance misuse research: Anthropological and cross-cultural factors. In *Rethinking Substance Abuse: What the Science Shows, and What We Should Do about It*, edited by William R. Miller and Kathleen M. Carroll, 201–219. New York: Guilford Press.

Clow, Barbara, Ann Pederson, Margaret Haworth-Brockman, and Jennifer Bernier. 2009. *Rising to the challenge: Sex-and gender-based analysis for health planning, policy and research in Canada*. Halifax, NS: Atlantic Centre of Excellence for Women's Health.

Crozier, Lorna, and Patrick Lane. 2006. *Addicted: Notes from the belly of the beast*. Vancouver, BC: Greystone Books.

Dankwa-Mullan, Irene, Kyu B. Rhee, David M. Stoff, Jennifer Reineke Pohlhaus, Francisco S. Sy, Nathaniel Stinson Jr., and John Ruffin. 2010. Moving toward paradigm-shifting research in health disparities through translational, transformational, and transdisciplinary approaches. *American Journal of Public Health* 100 (S1):S19–S24.

Derry, Sharon, and Gehard Fischer. 2005, April. "Toward a model and theory for transdisciplinary graduate education." Paper read at AERA Annual Meeting, Symposium, *Sociotechnical Design for Lifelong Learning: A Crucial Role for Graduate Education*, Montreal.

Durkheim, Emile. 1951. *Suicide: A study in sociology* (J. A. Spaulding and G. Simpson, Trans.). Glencoe, IL: Free Press. (Original work published 1897)

Erikson, Erik H. 1959. Identity and the life cycle: Selected papers. *Psychological Issues* 1, 1–171.

Ettorre, Elizabeth. 2007. *Revisioning women and drug use: Gender, power and the body*. New York: Palgrave.

The Fix. 2011. *The controversial heretic who's taking on AA* [cited September 22, 2014]. Available from www.thefix.com/content/heretic.

Food and Drug Administration. 1993. Guideline for the study and evaluation of gender differences in the clinical evaluation of drugs. *Federal register* 58 (139):39406–39416.

Fox, Helen C., and Rajita Sinha. 2009. Sex differences in drug-related stress-system changes: Implications for treatment in substance-abusing women. *Harvard Review of Psychiatry* 17 (2):103–119.

Frankl, Viktor E. 1985. *Man's search for meaning*. New York: Simon & Schuster.

Gadsby, Joan E. 2000. *Addiction by prescription: One woman's triumph and fight for change*. Toronto, ON: Key Porter Books.

General Accounting Office. 2000. *Women's health: NIH has increased its efforts to include women in research*. Washington, DC: Author.

Godemann, Jasmin. 2008. Knowledge integration: A key challenge for transdisciplinary cooperation. *Environmental Education Research* 14 (6):625–641.

Grant, Karen, and Penny Ballem. 2000. *A women's health research institute in the Canadian Institutes for Health Research*. Vancouver: BC Centre of Excellence for Women's Health.

Greaves, Lorraine. 1996. *Smoke screen: Women's smoking and social control*. Black Point, NS: Fernwood.

Greaves, Lorraine. 2006. Mental health and addictions mergers and acquisitions: Making them work for women. *Centres of Excellence for Women's Health Research Bulletin* 5 (1):1–3.

Greaves, Lorraine. 2009. Women, gender and health research, 3–20. In *Women's Health: Intersections of Policy, Research, and Practice*, edited by P. Armstrong and J. Deadman. Toronto, ON: Canadian Scholars' Press.

Greaves, Lorraine, Penny Ballem, BC Centre of Excellence for Women's Health, and Symposium on Integrated Research. 2001. *Fusion: A model for Integrated Health Research*. Vancouver: British Columbia Centre of Excellence for Women's Health.

Greaves, Lorraine, Olena Hankivsky, Carol Amaratunga, Penny Ballem, Donna Chow, Maria De Koninck, Karen Grant, Abby Lippman, Heather MacLean, Janet Maher, Karen Messing, and Bilkis Vissandjee. 1999. *CIHR 2000: Sex, gender and women's health*. Vancouver, BC: BC Centre of Excellence for Women's Health.

Greenfield, Shelly F., and Grace O'Leary. 2002. Sex differences in substance use disorders, 467–533. In *Psychiatric Illness in Women: Emerging Treatments and Research*, edited by F. Lewis-Hall, T.S. Williams, J.A. Panetta and J.M. Herrera. Arlington, VA: American Psychiatric Publishing.

Grella, Christine E. 2003. Effects of gender and diagnosis on addiction history, treatment utilization, and psychosocial functioning among a dually-diagnosed sample in drug treatment. *Journal of Psychoactive Drugs* 35 (Suppl. 1):169–179.

Haire-Joshu, Debra, and Timothy D. McBride. 2013. *Transdisciplinary public health: Research, education, and practice*. Vol. 49. New York: John Wiley & Sons.

Hall, Kara L., Annie X, Feng, Richard P. Moser, Daniel Stokols, and Brandie K. Taylor. 2008. Moving the science of team science forward: Collaboration and creativity. *American Journal of Preventive Medicine* 35 (2):S243–S249.

Hall, Lindsey, and Leigh Cohn, eds. 1987. *Recoveries*. Carlsbad, CA: Gurze Books.

Health Canada. 2003. *Exploring concepts of gender and health*. Ottawa: Women's Health Bureau: Health Canada.

Jellinek, Elvin M. 1960. The disease concept of alcoholism. *New Haven* 343:63.

Johnson, Joy L., Lorraine Greaves, and Robin Repta. 2007. *Better science with sex and gender: A primer for health research*. Vancouver, BC: Women's Health Research Network.

Johnson, Joy L., Lorraine Greaves, and Robin Repta. 2009. Better science with sex and gender: Facilitating the use of a sex and gender-based analysis in health research. *International Journal for Equity in Health* 8:14.

Johnston, Ann D. 2013. *Drink: The intimate relationship between women and alcohol*. New York: HarperCollins.

Kessel, Frank, and Patricia L. Rosenfield. 2008. Toward transdisciplinary research: Historical and contemporary perspectives. *American Journal of Preventive Medicine* 35 (2):S225–S234.

Leibschutz, Jane, Jacqueline B. Savetsky, Richard Saitz, Nicholas J. Horton, Christine Lloyd-Travaglini, and Jeffrey H. Samet. 2002. The relationship between sexual and physical abuse and substance abuse consequences. *Journal of Substance Abuse Treatment* 22 (3):121–128.

Lemke, Sonne, Kathleen K. Schute, Penny L. Brennan, and Rudolf H. Moos. 2008. Gender differences in social influences and stressors linked to increased drinking. *Journal of Studies on Alcohol & Drugs* 69 (5):695–702.

Maté, Gabor. 2010. *In the realm of hungry ghosts: Close encounters with addiction*. Berkely, CA: North Atlantic Books.

National Institutes of Health. 1993. NIH Revitalization Act: Subtitle B, Part 1. *Sec* 131:103–143.

National Institutes of Health. 2011. *Including women, children, and minorities in clinical research*. Bethesda, MD: National Institutes of Health.

National Institutes of Health. 2013. New system and procedures for reporting sex/gender, race, and ethnicity information to the NIH. Bethesda, MD: National Institutes of Health.

Nicolescu, Basarab. 1998. *The transdisciplinary evolution of the university, condition for sustainable development* (Cern Document Server: SCAN-9809055).

NIDA. 2013, June 16. *Program announcement—Women, gender differences and drug abuse*. National Institute on Drug Abuse [cited July 30 2013]. Available from http://grants1.nih.gov/grants/guide/pa-files/PA-03-139.html.

Oliffe, John L., and Lorraine Greaves. 2011. *Designing and conducting gender, sex, and health research.* Thousand Oaks, CA: SAGE.

Orozco, Fadya, and Donald C. Cole. 2008. Development of transdisciplinarity among students placed with a sustainability for health research project. *EcoHealth* 5 (4):491–503.

Peele, Stanton. 1987. A moral vision of addiction. *Journal of Drug Issues* 17 (2):187–215.

Poole, Gary, John P. Egan, and Isabeau Iqbal. 2009. Innovation in collaborative health research training: The role of active learning. *Journal of Interprofessional Care* 23 (2):148–155.

Poole, Nancy, and Lorraine Greaves, eds. 2007. *Highs and lows: Canadian perspectives on women and substance use.* Toronto: Centre for Addiction and Mental Health.

Schaef, Anne W. 1987. *When society becomes an addict.* San Francisco: Harper & Row.

Schaef, Anne W., and Diane Fassel. 1988. *The addictive organization.* San Francisco: Harper & Row.

Snow, Mary E., Amy Salmon, and Richard Young. 2010. Teaching transdisciplinarity in a discipline-centered world. *Collected Essays in Learning and Teaching* 3:159–165.

Tupper, Kenneth W. 2008. The globalization of ayahuasca: Harm reduction or benefit maximization? *International Journal of Drug Policy* 19 (4):297–303.

Wizemann, Theresa M., and Mary-Lou Pardue. 2001. Exploring the biological contributions to human health: Does sex matter? Washington, DC: Institute of Medicine, National Academies Press.

2

FOSTERING TRANSDISCIPLINARITY IN ADDICTIONS RESEARCH TRAINING

Ellexis Boyle, Mary Elizabeth Snow and Nicole Vittoz

Addiction is one of society's most complex and vexing health problems. A wide range of issues often co-occur with addiction, including trauma, violence and mental illness, and all of these co-occurring issues are influenced by gender and other social determinants of health. The issue of addiction demands an understanding of the full range of influencing factors, including those related to the biological, psychosocial, political and economic. Given this complexity, it is recognized by health and funding agencies, policy makers, researchers, clinicians and service providers that multiple perspectives and collaborative approaches are necessary for developing effective treatment and prevention strategies. In this chapter, we argue that one area where we can make inroads towards this goal is through innovative *research training* that equips researchers with both an understanding of the multiple and intersecting factors that shape addiction, and the skills to engage in cross-pillar collaborations.

The Intersections of Mental Health Perspectives and Addictions Research Training (IMPART) program emerged out of this recognized need for enhanced approaches to addiction and has been a twelve-year endeavor towards preparing new researchers to develop more complex approaches to addiction and its intersecting issues. IMPART received support from a Canadian Institutes of Health Research (CIHR) strategic funding opportunity titled, "Health Researchers for the 21st Century." Launched in 2001, this initiative was designed to support innovative and transdisciplinary research training of Canadian health researchers, who could develop more effective solutions to complex health issues.[1] A group of ten leading addiction researchers, together with partners from educational and community settings, made a successful bid for a training program focused on women, gender and addiction, called the Integrated Mentor Program in Addictions Research Training (IMPART). Six years later, the program was renewed and re-funded under an evolved name (Intersections of Mental Health Perspectives in Addictions Research Training). In both iterations, the IMPART program was designed to enhance the capacity of health researchers to apply sex- and gender-based analysis to the study of addiction to increase knowledge and appreciation of the complexities and breadth of addiction, particularly in girls and women. Additionally, IMPART was designed to train new researchers in a transdisciplinary approach. IMPART trained over eighty researchers and clinicians across Canada, representing over a dozen disciplines, including cellular and physiological sciences, neuroscience, psychology, epidemiology, nutrition, sociology, education, social work and interdisciplinary studies. Research topics covered a range of addictions (i.e. tobacco, marijuana, alcohol, crack cocaine, gambling) in diverse populations (i.e. men, women, Aboriginal, sex workers, individuals with severe mental illnesses) and integrated complex co-morbidities, such as cardiovascular disease, diabetes, mental illness as well as incorporated intersecting issues of violence, trauma and mental health.

Transdisciplinarity remains under-utilized and not well understood in health research and research training (Nash et al. 2003). This is despite efforts by health agencies, funders and individuals to promote more integrated forms of health research and care. In this chapter, we draw on our experience with the IMPART program to share practical insights and strategies for a) fostering transdisciplinary community and b) supporting transdisciplinary communities to practice communication and exchange. We begin by discussing key factors that foster transdisciplinary community such as *diversity* of perspectives among members and *flexibility* in roles and forms of engagement. Next, we share knowledge translation strategies and innovative pedagogical approaches that can support a transdisciplinary community to communicate and thus move towards transdisciplinary collaboration. Finally, and drawing on examples from the IMPART program, we demonstrate some key benefits of transdisciplinary training that include transformation of disciplinary and personal identities and increased responsiveness to the complexities of addiction. Indeed, fostering transdisciplinarity is not without its challenges, and throughout our discussion we share the difficulties we encountered and the innovations we developed to minimize them.

While our discussion is specific to research training, our insights about strategies for and benefits of building transdisciplinary community and collaboration apply in multiple contexts. These include clinical and health services settings, where the complex needs of clients can be better addressed by bridging the expertise of diverse experts, and in health policy arenas, where the deliberate integration of diverse experts stand to improve policy making on addiction and mental health issues. Transdisciplinarity truly is for everyone; because it is about embracing complexity and creating environments in which diverse perspectives can be shared and cross-fertilized in ways that allow for the emergence of new and enhanced approaches to addiction.

Key Factors for Building a Transdisciplinary Community

Fundamental to fostering transdisciplinarity is the development of a community of members who represent a range of disciplines, areas, sectors and experience and who are open to sharing and learning from others. Diversity is thus a fundamental element in the development of successful transdisciplinary environments so that members are exposed to and learn to respect the different perspectives and approaches of their peers.

The IMPART community is comprised of participants with diverse expertise in the areas of women, mental health and addiction and who represent perspectives from across research pillars, clinical, policy and health-service settings. Furthermore, as a training program, members of the IMPART community held specific roles: 1) research mentors, who were expert academic and clinical researchers and who provided mentorship to trainees; 2) research trainees, who were enrolled in a master's degree or doctorate program or were a postdoctoral fellow or clinician researcher and undertook the IMPART training and 3) community members who represented the health systems and services sectors and whose perspectives, through guest lectures or site visits, provided trainees with insight into addictions issues beyond academic settings. In addition to these key roles, the IMPART community was managed by a program director—an individual trained in an area relevant to IMPART and with expertise in adult education. The program director was responsible for supporting and facilitating relationships among mentors, trainees and community representatives so as to foster transdisciplinary community. Orozco and Cole (2008) concur that a central support person or "broker" is key for fostering transdisciplinary relationships through role modeling and facilitation of communication among community members.

Research mentors were a cornerstone of the IMPART community. The mentor cohort was composed of academic and clinical researchers specializing in a range of areas and disciplines relating to addiction that included neuroscience, nursing, sociology, psychology, social work and epidemiology. The role of mentors was to provide research supervision to individual trainees as well as to the program as a whole through teaching presentations in seminars, hosting of clinical site visits or leading workshops. By exposing trainees (and other mentors) to the entire mentor cohort, it was hoped that transdisciplinary community would flourish through collaboration and cross-fertilization of ideas. This deliberate mixing of mentors and trainees within a diverse community resulted in various collaborative research projects and products including webinars, grant applications, innovative research agendas and peer-reviewed journal publications. Importantly, while the mentors were positioned as "experts" to guide the trainees, the IMPART community was built on the recognition that knowledge should flow in multiple directions. This is to say that trainees who came with varying levels of research experience and from diverse disciplinary backgrounds were also recognized as experts in their own areas who had much to teach each other and their mentors.

Over the years we encountered some challenges to maintaining the diversity that is necessary for fostering transdisciplinary community. Early on, it became clear that maintaining the involvement of service providers and policy advocates as part of a research based training program was easier said than done. Despite our goal for sectoral integration, IMPART was a *research*-based training program, and its key operations (i.e. adjudicating trainee applications, developing curriculum and making decisions about program policies) did not fit with the expertise of representatives from health authorities and community services. The realities of their busy schedules also contributed to low engagement. This initial problem lead to an improved system, where community representatives from health systems and services were engaged on a more *ad hoc* but relevant basis, such as presenting a seminar on specific issues facing them and their clients or hosting visits to community or clinical programs for on-site training.

Another challenge for building transdisciplinary community arose in the form of imbalances in the representation of research pillars among our mentors and trainees (i.e. biomedical, clinical, health systems and services, population and public health). Due to annual turnover in both the mentor and trainee cohorts, we sometimes had overrepresentation from some research pillars over others. While these imbalances were not problematic they reduced the diversity of perspectives necessary for a transdisciplinary learning environment. We addressed this problem through the careful balancing of research pillars and research areas during the annual selection of new trainees and through annual assessment and strategic recruitment of mentors each year. While these adjustments led to a greater turnover of mentors, it also meant that we retained a more engaged and dynamic community of experts who were better able to attend to the needs of trainees and who could invest in the program as a whole.

Another challenge for some transdisciplinary communities is that members are often geographically dispersed. Indeed, wide nets must often be cast in order to create the diversity required for an effective transdisciplinary training environment. IMPART evolved into a national training program and thus included members from across Canada and across time zones, with mentors who were often mobile. Derry and Fischer (2005) note the importance of fostering "sociotechnical environments" and fluency among trainees in using new media for conducting meaningful and flexible collaborations. Technology was vital to the IMPART program for delivering curriculum but also for fostering and maintaining community among a geographically dispersed group. Foundational to the field of distance education is the theory of "transactional distance" (Moore 1997). This theory describes the particular and unique configuration of relationships between teachers and students, and among students when separated via space and time. One strategy that we used to overcome transactional distances was the organization of an annual face-to face meeting held at the beginning of each training cycle. Known as the IMPART Annual Research Retreat, this event provided an opportunity for community and team building among new and existing members. Relationships established from these face-to-face interactions could then be continued in the online environment.

Following our Annual Research Retreat, we utilized strategic communications technologies to support connection and community amongst our geographically dispersed group. Early on we used a combination of room-based videoconferencing to connect groups of trainees at the same sites and desktop videoconferencing to link in individuals. Alienation arose where trainees who could only connect via desktop conferencing lacked the same ability to interact with the larger groups who had access to room-based videoconferencing and who could visually interact with peers. This led to our eventual abandonment of room-based videoconferencing and our exclusive use of desktop web conferencing. This decision effectively equalized transactional distances for all trainees because they now connected in the same way and experienced the same opportunities and limitations of online interaction. Interestingly, all trainees reported greater satisfaction with the web-based conferencing model because it allowed them greater flexibility to attend seminars and events among busy work and school schedules.

While not all transdisciplinary communities are geographically dispersed, our focus on this point highlights another key factor for fostering transdisciplinary communities: *flexibility*. In addition to diversity of members, transdisciplinary communities require a certain amount of flexibility in order to thrive. We have touched on this in our earlier discussion of how IMPART shifted mentor and community representative roles from fixed to more short-term and flexible engagements that resulted in more meaningful and quality interactions. By being more flexible in the recruitment of mentors and trainees we were also able to enhance the level of diversity that is necessary for transdisciplinary community building and exchange. Also, through the strategic use of technology, we were able to increase the flexibility and thus quality of trainee engagement. Certainly, building a diverse and engaged transdisciplinary community requires constant vigilance, through assessment and revision, in order to address gaps in representation and involvement. The importance of diversity and flexibility in generating a balanced and engaged community cannot be underestimated in a training program with transdisciplinary goals.

Strategies for Supporting Transdisciplinary Communities to Move Towards Collaboration and Exchange

> Transdisciplinary researchers work together to consciously transcend their discipline's conceptual, theoretical and methodological orientation to develop a "shared approach" to research and build a common framework that is used to define, analyze and develop new approaches to the problem. (Snow et al., 2010)

Building a diverse and flexible community is only the first step towards the creation of a successful transdisciplinary training environment. It is one thing to create a community of diverse and open learners but quite another to support them in moving towards transdisciplinary engagement. As the definition of transdisciplinarity suggests, community members must be open to stretching themselves beyond their disciplinary boundaries in order for transformative research questions, agenda and methods to emerge. In IMPART, we have learned that the key to moving towards transdisciplinarity is communication. Transdisciplinarity requires that individuals develop enhanced communication skills in order to create shared understandings and approaches to research. Indeed, communicating across disciplinary divides is cited as among the greatest challenges of transdisciplinary research training (Mitrany and Stokols 2005; Hall et al. 2008; Holmes et al. 2008; Nash et al. 2003; Nash 2008; Orozco and Cole 2008; Tress et al. 2009; Songca 2007). Barriers to effective communication include entrenchments in disciplinary jargon (Holmes et al. 2008), reluctance of members to fully integrate ideas and evidence from other fields (Nash et al. 2003) and difficulties determining the order of authorship on collaborative projects (Nash 2008). These challenges are underscored by disciplinary and institutional entrenchments in esoteric discourse, attitudes towards multi-authored papers and the meanings assigned to the order of authorship (Nash 2008; Snow et al. 2010). Certainly, IMPART was not exempt from these challenges, and there were many moments in which entrenchments in disciplinary jargon and lack of agreement on the meaning of key terms highlighted communications issues among the trainees. However, armed with the knowledge that lack of communication is a barrier for transdisciplinary exchange, IMPART implemented several knowledge translation strategies and utilized innovative pedagogies to support communication and help our members move towards transdisciplinarity.

Knowledge Translation Strategies for Supporting Transdisciplinary Communication

From the outset, dialogue and interactions among IMPART members was deliberately framed by a transdisciplinary approach. Similar to many graduate programs, IMPART trainees were required to complete an eight-month seminar series that covered transdisciplinary perspectives on addiction. As part of their training, trainees were required to present to their peers on one of the assigned themes. To guide them towards transdisciplinarity, the trainees were assembled in multidisciplinary teams and assigned a seminar topic. In addition to having to work with other disciplines in their teams, trainees were provided with a PowerPoint template that required them to present their content according to a transdisciplinary frame (see Figure 2.1). This template includes a requirement to present an issue from multiple perspectives and methods as well as to design activities that would facilitate transdisciplinary group discussion. The template was designed to promote

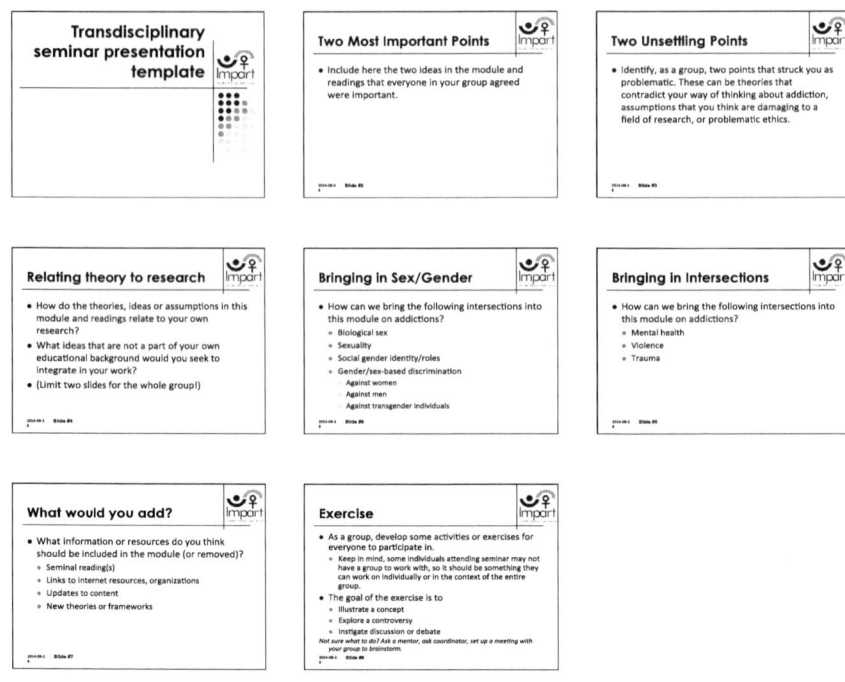

FIGURE 2.1 Presentation template for facilitating transdisciplinary exchange.

integrative thinking and prevent regression into comfortable, silo-friendly presentation structure.

While the seminar template was an effective tool for helping trainees to structure information for a transdisciplinary audience, it did not necessarily foster enhanced communication skills. Transdisciplinarity requires that members are open to interrogating their own disciplinary beliefs and ideas and be open to learning about others perspectives. To support this, we created an online training module and complementary seminar called Transdisciplinary Definitions of Addiction. Positioned at the beginning of the training, the online module required trainees to first read about various disciplinary approaches to addiction (i.e. neurobiological, psychosocial, epidemiological, health systems and services) and then share and discuss their own and each other's definitions of addiction in the seminar. This exercise was designed to move trainees towards transdisciplinarity through recognizing the assumptions and limitations of their own definitions and epistemologies via exposure to others' perspectives.

This was always a challenging exercise as the same terms (i.e. *sex, gender, addiction, trauma, abuse, disorder*) differed in meaning or usage across disciplines and could often be narrowly defined. As an example, the term *addiction* was interpreted by some as a clinical disorder. Others saw addiction as resulting from biological factors or social influences, drawing conclusions about to the effects of human agency on its development and persistence. The continuum of terms *substance abuse, substance misuse* and *substance use* produced debates over which terms were "correct" as well as which terms were most ethical and best captured nuanced meanings without stigmatizing individuals who struggled with these issues. Similar differences in usage and understanding were evident with the terms sex and gender, which in Canada are understood to refer to biological-related factors and social and culturally related factors respectively (Johnson et al. 2007). However, some biomedical and clinical disciplines sometimes use gender instead of sex, with many social scientists making clear and nuanced distinctions between these concepts. This is further confused as gender is used in place of sex and/or gender in some countries, disciplines, and journals, so interpreting scientific literature required some training in distinguishing these concepts. *Trauma* is also a key term in addictions, and its multiple perspectives and meanings are discussed in Chapter 3 of this book.

Despite struggles over meaning and authority to define key terms, this exercise also pushed trainees to bridge across disciplinary differences. In one inspiring moment, and amid frustration about differing definitions for similar concepts across disciplines, a trainee declared the need for an "addictions thesaurus" and proceeded to launch what became known as a Transdisciplinary Thesaurus of Addiction. The thesaurus contained key terms, such as those mentioned above and which traversed multiple disciplines. Trainees contributed their disciplinary-based definitions for each term. Contributions to the thesaurus effectively opened a key space for a discussion of the underpinning of terms, and the frameworks and theories that they reflect. It also gave an opportunity for generations of trainees to work towards more nuanced understandings of both the terms and the issues related to addiction, as well as for reflecting on the impact of the terms on individuals and social groups to whom similar labels are applied. The thesaurus is an example of the potential of transdisciplinary training to develop organically from among the trainees and provide a collaborative, flexible, and iterative "space" for trainees to explore multiple perspectives and practice open communication. These are foundational skills for successful transdisciplinary collaboration (Rosenfield 1992; Derry and Fischer 2005; McWilliams et al. 2008).

Teaching members of a transdisciplinary community to effectively communicate with one another is essential to foster transdisciplinary exchange. Teaching participants to communicate their knowledge to non-research audiences is another important aspect of transdisciplinary exchange. IMPART deployed several knowledge translation strategies towards this goal. First, as part of trainee orientation, trainees attended an annual retreat with the entire IMPART community and were required to give a three-minute presentation about their research focus. While trainees often expressed resistance to compressing their research into three minutes, they also came to recognize the power of using simplified language to reach a diverse audience and for inspiring cross-disciplinary dialogue. Second, we ran an annual workshop led by professional journalists, designed to introduce principles of good communication and which included constructive feedback for each trainee on their written and verbal communication skills. Through group critique of one another's writing and individual interviews with a journalist about their research, trainees were taught to a) recognize the limitations of their own esoteric discourses and b) integrate principles of good communication to better convey their key messages to a general audience.

Innovative Approaches to Pedagogy

Given that transdisciplinarity requires members to stretch beyond their own disciplinary boundaries and areas of expertise, transdisciplinary training requires innovative approaches to curriculum and pedagogy. In IMPART, we found that trainees were best supported in their learning through a "flipped classroom" approach. Flipped classroom or "flipped teaching" approaches are characterized by a reversal of traditional didactic teaching methods. Students typically study content at home and then work though problems in class with their instructor and peers. This approach encourages greater interaction and learner-centered development than is enabled by traditional lecture formats.

IMPART adopted a flipped classroom approach after experiencing the challenges of applying traditional teaching methods to a transdisciplinary model. Initially, our seminar course tended to be mentor-led, unidisciplinary, content-heavy, didactic and lacking in space for trainee dialogue. Trainees quickly recognized the limitations of this pedagogy for fostering transdisciplinary learning. Instead, they called for recognition of their expertise and more space for collective dialogue to share perspectives with one another. As a result, trainees were provided with a new responsibility for their own learning through the requirement that seminars be developed and delivered by teams of trainees with mentors playing supportive rather than leadership roles. This innovation placed greater emphasis on team building, increased trainee confidence through the recognition of their skills and abilities and improved their communication skills through the fostering of greater cross-disciplinary dialogue.

In addition to inverting traditional didactic teaching formats, flipped classroom pedagogies tend to utilize a blended model of learning. This is well suited to a transdisciplinary environment because while learners need the flexibility to interact, they also require an element of core curriculum in order to gain grounding in key areas of knowledge. Indeed, one of the main concerns raised in the literature on transdisciplinary training is that if training is too broad and diverse, trainees will become "jack of all trades and master of none" (Nash 2008). To address this concern, we developed a core curriculum on addictions and its intersections in the form of an online course. This course consisted of eight modules covering multi pillar and sectoral perspectives on addictions (i.e. biomedical, clinical, population and public health, health systems and services) as well as specific modules on methodologies, research ethics and knowledge translation. Each module was created to synchronize with one of the monthly seminars and was intended to provide trainees with the necessary background in an area so that they could engage in richer dialogue during each seminar that followed. As McWilliam et al. (2008) point out, flipped classroom approaches are particularly suited to transdisciplinary training because they place practice at the heart of research: "Practice-led research as distinct from traditional 'problem led research' does not start with a research problem but rather encourages researchers to dive in and start practicing to see what emerges" (p. 250). This confirms our insight that transdisciplinarity is achieved or approximated through active involvement in learning and exchange, not through didactic teaching or passive learning methods.

Our shift from a didactic teaching model to a flipped classroom model enabled the emergence of what we call "transdisciplinary moments." These were moments in which trainees demonstrated movement towards transdisciplinarity through an insight about the limitations of their own science or the value of another, or the merging of insights from more than one discipline that enlightened the group. For example, a neuroscience-based trainee exclaimed sudden insight into the fact that rats do not have culturally constructed gender like humans do, which might explain the mismatch in predictions from studies of the neurobiology of addiction and the reality revealed by clinical and population health studies. In other examples, students trained in critical social theory and who were acutely wary of knowledge and evidence hierarchies, acknowledged a new willingness to consider the validity of biomedical approaches, despite the problems associated with positivist claims to "objectivity." Throughout the IMPART program, "transdisciplinary moments" were deliberately named, honored and discussed as they occurred, as a way to highlight and encourage the deliberate practice of transdisciplinarity.

In our experience, surmounting barriers to communication is critically important and creating conscious growth and learning in a transdisciplinary training environment requires the explicit use of knowledge translation strategies and innovative approaches to pedagogy. As described, these tools and strategies should be used to prepare the training environment as well as be integrated into training activities so that each and every interaction among trainees becomes an opportunity to practice transdisciplinary exchange.

Key Benefits of Transdisciplinary Training

So far, we have outlined key factors that foster transdisciplinary community as well as have shared some tools and strategies that support movement towards transdisciplinary communication and exchange. In this final section we highlight and discuss some of the key benefits that are outcomes of this approach: transformation of disciplinary and personal identities and increased responsiveness to the complexities of addiction.

Disciplinary and Personal Transformation

Transdisciplinary research training in which members are required to share and examine the limitations and boundaries of their knowledge and expertise has the potential to produce higher standards of critical thinking than can be achieved in unidisciplinary training environments. Exposure to multiple perspectives creates increased challenges to one's own beliefs and practices and thus a greater capacity for reflexivity. Derry and Fischer (2005) observe: "Unlike interdisciplinary, transdisciplinary collaboration may create new knowledge domains outside or in between disciplines and in the process fundamentally transform the disciplinary identities of the collaborating researchers" (p. 4). More than transforming the disciplinary identities of transdisciplinary community members, transdisciplinary training also promotes changes in personal identity and beliefs (Lambert and Monnier-Barbarino 2005). Orozco and Cole assert:

> The passage from unidisciplinary thinking towards holistic understandings capable of responding to real-world social–ecological problems is often associated with growing commitments to social and even political action among students, as future innovators able to create alternatives for sustainability. (Orozco and Cole 2008, p. 496)

The potential that transdisciplinary training holds for promoting higher standards of critical thinking and transformation, both disciplinary and personal, is evident in the following reflections by IMPART graduates on their training[2]:

> As a PhD student in Behavioral Neuroscience at UBC, IMPART significantly impacted my training experience in many essential ways. I developed translational skills to effectively communicate my jargon filled, and often highly complex, research results to a variety of audiences. My growth as a neuroscience researcher has been greatly enhanced by the IMPART program. The transdisciplinary emphasis and practice that IMPART provides has provided me with an experience that I believe has been invaluable to my training as an academic researcher (PhD trainee, Neuroscience).
>
> IMPART helped me broaden my knowledge beyond the clinical psychology "silo" and learn how other disciplines approach mental health and substance use. Indeed, through my seminar presentations my interest was sufficiently piqued in the biological and neurological components of mental health that I am now enrolled in a neuro-anatomy course. Perhaps what I gained most from the IMPART process was hearing the often divergent but always fascinating view points of the other IMPART members, each person coming from a different background with a different focus of research but a similar passion for creating dialogue regarding substance use and gender (MA trainee, Clinical Psychology).

Previous to my fellowship, I had this feeling that the medical model of addiction just didn't cover everything, it was missing something, but I did not have enough education in the field to figure out exactly what the missing pieces were. The opportunity presented to me by IMPART to receive training, and attend and present at seminars, enabled me to figure out just what those missing and disjointed pieces were. My fellowship helped me develop greater understanding, knowledge, and compassion so I can be effective in the field (MA trainee, Epidemiology).

In addition to the effects on trainees, we have also witnessed how transdisciplinary training can transform the trainers. In our twelve year experience of the IMPART program, it is safe to say that the thinking of every mentor, director, and partner towards research training and towards addiction itself has been altered by the process of embracing and fostering transdisciplinarity. Each mentor has been enriched by accepting a more holistic and complex approach to addiction and has opened up to different perspectives. Such transformation is necessary for approaching the complexity of addiction and the range of intersecting issues, and for developing new and holistic approaches to research, health promotion, prevention, harm reduction and treatment.

Enhanced Responsiveness to the Complexities of Addiction and Its Intersections

To build upon the previous insight, we have learned that transdisciplinary work leads to the enhanced ability of members to embrace complexity and to respond to addiction. Transdisciplinary training supports recognition of complexity and identification of diverse ways to approach it, integrating multiple perspectives and approaches. For example, IMPART members noted that there were strong associations among substance use, trauma, violence and mental health problems, as key co-occurring issues for many women and are gendered issues for women and men, girls and boys, but that limited research had synthesized their complex interrelationships (Anda et al. 2006). At the same time, clinicians were calling for integrated treatment models for trauma and substance use, as opposed to the separate and often contradictory models that are commonly used (Finkelstein et al. 2004; Harris and Fallot 2001; Najavits, Weiss, and Shaw 1997). Research training on these issues continued to be largely segmented and discipline-specific. Thus, in 2009 when we applied for renewed funding, the proposal sought to fill these gaps with a focus on the intersections of addiction with mental health issues, violence, and trauma in addition to applying a sex/gender lens.

To reflect IMPART's embrace of increased complexity, the name of the program was changed from the Integrated Mentor Program in Addictions Research Training to Intersections of Mental Health Perspectives in Addictions Research Training. The new name emerged out of a collaboration among trainees to reflect the new foci and objectives of the renewed IMPART framework. Indeed, the development of the renewal grant itself was a transdisciplinary process in which all members of the IMPART community participated, contributing their knowledge in specific areas towards the development of a cross-pillar perspective on addictions and its intersections as an increasingly complex terrain. As a training exercise, trainees were invited to take part in the literature review portion of the grant application. Teams of trainees from key research pillars were assembled and tasked with summarizing the literature on the intersections of violence, trauma, mental health, addictions and gender from their respective fields. Their summaries were then brought together, and the group as a whole, collaborated to create the transdisciplinary literature review. Though not devoid of challenges, this exercise in grappling with the increased complexity of the problem of addiction was illustrative of the potential for transdisciplinary training to prepare individuals to cope with greater complexity. As we have described in this chapter, in order to support this enhanced capacity in learners, the training structure and environment requires continual assessment, refreshment, and flexibility in order to keep up with the needs of learners as well as developments in the area being studied.

Conclusion: Transdisciplinarity Is for Everyone

In this chapter, we have shared our insights into what is takes to foster a transdisciplinary community and support its capacity to move towards transdisciplinary exchange. In the context of an addiction research training program, we found that *diversity* of perspectives among members and flexibility in their roles and options for engagement support a transdisciplinary community to thrive. In contrast to more traditional, unidisciplinary training approaches in which a reliable and comfortable script can be followed, we have demonstrated that transdisciplinary training requires innovative pedagogy and deliberate use of knowledge translation strategies within a flexible structure that can accommodate change over time. Holmes et al. (2008) confirms this approach:

> Transdisciplinarity does not exist automatically, nor all at once; rather, it emerges over time, within and among individuals, groups of individuals, departments, schools, institutions, and organizations. Ultimately there is a need to foster team science so that transdisciplinarity is given a chance to emerge. (p. S191)

While transdisciplinarity is a less charted and more challenging approach to research than other types of collaboration, this should not be viewed as an inherent problem. Rather, the challenges we have described in this chapter are a reflection of the transformative goals and potential of transdisciplinary approaches to addiction. As we have discussed, in transdisciplinary approaches there is recognition and embracing of complexity, and exchange of multiple perspectives with the end goal of generating innovative and effective solutions to a problem. Through our discussion, we have also identified key benefits of the transdisciplinary training that include the potential for disciplinary and personal transformation and increased ability to respond to the complexity of addiction and its various intersections. These are indeed skills helpful to all living and learning and dealing with vexing human problems like addiction with its myriad of historical and contemporary perspectives.

Our final and overarching insight is that transdisciplinarity is by no means limited to a research context. It has relevance across health contexts, environments and sectors. Examples include treatment contexts such as are described in following chapters where teams of multidisciplinary practitioners can more effectively treat clients through shared understandings of each other's perspectives, of addiction and their clients' needs.

Discussion Questions

1. How does transdisciplinarity apply in your own workplace, team or environment?
2. Thinking about the factors that foster transdisciplinarity described in this chapter, which ones might apply for supporting transdisciplinary community and exchange in your own team or environment?
3. Taking the idea of the IMPART transdisciplinary thesaurus, discuss core terms used by your team. Record the different definitions of core terms and discuss the underlying assumptions of each.

Notes

1 For an archived description of the STIHR program, see www.cihr-irsc.gc.ca/e/22174.html
2 Testimonials by graduating trainees as posted on the IMPART website (www.addictiornsresearchtraining.ca/about/about.html#testimonials). Graduates were routinely surveyed at the end of their training about their experience with IMPART as part of our own evaluation efforts.

References

Anda, Robert F., Vincent J. Felitti, J. Douglas Bremner, John D. Walker, Charles Whitfield, Bruce D. Perry, Shata R. Dube, and Wayne H. Giles. 2006. "The enduring effects of abuse and related adverse experiences in childhood: A convergence of evidence from neurobiology and epidemiology." *European Archives of Psychiatry and Clinical Neuroscience* 256:174–186. DOI: 10.1007/s00406-005-0624-4

Derry, Sherry J., and Gerhard Fischer. 2005. "Toward a model and theory for transdisciplinary graduate education." Paper presented at the annual meeting for the American Educational Research Association, Montreal, Canada April 11–15.

Finkelstein, Norma, Nancy VandeMark, Roger Fallot, Vivian B. Brown, Sharon Cadiz, and Jennifer Heckman. 2004. *Enhancing substance abuse recovery through integrated trauma treatment.* Sarasota, FL: National Trauma Consortium.

Hall, Kara L., Daniel Stokols, Richard P. Moser, Brandie K. Taylor, Mark D. Thornquist, Linda C. Nebeling, Carolyn C. Ehret et al. 2008. "The collaboration readiness of transdisciplinary research teams and centers: Findings from the National Cancer Institute's TREC Year-One evaluation study." American Journal of Preventive Medicine 35 (2): S161–S172.

Harris, Maxine, and Roger Fallot. 2001. *Using trauma theory to design service systems.* San Francisco, CA: Jossey Bass.

Holmes, John H., Amy Lehman, Erinn Hade, Amy K. Ferketich, Sarah Gehlert, Garth H. Rausher, Judith Abrams, and Chloe E. Bird. 2008. "Challenges for multi-level health disparities research in transdisciplinary environment." *American Journal of Preventive Medicine* 35(2S): S182–S192. DOI: 10.1016/j.amepre.2008.05.019

Johnson, Joy. L., Lorraine Greaves, and Robin Repta. 2007. *Better Science with sex and gender: A primer for health research.* Vancouver: Women's Health Research Network.

Lambert, Robert, and Patricia Monnioer-Barbarino. 2005. "Transdisciplinary training in reproductive health through online multidisciplinary problem-solving: A proof of concept." *European Journal of Obstetrics and Gynecology and Reproductive Biology* 123(1):82–86. DOI: 10.1016/j.ejogrb.2005.07.001

McWilliam, Erica, Greg Hearn, and Brad Haseman. 2008. "Transdisciplinarity for creative futures: What barriers and opportunities?" *Innovations in Education and Teaching International* 45(3): 247–253. DOI: 10.1080/14703290802176097

Mitrany, Michael, and Daniel Stokols. 2005. "Gauging the transdisciplinary qualities and outcomes of doctoral training programs." *Journal of Planning and Education Research* 24: 437–449. DOI: 10.1177/0739456X04270368

Moore, Michael. 1997. "Theory of transactional distance." In *Theoretical Principles of Distance Education*, edited by Desmond Keegan, 22–38. New York: Routledge.

Najavits, Lisa, Roger D. Weiss, and Sarah R. Shaw. 1997. "The link between substance abuse and posttraumatic stress disorder in women." *American Journal on Addictions* 6(4): 273–283. DOI: 10.1111/j.1521-0391.1997.tb00408.x

Nash, Justin M. 2008. "Transdisciplinary training: Key components and prerequisites for success." *American Journal of Preventive Medicine* 35 (2): S133–S140 DOI: 10.1016/j.amepre.2008.05.004

Nash, Justin M., Bradley N. Collins, Sandra E. Loughlin, Marylou Solbrig, Richard Harvey, Suchitra Krishnan-Sarin, Jennifer Unger et al. 2003. "Training the transdisciplinary scientist: A general framework applied to tobacco use behavior." Nicotine & Tobacco Research 5 (Suppl 1): S41–S53.

Orozco, Fadya, and David Cole. 2008. "Development of transdisciplinarity among students placed with a sustainability for health research project." *EcoHealth* 5: 491–503. DOI: 10.1007/s10393-009-0210-8

Rosenfield, Patricia. 1992. "The potential of transdisciplinary research for sustaining and extending linkages between the health and social sciences." *Social Science & Medicine* 35(11): 1343–1357.

Snow, Mary Elizabeth, Amy Salmon, and Richard Young. 2010. "Teaching transdisciplinarity in a discipline-centered world." *Collected Essays on Learning and Teaching* 3: 159–165.

Songca, Rushiella. 2007. "Transdisciplinarity: The dawn of an emerging approach to acquiring knowledge." *International Journal of African Renaissance Studies- Multi-, Inter- and Transdisciplinarity* 1(2):221–232. DOI: 10.1080/18186870608529718

Tress, Barbel, Gunther Tress, and Gary Fry. 2009. "Integrative research on environmental and landscape change: PhD students' motivations and challenges." *Journal of Environmental Management* 90: 2921–2929. DOI: 10.1016/j.jenvman.2008.03.015

Suggestions for Further Reading

Albrecht, G., Sonia Freeman, and Nick Higginbotham. 1998. Complexity and human health: The case for a transdisciplinary paradigm. *Culture, Medicine, Psychiatry* March 22 (1): 55–92.

Kessel, Frank, and Patricia L. Rosenfield. 2008. Towards transdisciplinary. *American Journal of Preventative Medicine*, 35(2), S225–S234. DOI: http://dx.doi.org/10.1016/j.amepre.2008.05.005

Songca, Rushiella. 2007. Transdisciplinarity: The dawn of an emerging approach to acquiring knowledge. *International Journal of African Renaissance Studies- Multi-, Inter- and Transdisciplinarity* 1(2):221–232. DOI: 10.1080/18186870608529718

3
INTEGRATING TRAUMA WITH ADDICTION RESEARCH AND TREATMENT

Nancy Poole

Trauma is a key element in understanding addiction. The links between addiction and other determinants of and influences on women's and men's health—such as the experience of trauma and violence—are important to all disciplines interested in addiction treatment, prevention and harm reduction. Despite strong associations among substance use, trauma, gender-based violence and mental health concerns, and the range of social determinants of health including gender, there has been insufficient research synthesizing their complex interrelationships. When it has occurred, the study of these intersections and their treatments has typically remained discipline-specific.

That situation needs to change and is changing. Women's health researchers and advocates have long worked at raising awareness of the intersections between substance use, mental health problems, trauma, gender-based violence and the social determinants of health for girls and women (Poole and Greaves 2012; Humphreys, Thiara, and Regan October 2005; Herman 1992; Covington et al. 2008). More recently, clinicians in the field of primary health care and addictions have called for integrated treatment models for trauma and substance use (Klinic 2013; SAMHSA 2014). At the same time, Indigenous scholars are identifying the importance of decolonizing approaches to historical and intergenerational trauma and problematic substance use experienced by Indigenous women and men (Wesley-Esquimaux and Snowball 2010; Brave Heart et al. 2012). In addition, neuroscientists are showing how sympathetic nervous system activation and the HPA axis are involved in trauma responses (Panksepp and Biven 2012) and offering additional avenues for how to intervene (Briere 2006; Ogden, Minton, and Pain 2006; Shapiro 2012). The simultaneity and critical mass of this awareness about the associations between trauma, addiction and gender arising from so many different perspectives, locations and fields is creating an important transdisciplinary juncture in the addictions field. This chapter explores these linkages and describes the potential for advancing treatment and research through a more comprehensive understanding of the role of trauma in peoples' lives, addiction processes, and recovery.

Surveying the Various Literatures on Trauma, Gender and Addiction Intersections

In 2009 IMPART trainees[1] from the four pillars of research recognized by the Canadian Institutes of Health Research—biomedical, clinical, health services, and population health—undertook a literature search to identify existing evidence and perspectives on the intersections of addiction and trauma.[2] Researchers from a wide range of disciplines had to determine search terms and relevant databases appropriate to their pillar to highlight what was known about the intersections between addiction and trauma. The findings were subsequently overlaid with a sex- and gender-based analysis. This would allow a comparison of the various disciplinary perspectives and to identify avenues for future transdisciplinary research, policy and practice collaborations. The findings from this exercise, organized by pillar, are captured in Figure 3.1.[3]

The biomedical team found literature on the interplay of sex-related hormones, genetics and epigenetics, environment and development. In addition, psychological trauma was modeled in the biomedical literature by studies examining the neurobiological systems that underlie stress responsivity (Gunnar and

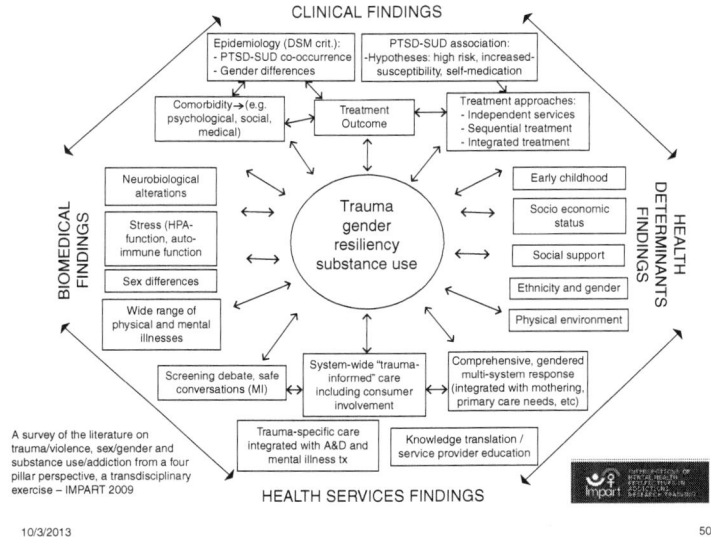

FIGURE 3.1 Literature search findings on trauma and addiction, by research pillar

Quevedo 2007). The hormones released by body and brain in response to stressors were described as interacting with sex hormones and with brain systems involved in addiction (Becker et al. 2007; Kajantie and Phillips 2006). The evidence suggested that women are more prone to long-term alterations in their stress systems, conferring increased vulnerability to adverse trauma-related health outcomes (MacMillan et al. 2001; Nemeroff et al. 2006). The interplay between early environment, childhood or adult trauma and alterations in stress and sex hormones is still remarkably understudied in biomedical research on mental health and substance use. However, all available evidence points to the intersections of these factors as "a perfect storm" for women and girls in neurobiological terms, given the prevalence of early sexual abuse and gendered violence in women's lives and the higher rates of poverty and stress-related lone motherhood.

The clinical team recognized that the definition of trauma in their disciplines was often defined specifically using the diagnostic term, post-traumatic stress disorder (PTSD). PTSD is characterized by the re-experiencing and avoidance of the trauma and increased arousal, with longstanding symptoms causing significant distress and impairment (American Psychiatric Association, 2000). Importantly, women are more likely to develop PTSD. In a Canadian sample of women and men who had experienced at least one traumatic event, 8.2% of women and 1.8% of men had PTSD (Stein, Walker, and Forde 2000). Similarly, a USA-based study observed higher lifetime prevalence of traumatic events among men, yet the risk of PTSD was twice as likely among women (Breslau 2001). Men and women with PTSD and substance-use disorders often differ in their prior experiences. For example, women are more likely than men to report sexual assault and less likely to report physical assault (Cottler, Nishith, and Compton 2001; Peirce et al. 2008; Tolin and Foa 2006). Compared to men, women who have experienced a traumatic event have a greater risk of substance abuse (Danielson et al. 2009) and appear to use more avoidance and emotion-focused coping strategies (Matud 2004). Thus, compared to men, women may experience different forms of trauma and may develop more serious health consequences as a result of this trauma (including anxiety disorders and substance dependence). Again, the intersections of sex, gender and trauma play a big role in determining the experiences of PTSD in a clinical frame.

The population health team found studies that were concerned with identifying the broad factors that confer risk and resilience related to substance use problems for women and men in varying situations. They also found that a gendered investigation of childhood trauma and interpersonal violence may be a key issue to consider. Women who report serious childhood abuse are significantly more likely to report abusing prescription drugs, illegal drugs, tobacco and alcohol than women who did not report childhood abuse (Logan et al. 2002; Agrawal et al. 2005). Interestingly, while they found that social support (one of the social determinants of health) can be a buffer against interpersonal violence among many impoverished women, this support does not protect the women who use drugs or alcohol from interpersonal violence (Golinelli, Longshore, and Wenzel 2008). They also found that population level data show that the historical gender gap in use of alcohol is disappearing. This trend may have implications for vulnerability to trauma and violence as women and men begin to use alcohol at more similar rates, and consequent experiences of violence and trauma may increase for women (Poole and Dell 2005).

The team members from the health services pillar looked for research that captured the topics of trauma, addiction and service system responses. They identified the groundbreaking Women Co-occurring Disorders and Violence Study (WCDVS) from the USA, which generated and applied knowledge about clinical and other interventions nested in an integrated service approach. This approach included an appropriate blend of services and interventions for the target populations of women (and their children) with co-occurring experience of trauma/violence, mental illness and substance use disorders. The results showed that women with these complex co-existing problems were able to reduce these problems when provided with integrated service models that were trauma-informed and financially accessible (Cocozza et al. 2005). Indeed, integrated counseling in a trauma-informed policy and service context was more effective than services as usual (Amaro et al. 2007). Supporting this integration, complex collaboration included consumers, providers and system planners in all aspects of the policy, design, implementation and evaluation of services to improve the quality of the work (Markoff, Reed, et al. 2005). Importantly, from a systems perspective, the costs of such integrated care were not higher (Domino et al. 2005). As this study showed, the integration and coordination of services informed by evidence from the other pillars of health research was central to addressing the interconnections of gender, trauma, mental health concerns and substance use.

While these pillar-specific findings were all rich and critically important in their own disciplinary contexts, the IMPART researchers found surprisingly little overlap or interdisciplinary study as they engaged in this exercise. The notable exception was the WCDVS. The multidisciplinary and multi-sectoral involvement in the WCDVS study seemed to generate a transdisciplinary process and the testing of complex, multi-faceted, clinical and social interventions.

The processes of the IMPART researchers who embarked on the scoping reviews in their respective pillars or disciplines of research are also of interest. While they did not immediately identify transdisciplinary opportunities for their own collaborative involvement, since that time they have had further discussions and developed research ideas. For example, several social scientists associated with IMPART working on the design and delivery of holistic services for pregnant women with substance use problems have engaged with IMPART's lab-based biomedical researchers who are doing research on alcohol consumption with rats, to examine the relative roles of social support and nutrition in the prevention of fetal alcohol spectrum disorder. The potential knowledge gained will offer key translational opportunities for possible interventions with pregnant women at risk for or using substances. This emerging collaboration holds the promise of merging disciplinary perspectives and ultimately joining forces to forge a transdisciplinary approach. Such efforts could be expanded across all pillars, given the increased interest in trauma across disciplines.

Two Recent Trauma-Based Transdisciplinary Approaches

The increased interest in trauma based research as it links to addiction offers a critical opportunity for a transdisciplinary consolidation of understanding. The processes of doing transdisciplinary work offer detail on the issues in developing future thinking that would bring trauma into a transdisciplinary framework. Two divergent examples are discussed in this section. First, the integration of the response to trauma and addiction experienced by women by a multi-sectoral team who linked health service and clinical disciplines/sectors and second, a culturally safe response to historical trauma experienced by Indigenous people achieved through linking the disciplines of neurobiology and social work.

Women's Addiction and Mental Health Treatment

The WCDVS was undertaken between 1998 and 2003 in nine sites in the USA. It remains the key study demonstrating the benefits of an integrated approach to mental health, substance use/addiction and violence/trauma concerns for women. The study was initiated by the Substance Abuse and Mental Health Services Administration (SAMHSA), which recognized a significant lack of appropriate services for women with alcohol, drug abuse and mental health disorders and histories of violence; and the need for evidence about comprehensive, integrated service approaches. In this five-year study, numerous multisectoral and multidisciplinary collaborations were built and maintained to design, implement and then evaluate transdisciplinary approaches to serving women with complex needs and their children. The study involved a cross-section of players including researchers, treatment service system providers, system administrators, policy makers and women who were *consumers* of mental health system services, *survivors* of violence and trauma, and/or in *recovery* from substance use problems (C/S/R women), as well as local and statewide collaborating organizations from multiple systems of care. The first two years of the study were dedicated to relationship building, engaging people from a wide range of organizations and from multiple systems, engaging C/S/R women, delivering cross-training, developing a shared vision for system integration, and developing a system integration approach (Moses, Huntington, and D'Ambrosio 2004). This extensive relational work, to support "relational system change" (system change built on interagency and cross-sector relationships, not on edicts or protocols) (Markoff, Finkelstein, et al. 2005) was fundamental to the achievement of trauma-informed, integrated and transdisciplinary approaches.

The preparatory work to such cross-system and transdisciplinary work can be daunting. In transdisciplinary endeavours, finding common language, understanding each field's philosophical underpinnings and discussing opportunities for linked and integrated approaches is critically important. In the WCDVS personnel from differing systems (mental health, addictions, violence and parenting) often had little knowledge of the assumptions, theories, and practices of other areas (Moses, Huntington, and D'Ambrosio 2004), making shared visioning of integrated responses and services challenging. One such challenge in the WCDVS was related to the timing of substance use/addiction interventions. Prior to the study, most of the addictions treatment personnel deemed it necessary to treat substance *before* getting support for trauma-related and mental health concerns such as depression. Further, they often required women to be abstinent from all substances prior to entering treatment. In the WCDVS women, service providers, system planners and researchers collectively forged new understandings of multiple co-existing problems, and learned how to co-deliver and study multifaceted interventions. This became the foundation to creating a responsive, integrated and transdisciplinary practice. To support this, the first two years were invested in building cross system understanding, awareness, values clarification and consensus, using cross-training, coordinating committees of various sizes, memoranda of agreements, advocacy for system change and other mechanisms (Moses, Huntington, and D'Ambrosio 2004).

The nine sites of the study were distributed across the USA, but all provided a core set of services that included trauma-informed outreach and engagement; screening and assessment; treatment activities including psycho-educational groups; parenting skills; resource coordination and advocacy; trauma-specific services; crisis intervention and peer-run services. Groups were often co-led by practitioners from different disciplines (or different backgrounds such as a consumer and a clinician) enhancing their integrative nature. Many sites reported success with multidisciplinary case conferences and co-facilitation of committees that supported clinical integration and system integration strategies.

Nonetheless, the logistical details of service integration were monumental, and included challenges with transportation and the need to recognise the importance of children, child care and the role of mothering in women's lives. Women's (often realistic) fears of losing custody of their children were respected and addressed. When women reported struggling to meet basic needs for food and shelter, which made it difficult to participate in services, these issues were listened to. Indeed the study sites concluded that systemic changes in approaches to financial aid, housing, health care, employment, child care, children's services, family supports, legal rights, and gendered division of labor in the family were all part of a more comprehensive and tailored response to women with addictions, mental health and trauma-related concerns. The multi-site commitment to participatory processes involving diverse multidisciplinary groups of service providers, administrators, researchers and the C/R/Ss helped ensure that the services were responsive to the needs of all these stakeholders, as well as to local contexts.

Within these participatory and collaborative groups integrating support on trauma became central for mental health and substance use services. This focus was based on the understanding that violence against women is pervasive and clearly implicated in the development of addiction and mental health issues, and therefore needs to be a foundation for safe and relevant service delivery (Finkelstein et al. 2004). Innovative models for delivering integrated trauma, mental health and substance use interventions were utilized and tested such as Seeking Safety (Najavits 2002); and Trauma Recovery and Empowerment (TREM) (Fallot and Harris 2002).

Ultimately, trauma-informed practice was agreed upon as a key approach. All of the sites "arrived at a consensus understanding of the key principles of trauma-informed services and outlined, at both the systems and services levels, several specific ways that mental health and substance abuse service providers could begin to utilize this approach" (Elliott et al. 2005, 462). This principle based approach to address experiences of trauma and integrate this into addictions and mental health treatment emerged as a transdisciplinary bridge between the sites and between the various participating sectors. Principles such as trauma awareness, empowerment, relational collaboration, safety and supporting strengths over pathology (Elliott et al. 2005), made it possible to draw on evidence from psychiatry, psychology, neurobiology, sociology, social work, primary health care, maternal and child health as well as from systems theory in the design of interventions. Indeed, in trauma-informed approaches the focus is on building awareness of connections among issues, and building skills among both practitioners and clients in understanding how trauma affects present functioning, and adaptive skills for coping.

Within the WCDVS, recovery from trauma became a primary goal, not to be addressed in a sequential or parallel way with addictions and mental health treatment, but at the same time. The service providers in the study found it helpful to place less emphasis on exploring women's past abusive experiences and on deficits and labels, and to strengthen the focus on trauma-informed approaches. Other aspects of trauma-informed approaches that were important were maintaining consistency, safety and trustworthiness in service delivery. Logically, this shift to trauma-informed practice led to a re-conceptualization of client "success" from focusing solely on abstinence from substance use and mental health symptom reduction to supporting women's overall "recovery" in multiple domains. The changes seen in this context were significant. As described by one of the study's leads, they included an enhanced ability in women to manage current symptoms and increased understanding of symptoms as attempts to cope (Finkelstein 2002). Women increased their understanding of the way trauma, mental illness and substance abuse had impacted their lives and developed complex new identities integrating all three (Finkelstein 2002). They developed increased empowerment, agency, self esteem and quality of life and increased capacity for mutuality, empathy, authenticity in relationships (Finkelstein 2002). In short, this groundbreaking study is a clear example of the benefits of taking an integrated approach to addiction treatment, and the consequent effects of reaching transdisciplinary consensus and practice.

From Indigenous Health and Social Work

A second illustration of an approach to trauma that offer insights into transdisciplinarity has emerged from Indigenous researchers and clinicians. Indigenous people have experienced a range of traumas and have struggled to conceptualize and respond to trauma in culturally specific ways. Historical trauma, or the wounding that is evident across generations and which often emanates from group trauma, is seen as a critical underpinning of addiction problems for Indigenous peoples (Brave Heart 1998). Indigenous health researchers and clinicians have responded to this by describing some important trauma-specific approaches that link spiritual, psychological and physical health approaches to the healing of historical trauma. For example, Walters and colleagues (Walters et al. 2011, 181) describe how for American Indian or Alaskan Natives (AI/AN):

> Historical [trauma] and contemporary events [contemporary lifetime trauma and chronic stressors] undermine AIAN physical, spiritual, and psychological health and well-being in complex and multifaceted ways.

In a key example of transdisciplinarity, Michael Yellow Bird, an Indigenous clinician, has explored how neurobiology research can be incorporated into social work practice with indigenous people who have experienced historical trauma. He has developed the concept of neurodecolonization: the undoing of negative brain processes and replacing them with positive brain processes. He states that "understanding how the mind and brain are affected by colonization is an important paradigm in decolonizing social work" (Yellow Bird 2013, 293) and that "mindfulness practices offer powerful antidotes to the negative sequelae of colonialism" (306).

Yellow Bird draws on neuroscience research on brain structure, activity and neuroplasticity (Luu and Posner 2003; Schwartz and Begley 2003; Doidge 2007), traditional Indigenous knowledge, and Buddhist teachings on regulation of negative emotions (Goleman 2003) to promote understanding of how "mind and brain function are shaped by the stresses of colonialism and compromise the wellbeing of Indigenous people" (298). He links stressors such as racism and loss of culture to ineffective brain networks that support destructive thoughts, emotions, memories and behaviors, and identifies the need for "the building of new empowered neural networks" (298). Thus, neurodecolonization involves the growth of new beneficial brain networks that enable optimistic thinking, resilience and confidence in order to challenge oppression. Yellow Bird advocates the practice of mindfulness, as practice built on neuroscientific evidence and showing beneficial outcomes for complex health and social problems associated with trauma, addictions and mental illness (Baer 2005). In this way Yellowbird uses transdisciplinary processes to address the goal for social work to be a decolonizing profession.

In addition to linking neuroscience and social work disciplines, neurodecolonization also involves cross-cultural work. Canadian researchers interested in addictions and historical trauma recovery have also employed a cross-cultural and transdisciplinary approach in the study of integrated responses by treatment centers working with Indigenous people with substance use problems (Rowan et al. 2014). In the identification of cultural interventions to support the wellness of Indigenous people with substance use concerns, the Honouring our Strengths: Culture as Intervention research team used a Two-Eyed Seeing approach originated with Mi'kmaq Elders Murdena and Albert Marshall (Bartlett, Marshall, and Marshall 2012). Their approach draws together the strengths of Western and Indigenous knowledge. It involves a flexible and reflexive process of weaving back and forth to integrate or connect the best of Indigenous and Western knowledge systems, both of which are founded on different values and evidentiary sources (Fornssler et al. 2013; Castellano 2000). This intercultural research team identified a range of Indigenous practices and transitions adapted by Indigenous communities for use alongside Western approaches that are designed to be place- and person-specific. For example, participation in sweat lodges, story telling, and ceremonial feasts (Rowan et al. 2014) are culturally based interventions that improve functioning in all areas of wellness, including reducing trauma symptoms for Indigenous people in treatment for substance use problems and addiction. In the course of this work, a bio-psycho-social-spiritual approach, long advocated in the addictions field, is being realized.

These developments in neurodecolonization approaches and in folding cultural/spiritual practices into addictions treatment create new avenues and possibilities for integrated healing, catalyzed by the need to address trauma with substance use. Renee Linklater (2014), author of *Decolonizing Trauma Work: Indigenous Stories and Strategies*, sees the challenge for Indigenous communities when creating programming as one of balancing "the realities of self-medicating survival strategies with the implementation of treatment and healing programs that are accessible, culturally relevant and based on trauma informed approaches" (2014, 41). The recognition of substance use as an adaptive strategy for coping with trauma, together with the need to intervene on trauma simultaneously with addiction, also prompts those working on culturally safe approaches to addiction to engage with harm reducing approaches. As found in the WCDVS study, integrated responses force and facilitate more complex and nuanced responses on multiple issues. Clearly, Indigenous cultures and philosophies have much to offer to assist such multifaceted healing.

Trauma as a Bridge between Neuroscience, Clinical, Population Health and Health Service Approaches

These two exemplars of transdiciplinarity offer insights that can be replicated and learned from. Significant, inspiring transdisciplinary thinking and action has emerged from the WCDVS and those interested in decolonizing approaches to substance use problems and addictions experienced by Indigenous people. These interventions bridge clinical and population health pillars as in the WCDVS, and bridge neuroscience-clinical-population health as illustrated by Indigenous neurodecolonization. Together, they illustrate the possibilities for drawing together the best of the seemingly disparate philosophies and approaches to addiction described in Chapter 1 and for addressing gender and diversity in trauma- and gender-informed and gender-specific ways. As such, they present a real opportunity and juncture for the addictions field where integrated, gendered, and transdisciplinary approaches can fundamentally shift practice and policy.

Is trauma a unifying concept in addiction? It is possible that the importance of trauma in addiction may assist the addictions and mental health fields in integrating approaches in a way that is not acquisitive, with one field subsuming the other (Greaves 2006; Greaves and Poole 2007) but rather in a mutually supportive and progressive manner. It may also catalyze the adoption of harm-reducing approaches, as trauma-informed approaches have comparable engagement oriented benefits, enabling a wider access to treatment. The translation of trauma and neuroscience into affect regulation interventions that are linked to ancient spiritual traditions have the potential to affirm the bio-psycho-social-spiritual approaches that are seldom fully enacted by the addictions field. The different experiences of trauma across ages, genders and cultures and the emerging and promising responses in child welfare, child and youth mental health, women's treatment, refugee and Indigenous settings, have the potential to help the addictions field embrace gendered and culturally competent approaches for all groups. The tremendous alliances that were built and maintained across multiple systems of care in the WCDVS—which involved women, service providers, administrators, system planners, decision makers and researchers in collectively forging new gendered understandings—birthed responsive, integrated principle-based, transdisciplinary interventions. Similarly, the innovative cross-fertilization of perspectives and approaches in reaching for neurodecolonization is a model for other culturally competent transdisciplinary efforts. Both of these examples are an inspiration to forging new transdisciplinary projects that are integrated and trauma-informed. The opportunities afforded by studying the WCDVS and emerging Indigenous approaches to melding complex responses to trauma and addiction are critically important and worth seizing.

Discussion Questions

1. What have you noticed about the links among trauma and substance use problems/addictions, when undertaking work in one or more of the pillars investigated by the IMPART trainees (biomedical, clinical, health services and/or population health pillars)?
2. Do you see trauma as central to substance use and mental health disorders as did the researchers in the Women Co-occurring Disorders and Violence Study? Regardless of its centrality, how do you see addiction treatment enhanced by the integration of trauma-informed approaches?

3. What other transdisciplinary opportunities might be pursued beyond those created through linking neuroscience and decolonizing social work practices, or linking health services, clinical and parenting approaches for women, as described here?

Notes

1 See Chapter 2 for a description of the Intersections of Mental Health Perspectives in Addictions Research Training (IMPART) program.
2 The IMPART trainees and coordinators involved in this literature search exercise were: Michelle Coghlan, Erin Gibson, Kim Hellemans, Warren Michelow, Nancy Poole, Hajera Rostam, Joanna Sliwowska, Elizabeth Snow, Iris Torchalla, Kristina Uban and Nicole Vittoz. Two unpublished papers—the complete findings and a short summary titled "What a Difference Trauma Makes (in the Lives of Women): Looking Through a Transdisciplinary Lens"—were generated following the search.
3 This diagram summarizes the multi-pillar findings from this literature search. The layout for this diagram was inspired by a diagram found in an article identified in the search authored by Logan, Walker, Cole and Leukefeld (2002).

References

Agrawal, A., P.A.F. Madden, A. C. Heath, M. T. Lynskey, K. K. Bucholz, and N. G. Martin. 2005. Correlates of regular cigarette smoking in a population-based sample of Australian twins. *Addiction* 100 (11):1709–1719.

Amaro, Hortensia, Miriam Chernoff, Vivian Brown, Sandra Arévalo, and Margaret Gatz. 2007. Does integrated trauma-informed substance abuse treatment increase treatment retention? *Journal of Community Psychology* 35 (7):845–862.

American Psychiatric Association. 2000. *Diagnostic and statistical manual of mental disorders, 4th ed., text revision.* Washington, DC: American Psychiatric Association.

Baer, Ruth. 2005. *Mindfulness-based treatment approaches: Clinician's guide to evidence base and applications.* London: Elsevier.

Bartlett, Cheryl, Murdena Marshall, and Albert Marshall. 2012. Two-eyed seeing and other lessons learned within a co-learning journey of bringing together indigenous and mainstream knowledges and ways of knowing. *Journal of Environmental Studies and Sciences* 2 (4):331–340.

Becker, Jill B., Lisa M. Monteggia, Tara S. Perrot-Sinal, Russell D. Romeo, Jane R. Taylor, Rachel Yehuda, and Tracy L. Bale. 2007. Stress and disease: Is being female a predisposing factor? *The Journal of Neuroscience* 27 (44):11851–11855.

Brave Heart, Maria Yellow Horse. 1998. The return to the sacred path: Healing the historical trauma response among the Lakota. *Smoth College Studies in Social Work* 68 (3):287–305.

Brave Heart, Maria Yellow Horse, Jennifer Elkins, Greg Tafoya, Doreen Bird, and Melina Salvador. 2012. Wicasa Was'aka: Restoring the traditional strength of American Indian boys and men. *American Journal of Public Health* 102 (Suppl. 2):S177–S183.

Breslau, Naomi. 2001. Gender differences in trauma and posttraumatic stress disorder. *The Journal of Gender-Specific Medicine: JGSM: The Official Journal of the Partnership for Women's Health at Columbia* 5 (1):34–40.

Briere, J. 2006. *Principles of trauma therapy: A guide to symptoms, evaluation, and treatment.* Thousand Oaks, CA: Sage.

Castellano, M. B. 2000. Updating aboriginal traditions of knowledge. In *Indigenous Knowledges in Global Contexts: Multiple Readings of Our World*, edited by G.J. Sefa Dei, B.L. Hall, and D.G. Rosenberg. Toronto, ON: University of Toronto Press.

Cocozza, Joseph J., Elizabeth W. Jackson, Karen Hennigan, Joseph P. Morrissey, Beth Glover Reed, Roger Fallot, and Steve Banks. 2005. Outcomes for women with co-occurring disorders and trauma: Program-level effects. *Journal of Substance Abuse Treatment* 28 (2):109–119.

Cottler, L. B., P. Nishith, and W.M. Compton. 2001. Gender differences in risk factors for trauma exposure and post-traumatic stress disorder among inner-city drug abusers in and out of treatment. *Comprehensive Psychiatry* 42 (2):111–117.

Covington, Stephanie S., Cynthia Burke, Sandy Keaton, and Candice Norcott. 2008. Evaluation of a trauma-informed and gender-responsive intervention for women in drug treatment. *Journal of Psychoactive Drugs*: 387–398.

Danielson, Carla Kmett, Ananda B. Amstadter, Ruth E. Dangelmaier, Heidi S. Resnick, Benjamin E. Saunders, and Dean G. Kilpatrick. 2009. Trauma-related risk factors for substance abuse among male versus female young adults. *Addictive Behaviors* 34 (4):395–399.

Doidge, Norman. 2007. *The Brain that Changes Itself: Stories of personal triumph from the frontiers of brain science*. New York: Penguin Books.

Domino, Marisa E., Joseph P. Morrissey, Terri Nadlicki-Patterson, and Sukyung Chung. 2005. Service costs for women with co-occurring disorders and trauma. *Journal of Substance Abuse Treatment* 28 (2):135–143.

Elliott, Denise E., Paula Bjelajac, Roger D. Fallot, Laurie S. Markoff, and Beth Glover Reed. 2005. Trauma-informed or trauma-denied: Principles and implementation of trauma-informed services for women. *Journal of Community Psychology* 33 (4):461–477.

Fallot, Roger D., and Maxine Harris. 2002. The Trauma Recovery and Empowerment Model (TREM): Conceptual and practical issues in a group intervention for women. *Community Mental Health Journal* 38 (6):475–485.

Finkelstein, Norma. 2002. Enhancing substance abuse treatment with women through integrated trauma treatment. In *Seminar on Women's Substance Use Treatment*. Vancouver, BC: Co-Sponsored by the Aurora Treatment Centre at BC Women's Hospital and the BC Centre of Excellence for Women's Health.

Finkelstein, Norma, Nancy VandeMark, Roger Fallot, Vivian Brown, Sharon Cadiz, and Jennifer Heckman. 2004. Enhancing substance abuse recovery through integrated trauma treatment. Sarasota, FL: National Trauma Consortium.

Fornssler, Barbara, Holly A. McKenzie, Colleen Anne Dell, Larry Laliberte, and Carol Hopkins. 2013. "I got to know them in a new way": Rela(y/t)ing rhizomes and community-based knowledge (brokers') transformation of western and Indigenous knowledge. *Cultural Studies Critical Methodologies*. DOI: 10.1177/1532708613516428

Goleman, D. 2003. *Destructive emotions and how we can overcome them: A dialogue with the Dalai Lama*. London, UK: Bloomsbury.

Golinelli, Daniela, Douglas Longshore, and Suzanne L. Wenzel. 2008, June 6. Substance use and intimate partner violence: clarifying the relevance of women's use and partner's use. *Journal of Behavioural Health Services and Research* Special Issue. DOI: 10.1007/s11414-008-9114-6

Greaves, Lorraine. 2006. Mergers and acquisitions: Making them work for women. *Research Bulletin of the Canadian Centres of Excellence for Women's Health* 5 5 (1):1–3.

Greaves, Lorraine, and Nancy Poole. 2007, October. *Brief to the Mental Health Commission on applying a sex and gender based analysis to mental health and addiction*. Vancouver, BC: British Columbia Centre of Excellence for Women's Health.

Gunnar, Megan, and Karina Quevedo. 2007. The neurobiology of stress and development. *Annual Review of Psychology* 58:145–173.
Herman, Judith L. 1992. *Trauma and recovery*. New York: HarperCollins.
Humphreys, Cathy, Ravi Thiara, and Linda Regan. 2005, October. *Domestic violence and substance use: Overlapping issues in separate services*. London, UK: Home Office and Greater London Authority.
Kajantie, Eero, and David I.W. Phillips. 2006. The effects of sex and hormonal status on the physiological response to acute psychosocial stress. *Psychoneuroendocrinology* 31 (2):151–178.
Klinic. 2013. *Trauma-informed: The trauma toolkit*. Winnipeg, MB: Klinic Community Health Centre. http://trauma-informed.ca/wp-content/uploads/2013/10/Trauma-informed_Toolkit.pdf. (accessed November 15, 2014).
Linklater, Renee. 2014. *Decolonizing trauma work: Indigenous stories and strategies*. Halifax, NS: Fernwood.
Logan, T. K., Robert Walker, Jennifer Cole, and Carl Leukefeld. 2002. Victimization and substance use among women: Contributing factors, interventions and implications. *Review of General Psychology* 6 (4):325–397.
Luu, Phan, and Michael I. Posner. 2003. Anterior cingulate cortex regulation of sympathetic activity. *Brain* 126 (10):2119–2120.
MacMillan, H. L., J. E. Fleming, D. L. Streiner, E. Lin, M. H. Boyle, E. Jamieson, E. K. Duku, C. A. Walsh, M. Y. Wong, and W.R. Beardslee. 2001. Childhood abuse and lifetime psychopathology in a community sample. *American Journal of Psychiatry* 158:1878–1883.
Markoff, Laurie S., Norma Finkelstein, Nina Kammerer, Peter Kreiner, and Carol A. Prost. 2005. Relational systems change: Implementing a model of change in integrating services for women with substance abuse and mental health disorders and histories of trauma. *Journal of Behavioral Health Services & Research* 32 (2):227–240.
Markoff, Laurie S., Beth Glover Reed, Roger D. Fallot, Denise E. Elliott, and Paula Bjelajac. 2005. Implementing trauma-informed alcohol and other drug and mental health services for women: Lessons learned in a multisite demonstration project. *The American Journal of Orthopsychiatry* 75 (4 Print):525–539.
Matud, M. Pilar. 2004. Gender differences in stress and coping styles. *Personality and Individual Differences* 37:1401–1415.
Moses, Dawn Jahn, Nicholas Huntington, and Brandy D'Ambrosio. 2004, April. *Developing integrated services for women with co-occurring disorders and trauma histories: Lessons from the SAMSHA Women with Alcohol, Drug Abuse and Mental Health Disorders Who have Histories of Violence study*. Washington, DC: National Center on Family Homelessness.
Najavits, Lisa M. 2002. *Seeking safety: A treatment manual for PSTD and substance abuse*. New York: Guilford Press.
Nemeroff, Charles B., J. Douglas Bremner, Edna B. Foa, Helen S. Mayberg, Carol S. North, and Murray B. Stein. 2006. Posttraumatic stress disorder: A state-of-the-science review. *Journal of Psychiatric Research* 40 (1):1–21.
Ogden, Pat, Kejuni Minton, and Claire Pain. 2006. *Trauma and the body: A sensorimotor approach to psychotherapy*. New York: W.W. Norton.
Panksepp, Jaak, and Lucy Biven. 2012. *The archaeology of mind: Neuroevolutionary origins of human emotion*. New York: W.W. Norton.
Peirce, Jessica M., Kori A. Kindbom, Mathew C. Waesche, Abigail S. E. Yuscavage, and Robert K. Brooner. 2008. Posttraumatic stress disorder, gender, and problem profiles in substance dependent patients. *Substance Use & Misuse* 43 (5):596–611.

Poole, Nancy, and Colleen A. Dell. 2005. Girls, women and substance use. Ottawa, ON: British Columbia Centre of Excellence for Women's Health and the Canadian Centre on Substance Abuse.

Poole, Nancy, and Lorraine Greaves, eds. 2012. *Becoming trauma informed*. Toronto, ON: Centre for Addiction and Mental Health

Rowan, Margo, Nancy Poole, Beverley Shea, Joseph Jones, David Myota, Marwa Fang, Carol Hopkins, Laura Hall, Christopher Mushquash, and Colleen Dell. 2014. Cultural interventions to treat addictions in Indigenous populations: Findings from a scoping study. *Substance Abuse Treatment, Prevention, and Policy* 9 (34).

SAMHSA. 2014. *Trauma-informed care in behavioral health services: Treatment Improvement Protocol (TIP) Series 57.* Rockville, MD: Substance Abuse and Mental Health Services Administration.

Schwartz, Jeffrey M., and Sharon Begley. 2003. *The mind and the brain: Neuroplasticity and the power of mental force.* New York: ReganBooks.

Shapiro, Francine. 2012. *Getting past your past: Take control of your life with self-help techniques from EMDR.* New York: Rodale.

Stein, Murray B., John R. Walker, and David R. Forde. 2000. Gender differences in susceptibility to posttraumatic stress disorder. *Behaviour Research and Therapy* 38 (6):619–628.

Tolin, David F., and Edna B. Foa. 2006. Sex differences in trauma and posttraumatic stress disorder: A quantitative review of 25 years of research. *Psychological Bulletin* 132 (6):959.

Walters, Karina L., Selina A. Mohammed, Teresa Evans-Campbell, Ramona E. Beltrán, David H. Chae, and Bonnie Duran. 2011. Bodies don't just tell stories, they tell histories. *Du Bois Review: Social Science Research on Race* 8 (01):179–189.

Wesley-Esquimaux, Cynthia C., and Andrew Snowball. 2010. Viewing violence, mental illness and addiction through a wise practices lens. *International Journal of Mental Health & Addiction* 8 (2):390–407.

Yellow Bird, Michael. 2013. Neurodecolonization: Applying mindfullness research to decolonizing social work. In *Decolonizing Social Work*, edited by M. Gray, J. Coates, M. Yellow Bird, and T. Heatherington. Burlington, VT: Ashgate.

Suggestions for Further Reading

Bloom, Sandra L., and Brian Farragher. 2013. *Restoring Sanctuary: A new operating system for trauma-informed systems of care.* New York, NY: Oxford University Press.

Jakovljević, Miro, Lovorka Brajković, Nenad Jakšić, Mladen Lonćar, Branka Aukst-Margetić, and Davor Lasić. 2012. "Posttraumatic stress disorders (PTSD) from different perspectives: A transdisciplinary integrative approach." *Psychiatria Danubina* 24 (3): 246–255.

Poole, Nancy, and Lorraine Greaves. 2012. *Becoming trauma informed.* Toronto, ON: Centre for Addiction and Mental Health

SAMHSA. 2014. Trauma-informed care in behavioral health services: Treatment Improvement Protocol (TIP) Series 57. Rockville, MD: Substance Abuse and Mental Health Services Administration.

4

OF MICE AND WO/MEN: TRANSDISCIPLINARITY IN THE LABORATORY

Travis E. Baker, Vivian Lam, Ni Lan, Kristina Andrea Uban and Joanne Weinberg[1]

Substance use disorders (SUDs) are extremely complex, resulting from a confluence of risk factors related to biology/neurobiology, stress, sex and gender, cognition, personality, genetics, mental health, culture and the social environment (W.R. Miller and Carroll 2006). An understanding of the neurobiological, behavioural and cognitive mechanisms that underlie substance use disorders, together with alterations in cognitive control and decision making, and the role of biological, social, environmental and sex- and gender-related variables could act as a pivotal point within the confluence of risk factors that comprise these disorders, and ultimately help to reduce or alleviate this serious public health problem.

This chapter explores the relationships among neurobiology, sex and gender, stress/trauma, addiction and mental health, as well as theories of decision making and cognitive neuroscience from a transdisciplinary perspective. The Intersections of Mental Health Perspectives in Addictions Research Training (IMPART) program provided us with the invaluable experience of interacting with researchers from across disciplines, sectors and settings to understand how to conduct sex- and gender-based analyses with a focus on the intersections of stress, trauma and mental health with addictions. Here, we deconstruct the neurobiological, cognitive, behavioural, stress-, sex- and gender-related factors underlying individual differences in vulnerability to drugs and the transition to addiction. While previous studies have examined many of these variables, these studies have often focused solely on male subjects and have not considered sex and gender issues. The possible role of early life experience as a vulnerability factor for the development of addiction is also often overlooked. This chapter brings together the work of an interdisciplinary team of investigators working with both animal models and human subjects and is motivated by their multiple interrelated areas of investigation, towards understanding addiction from a transdisciplinary perspective. This approach provides an important step forward in addressing some of the gaps in the literature and providing a comprehensive view of addiction and SUDs. As an exemplar, we explore fetal alcohol spectrum disorder (FASD), focusing on both animal and clinical studies and highlighting how knowledge of the multiple factors that influence addiction and SUDs has important implications for understanding the range of phenotypes observed in FASD. The work of our group is a powerful example of how a transdisciplinary approach, with a focus across the life cycle, can begin to elucidate possible mechanisms underlying vulnerability to mental health problems in later life.

Neurobiology of Addiction and Substance Use Disorders (SUDs)

Research suggests that the dopamine and stress (hypothalamic-pituitary-adrenal [HPA]) systems and their extended central neurocircuitries play critical roles in addiction. In turn, these systems not only interact extensively with each other, but their circuitries overlap with those underlying depression, anxiety and other mental health disorders. Moreover, all of these circuitries are typically sexually dimorphic in function. The following sections discuss our current understanding of addiction as a disorder of learning and memory/cognitive control and decision making, the role of the dopamine and stress systems and their interactions in mediating behavioural changes observed in addiction, and the sex and gender differences known to occur in the functions and interactions of these systems.

Dysregulation of Dopamine Systems and Vulnerability to Substance Use Disorders

Dopaminergic cell bodies are located in two major brain areas: the ventral tegmental area (VTA) and the substantia nigra (see Figure 4.1).

Of particular relevance, the VTA projects to limbic and cortical areas (the mesocorticolimbic pathway) involved in cognitive control and decision-making, namely the medial prefrontal, orbitofrontal and anterior cingulate cortices, and the basal ganglia, including the nucleus accumbens (Volkow et al. 2011). This neuromodulatory system plays important roles in motor function, motivation, reward and reinforcement, learning and memory, executive function (saliency of stimuli or events, attention, planning, organizing) and emotional regulation.

In this context, addiction has recently been hypothesized to be fundamentally a problem of learning and memory (Hyman 2005). Data suggest that addictive drugs drive maladaptive behaviours through interactions with dopaminergic mechanisms evolved for reward processing, cognitive control and decision making (Redish, Jensen, and Johnson 2008), making dopamine a central component to SUDs. Whereas natural rewards and associated cues produce transient increases in dopamine activity only when these events are unexpected, addictive drugs and

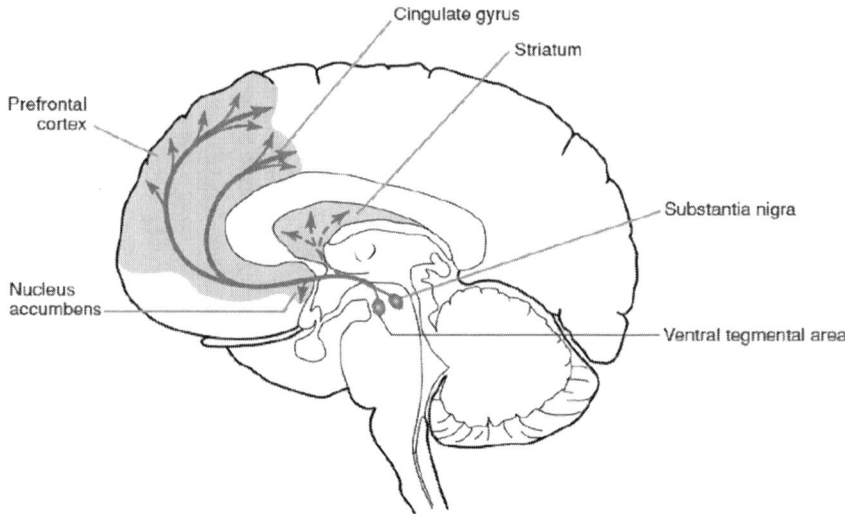

FIGURE 4.1 The major dopamine pathways in the brain

Illustrated are projections from dopamine cell bodies in the ventral tegmental area to the nucleus accumbens and the prefrontal and anterior cingulate (cingulate gyrus) cerebral cortex, and projections from the substantia nigra to the basal ganglia (dorsal striatum—caudate, putamen and nucleus accumbens).
From Hyman, Malenka, and Nestler, 2006.

drug-related cues increase dopamine levels even when these events are expected (Rice and Cragg 2004). Thus, drugs of abuse effectively increase the magnitude of dopaminergic signals (Di Chiara and Imperato 1988). In turn, potentiated dopamine activity induces alterations in the cortical targets of the dopamine system (Robinson and Kolb 2004). Moreover, because these brain areas underlie neural processes that are central to cognitive control and decision making, including goal-directed action selection, response activation and inhibition, performance monitoring and reward-based learning (Holroyd and Coles 2002; E.K. Miller and Cohen 2001), addictive drugs are sometimes said to "usurp" the cognitive control system (Hyman 2007). Thus, the control system withdraws control over behaviours that it should inhibit, and facilitates behaviours that it should not. Inevitably, the consequence of overconsumption of drugs of abuse can be a desensitization to the drugs' reinforcing effects, hypersensitivity to drug-associated stimuli (i.e., drug 'wanting'), and a decrease in the reinforcing strength of alternative reinforcers (Koob and Le Moal 2008a), possibly mediated by the dopamine receptor downregulation and reduced dopamine system function that occur with chronic drug intake (Volkow et al. 2011). Functional consequences of these maladaptive processes are that drug rewards become overvalued at the expense of other natural rewards, contributing to the compulsion to obtain and use drugs (Hyman, Malenka, and Nestler 2006). This dysregulation is of central importance for vulnerability to, or resilience against, addiction and SUDs (Di Chiara and Bassareo 2007; Volkow et al. 2011), and can be very long lasting, even following long periods of abstinence.

Together, these observations have profoundly influenced contemporary notions regarding the role of dopamine in reinforcement learning and addiction. Interestingly, the neural changes described above can result from chronic use of a broad range of substances, including alcohol, nicotine, heroin and cocaine (Volkow et al. 2009), supporting the idea that there may be common substance-induced neurobiological alterations, and suggesting a "universal" neurobiological pathway to increased vulnerability to subsequent SUDs.

Sex and Gender Differences in Dopamine Dysregulation and Vulnerability to Mental Health Problems

The gonadal or sex hormones (e.g., estradiol, progesterone and testosterone) are known to modulate the dopaminergic reward system (Anker and Carroll 2011). In animal studies, variation in behavioural and neurochemical responses of males and females to drugs such as cocaine can occur due to modulatory effects of gonadal hormones on dopamine activity (Carroll and Anker 2010; Becker, Perry, and Westenbroek 2012). A recent human study found that the response of the dopaminergic system in females depends on the phase of the menstrual cycle (Dreher et al. 2007). Brain regions involved in processing emotions, such as the amygdala and orbitofrontal cortex are activated to a greater extent during the follicular phase (4 to 8 days after the start of the menstrual period) than during the luteal phase (6 to 10 days after the luteinizing hormone surge) of the cycle. Conversely, when men anticipate rewards, they mainly activate the ventral striatum, another region involved in motivation for obtaining rewards. Data such as these have important implications for understanding sex and gender differences in susceptibility to addiction.

Consistent with these findings, the sex hormones appear to play a key role in the sex and gender differences observed in mental health problems, including SUDs (Becker and Hu 2008). Findings from both clinical and basic research suggest that females tend to escalate their consumption of substances more quickly and at lower doses, and are more prone to stress-induced relapse than males, especially when levels of circulating estradiol are increased (Becker and Hu 2008). Although psychosocial factors likely have an impact, converging evidence from animal studies suggests that the sex hormones play an important role in these differences. In rats, for example, cocaine self-administration varies across the estrous cycle (Roberts, Bennett, and Vickers 1989), with high doses of estradiol facilitating self-administration (Lynch et al. 2001). Moreover, the enhanced cocaine self-administration in females is abolished by removing the ovaries, and can be reinstated by administration of estradiol (Hu et al. 2004). Thus, similar to their effect on HPA function (discussed below), estrogens appear to facilitate dopaminergic function.

Despite evidence that females may be more vulnerable to SUDs on a neurobiological level, substance abuse and dependence disorders are 2–3 times more likely in men than women in adulthood (Van Etten and Anthony 2001). These contradictory findings may reflect effects of the social environment (Becker and Hu 2008), including gendered prescribing practices, gender norms, roles and expectations and gendered drug use patterns and preferences or could reflect fluctuating hormone levels during the menstrual cycle, which could alter drug-seeking/wanting cognitions and thus change the perceptual experience surrounding substance use. Interestingly, steadily increasing rates of illicit and non-illicit drug use in adolescent girls compared to adolescent boys suggest that the gender difference observed to date may be changing (Becker and Hu 2008). Moreover, these findings speak to the value of using animal models to investigate neurobiological underpinnings of SUDs, as biological, genetic, nutritional and environmental variables can be controlled in ways not possible in the human situation. Conversely, complex emotion, behaviour, cognitive processes, environment, nutritional status and genetic variability that exist among humans cannot always be modeled with animals. Thus, transdisciplinary perspectives are needed to apply and evaluate working hypotheses across basic, clinical and community-based studies. This transdisciplinary flow of hypotheses accelerates knowledge, and provides a rigorous platform upon which competing hypotheses can be evaluated. Ultimately, we can form universal theories about SUDs that encompass the intersections of dopamine and stress dysregulation, sex and gender differences and co-morbid mental health problems.

Dysregulation of the HPA Axis and Vulnerability to Substance Use Disorders

The HPA axis responds to real and potential environmental threats to homeostasis or baseline function (i.e., stressors), and mediates activation of behavioural and physiological responses that facilitate coping (McEwen 2008). The activity of the HPA axis involves a cascade of hormones (see Figure 4.2).

An area at the base of the brain called the hypothalamus releases corticotropin-releasing hormone (CRH), which stimulates the pituitary to release a hormone called adrenocorticotropic hormone (ACTH), which in turn stimulates the adrenal gland to release glucocorticoid hormones (cortisol in humans, corticosterone in most rodents). These hormones exert significant effects on virtually all systems in the body including the brain and are critical in initiating responses that enable the organism to respond to and cope with stressors and feed back to multiple brain areas to return the system to homeostasis.

Stress responses are adaptive in the short term, utilizing a range of neural, metabolic and immune systems (McEwen 2008). However, long-term activation of these short-term adaptive processes can lead to dysregulation of these same systems (McEwen 2008; Sinha 2009), and ultimately, the development of pathology

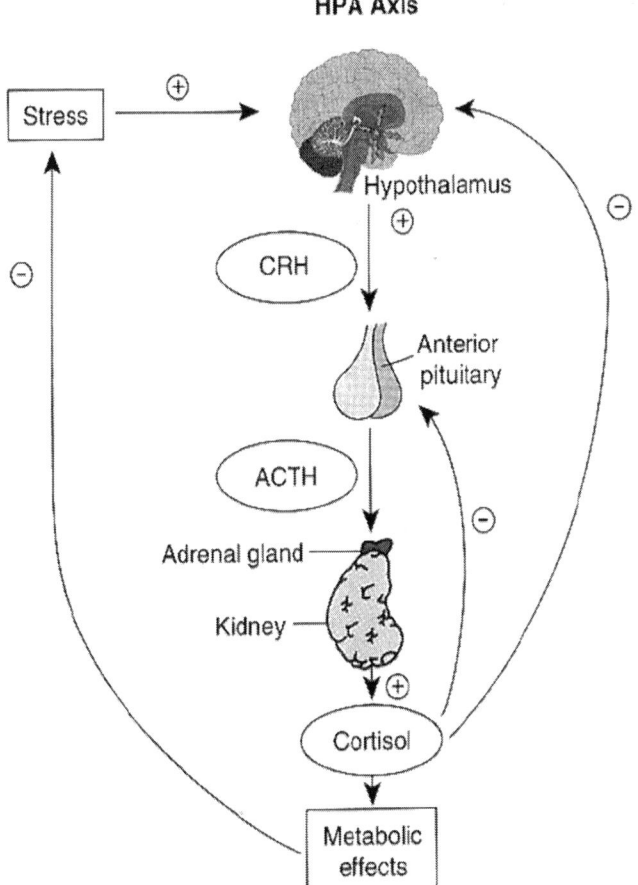

FIGURE 4.2 The hypothalamic-pituitary-adrenal (HPA) axis

The hypothalamus is activated by stressors, and stimulates the release of hormones such as corticotropin-releasing hormone (CRH), that act on the anterior pituitary to stimulate the release of adrenocorticotropic hormone (ACTH). ACTH then circulates in the blood and stimulates the release of glucocorticoids (cortisol in humans, corticosterone in most rodents) from the adrenal gland. Glucocorticoids provide negative feedback to all levels of the HPA axis to bring the system back to normal levels. Glucocorticoids also have numerous metabolic effects throughout the body and help us respond to and cope with stress.

(Juster, McEwen, and Lupien 2010), including depression, anxiety and SUDs (Koob 2008). Continued exposure to stressors can potentially result in further deviation of stress responses from baseline functioning, and in turn alter other systems with which they interact, including dopamine systems (Koob and Le Moal 2008a). Both basic and clinical studies suggest that the long-term neurobiological effects of stress and adversity, during childhood or adulthood can result in stress system dysregulation, with subsequent susceptibility to a range of mental health problems including SUDs (Koob 2008; Sinha 2008). Due to the considerable overlap between central dopamine and HPA systems, stress interacts with neurobiological pathways implicated in drug reward, and conversely, drug intake alters stress system activity (Koob and Kreek 2007). Alterations in stress systems appear to be involved in the transition from acute to chronic drug intake and contribute to both positive (binge stage) and negative (withdrawal) reinforcement aspects of addiction (Koob 2008). Furthermore, evidence from both basic and clinical studies demonstrates a relationship between chronic use of drugs of abuse and enhanced responses to stressors. In rats: basal stress hormone levels are known to correlate with amount of self-administered cocaine (Mantsch et al. 2000); acute cocaine use activates, while chronic use attenuates, HPA activity; and CRH is released if cocaine intake increases during self-administration (Sarnyai, Shaham, and Heinrichs 2001). Similarly, HPA activity increases with acute alcohol consumption, but decreases with repeated exposure (Lee et al. 2001; Brick and Pohorecky 1983). Alcoholics in acute withdrawal have elevated CRH levels in their cerebrospinal fluid (Adinoff et al. 1996). Conversely, increased alcohol consumption, craving and relapse to drinking have been reported in abstinent alcoholics with high levels of stress and anxiety (Hore 1971; Kushner, Sher, and Beitman 1990). As well, stress sensitizes (response is increasingly amplified) healthy individuals to the rewarding effects of substances, and can induce relapse after abstinence (Sarnyai, Shaham, and Heinrichs 2001). Furthermore, the dopamine reward system is activated following psychological stress, which increases sensitivity to the rewarding effects of drugs (Koob and Le Moal 2008b). HPA alterations thus appear to provide a pathway for increased vulnerability to drug use. Understanding the bi-directional interactions between the HPA and dopamine pathways will help to elucidate mechanisms underlying individual vulnerability to addiction (Koob and Kreek 2007).

It is noteworthy that although stress-dopamine interactions have been widely investigated in animal and human studies, the subjects have been predominantly male. Given the known sex and gender differences in these systems, future research should reexamine some of these 'classic' stress-dopamine effects in females. This is a gap in both basic and clinical research focused on the role of stress-dopamine interactions in vulnerability to mental health problems and SUDs.

Fetal Alcohol Spectrum Disorder (FASD): Fetal Programming, Sex and Gender Differences, Stress and Vulnerability to Substance Use Disorders

The link between the prenatal environment and later physical and mental health in adulthood has long been recognized (Seckl and Holmes 2007), specifically as it pertains to adverse intrauterine environments including poor nutrition, exposure to teratogenic substances such as alcohol or nicotine, and maternal stress. Increasing evidence suggests that some adult diseases may have common developmental origins, i.e., the "Developmental Origins of Health and Disease" (DOHaD) concept. Links between an adverse intrauterine environment and development of chronic diseases, including cardiovascular disease, Type 2 diabetes, and mental health disorders have been described across the life span (Barker 1998). At the same time, evidence supporting fetal programming, as a possible mechanism underlying the long-term consequences of early life experiences has also been published (Seckl and Holmes 2007). Fetal programming refers to the concept that adverse pre-/perinatal environments can program developing and/or maturing neurobiological systems, resulting in altered sensitivity of these systems throughout life. The HPA axis is particularly vulnerable to programming by early life events and may provide a final common pathway through which different early life events can alter long-term outcomes (Meaney and Szyf 2005; Weaver et al. 2004).

Fetal Alcohol Spectrum Disorder (FASD)

FASD refers to the broad range of deficits that can occur in offspring whose mothers consumed alcohol during pregnancy. Long-lasting alcohol-related effects can include growth deficiencies, physical abnormalities (including a characteristic facial dysmorphology in children most severely affected), and/or damage to the central nervous system, including neurodevelopmental and neurobehavioural abnormalities (Calhoun and Warren 2007). Mental health problems in children with FASD are often referred to as "secondary disabilities," i.e., deficits that occur secondarily to and often as a consequence of the primary deficits. However, animal studies, supported by imaging studies on human subjects, suggest that mental health problems may have a primary basis as well, as alcohol-induced alterations in neurobiology, including HPA, dopamine, and other systems, likely influence an individual's vulnerability to developing mental health problems, including SUDs.

Research in our laboratory has utilized an animal model of prenatal alcohol exposure (PAE) to investigate adverse effects of alcohol on developmental outcomes, with particular focus on vulnerability to stress-related mental health problems, such as depression, anxiety and SUDs.

The Contribution of Animal Models to Understanding Alcohol as a Teratogen

Experimental animal models have been critically important to research in the field of FASD. *In vivo* models, including rodents, chicks, dogs, pigs, sheep and non-human primates, have been complemented over the years by *in vitro* studies examining direct effects of alcohol on cells and tissues in culture. These models provide control over environmental (dose and timing of alcohol exposure, other drugs, maternal nutrition and health, pre and postnatal environments) and genetic (sensitivity to alcohol, differences in alcohol absorption, distribution and metabolism) variables not possible in human studies. Many of the physical, biological and neurobehavioural effects of PAE described in children have been paralleled in studies using animal models, confirming the teratogenic effects of alcohol. These models thus provide valuable tools for investigating both direct and indirect mechanisms underlying alcohol's adverse effects on the brain and behaviour, which will ultimately allow for the development of more targeted and effective intervention and treatment strategies.

Animal studies have been important in informing the ongoing debate about the impact of low to moderate alcohol consumption [1–4 glasses of alcohol per week (Dufour 1999)] during pregnancy on children's neurodevelopmental outcome. Studies have demonstrated significant adverse effects of low-moderate alcohol exposure on the brain (e.g., Valenzuela et al. 2012), on placental gene expression, and on anxiety- and depressive-like behaviour in adult offspring (Brocardo et al. 2012; Cullen et al. 2013; Rosenberg et al. 2010). Other clinically relevant issues, including the effects of alcohol consumption during the periconceptional period, and the impact of paternal drinking, have also benefitted from the use of animal models. The periconceptional effects of alcohol are difficult to explore in clinical studies. Utilizing a mouse model, it was shown that fetuses of females but not males exposed to alcohol for 60 days prior to conception were significantly growth retarded compared with control fetuses (Livy, Maier, and West 2004). A direct relationship between paternal alcohol exposure and offspring health and behaviour has also been observed in animal models (Abel 1995; Haycock 2009). Such findings are not only clinically relevant and help to elucidate the effects of alcohol dose and exposure period on outcome, but also support other research to date suggesting that there is no safe amount of alcohol or safe time to drink during pregnancy.

Prenatal Alcohol Exposure, Stress, Sex and Gender Differences, and Long-term Mental Health Outcomes

Prenatal Alcohol Exposure Alters Development and Activity of the Dopamine System

PAE delays development of dopamine systems, reduces the size, structure and electrical activity of dopaminergic neurons, and reduces dopamine synthesis, binding and metabolism (Cooper and Rudeen 1988; Druse et al. 1990; Shen, Hannigan, and Kapatos 1999). While these alterations reduce tonic or baseline dopaminergic activity, sensitivity of dopamine systems to drug insults appears to increase (Uban et al. 2014). Like the effects of PAE on the HPA axis, dysregulation of dopamine systems following PAE is likely a result of both direct and indirect effects of maternal alcohol consumption. Given the bi-directional interaction of dopamine and stress systems, alcohol-induced alterations in the HPA axis likely produce additional dysregulation of already altered dopamine systems, and conversely, altered dopaminergic function is likely exacerbated by dysregulation of the stress system that may occur through fetal programming mechanisms.

We recently utilized an amphetamine sensitization paradigm to investigate the possibility that prenatal alcohol-induced alterations in stress-dopamine system interactions may be involved in mediating vulnerability to SUDs in adult males and females (Uban et al. 2014). Previous work had shown that hypersensitivity of dopaminergic systems can be produced with repeated exposure to stimulants, such as amphetamine, resulting in an enhanced behavioural response to the drug, referred to as behavioural sensitization (Vanderschuren and Pierce 2010). Moreover, behavioural sensitization was shown to be positively correlated with stimulant self-administration and increased propensity for reinstatement following abstinence (Vanderschuren and Pierce 2010). We found that amphetamine sensitization occurred earlier and at a lower threshold in PAE compared to control males and females, and furthermore, that PAE but not control offspring showed cross-sensitization between amphetamine and stress. These findings demonstrate that PAE increases sensitivity of dopamine and stress systems to drug exposure in adulthood, and alters stress-dopamine interactions. These changes are consistent with the hypothesis that PAE results in neurobiological alterations that enhance vulnerability to SUDs. Indeed, children with FASD exhibit a wide range of mental health problems, including alcohol and drug use (Alati et al. 2006; Baer et al. 2003; Barr et al. 2006; O'Connor and Paley 2009; Spohr, Willms, and Steinhausen 2007). For example, individuals exposed to alcohol *in utero* are more likely to present with alcohol use problems themselves, beginning in adolescence and often persisting into adulthood (Baer et al. 2003). This increased prevalence is observed even after controlling for environmental and genetic variables such as home environment, parenting styles and family history of substance use.

Prenatal Alcohol Exposure Alters Activity of The HPA Axis in a Sexually Dimorphic Manner

Studies in both human infants and animal models have shown that PAE reprograms the fetal HPA axis, such that basal HPA tone is increased, and offspring are hyperresponsive to stressors. For example, heavy drinking at conception and during pregnancy was associated with higher basal and post-stress (blood draw) cortisol concentrations in 13-month-old infants (Jacobson, Bihun, and Chiodo 1999), and 2-month-old infants exposed *in utero* to alcohol or cigarettes had higher basal cortisol levels than control infants (Ramsay, Bendersky, and Lewis 1996). Haley, Handmaker and Lowe (2006) found altered cortisol, heart rate and negative affect in 5–7-month-old infants during a modified "still face" procedure, a paradigm used to study emotion and stress regulation. Of note, these effects were sexually dimorphic, with girls showing greater changes in heart rate and negative affect, and boys showing greater changes in cortisol, indicating that gender differences can occur even prior to puberty.

In animal models, we and others have shown that PAE results in increased HPA responses to a variety of stressors and to challenges with drugs such as ethanol and morphine (Kim, Osborn, and Weinberg 1996; Lee et al. 2000; Taylor et al. 1988; Weinberg et al. 2008). Interestingly, while HPA hyperresponsiveness is a robust phenomenon, sex differences are often observed in animal models as well, depending on the nature and intensity of the stressor, time course of testing, and hormonal endpoint (Weinberg et al. 2008; Hellemans et al. 2010). Similarly, the combination of moderate prenatal alcohol and noise stress reduced birth weights in male but not female rhesus monkey offspring, although both males and females showed increased HPA responses to maternal separation (Schneider et al. 2002). Importantly, our studies have shown that sex differences in HPA responses of male and female offspring might be mediated by alcohol-induced changes in sex hormone activity and/or altered interactions between HPA and sex hormones. We found that PAE males showed changes in both HPA and sex hormone regulation, as well as reduced HPA sensitivity to the normal inhibitory effects of testosterone (Lan, Hellemans, et al. 2009). In females, on the other hand, HPA activity was affected by the estrous cycle (analogous to the menstrual cycle in women). PAE females had increased basal corticosterone levels during proestrus, the cycle phase when estradiol levels are high, and responded differentially to stress at different phases of the cycle compared to their control counterparts, suggesting that, similar to PAE males, PAE females exhibit differential sensitivity to the sex hormones (Lan, Yamashita, et al. 2009; Sliwowska et al. 2008).

Stress, Trauma, Mental Health and FASD

One framework for thinking about the mediating role of the HPA axis for later life outcomes in individuals with FASD is the stress-diathesis hypothesis. Accordingly, adverse early life experiences sensitize or prime stress systems, which will then be hyperresponsive to subsequent, even mild, stressful life events. Thus, although stress *per se* can induce adverse later life effects, stressors acting on an already sensitized system may have even greater long-term effects. Importantly, individuals who experience adverse prenatal environments, such as prenatal drug or stress exposure, also often experience adversity in the early postnatal period when brain development is still occurring: the diathesis. For example, individuals with FASD are more likely to be raised outside the birth family, with a high proportion entering the foster care system, and many experiencing multiple placements, instability, neglect or abuse and other stressors, which increase adverse outcomes. In addition, even those who remain in the family home sometimes experience adversity resulting from a chaotic and unstable environment, particularly if the mother, father, or other family members drink and/or use other drugs (Mengel, Searight, and Cook 2006). Thus, both prenatal and postnatal stress/adversity may be mediating factors in the outcome of prenatal alcohol exposure, and it may not be easy to separate the impact of these factors from those of alcohol itself (O'Connor and Paley 2009). Furthermore, although early life adversities have been broadly associated with disease susceptibility, sex-, gender-, and temporal-specific programming of offspring stress responsivity have been demonstrated (Bale 2011).

A related framework for understanding the mediating role of the HPA axis for later life outcomes is the three-hit hypothesis of vulnerability and resilience (Daskalakis et al. 2013). In the context of prenatal alcohol exposure, hit-1 corresponds to genetic/biological predisposition, and can include changes in neurobiological systems and gene expression induced directly or indirectly by alcohol. Hit-2 corresponds to postnatal, early life, or adolescent stress or adversity often experienced by individuals prenatally exposed to alcohol, which could further influence later life outcomes. Hit-3 represents the later-life environment and can include exposure to stress or trauma, including illness or infection, in adulthood. It is also important to consider the interplay between sex and/or gender and each of the three hits. For example, we have demonstrated that exposure to chronic mild stress in adulthood differentially alters depressive- and anxiety-like behaviour in PAE males and females (Hellemans et al. 2010; Hill et al. 2012). We have also shown that PAE results in sexually dimorphic dysregulation of the neurocircuitry that underlies stress and emotional regulation, and that chronic mild stress differentially affects these networks in both PAE and control males and females (Raineki et al. 2014). In addition, research utilizing non-human primates reported that the double insult of prenatal alcohol and prenatal stress appeared to augment behavioural responses related to dopamine function, but without significantly altering dopamine content and receptor activity, suggesting a role for additional biological or environmental factors in the behavioural outcomes observed (Schneider et al. 2002; Schneider et al. 2005).

In the clinical situation, one must be equally aware of possible gender differences in the effects of prenatal, early life or later life experience/adversity on behavioural, physiological and health outcomes (e.g., Van Os and Selten 1998). However, results in clinical studies can only suggest correlational relationships among variables such as sex and gender, prenatal/early life/later life stress or adversity and neurobiological alterations. In contrast, animal models enable the manipulation and control of parameters of interest, as well as direct access to the brain. As such, animal models are instrumental in filling the gaps in our understanding of the effects of interactions among biological sex, prenatal alcohol exposure and stress/trauma (e.g., prenatal stress, maternal abuse/neglect, chronic stress) on neural networks of the brain. Moreover, while it is difficult to create the conditions of a gendered environment in a lab, and thus animal research cannot go beyond studying the effects of biological sex, nevertheless, these findings provide a basis for making inferences about interactions of these variables with gender.

Mental health disorders, such as depression and anxiety, are common disabilities in FASD populations, occurring at significantly higher rates than in the general population (O'Connor and Paley 2009). Although the etiology of such disorders is currently unclear, it is generally accepted that the incidence of mental health problems occurs at a higher rate among vulnerable populations that are exposed to adverse early life experiences, as is often the case for children with FASD. Of note, gender differences in the prevalence of mental illness that occur in the general population (incidence in women almost twice that in men)

(Kessler 2003; Young and Korszun 2010), are also apparent in FASD populations (O'Connor and Paley 2009). Programming of neuroendocrine function by prenatal alcohol exposure may be one underlying factor or "final common pathway," and PAE-induced changes in gonadal hormone secretion or HPA sensitivity to gonadal hormones may contribute to the sex-biased HPA dysregulation seen in FASD.

Mental illnesses are often comorbid with SUDs (Conway et al. 2006). While comorbidity does not imply causality or directionality, drugs of abuse may lead to symptoms of mental illness, and mental illness may lead to substance use, sometimes as a way to cope with the mental illness itself. Thus, research on addiction would not be complete without a mental health perspective, an approach that has shaped the IMPART training program and research by IMPART-associated investigators. Furthermore, a transdisciplinary approach to research on FASD highlights how an understanding of neurobiology, fetal programming and sex and gender differences can help to explain vulnerability to mental health problems. Such an approach has been essential for elucidating the impact of prenatal alcohol exposure on brain development, sex and gender differences in the impact of prenatal alcohol exposure, and the role of early and later life stress/trauma in shaping subsequent vulnerability to, or resilience against, a range of mental health problems, including SUDs, in FASD.

Conclusion

Multiple complex factors come together to influence both vulnerability and resilience to mental health problems, including SUDs. An understanding of how these variables interact is critical for understanding the complex etiology of SUDs, and for developing evidence-based approaches to treatments and interventions. The research of our interdisciplinary team is uniquely positioned to explore, from a transdisciplinary perspective, the relationships among the multiple variables discussed. This approach holds great promise for gaining insight into individual differences in vulnerability/resilience to drugs, the transition to addiction, and the processes of relapse and recovery. Our group also exemplifies the value of bi-directional interactions between basic and clinical approaches. We can test hypotheses from 'bench to bedside and back,' and within the larger societal context. Our research on FASD illustrates how the DOHaD approach, utilized across multiple disciplines, is essential for understanding the role of early life experiences in later vulnerability/resilience to mental health problems. Clinically informed animal models must continue to have a central role in the addictions and mental health fields. In turn, human studies provide a rigorous platform upon which basic science hypotheses and findings can be tested within the context of complex genetic variability, gender constructs, nutritional status and environments. The knowledge gained from basic science studies can not only inform evidence-based and sex- and gender-based approaches to the development of novel and targeted treatment and intervention strategies, consistent with today's current focus on personalized medicine, but also provide critical knowledge to inform both policy and practice.

Discussion Questions:

1. Why is it important to understand sex and gender differences in addiction/ substance use disorders?
2. How does a transdisciplinary perspective benefit research on addictions/substance use disorders?
3. In your own field of research, how can you include transdisciplinarity and sex/gender-based analyses?

Note

1 Dr. Joanne Weinberg is senior author on this chapter. All other authors contributed equally and are listed in alphabetical order. The research in Dr. Weinberg's laboratory is supported by grants from the US National Institutes of Health/National Institute on Alcohol Abuse and Alcoholism; NeuroDevNet, a Canadian Network of Centres of Excellence; and the Canadian Foundation On Fetal Alcohol Research. The authors are grateful to Drs. Ellexis Boyle, Nancy Poole and Lorraine Greaves for helpful comments and suggestions on earlier drafts of this chapter.

References

Abel, E. L. 1995. "A Surprising Effect of Paternal Alcohol Treatment on Rat Fetuses." *Alcohol* 12 (1): 1–6.

Adinoff, B., J. M. Kiser, P. R. Martin, and M. Linnoila. 1996. "Response of Dehydroepiandrosterone to Corticotropin-Releasing Hormone Stimulation in Alcohol-Dependent Subjects." *Biological Psychiatry* 40 (12): 1305–7.

Alati, R., A. Al Mamun, G. M. Williams, M O'Callaghan, J M Najman, and W Bor. 2006. "In Utero Alcohol Exposure and Prediction of Alcohol Disorders in Early Adulthood: A Birth Cohort Study." *Archives of General Psychiatry* 63 (9): 1009–16. doi:63/9/1009 [pii] 10.1001/archpsyc.63.9.1009.

Anker, J. J., and M. E. Carroll. 2011. "Females Are More Vulnerable to Drug Abuse Than Males: Evidence from Preclinical Studies and the Role of Ovarian Hormones." *Current Topics in Behavioral Neurosciences* 8: 73–96. doi:10.1007/7854_2010_93.

Baer, J. S., P. D. Sampson, H. M. Barr, P. D. Connor, and A. P. Streissguth. 2003. "A 21-Year Longitudinal Analysis of the Effects of Prenatal Alcohol Exposure on Young Adult Drinking." *Archives of General Psychiatry* 60 (4): 377–85. doi:10.1001/archpsyc.60.4.377 60/4/377 [pii].

Bale, T. L. 2011. "Sex Differences in Prenatal Epigenetic Programming of Stress Pathways." *Stress* 14 (4): 348–56. doi:10.3109/10253890.2011.586447.

Barker, D. J. 1998. "In Utero Programming of Chronic Disease." *Clinical Science (London, England: 1979)* 95 (2): 115–28.

Barr, H. M., F. L. Bookstein, K. D. O'Malley, P, D. Connor, J. E. Huggins, and A. P. Streissguth. 2006. "Binge Drinking during Pregnancy as a Predictor of Psychiatric Disorders on the Structured Clinical Interview for DSM-IV in Young Adult Offspring." *The American Journal of Psychiatry* 163 (6): 1061–5. doi:10.1176/appi.ajp.163.6.1061.

Becker, J. B., and M. Hu. 2008. "Sex Differences in Drug Abuse." *Frontiers in Neuroendocrinology* 29 (1): 36–47. doi:10.1016/j.yfrne.2007.07.003.

Becker, J. B., A. N. Perry, and C. Westenbroek. 2012. "Sex Differences in the Neural Mechanisms Mediating Addiction: A New Synthesis and Hypothesis." *Biology of Sex Differences* 3 (1): 14. doi:10.1186/2042-6410-3-14.

Brick, J., and L. A. Pohorecky. 1983. "The Neuroendocrine Response to Stress and the Effect of Ethanol." In *Stress & Alcohol Use*, edited by L. A. Pohorecky and J. Brick, 389–402. New York, NY: Elsevier Biomedical.

Brocardo, P. S., F. Boehme, A. Patten, A. Cox, J. Gil-Mohapel, and B. R. Christie. 2012, March. "Anxiety- and Depression-like Behaviors Are Accompanied by an Increase in Oxidative Stress in a Rat Model of Fetal Alcohol Spectrum Disorders: Protective Effects of Voluntary Physical Exercise." *Neuropharmacology*. doi:10.1016/j.neuropharm.2011.10.006.

Calhoun, F., and K. Warren. 2007. "Fetal Alcohol Syndrome: Historical Perspectives." *Neuroscience and Biobehavioral Reviews* 31 (2): 168–71. doi:10.1016/j.neubiorev.2006.06.023.

Carroll, M. E., and J. J. Anker. 2010. "Sex Differences and Ovarian Hormones in Animal Models of Drug Dependence." *Hormones and Behavior* 58 (1): 44–56. doi:10.1016/j.yhbeh.2009.10.001.

Conway, K. P., W. Compton, F. S. Stinson, and B. F. Grant. 2006. "Lifetime Comorbidity of DSM-IV Mood and Anxiety Disorders and Specific Drug Use Disorders: Results from the National Epidemiologic Survey on Alcohol and Related Conditions." *The Journal of Clinical Psychiatry* 67 (2): 247–57.

Cooper, J. D., and P. K. Rudeen. 1988. "Alterations in Regional Catecholamine Content and Turnover in the Male Rat Brain in Response to in Utero Ethanol Exposure." *Alcoholism: Clinical and Experimental Research* 12 (2): 282–85.

Cullen, C. L., T.H.J. Burne, N. A. Lavidis, and K. M. Moritz. 2013. "Low Dose Prenatal Ethanol Exposure Induces Anxiety-like Behaviour and Alters Dendritic Morphology in the Basolateral Amygdala of Rat Offspring." *PloS One* 8 (1): e54924. doi:10.1371/journal.pone.0054924.

Daskalakis, N. P., R. C. Bagot, K. J. Parker, C. H. Vinkers, and E. R. de Kloet. 2013. "The Three-Hit Concept of Vulnerability and Resilience: Toward Understanding Adaptation to Early-Life Adversity Outcome." *Psychoneuroendocrinology* 38 (9): 1858–1873. doi:10.1016/j.psyneuen.2013.06.008.

Di Chiara, G., and V. Bassareo. 2007. "Reward System and Addiction: What Dopamine Does and Doesn't Do." *Current Opinion in Pharmacology* 7 (1): 69–76. doi:10.1016/j.coph.2006.11.003.

Di Chiara, G., and A. Imperato. 1988. "Drugs Abused by Humans Preferentially Increase Synaptic Dopamine Concentrations in the Mesolimbic System of Freely Moving Rats." *Proceedings of the National Academy of Sciences of the United States of America* 85 (14): 5274–8.

Dreher, J-C., P. J. Schmidt, P. Kohn, D. Furman, D. Rubinow, and K. F. Berman. 2007. "Menstrual Cycle Phase Modulates Reward-Related Neural Function in Women." *Proceedings of the National Academy of Sciences of the United States of America* 104 (7): 2465–70. doi:10.1073/pnas.0605569104.

Druse, M. J., N. Tajuddin, A. Kuo, and M. Connerty. 1990. "Effects of in Utero Ethanol Exposure on the Developing Dopaminergic System in Rats." *Journal of Neuroscience Research* 27 (2): 233–40. doi:10.1002/jnr.490270214.

Dufour, M. C. 1999. "What Is Moderate Drinking? Defining 'Drinks' and Drinking Levels." *Alcohol Research & Health : The Journal of the National Institute on Alcohol Abuse and Alcoholism* 23 (1): 5–14.

Haley, D. W., N. S. Handmaker, and J. Lowe. 2006. "Infant Stress Reactivity and Prenatal Alcohol Exposure." *Alcoholism: Clinical and Experimental Research* 30 (12): 2055–64. doi:10.1111/j.1530-0277.2006.00251.x.

Haycock, P. C. 2009. "Fetal Alcohol Spectrum Disorders: The Epigenetic Perspective." *Biology of Reproduction* 81 (4): 607–17. doi:10.1095/biolreprod.108.074690.

Hellemans, K.G.C., J. H. Sliwowska, P. Verma, and J. Weinberg. 2010. "Prenatal Alcohol Exposure: Fetal Programming and Later Life Vulnerability to Stress, Depression and Anxiety Disorders." *Neuroscience and Biobehavioral Reviews* 34 (6): 791–807. doi:10.1016/j.neubiorev.2009.06.004.

Hill, M. N., K.G.C. Hellemans, P. Verma, B. B. Gorzalka, and J. Weinberg. 2012. "Neurobiology of Chronic Mild Stress: Parallels to Major Depression." *Neuroscience and Biobehavioral Reviews* 36 (9): 2085–2117. doi:10.1016/j.neubiorev.2012.07.001.

Holroyd, C. B., and M.G.H. Coles. 2002. "The Neural Basis of Human Error Processing: Reinforcement Learning, Dopamine, and the Error-Related Negativity." *Psychological Review* 109 (4): 679–709.

Hore, B. D. 1971. "Factors in Alcoholic Relapse." *Addiction* 66 (2): 89–96. doi:10.1111/j.1360-0443.1971.tb02371.x.

Hu, M., H. S. Crombag, T. E. Robinson, and J. B. Becker. 2004. "Biological Basis of Sex Differences in the Propensity to Self-Administer Cocaine." *Neuropsychopharmacology* 29 (1): 81–85. doi:10.1038/sj.npp.1300301.

Hyman, S. E. 2005. "Addiction: A Disease of Learning and Memory." *The American Journal of Psychiatry* 162 (8): 1414–22. doi:10.1176/appi.ajp.162.8.1414.

———. 2007. "The Neurobiology of Addiction: Implications for Voluntary Control of Behavior." *The American Journal of Bioethics* 7 (1): 8–11. doi:10.1080/15265160601063969.

Hyman, S. E., R. C. Malenka, and E. J. Nestler. 2006. "Neural Mechanisms of Addiction: The Role of Reward-Related Learning and Memory." *Annual Review of Neuroscience* 29: 565–98. doi:10.1146/annurev.neuro.29.051605.113009.

Jacobson, S. W., J. T. Bihun, and L. M. Chiodo. 1999. "Effects of Prenatal Alcohol and Cocaine Exposure on Infant Cortisol Levels." *Development and Psychopathology* 11 (02): 195–208.

Juster, R. P., B. S. McEwen, and S. J. Lupien. 2010. "Allostatic Load Biomarkers of Chronic Stress and Impact on Health and Cognition." *Neuroscience and Biobehavioral Reviews* 35 (1): 2–16. doi:10.1016/j.neubiorev.2009.10.002.

Kessler, R. C. 2003. "Epidemiology of Women and Depression." *Journal of Affective Disorders* 74 (1): 5–13.

Kim, C. K., J. A. Osborn, and J. Weinberg. 1996. "Stress Reactivity in Fetal Alcohol Syndrome." In *Fetal Alcohol Syndrome: From Mechanism to Prevention*, edited by E. Abel, 215–36. Boca Raton, FL: CRC Press.

Koob, G. F. 2008. "A Role for Brain Stress Systems in Addiction." *Neuron* 59 (1): 11–34. doi:10.1016/j.neuron.2008.06.012.

Koob, G. F., and M. J. Kreek. 2007. "Stress, Dysregulation of Drug Reward Pathways, and the Transition to Drug Dependence." *The American Journal of Psychiatry* 164 (8): 1149–59. doi:10.1176/appi.ajp.2007.05030503.

Koob, G. F., and M. Le Moal. 2008a. "Addiction and the Brain Antireward System." *Annual Review of Psychology* 59: 29–53. doi:10.1146/annurev.psych.59.103006.093548.

———. 2008b. "Review: Neurobiological Mechanisms for Opponent Motivational Processes in Addiction." *Philosophical Transactions of the Royal Society of London. Series B, Biological Sciences* 363 (1507): 3113–23. doi:10.1098/rstb.2008.0094.

Kushner, M. G., K. J. Sher, and B. D. Beitman. 1990. "The Relation between Alcohol Problems and the Anxiety Disorders." *The American Journal of Psychiatry* 147 (6): 685–95.

Lan, N., K.G.C. Hellemans, L. Ellis, V. Viau, and J. Weinberg. 2009. "Role of Testosterone in Mediating Prenatal Ethanol Effects on Hypothalamic-Pituitary-Adrenal Activity in Male Rats." *Psychoneuroendocrinology* 34 (9): 1314–28. doi:10.1016/j.psyneuen.2009.04.001.

Lan, N., F. Yamashita, A. G. Halpert, J. H. Sliwowska, V. Viau, and J. Weinberg. 2009. "Effects of Prenatal Ethanol Exposure on Hypothalamic-Pituitary-Adrenal Function across the Estrous Cycle." *Alcoholism: Clinical and Experimental Research* 33 (6): 1075–88. doi:10.1111/j.1530-0277.2009.00929.x.

Lee, S., D. Schmidt, F. J. Tilders, and C. Rivier. 2000. "Increased Activity of the Hypothalamic-Pituitary-Adrenal Axis of Rats Exposed to Alcohol in Utero: Role of Altered Pituitary and Hypothalamic Function." *Molecular and Cellular Neurosciences* 16 (4): 515–28. doi:10.1006/mcne.2000.0890.

Lee, S., E. D. Schmidt, F. J. Tilders, and C. Rivier. 2001. "Effect of Repeated Exposure to Alcohol on the Response of the Hypothalamic-Pituitary-Adrenal Axis of the Rat: I. Role of Changes in Hypothalamic Neuronal Activity." *Alcoholism: Clinical and Experimental Research Clinical and Experimental Research* 25 (1): 98–105.

Livy, D. J., S. E. Maier, and J. R. West. 2004. "Long-Term Alcohol Exposure prior to Conception Results in Lower Fetal Body Weights." *Birth Defects Research. Part B, Developmental and Reproductive Toxicology* 71 (3): 135–41. doi:10.1002/bdrb.20007.

Lynch, W J, M E Roth, J L Mickelberg, and M E Carroll. 2001. "Role of Estrogen in the Acquisition of Intravenously Self-Administered Cocaine in Female Rats." *Pharmacology Biochemistry & Behavior* 68 (4): 641–6.

Mantsch, J. R., S. D. Schlussman, A. Ho, and M. J. Kreek. 2000. "Effects of Cocaine Self-Administration on Plasma Corticosterone and Prolactin in Rats." *The Journal of Pharmacology and Experimental Therapeutics* 294 (1): 239–47.

McEwen, B. S. 2008. "Central Effects of Stress Hormones in Health and Disease: Understanding the Protective and Damaging Effects of Stress and Stress Mediators." *European Journal of Pharmacology* 583 (2–3): 174–85. doi:10.1016/j.ejphar.2007.11.071.

Meaney, M. J., and M. Szyf. 2005. "Environmental Programming of Stress Responses through DNA Methylation: Life at the Interface between a Dynamic Environment and a Fixed Genome." *Dialogues in Clinical Neuroscience* 7 (2): 103–23.

Mengel, M. B., H. R. Searight, and K. Cook. 2006. "Preventing Alcohol-Exposed Pregnancies." *The Journal of the American Board of Family Medicine* 19 (5): 494–505.

Miller, E. K., and J. D. Cohen. 2001. "An Integrative Theory of Prefrontal Cortex Function." *Annual Review of Neuroscience* 24: 167–202. doi:10.1146/annurev.neuro.24.1.167.

Miller, W. R., and K. M. Carroll, ed. 2006. *Rethinking Substance Abuse: What the Science Shows and What We Should Do About It*. New York: Guildford Press.

O'Connor, M. J., and B. Paley. 2009. "Psychiatric Conditions Associated with Prenatal Alcohol Exposure." *Developmental Disabilities Research Reviews* 15 (3): 225–34. doi:10.1002/ddrr.74.

Raineki, C., K.G.C. Hellemans, T. Bodnar, K. M. Lavigne, L. Ellis, T. S. Woodward, and J. Weinberg. 2014. "Neurocircuitry Underlying Stress and Emotional Regulation in Animals Prenatally Exposed to Alcohol and Subjected to Chronic Mild Stress in Adulthood." *Frontiers in Endocrinology* 5: 5. doi:10.3389/fendo.2014.00005.

Ramsay, D. S., M. I. Bendersky, and M. Lewis. 1996. "Effect of Prenatal Alcohol and Cigarette Exposure on Two- and Six-Month-Old Infants' Adrenocortical Reactivity to Stress." *Journal of Pediatric Psychology* 21 (6): 833–40.

Redish, A. D., S. Jensen, and A. Johnson. 2008. "A Unified Framework for Addiction: Vulnerabilities in the Decision Process." *The Behavioral and Brain Sciences* 31 (4): 415–37; discussion 437–87. doi:10.1017/S0140525X0800472X.

Rice, M. E., and S. J. Cragg. 2004. "Nicotine Amplifies Reward-Related Dopamine Signals in Striatum." *Nature Neuroscience* 7 (6): 583–4. doi:10.1038/nn1244.

Roberts, D. C., S. A. Bennett, and G. J. Vickers. 1989. "The Estrous Cycle Affects Cocaine Self-Administration on a Progressive Ratio Schedule in Rats." *Psychopharmacology* 98 (3): 408–11.

Robinson, T. E., and B. Kolb. 2004. "Structural Plasticity Associated with Exposure to Drugs of Abuse." *Neuropharmacology* 47 Suppl 1: 33–46. doi:10.1016/j.neuropharm.2004.06.025.

Rosenberg, M. J., C. R. Wolff, A. El-Emawy, M. C. Staples, N. I. Perrone-Bizzozero, and D. D. Savage. 2010. "Effects of Moderate Drinking during Pregnancy on Placental Gene Expression." *Alcohol* 44 (7–8): 673–90. doi:10.1016/j.alcohol.2009.10.002.

Sarnyai, Z., Y. Shaham, and S. C. Heinrichs. 2001. "The Role of Corticotropin-Releasing Factor in Drug Addiction." *Pharmacological Reviews* 53 (2): 209–43.

Schneider, M. L., C. F. Moore, T. E. Barnhart, J. A. Larson, O. T. DeJesus, J. Mukherjee, R. J. Nickles, A. K. Converse, A. D. Roberts, and G. W. Kraemer. 2005. "Moderate-Level Prenatal Alcohol Exposure Alters Striatal Dopamine System Function in Rhesus Monkeys." *Alcoholism: Clinical and Experimental Research* 29 (9): 1685–97.

Schneider, M. L., C. F. Moore, G. W. Kraemer, A. D. Roberts, and O. T. DeJesus. 2002. "The Impact of Prenatal Stress, Fetal Alcohol Exposure, or Both on Development: Perspectives from a Primate Model." *Psychoneuroendocrinology* 27 (1–2): 285–298. doi:10.1016/S0306-4530(01)00050-6.

Seckl, J. R., and M. C. Holmes. 2007. "Mechanisms of Disease: Glucocorticoids, Their Placental Metabolism and Fetal 'Programming' of Adult Pathophysiology." *Nature Clinical Practice Endocrinology & Metabolism* 3 (6): 479–88. doi:10.1038/ncpendmet0515.

Shen, R. Y., J. H. Hannigan, and G. Kapatos. 1999. "Prenatal Ethanol Reduces the Activity of Adult Midbrain Dopamine Neurons." *Alcoholism: Clinical and Experimental Research* 23 (11): 1801–7. doi:00000374-199911000-00013 [pii].

Sinha, R. 2008. "Chronic Stress, Drug Use, and Vulnerability to Addiction." *Annals of the New York Academy of Sciences* 1141: 105–30. doi:10.1196/annals.1441.030.

———. 2009. "Stress and Addiction: A Dynamic Interplay of Genes, Environment, and Drug Intake." *Biological Psychiatry* 66 (2): 100–1. doi:10.1016/j.biopsych.2009.05.003.

Sliwowska, J. H., N. Lan, F. Yamashita, A. G. Halpert, V. Viau, and J. Weinberg. 2008. "Effects of Prenatal Ethanol Exposure on Regulation of Basal Hypothalamic-Pituitary-Adrenal Activity and Hippocampal 5-HT1A Receptor mRNA Levels in Female Rats across the Estrous Cycle." *Psychoneuroendocrinology* 33 (8): 1111–23. doi:S0306-4530(08)00136-4 [pii] 10.1016/j.psyneuen.2008.05.001.

Spohr, H. L., J. Willms, and H. C. Steinhausen. 2007. "Fetal Alcohol Spectrum Disorders in Young Adulthood." *The Journal of Pediatrics* 150 (2): 175–9, 179.e1. doi:10.1016/j.jpeds.2006.11.044.

Taylor, A. N., B. J. Branch, J. E. Van Zuylen, and E. Redei. 1988. "Maternal Alcohol Consumption and Stress Responsiveness in Offspring." *Advances in Experimental Medicine and Biology* 245: 311–17.

Uban, K. A., W. L. Comeau, T. Bodnar, W. K. Yu, J. Weinberg, and L.A.M. Galea. 2014. "Amphetamine Sensitization and Cross-Sensitization with Acute Restraint Stress: Impact of Prenatal Alcohol Exposure in Male and Female Rats." *Psychopharmacology* (Berl). 2014 Nov 26. [Epub ahead of print]

Valenzuela, C. F., R. A. Morton, M. R. Diaz, and L. Topper. 2012. "Does Moderate Drinking Harm the Fetal Brain? Insights from Animal Models." *Trends in Neurosciences* 35 (5): 284–92. doi:10.1016/j.tins.2012.01.006.

Van Etten, M. L., and J. C. Anthony. 2001. "Male-Female Differences in Transitions from First Drug Opportunity to First Use: Searching for Subgroup Variation by Age, Race, Region, and Urban Status." *Journal of Women's Health & Gender-Based Medicine* 10 (8): 797–804. doi:10.1089/15246090152636550.

Van Os, J., and J. P. Selten. 1998. "Prenatal Exposure to Maternal Stress and Subsequent Schizophrenia. The May 1940 Invasion of The Netherlands." *The British Journal of Psychiatry: The Journal of Mental Science* 172: 324–6.

Vanderschuren, L.J.M.J., and R. C. Pierce. 2010. "Sensitization Processes in Drug Addiction." *Current Topics in Behavioral Neurosciences* 3: 179–95. doi:10.1007/7854_2009_21.

Volkow, N. D., J. S. Fowler, G-J. Wang, R. Baler, and F. Telang. 2009. "Imaging Dopamine's Role in Drug Abuse and Addiction." *Neuropharmacology* 56 Suppl 1: 3–8. doi:10.1016/j.neuropharm.2008.05.022.

Volkow, N. D., G-J. Wang, J. S. Fowler, D. Tomasi, and F. Telang. 2011. "Addiction: Beyond Dopamine Reward Circuitry." *Proceedings of the National Academy of Sciences of the United States of America* 108 (37): 15037–42. doi:10.1073/pnas.1010654108.

Weaver, I. C., N. Cervoni, F. A. Champagne, A. C. D'Alessio, S. Sharma, J. R. Seckl, S. Dymov, M. Szyf, and M. J. Meaney. 2004. "Epigenetic Programming by Maternal Behavior." *Nature Neuroscience* 7 (8): 847–54. doi:10.1038/nn1276.

Weinberg, J., J. H. Sliwowska, N. Lan, and K.G.C. Hellemans. 2008. "Prenatal Alcohol Exposure: Foetal Programming, the Hypothalamic-Pituitary-Adrenal Axis and Sex Differences in Outcome." *Journal of Neuroendocrinology* 20 (4): 470–88. doi:10.1111/j.1365-2826.2008.01669.x.

Young, E. A., and A. Korszun. 2010. "Sex, Trauma, Stress Hormones and Depression." *Molecular Psychiatry* 15 (1): 23–8. doi:10.1038/mp.2009.94.

Suggestions for Further Readings

Becker, J.B., A.N. Perry, and C. Westenbroek (2012). "Sex Differences in the Neural Mechanisms Mediating Addiction: A New Synthesis and Hypothesis. *Biology of Sex Differences*, 3 (1): 14. doi:10.1186/2042-6410-3-14.

Hyman, S.E., R.C. Malenka, and E.J. Nestler (2006). "Neural Mechanisms of Addiction: The Role of Reward-Related Learning and Memory." *Annual Review of Neuroscience*, 29: 565–98. doi:10.1146/annurev.neuro.29.051605.113009.

Sinha, R. (2007). "The Role of Stress in Addiction Relapse." *Current Psychiatry Reports*, 9: 388–95.

5
TWO-EYED SEEING IN INDIGENOUS ADDICTION RESEARCH AND TREATMENT

Laura Hall

Laura Hall is of Haudenosaunee/English-Canadian descent and is currently working toward a PhD in Environmental Studies on the importance of Indigenous gendered and temporal understandings within movements and studies of sustainable community development. Hall is part of a research team for a study entitled "Honouring Our Strengths: Indigenous Culture as Intervention in Addiction Treatment." The project is examining the use of cultural interventions to support healing within addictions treatment for Indigenous people. Its aim is to develop a wellness instrument to measure the impact of culturally based addictions treatment services on client wellness. The project uses a range of methods for ensuring that Indigenous ways of knowing involving community-based wisdom are central to the study, including focus groups with Indigenous staff at 12 community treatment centers from across Canada. The team has used a Two-Eyed Seeing Indigenous-centered guiding lens in the course of evidence gathering and assessment. Two-Eyed Seeing integrates and connects the best of Indigenous and Western knowledge systems, even though they are founded on different values and sources, by reflexively weaving back and forth. This approach originated with Mi'kmaq Elders Murdena and Albert Marshall in their development of an integrative science curriculum for post-secondary education. In this conversation with Nancy Poole and Lorraine Greaves, Hall discusses her understanding of transdisciplinarity, and its relationship to Indigenous ways of knowing and Two-Eyed Seeing approaches to conducting addictions research, which involve Indigenous peoples.

Q: Can you tell us about your current work with the Honoring Our Strengths project?
A: The project is a culturally rooted, culturally grounded investigation into culturally rooted addiction treatment for Indigenous people. I started with the project by travelling to treatment centers with Elder Jim Dumont. The stories from the treatment centers in this project were about how they approach culture, how they utilize culture, and how they understand culture in their

treatment processes. After that, I worked with a group of knowledge keepers and elders from the research team—Jim Dumont, Carol Hopkins, Virgil Tobias, Mary Deleary—who were able to speak to the information gathered and filter it through an Indigenous lens. They were able to analyze the information that way and reorganize it, and from there came up with a set of wellness indicators, all culturally appropriate, all culturally relevant, all speaking to what it means to be a whole and healthy Anishinaabe or Indigenous person. We came up with a set of twenty-two cultural activities that were similar across the country. Everyone conducted certain ceremonies in their First Nations treatment center; almost everybody had some kind of food gathering or gardening and other kinds of work on the land. After that we ran the same information through the qualitative coding software, NVivo, so it was a much more of a picking the words apart approach. From this, we realized that the two approaches were fairly complete and found what we needed in both ways, one using computers, one using the minds of knowledge keepers, which are almost like human computers. Except that the Elder and knowledge keepers were able to interpret the information more accurately. Then, we met again with the treatment center specialists and discussed all the findings and worked together as a larger team. I think there were thirty of us. Right now I'm helping with the publication side of things and doing quite a bit of writing and reading about Two-Eyed Seeing and what it really means when you're working with a decolonizing and Two-Eyed Seeing approach.

Q: It is a very complex challenge to bring all these ways of knowing together. I was wondering if you could just talk a little bit about the Two-Eyed Seeing approach as you see it being applied in this context.

A: In some ways it has been really simple and in other ways really complex, and I think we're still figuring it out, reflexively and retroactively. When we began, we talked about ethical space and decolonizing methodology. The more I read about Two-Eyed Seeing, the more it sounded like decolonizing methodology, but with a different balancing between Western scientific and Indigenous scientific approaches. For example, when we ran information through NVivo, we had some trip-ups when it came to culturally appropriate understandings, so moments of trying to figure out how to translate a word, like "sacred item," without imposing meaning but knowing that a sacred item is a sacred item. So, the priority, similar to decolonizing methodology, had to be on Indigenous knowledge for Indigenous peoples. Then, how we negotiated from within that and how we borrowed tools, borrowed theories, borrowed analysis is work that is ongoing.

At every treatment center visit, Elder Jim Dumont spoke the creation story. Jim is a really well-respected, extremely knowledgeable knowledge keeper and Elder, and his ability to steer the process to say, that our creation stories are the basis of who First Nations people are, that our creation stories are how we see the world, and our creation stories are ongoing truths of our lives. He kept referring to as "speaking from within the worldview." That approach contextualized things in a way that allowed us to use our good intellectual minds, and then bring our best minds together with the best minds of the West. The question then becomes, how do we do that as friends? The other question is, how do we take the culturally relevant information we were receiving in the treatment centers and filter it through a culturally-relevant framework and then put it into a culturally rooted and culturally relevant measurement tool? The measurement tool is really pushing the boundaries of what's been done before because we need to be able to borrow those tools while also ensuring the cultural integrity (because of the in depth involvement of knowledge keepers at every stage) of the measurement instrument. We hope that at the end of the project the clients are able to answer questions about culture and about their wellness and do so in a way that's appropriate and comfortable and truthful, but also have this valid measurement tool. It's almost a range of approaches that culminates in this measurement tool but that begins with creation, begins with culturally appropriate research, begins with gifting, ensuring that we go to each treatment center with gifts, with capacity building in mind and that costs are shared so that people can free up their time to do this work. We also need to ensure that money is available so that food is shared, to free up the space for truer sharing. I would say that right from the time of the environmental scan and the treatment center visits we've tried to understand the relationships between cultural integrity and borrowing of Western approaches. Are the two eyes equal? Is it a sense of relationship or relationality?

Q: In some ways it seems that it's a little bit about constantly have the two kinds of knowledge weaving together rather than seeing them as two parallel processes. It seems a fluid process. Would you agree?

A: I would certainly say that that's kind of the paradox of the situation. In a sense there is separateness, there is that parallel—almost like the Two-Row Wampum when the parallel vessels go side by side but then come together to take care of the water in between, the water being wellness in a sense, the river that we share. The weaving that you mention, Colleen Dell (Research Chair in Addictions at the University of Saskatchewan) calls it "the dance," when you step in and step back, that was ongoing especially during times when we had to go back and forth to discuss something in depth such as creation of the measurement tool and in the publication stage and even going right back to the original questions because the questions had to be strengths-based. The questions could not assume that in a colonial context we should ever ask if culture works because there are pressures to, as Indigenous people, to have to prove that our cultures work. So, the questions had to be kind of danced through as well. Carol Hopkins provided a key point, of bringing back the final question about challenges in addictions treatment and reiterating the importance of culture in saying, "How does culture help us to face these challenges that we face?" She wove it back around in this way that I thought was really amazing.

Q: How do you see transdisciplinarity fitting into that approach, either in this team and or in general, as a piece that may be useful in addictions research?

A: That is something that I've thought a lot about. I did an undergraduate degree in Canadian Studies, and our professor, Pauline Rankin, would always talk about how we were doing a disservice to ourselves by not asking about transdisciplinarity or interdisciplinarity until the end of our degrees, that we as students really needed to kind of build in the question about what exactly we were doing right from the start. I think it's really a levering question for me in the sense that transdisciplinarity, working across disciplines, weaving together disciplines, puts together the wholeness of the knowledge project again. The wholeness of understanding that Indigenous science, Indigenous spirituality, Indigenous medicine, Indigenous art and aesthetics, environmental knowledge, is all woven together in a way that the transdisciplinary project in the west is able to complement. I think that it's another opportunity for parallel work and for collaborative work so that we can start to really work across some of the constructed divides of each discipline but I wouldn't want to dismiss the boundaries that quickly. I think that there's always usefulness in designating some of our different knowledge, our different inquiries. In terms of the project, it's been a practice, a project of bringing together measurement specialists with sociologists and psychologists and therapeutic front-line workers and management specialists and executive directors as well as Indigenous knowledge keepers and interdisciplinary anti-colonial gender theorists like myself and others on the team, and working through the dance on a level so that the dance isn't just between Indigenous and Western. Knowing it's also about the disciplines within Western and Indigenous knowledges and sciences. As an example, my mind's going back to Elk Ridge (the site of a project team meeting in Saskatchewan) and I'm remembering interesting conversations between the representative from the Centre for Addiction and Mental Health (CAMH) and measurement folks talking about how exactly you measure wellness, and really having interesting, deep discussions about the possibility of measuring wellness.

Q: You have given a great, concrete example of it, struggling together at Elk Ridge. We were just meeting each other. We came from really a lot of different disciplines and sectors and locations, and we had to come up with a new understanding that was greater than the sum of the parts in some ways.

A: I would agree. I think that there's a multi-layered discussion, dialogue happening. And it's just such a pressing set of issues we're up against. The task ahead is really amazing but at the same time we have so much to teach the larger society. It is a strengths-based project and our approach to Two-Eyed Seeing can be a little bit provocative because we are trying to push the boundaries, and we are trying to inform something that's going to be helpful to other teams who need to work across kind of either small or vast differences.

Q: Can you talk a little bit about how transdisciplinarity links to Two-Eyed Seeing, or doesn't link to Two-Eyed Seeing? How do you see them in relation to each other?

A: It's almost like a schematic in my mind. When I think of Two-Eyed Seeing, I think of the Two Row Wampum. In my mind I imagine the Indigenous canoe on the river and I imagine the Western canoe. I imagine in the Two-Eyed Seeing process, we're coming together from distinct world views but at the same time within the West, there is that need and that recognized need to decolonize across the disciplines, to challenge as has been done for decades and decades the notions of objectivity and to bring our own subjectivities and stories into our understanding of how knowledge is constructed. Transdisciplinarity complicates the notion of a Western lens. The distinctness of Indigeneity and Western ways of thinking are still maintained in the sense of ensuring that Indigenous knowledge is kind of protected, or maintained by the knowledge keepers while also acknowledging that the lens on the other side of the river has been changing and shifting and challenging from within. Another layer of that is the project of transdisciplinarity and then another layer is the gender-race-class analysis that needs to be done and then somehow that needs to be regrounded in Indigenous knowledge. That conversation becomes a new layer, a new kind of dialogue. In terms of concrete processes, those are good questions to take to the larger team that we haven't really yet asked of ourselves.

Q: Can you talk about how gender is addressed within a Two-Eyed Seeing or transdisciplinary framework?

A: It is challenging. I was sitting and I was reading through some National Native Addiction Partnership Foundation documents, and some of them were looking at the disproportionate pressures on certain members of Indigenous communities. I was thinking to myself, "How is it that we do this? How do we do gendered analysis? How do we do two-spirited analysis? How do we do this without borrowing too heavily from Western theories that are grounded in a (gender) binary that our knowledge systems are not grounded in? How do we do this to honor the people in communities who are more heavily pressured and at times excluded because of what impact residential schooling has had?" There are a growing number of Indigenous theorists who are trying to attend to these questions in ways that also attend to creation and our understanding of our laws and our governance structures and to the very basic understanding that, if something was true prior to colonization, it doesn't have to remain unchanged over time. We know that that piece can free us up from a lot of rather anguished questioning, but I think we have such a capacity to attend to questions of gender and sexuality and class, an ability within our world view, and we just more space and more time to do that analysis.

Q: I think these kinds of questions around gender and other places where there may need to be more space created in Indigenous discourse will also be an outcome of this project, so we will all learn.

A: Dan Longboat and Joe Sheridan (Indigenous scholars affiliated with Trent and York Universities) wrote an amazing essay a few years back where they talk about the major sort of difference in world view between believing that knowledge comes from the human mind and believing that knowledge comes from the spirit helpers and animal helpers of the land. That our collective knowledge base can actually inform these questions around gender and we can do so by delving further into our traditions rather than away, while also freeing ourselves up to do that kind of borrowing, knowing that we're safe, we're secure, we're grounded where we need to be. The phrase 'attend to,' this is something Jim talks a lot about. I really like it. It's a very gentle approach as opposed to interrogating questions. So, really attending to the people in communities who are most in need. In terms of addiction, it certainly, certainly touches on the need to attend to community members who are most in need.

Q: How might Two-Eyed Seeing help us in addictions research?
A: The first layer for me is the ability that Two-Eyed Seeing provides toward ensuring the centrality of Indigenous knowledge within Indigenous-centered questioning. So if you're working in First Nations communities, being able to actually turn to the culture to ask questions, to center Indigenous spirits and Indigenous researchers, building up that capacity to do culturally rooted research is a huge piece of the benefit of Two-Eyed Seeing to addictions research. From there, Two-Eyed Seeing allows that centering within the actual work itself, so that the work of addictions treatment and addressing addictions treatment allows us to center culture in a way that certainly has been done, but now it's calling for more support for the work. The next layer, for me, is about the broader question of Two-Eyed Seeing in research in addictions that is not necessarily focused only on Indigenous communities. This project has provided some unique products such as the Indigenous Knowledge Framework, specifically the Wellness Framework—mind-body-heart-and-spirit. I think that there are connections, that using a Two-Eyed Seeing approach has meant that we've been able to make these kinds of deeper connections between parts of the self that the mainstream field of addictions have certainly brought together—aspects of emotional and physical and intellectual and physical well-being—but this is providing a set of kind of ethically bounded questions around how spirit also works in the question of research and also in the question of addictions treatment.

Q: How do you explain what Two-Eyed Seeing to people who are in particular Western-based disciplines? Have you had those experiences and how you had addressed them?
A: I have had those experiences in very specific instances. Barb Fornssler, our project manager, and I have talked about the applicability of certain Western theorists within Indigenous knowledge inquiry. The arrow of borrowing tends to go only in one direction and we need to look not only at the way the Western theorists have actually borrowed from Indigenous knowledge thinkers but also look at the applicability of world view—applicability of ideas within the world view. I've had very specific conversations in which Two-Eyed Seeing

becomes almost a set of ethical protocols for checking one's assumptions about what counts as knowledge within a certain discipline, and then checking those assumptions in relation to where the history of ideas comes into play. Barbara Alice Mann (an author on Iroquoian history and culture, affiliated with the University of Toledo) has written an amazing analysis about the influence of Iroquois or Haudenosaunee knowledge on Marxist theory. It's a matter of going back to each dialogue, looking at where dialogue has happened or where dialogue is needed and ensuring that the integrity of an Indigenous worldview is really respected.

Q: This is a big question, but what would be your ideal outcome of any communication with Western discipline-based people?
A: One of my ideal outcomes is about capacity building and about shaking up some of the hierarchies of the academy. I really like the writing that the Gift-Economy Network[1] has done around the hierarchies of the academy, and sharing the various gifts of the academy around knowledge, sharing the wealth a bit, and how to keep that work going? Another part of the ideal is about facing difficult truths. Given where Canada is at in the truth and reconciliation process, still facing the vast numbers of Indigenous children in care, and facing some of the harder realities of the state system, Barb and I talk a lot about the role of the ally. The ally is a friend and someone who doesn't get off the ride when it gets hard, who keeps plugging away and keeps hearing difficult truths. As well, we should have space to keep moving our knowledge systems along so that we can keep asking these tough, interesting questions and unique questions, and asking them in reflexive ways that allow the space and time that Indigenous people need to renew complex knowledge systems, protect some aspects of those systems, articulate things that perhaps need to be challenged, but in a safe way. Going back to capacity building, there's the overarching question of land. All of our academic labor is still grounded in our relationality to land and to these corporate structures that we do our academic work within, and land-owning structures that we do our academic work within, or are affiliated with. So it's also about attending to questions of land and questions of treaty, questions of peace and friendship, and grounding in the work that we need to do to decolonize.

Note

1 See http://gift-economy.com/

PART 2

How Does Transdisciplinarity Work?

This section offers insights into the thinking and approaches of a range of contributors to doing transdisciplinary research and practice. It is clear that there are many different approaches and entry points into transdisciplinarity. Sometimes, it is a result of observation, or a thought experiment, to solve a problem, or in reaction to a prevailing approach. Marcellus takes us in the neonatal intensive care unit (NICU) as a nurse and researcher, and contemplates the approach to infants born to mothers who have addiction issues. She critiques the prevailing family-centered approach by using a transdisciplinary lens to underscore how much about women's health is ignored, and how taking a view that includes gender and trauma and engages multiple disciplines is preferable. Einstein asks a critical question about how the body and the brain are linked, and how pain figures in this link. She offers an illustration of bringing a transdisciplinary team together to use a range of methods to understand the effects of female genital cutting (FGM/C) on the brain and psychosocial health of women, and applies this learning to addiction.

Torchalla and colleagues review three projects done with women with addiction, who were experiencing homelessness, trauma or mental health issues and were living in a disadvantaged urban neighborhood. They document the challenges in doing this research, the adjustments required in working with the women and their helping agencies, and how transdisciplinarity helped. Clark and colleagues reveal how, as nurses and social workers and researchers, they have been in situations where honing the tools of reflexivity and being aware of intersectional issues affecting women became critically important. They offer some examples of when and how reflexivity was important to understanding a research or practice question differently.

In an interview with the editors, Bradshaw reflects on how running a treatment center for women with addiction issues demands a transdisciplinary approach in order to address and integrate gender-related issues, and a trauma-informed approach. Finally, Hemsing et al. address a key question about systematic reviews and how they relate to practice. They argue that restricting our consideration of evidence to randomized control trials data in academic journals is insufficient for developing better practices and that many other data sources are required to guide us in action.

Taken together, these chapters take us through beginning thoughts, developing ideas, new methods, forming teams and critiquing current practices. They look at the challenges of doing research with community partners, providing progressive treatment to women with addiction issues, serving the needs of both mothers and infants in NICU and women and fetuses in addressing substance use during pregnancy. They offer us new ideas along the way, as well as revealing the internal and external processes, struggles and insights resulting from doing transdisciplinary work.

6
LINKING ADDICTION, GENDER AND TRAUMA IN THE NEONATAL INTENSIVE CARE UNIT

Lenora Marcellus

> *Crossing, as we have seen, is not easy, because borders, like the markings of a river, change again and again.*
>
> (Hayes and Cuban 1997)

The Neonatal Intensive Care Unit (NICU) is a clinical health care setting where families and team members are faced with life-defining and life-threatening circumstances such as preterm birth, the birth of an infant with a congenital anomaly or health crisis, or the death of an infant. The NICU has developed structurally and operationally as a location of care primarily for infants who are born prematurely or with significant congenital or physiological health conditions such as heart defects and respiratory illness, and as such, clinical services have been organized primarily to address the critical biomedical needs of the infant. Additional supports have been developed and integrated over the years to address parent and family needs, such as grief and bereavement counseling and peer support for addressing the stress and anxiety that often develops related to having an infant in the NICU.

Of infants born in Canada, 11.1% are admitted to an NICU in their first weeks of life (Fallah et al. 2011). The majority of these infants are admitted due to prematurity or low birth weight, with demographic and population health trends shifting over time to influence these conditions. In Canada and the United States, obstetrical trends include rising rates of caesarean delivery and labor induction, assisted reproductive technology with multiple births, maternal obesity, older age of women at birth, and an increasing number of women giving birth who have preexisting medical conditions. Societal trends that intersect with these factors include the erosion of social and community support, stress, poverty, racism, violence and trauma, and substance use (Bettegowda et al. 2011; Canadian Institute for Health Information 2009). Indeed, prematurity and low birth weight have sometimes been constructed and framed as "social diseases," as this broad and complex combination of medical and social factors is known to contribute to premature birth disproportionately affects socially disadvantaged and marginalized women.

With recent reported increases in the use and misuse of prescription opioids, there has been a simultaneous increase in the number of infants in NICUs requiring care for neonatal withdrawal (Kelly et al. 2011; O'Donnell et al. 2009; Patrick et al. 2012). Teams in some NICUs are reporting that up to half their clinical population are infants experiencing withdrawal in relation to prenatal substance exposure. Health care professionals and the media are declaring this increase an epidemic, repeating a cycle of moral panic that has developed each time a different substance becomes more mainstream. For example, Boyd (2004) reminds us that after almost 20 years of research, there is no evidence to support a condition or disorder that could be labeled a "crack baby," and that once again society is rushing to judge and label both women and their infants as deviant and damaged.

Although not identified as such, the growing population of infants with prenatal substance exposure in the NICU may be perceived as less legitimate clients and less deserving of intensive care services. Historically, women with substance use issues who have given birth to an infant requiring NICU care have been blamed, stigmatized, and positioned as a risk to their infants (Greaves et al. 2002; Poole and Isaac 2001; Young et al. 2007). Most health care providers rely largely on an individualized and moralized notion of what is problematic about substance use rather than acknowledging that substance use is both a commonly and widely culturally endorsed activity and contextualized by a range of socio-structural factors (Benoit et al. 2014).

In this chapter I share my story from the standpoint of being a registered nurse (RN) in an NICU setting, with highly developed technical and scientific skills, yet with little knowledge of addiction, mental health, violence, trauma, and their intersections. Not unlike the education and career trajectory of many RNs of my generation, I began my education in a hospital-based program with a typical curriculum of the time that was grounded in a biomedical perspective and focused on hospital-based care, with limited integration of contextual considerations such as social determinants of health. From a mental health and addiction practice perspective, my clinical exposure was limited to time spent in an acute psychiatric unit and an adult community detoxification program. At a young age of 20, with a middle class upbringing, these experiences were more stressful than educational.

As I developed my career in the NICU setting and cared for infants with prenatal substance exposure and their mothers and families, I realized that I had significantly limited capacity to support parents with their complex life circumstances and social needs. I began to establish and foster a transdisciplinary approach in my practice and knowledge development over different stages of my career and across practice, leadership, policy and research contexts.

Participating in the IMPART program during my doctoral studies and while still practicing as an RN in an NICU provided me with a unique opportunity to "cross the borders" of my personal disciplinary knowledge of sex and gender, substance use, mental health, violence and trauma. In this chapter I incorporate an intersectionality-based approach into my reflections on how the issue of substance use becomes visible in the NICU setting in the form of the medical diagnosis of Neonatal Abstinence Syndrome (NAS) and describe and critique the theoretical foundations of NICU care related to the infant, woman, and family. I provide an exemplar of participating in an international NAS quality improvement collaborative as a way to provide insight into the power and potential of a transdisciplinary evidence-to-action process when a researcher is able to embed in an area of clinical practice and bridge the gap between research and action that often exists, particularly between fields that have not historically been linked.

Confined Quarters: The NICU as a Location of Care

Although the NICU is a relatively recent construction within Western health care systems, its roots go back into the last century. Historically, the death of infants was seen fatalistically as a fact of life. The first major development in premature baby care addressed the physiological need of small infants for warmth. Dr. Stéphane Tarnier, a French obstetrician, invented the incubator in 1881 and reported a 28% reduction in infant mortality with the device (Davis et al. 2003). In 1922 a specialized unit was opened in a Chicago hospital to care for premature infants (Hess 1922). Following this introduction into more mainstream medical care, new innovations in the treatment of premature infants were developed, such as ventilators to support breathing and intravenous nutrition solutions to support growth. This development has continued to the present time, with new technologies and treatment options continuously being created that not only lower the gestational age at which viability is considered, but also expand the number of health conditions that are now considered treatable.

The NICU is an overwhelming, unpredictable, and technologically complex physical and social environment to both those who work within it and to parents who are required to spend time in it to be with their infants. Geographically, the NICU is a closed complex system in a tightly bounded location, suspended organizationally between obstetric and pediatric departments. NICU team composition has evolved over the years but primarily has been constructed to meet the needs of preterm infants. Team members usually include RNs, neonatologists, physical and occupational therapists, pharmacists, respiratory therapists. Many teams also include social workers and peer parent counselors to meet the needs of parents.

Within the discourse of infant safety, access to this environment is highly controlled, even for parents, as evidenced by gated entrances and strict visitation policies. There is some spatial reach by team members to other external units, for example to birthing rooms for infant resuscitation and to other areas of the hospital that may need neonatal skills, such as the emergency department or pediatric intensive care (Carroll 2009). Links to community are created in relation to discharge planning and supporting parents as they transition from having their infant being in a hospital to being with them at home.

The Construction of Neonatal Abstinence Syndrome as a Medical Diagnosis

The term *social construction* is familiar to those in the social sciences, but not necessarily to those in health science practice fields, including RNs. In Western medical care, we have for the most part studied health and illness without acknowledging their socially constructed nature (Conrad and Barker 2010). The tendency within our health care system has been to medicalize human conditions into social problems and to ignore or dismiss the effects of impoverished circumstances and social, moral, and political influences on health. This holds particularly true in the NICU setting, which is highly technical in nature.

Opioids have been used medicinally for centuries by cultures around the world. Women used opioids to manage "female problems" (such as painful menstruation, childbirth, and puerperal fever) and use during pregnancy was prevalent (Boyd 2004). In the early 20th century historical, political, moral, and economic factors began to shape drug laws; substances such as heroin were classified as illegal and other opioids were regulated with access only through physicians. The possibility that opioids were teratogens[1] was the subject of much research beginning in the 1970s, when heroin use was perceived to be a serious threat to society.

Although there were earlier publications on the subject, a 1975 article by Finnegan and colleagues in the journal *Addictive Diseases* is considered to be a seminal clinical publication on caring for infants experiencing withdrawal from opioids. The medical diagnosis of Neonatal Abstinence Syndrome (NAS) was created. Although it is a technically correct medical usage of the term *syndrome*, NAS in some cases became a label that remained with children long after the withdrawal symptoms disappeared. It may be more accurate to employ a term such as neonatal withdrawal to describe the experiences of the infant, reflect that they are limited to the neonatal period, and reduce the lifetime stigma of the label of syndrome (Marcellus 2007).

With these clinical developments, models of health service shifted, and it became recommended best practice to have infants transferred to an NICU for care. This care usually included regular systematic assessment of withdrawal symptoms, administration of medication to manage the symptoms, and care of the infant within a strictly controlled environment. These strict controls extended to how much parents were "allowed" to touch and care for their infants (Boyd 1999). There has been limited evolution of clinical management recommendations for NAS since the 1970s, and systematic, rigorous research in this field has lagged, possibly because NAS lacks the cachet of other neonatal intensive care health concerns and is often fundamentally seen as a social or moral issue.

A primary use of taking a social construction approach has been for raising consciousness. In the case of NAS, there is an opportunity to not only see this diagnosis as simply biomedical in origin, but as having multiple complex and interrelated social factors that require us to pursue further research on improving specific NICU clinical practices and to act together as a community to advocate for addressing inequities in broader determinants of health. Addressing these longer term inequities holds greater potential for improving the health outcomes for children and their families than focusing on managing the finite period of withdrawal and focusing on the impact of substances. Lester and colleagues (2004), leaders in the field of perinatal substance use outcome research, concluded that the greatest impediment to cognitive development in children is not substance use, but poverty. By focusing on only the substance as harmful and presenting misuse as an individual, deliberate, and a poor choice, key points of debate are hidden and missing, such as a full discussion of the barriers of care for substance-using women, the lack of treatment services, and the relationship of the substance use to the social conditions in women's lives (Marcellus 2004).

Dominant Cultures: Theoretical Approaches to Practice in the NICU

Because of the infant-centric context of the NICU, the theoretical approaches to practice that are considered foundational are focused on supporting the infants themselves and supporting the infant within a family. Although many maternity programs identify woman-centered care as their primary approach to care, this perspective becomes immediately invisible the moment that the NICU becomes the context for care. In this section I will briefly describe these three approaches and discuss critiques of and tensions between these three views of care.

Family-centered Care

Early medical efforts to care for premature babies meant that babies were separated from their family for extended periods of time. Until the late 1940s, visiting regulations in children's hospitals were very restrictive, considered necessary because of the fear that infections would be brought in from outside. Families were situated as vectors for disease and/or as visitors or attendants. Their presence was restricted, and often considered a nuisance and obstacle to care (Harrison 2010). At that time, having infants and children away from their families for extended periods was not seen as breaching the family unit but was seen as being responsible to both the child and the family.

In mid 1940s post-war Britain, John Bowlby, a child psychiatrist, and James Robertson, a social worker, demonstrated that child and parent separation could lead to significant emotional, psychological and developmental consequences (Harrison 2010). Exploration of the effects of separation then expanded to include the separation of hospitalized children from their families. Changes in practice emerged in response to this research, including increased "visiting" hours, opportunities for parents to stay with their children during hospitalization, and devolution of institutional models of care for children with complex health and developmental issues to home as location for care. These changes in practice were often credited to the strong advocacy of families of children with chronic health concerns, not necessarily to health care professionals, who have historically been reluctant to champion these changes (MacKean et al. 2005).

Family-centered care (FCC) is the predominant theoretical social value and approach to care within current neonatal and pediatric contexts. This approach has been formalized and institutionalized over the past 60 years and is now established as gold standard practice for all children and families in the health care system. It has become a legally mandated expectation of service delivery for children with special health care needs. Within this approach the pivotal role of the family is recognized and respected in the lives of children, as they provide the framework through which individuals enter and interact with society at large. Parents and professionals are theoretically positioned as equals in a partnership committed to the well being of the child.

Although this approach to care has been idealized, attainability of this approach to care is increasingly seen as questionable (Shields 2010). Despite 60 years of promotion, there is little evidence of its effectiveness and there are multiple barriers to its implementation. Health care continues to be dominated by the medical model where health care professionals are often the primary decision makers of the treatment a child receives and a controlling force that dictates the role that families may undertake (MacKean et al. 2005). Parents remain dissatisfied with opportunities for involvement, physician parent communication, and transition to home planning (Gooding et al. 2011). Heimer and Staffen (1998) have characterized parents in the NICU as impoverished social control agents as they face multiple obstacles to participating in, monitoring and evaluating the care of their infants.

Family-centered care as an approach, a model, and a philosophy has not been widely critically analyzed in mainstream health literature. There is limited examination of FCC from gender, cultural, racial, economic, social, diversity, and equity perspectives. As with society in general, providers in the NICU most likely hold embedded expectations of idealized and normative family states, in particular that of a mother and a father who have adequate social, emotional, and economic resources. There is some literature on mothers of preterm infants and their "struggle to mother" in a medically privileged environment (Fenwick et al. 2001). In particular it is challenging to find literature where the appropriateness and usefulness of FCC has been considered for women with complex social challenges, including substance use, mental health issues, violence and trauma. Most likely the additional obstacles of stigma and judgment experienced by women in health care settings would further reduce the possibility of establishing any kind of equitable partnership.

Developmental Care

Individualized, family-centered developmental care is a framework for providing neonatal care that enhances the neurodevelopment of the infant through clinical and educational interventions that support both the infant and family. The National Association of Neonatal Nurses (2009) defines developmental care as "a philosophy that embraces the concepts of dynamic interaction between the infant, family, and surrounding environment" (p. xi). This approach is based on research conducted in the 1970s and 1980s by psychologist Dr. Heidilise Als that demonstrated the positive effects of interventions such as adjusting the NICU environment and caregiving strategies to support the neurodevelopmental needs of each infant (Als et al. 1994). In this approach, the NICU environment was framed as primitive and hostile compared to the more favorable "in-utero environment" (mother's own touch, sound, movement, and nutrition) because of the noise, light, handling, treatment, and separation from mother and father. The physical environment and standardized NICU practices themselves were seen as detrimental to the growth and recovery of the infant. Dr. Als developed a vocabulary of infant cues and behaviors, a primitive language, that providers in the NICU could interpret and then develop actions to meet the needs of the infant.

The period of time during the 1970s and 1980s when the developmental approach was being developed and studied was when there was expanding research into fetal and neonatal neurodevelopment. Another significant milestone of neonatal practice and science at this time was the recognition and treatment of neonatal pain. Prior to this point it was felt that infants, in particular preterm infants, were not physiologically capable of experiencing pain and procedures such as surgery were conducted with minimal or no analgesia (Rodkey and Riddell 2013).

Developmental care is now considered a critical dimension of high quality neonatal care (Kenner and McGrath 2010; Symington and Pinelli 2009; Vandenberg 2007). Like family-centered care, it viewed the family as an integral part of the health care team. This shift in approach to care is still not universally implemented as it requires a change in culture from being protocol and technologically focused to being relationally based and reflective (McGrath et al. 2011). A Cochrane systematic review (Symington and Pinelli 2009) indicates that research on the effectiveness of the developmental approach is primarily conducted with preterm infants.

There is little research or reflection on the effectiveness of this approach with infants experiencing withdrawal, who may not necessarily have been born prematurely. Although there is little specific literature linking the NICU-based care of infants with prenatal substance exposure with developmental care, this approach theoretically holds possibilities for improving practice and outcomes as caregivers would be able to respond in an individualized manner to each infant and their family and provide opportunities to teach parents about how to read and respond to their infant's unique cues. Because mothers of infants with neonatal withdrawal in the NICU have reported that they have experienced judgment and blame from NICU providers and have restricted opportunities to actively care for their infant, the possibility of the developmental approach being helpful is reduced (Boyd 1999; McGuire et al. 2012; Murphy-Oiken et al. 2010). Within this approach parents are also seen as a whole instead of as mothers and fathers. In a leading developmental textbook there is a chapter on supporting parents and a chapter on supporting fathers, but no separate chapter on mothers. Inclusion of this chapter is justified by stating that the role of fathers is often not included and is deserving of exploration, whereas the authors most likely see the role of the mother as the default focus of support and therefore not of need of the same gendered exploration (National Association of Neonatal Care 2009).

Woman-Centered Care

Woman-centered care is positioned frequently as fundamental to the provision of maternity care. Woman-centered care is relationship-based and is an approach to clinical encounters that places value on a woman's needs within the context of her life circumstances. This approach incorporates the principles of equality, empowerment, autonomy, partnership, self-determination, and respect (Cory 2007). Woman-centered care is based on the view that women are valued as individuals, not only as partners, mothers, or workers.

Historically, once midwives were successfully displaced by male obstetricians in modern industrial and capitalist societies, childbirth became increasingly paternalistic and medicalized (Oakley 1984). Birthing moved from home to hospital, from being controlled by women to being socially controlled by men, and from being woman-centered to viewing women as the containers of fetuses. Women were subjected to an increasing number of procedures and technologies that had little scientific justification but were seen as being in the best interests of the infant's health. Experiences of antenatal care and birth also varied widely depending on women's social class, ethnicity, educational background, and geographical location (Leap 2008).

Emergence of the philosophy of woman-centered care may be traced back to the women's health movement that evolved during the second wave of feminism in the 1960s and 1970s. Similar shifts were occurring in the field of medical obstetrical care. Dr. Fernand Lamaze and Dr. Grantley Dick-Reed had the opportunity to observe childbirth practices in many countries and cultures, and returned to their home countries to promote the benefits of "more natural" childbirth strategies (Michaels 2014). Despite 40 years of a push toward demedicalizing childbirth in North America, providers are faced with increasing risk discourses, the domination of technology practices, and a neoliberal approach to health care system administration. Some women continue to report receiving care that is paternalistic, controlling, and traumatizing.

A key concern for some health care providers is that the term "woman-centered" means that the well-being of her infant, her partner, and family are ignored and marginalized. Thus, many prefer the term "family-centered." Proponents of woman-centered care claim that when there is a focus on individual women, there is the potential to create situations where the woman can become more powerful and in turn strengthen her family community and society (Leap 2008).

Most, if not all, of the NICU literature frames women within the context of family-centered care only, even when NICUs are co-located in an institution with obstetrical and other women's health services. The focus of care becomes the infant, even when a woman may have given birth just hours ago. The condition of the woman is situated within her new role as a mother and there will be little focus on her own physical or mental health. There will also be little acknowledgment of her life circumstances once she has left the hospital, unless these life circumstances present a risk for the infant.

From a gendered perspective, mother–child ties receive more scrutiny than father–child ties; mothers are expected to learn about infant care more than fathers, and are more likely to be labeled inappropriate (Heimer and Staffen 1998). The mothers of infants with NAS in particular are seen as problematic and as a risk to their infant. NICU RNs have described feeling stressed and resentful towards women who are pregnant and using substances (McGuire et al. 2012; Murphy-Oiken et al. 2010). They report experiencing personal struggles in balancing the competing priorities of caring for the infant and supporting families with psychosocial vulnerabilities. Concealed by idealistic family and developmental centered approaches to care, women and NICU health care providers are caught between a number of competing discourses informed by the Canadian public health abstinence policy for pregnancy and parenting women, the harm reduction movement, the medicalization and criminalization of substance use, and dominant cultural and moral constructions of the pregnant body and motherhood (Benoit et al. 2014).

Travelling into New Neighborhoods: Learning from Others

My first few years of practice in an NICU setting were consumed by mastering advanced neonatal psychomotor skills, such as intravenous insertion, ventilator support, chest tube care, orogastric tube feeds, and apnea and bradycardia management. An infant that demonstrated irritability or feeding challenges was labeled as colicky or temperamental. The issue of substance use and neonatal withdrawal did not enter into our diagnostic considerations at that time. If I situate the literature in the field of prenatal substance use with my early years of practice (the second half of the 1980s), this was about the same time that Dr. Loretta Finnegan and her colleagues in Philadelphia were conducting what is now considered groundbreaking work in the area of NAS (Finnegan 1986). They developed structured medication treatment regimes, designed a neonatal abstinence scoring system (which continues to be the most used instrument in the United States and Canada), and raised awareness of the impact of maternal opioid use on infant outcomes. Similarly, in Seattle, Washington, Drs. Ken Jones and David Smith were publishing early papers on fetal alcohol syndrome (FAS) after they noted a unique pattern of altered development and function in children of mothers who consumed alcohol during pregnancy (Benz et al. 2009; Jones and Smith 1975). More recently, researchers have also challenged the construction of FAS as a medical diagnosis (Golden 2006; Schellenberg 2007).

As awareness of the impact of substance use on fetal and neonatal outcomes increased within our NICU settings, we aimed to develop standardized practices to improve our care. In British Columbia, Canada, infants experiencing withdrawal were often transferred to Vancouver to a specialized pediatric unit at a children's rehabilitation hospital (Boyd 1999). In the late 1990s I began a special project with our child welfare ministry, the British Columbia Ministry for Children and Family Development (MCFD) to develop an education and support program for foster parents who cared for infants after their discharge from the hospital, as many of the infants who experienced withdrawal or who had confirmed or suspected prenatal substance exposure were removed from their birth families and placed in foster care (Marcellus 2000, 2004). During my search for innovative programs and core components for an education program, three key things happened that triggered the expansion of my disciplinary borders. First, MCFD had developed a provincial FAS resource and was holding a number of workshops around the province to support clinicians in integrating this resource into their practice. Second, guidelines for the care of women who were using substances during pregnancy and the care of infants with prenatal exposure to substances were released by a provincial perinatal practice organization at a provincial conference where some of the speakers were focusing on supporting the mother (British Columbia Reproductive Care Program 1999). At that time, these guidelines were considered innovative and incorporated approaches such as woman centered care and harm reduction, concepts that were unfamiliar to me as an NICU practitioner. Third, I read a book that was based on research conducted at the specialized pediatric unit in Vancouver (Boyd 1999). The researcher, a critical feminist sociologist, interviewed program team members and parents. Parents, mostly women, shared that they felt unwelcome, stigmatized, racialized, and blamed. After reading this book and beginning to meet a new group of clinical and community providers with knowledge of women's experiences, I experienced significant disruption of my taken-for-granted clinical practices. Someone with a different set of disciplinary knowledge, values, and behaviors was challenging my professional claims.

I chose to address this discomfort, and this disruption, by cultivating professional relationships far beyond the border of how I had previously conceptualized a multidisciplinary team. The knowledge that I knew I needed to improve my practice needed to come from different places and I sought out partners in other disciplinary worlds where this knowledge was available, such as sociology, psychology, gender studies, mental health and addictions, social work and violence against women fields.

I returned to university for doctoral studies and used that time to explore this field even more broadly and more deeply from perspectives such as ethics and philosophy. As I was searching for doctoral related opportunities to develop my research capacity, I was referred to information about the Intersections of Mental Health Perspectives in Addictions Research Training (IMPART) program and joined the first cohort in 2004. As an RN, I was able to interact and learn from scholars and researchers in diverse academic and practice fields, such as psychology, eating disorders, cellular medicine, addiction science, and sociology. This training provided me with the opportunity to theorize and reflect more deeply on the impact of social determinants of health and on the hidden and unacknowledged social processes that came into play in the course of my daily practice.

Following my doctoral program, I moved through a series of leadership positions in maternal and women's health in health authority and provincial organizations. Because of my IMPART involvement, I approached this new work with an expanded perspective that bridged settings that have traditionally been siloed in health care. As an initial step, I was more aware of these siloes such as between neonatology and obstetrics, and between neonatology and public health. For example, as someone responsible for strategic planning for perinatal health, I engaged with partners in obstetrics, neonatology, pediatrics and public health, but also addictions, mental health, women's violence and transition programs, early childhood development, psychology, and child welfare. In my work, I was able to situate perinatal health within the larger context of women's health, integrate sex and gender analysis into strategic planning, and profile the importance of considering health equity, social justice and social determinants of health when developing programs and services. I was also able to reflect on how impoverished my previous conceptualizations and understandings were about the politics and organization of health care delivery and the dominant approaches to care in my practice field that were taken for granted, and share these reflections with others.

A Story of Border Learning: A NICU Quality Improvement Collaborative as a Vehicle for Transdisciplinary Practice

Because of the infant-centered focus of team members, women who have had infants in the NICU setting have shared with us that often the care they receive is judgmental and stigmatizing, and that they are not comfortable being with their infant in this setting. The clinical case of NAS provides a useful exemplar for visualizing how the application of a transdisciplinary approach to practice provides new possibilities for improving care. Here I share a story of how this approach provided an opportunity to collectively take into account different perspectives, with the goal of integrating scientific and practice based knowledge to create solutions to improve clinical and relational practice in the NICU and beyond.

The Vermont Oxford Network (VON) is an international voluntary non-profit quality improvement collaborative organization that was formed in 1988 to improve the quality and safety of medical care for newborn infants and their families (Horbar et al. 2010). The Network today is composed of over 900 NICUs around the world. Each year, VON teams focus on one specific clinical issue. In past years, this has included issues related to ventilator care and oxygenation. In 2012 the VON team, with feedback from these participating units, identified NAS as their priority focus for the next two years. The leaders of this collaborative were particularly interested in exploring new and innovative ways of practice and disrupting entrenched practices. One of their priorities (identified as potentially better practices) within this collaborative was to "create a culture of compassion, understanding and healing for the mother infant dyad affected by the problem of NAS." I was invited to join this faculty because of my research and scholarship in the area of neonatal withdrawal. This presented to me a unique opportunity to bridge across what have been traditionally siloed areas of practice in health care. The leaders of the Network aimed to provide their collaborative members with access to the most current and innovative evidence and practice that is available. For this particular clinical topic, "better practices" are located not only in the NICU field, but in broader areas of health, social and community care. For example, integrated maternity care models (such as Breaking the Cycle in Ontario, Canada, and Sheway, Maxxine Wright, and HerWay Home in British Columbia, Canada) have emerged as effective one stop models for women with multiple complex issues including problematic substance use (Nathoo et al. 2013). Providers in these programs have developed advanced skills and knowledge in providing woman-centered, trauma-informed care. Better practices are also found in the Families in Recovery (FIR) Square program at BC Women's Hospital, the only hospital based clinical unit in North America for women who are pregnant and coping with problematic substance use. Within this program, practices such as keeping mother and baby together and supporting breastfeeding have contributed to outcomes such as fewer infants requiring medication for treatment, reduced numbers of days on medication, and fewer infants being placed in foster care (Abrahams et al. 2010).

As one of the faculty for this collaborative, I have harnessed this opportunity to introduce teams to the bodies of knowledge on substance use, sex and gender, violence, and trauma to an audience that typically has limited knowledge and skills related to these areas. I have provided online lectures on topics such as an introduction to trauma-informed care, photo voice and patient journey mapping, and partnering with birth families. The Network also collaborated with teams at

Sheway and FIR Square to develop a DVD of women's stories of receiving care and support through these programs. I developed a facilitator's guide for the DVD and integrated concepts such as trauma-informed care, harm reduction, stigma, social determinants of health, and cultural safety. Members of the Network leadership team felt it was critical to infuse family voices into quality improvement work, and in the case of neonatal withdrawal, the complexity of the issue and the vulnerability of women made it challenging to access deep stories of experience for each hospital team. The virtual stories shared in this DVD provided an alternate mechanism to bring these voices to this learning.

There are already early shifts in practice and successes being reported. In addition to improvements being noted in clinical practices such as improved consistency and reliability in withdrawal assessment, teams are reporting developing new partnerships, such as with public health, women's programs, local methadone clinics, and community addictions specialists. Team members are acknowledging and talking about their pre-existing attitudes and judgments and the impact that they have on providing compassionate care. NICU family support counselors are partnering with women to share their stories and engage them in changing practice to better meet their needs. The concept and practices of trauma-informed care teams are being discussed by teams and ideas are being generated about how to infuse these practices throughout institutional structures and also about how to create new structures or processes that are more able to support this approach.

One challenge has been related to situating the value of qualitative research and knowledge from non-medical disciplines. The privileged approach to evidence in the NICU is a highly medicalized and empirical one, with other forms of knowledge often marginalized. A simultaneous goal has been to introduce evidence from other fields and have it be seen as valid and useful as biomedical health science evidence. A second challenge has been coming to terms with how groups and disciplines are defining the common good. Most team members in the NICU consider the infant their primary patient, and the family as a support for this patient. From an ethical perspective, teams are grappling with how they balance for themselves the good of the infant versus the good of the woman, family, community or society (Marcellus 2004).

Conclusion: Moving Towards Transdisciplinarity in the NICU

Over ten years ago, the Institute of Medicine (IOM) issued a call to action for those who are involved in interdisciplinary research and training (IOM 2004). This call to action was intended to facilitate both incremental and transformative collaborative practices. In this report it was suggested that interdisciplinary thinking was rapidly becoming an integral feature of research as a result of four powerful drivers—the inherent complexity of nature and society, the desire to explore problems and questions that are not confined to a specific discipline, the need to solve societal problems and questions that are not confirmed to a single discipline, and the power of new technologies (pp. 2–332). Bridging the gap between academia and the wider community, meeting at the interfaces, is best generated through a collaborative, iterative process to create a more holistic understanding of a social problem (Messing et al. 2012).

Reynolds (2000) suggests that academics and academia suffer from an "acute hardening of the boundaries" (p. 559), in some cases positioning the boundaries as more important than the places themselves. Traditional disciplinary structures and bonds should not bind possibilities for improvement. We need to move together to reframe neonatal withdrawal and substance use during pregnancy as social concerns rather than strictly biomedical problems. Otherwise our attention will be restricted to limited and narrow practices, primarily physical and pharmacological care in a finite period of time. A critical view of population health will help to situate and provide direction for strengthening nursing practice and improving the care of women, children and families within communities. Application of this broader perspective expands the definition of vulnerability beyond health risk to address to social, cultural, environmental and political factors.

For myself as a research and scholar and for other RNs and health care providers, answering the question of "how has this come about?" challenges us to look beyond the accepted contemporary meaning of constructs of health and illness to the social realities of our nursing practice and the families with whom we work. Researchers in the medical industry continue to pursue knowledge production primarily within a positivist tradition, and sociology in some forms holds a conflictual relationship with biomedicine that risks leaving the everyday practice of nursing ungrounded (McPherson 2008).

Morrow and Brown (1994) contend that some form of ontological realism is required to maintain the connection between the sciences and human emancipation, and that immobilization can occur when all perspectives and forms of knowledge are considered to be equally legitimate. Because nursing and other health care disciplines are practice-oriented, it is not enough simply to deconstruct and critique health and social theories and practices. It is also vital that we pay attention to how mothering discourses are shaping the experiences of women in their own particular circumstances (Varcoe and Doane 2007). As health professionals, we need to admit that we are most likely pragmatically focusing on the immediate and short-term physical needs of mother and baby from a middle class, Western, biomedical perspective. Critical scholars in turn conduct ideological deconstruction without providing alternatives for reconstruction that are relevant to the everyday practice of RNs and other health professionals working with women and families (Marcellus 2004). However, unless a critical analysis of the constructs of neonatal withdrawal and prenatal substance use are undertaken and disseminated/translated to RNs, RNs risk becoming unintentional participants in marginalization and oppression. Nursing curricula are increasingly addressing this concern by being grounded in critical perspectives and developing critical thinking and reasoning skills in students. Participating in the IMPART program during my doctoral studies while still practicing as an RN in an NICU provided me with a unique opportunity to "cross the borders" of my personal disciplinary knowledge of sex and gender, addiction, mental health, violence and trauma and develop new languages and insights that help me reveal, discuss and address these questions.

Discussion Questions

1. What are the theoretical foundations in your place of practice? Do you see evidence of reflective thinking about the deep meaning of these foundations for your practice?
2. How do your daily routines and ways of practice work for families who experience many complex social challenges, including substance use? Can you identify any practice changes that you can make to improve how you are supporting women and families?
3. Reflect on your own personal stance and how you were taught about issues such as addiction, mental health and violence/trauma in your education programs. What gaps or tensions arise in professional education, and how might these be addressed?

Note

1 Agents, either viruses, radiation, or drugs, that cause malformation of the embryo or fetus.

References

Abrahams, Ronald, Marion MacKay-Dunn, Victoria Nevmerjitskaia, Scott MacRae, Sarah Payne and Zoe Hodgson. 2010. An Evaluation of Rooming-in Among Substance-Exposed Newborns in British Columbia. *Journal of Obstetrics and Gynaecology Canada* 32, no. 9: 866–871.

Als, Heidilise, Gretchen Lawhon, Frank Duffy, Gloria McAnulty, Rita Gibes-Grossman and Johan Blickman. 1994. Individualized Developmental Care of the Very Low-Birth-Weight Preterm Infant: Medical and Neurofunctional Effects. *Journal of the American Medical Association* 272, no. 11: 853–858.

Benoit, Cecilia, Lenora Marcellus, Rachel Phillips, Camille Stengel and Sinead O'Connor. 2014. Analyzing Provider's Constructions of Problematic Substance Use among Pregnant and Early Parenting Women. *Sociology of Health and Illness* 36, no. 2: 252–263.

Benz, Jennifer, Carmen Rasmussen and Gail Andrew. 2009. Diagnosing Fetal Alcohol Spectrum Disorder: History, Challenges and Future Directions. *Paediatrics and Child Health* 14, no. 4: 231–237.

Bettegowda, Vani, Eve Lackritz and Joann Petrini. 2011. Epidemiologic Trends in Perinatal Data. In *Toward Improving the Outcome of Pregnancy III: Enhancing Perinatal Health through Quality, Safety and Performance Initiatives*, edited by Scott Berns, 20–32. White Plains, NY: March of Dimes Foundation.

Boyd, Susan. 1999. *Mothers and Illicit Drugs: Transcending the Myths*. Toronto: University of Toronto.

Boyd, Susan. 2004. *From Witches to Crack Moms: Women, Law, and Policy*. Durham, NC: Carolina Academic Press.

British Columbia Reproductive Care Program. 1999. *Guidelines for the Care of Women with Substance Use Issues*. Vancouver, BC.

Canadian Institute for Health Information. 2009. *Too Early, Too Small: A Profile of Small Babies Across Canada*. Ottawa, Ontario.

Carroll, Katherine. 2009. *Unpredictable Predictables: Complexity Theory and the Construction of Order in Intensive Care*. Unpublished thesis: University of New South Wales.

Conrad, Peter and Kristin Barker. 2010. The Social Construction of Illness: Key Insights and Policy Implications. *Journal of Health and Social Behavior* 51, no. 1: S67-S79.

Cory, Jill. 2007. *Woman-Centered Care: A Curriculum for Health Care Providers*. Vancouver, BC: BC Women's Hospital and Health Centre.

Davis, Leigh, Heather Mohay and Helen Edwards. 2003. Mother's Involvement with Caring for Their Premature Infants: An Historical Overview. *Journal of Advanced Nursing* 42, no. 6: 578–586.

Fallah, Shafagh, Xi-Kuan Chen, Derek Lefebvre, Jacqueline Kurji, Joanne Hader and Kira Leeb. 2011. Babies Admitted to NICU/ICU: Province of Birth and Mode of Delivery Matter. *Healthcare Quarterly* 14, no. 2:16–20.

Fenwick, Jennifer, Lesley Barclay and Virginia Schmied. 2001. Struggling to Mother: A Consequence of Inhibitive Nursing Interactions in the Neonatal Nursery. *Journal of Perinatal and Neonatal Nursing* 15, no. 2: 49–64.

Finnegan, Loretta. 1986. Neonatal Abstinence Syndrome: Assessment and Pharmacotherapy. In *Neonatal Therapy: An Update*, edited by Firmino Rubatelli and Bruno Granadi, 122–146. New York: Exerpta Medica.

Finnegan, Loretta, J. Connaughton, R. Kron, and J. Emich 1975. Neonatal Abstinence Syndrome: Assessment and Management. *Addictive Diseases* 2(1–2): 141–158.

Golden, Janet. 2006. *Message in a Bottle: The Making of Fetal Alcohol Syndrome*. Boston: Harvard University Press.

Gooding, Judith, Liza Cooper, Arianna Blaine, Linda Franck, Jennifer Howse and Scott Berns. 2011. Family Support and Family-Centered Care in the Neonatal Intensive care Unit: Origins, Advances, Impact. *Seminars in Perinatology* 35: 20–28.

Greaves, Lorraine, Colleen Varcoe, Nancy Poole, Marina Morrow, Joy Johnson, Ann Pederson, and Lori Irwin. 2002. *A Motherhood Issue: Discourses on Mothering Under Duress*. Ottawa, ON: Status of Women Canada.

Harrison, Tondi. 2010. Family-Centered Pediatric Nursing Care: State of the Science. *Journal of Pediatric Nursing* 25: 335–343.

Hayes, Elisabeth and Sondra Cuban. 1997. Border Pedagogy: A Critical Framework for Service-Learning. *Michigan Journal of Community Service Learning* 4, no. 1: 75–82.

Heimer, Carol and Lisa Staffen. 1998. *For the Sake of the Children: The Social Organization of Responsibility in the Hospital and the Home*. Chicago: University of Chicago Press.

Hess, Julius. 1922. *Premature and Congenitally Diseased Infants*. Philadelphia: Lea and Febiger.

Horbar, Jeffrey, Roger Soll and William Edwards. 2010. The Vermont Oxford Network: A Community of Practice. *Clinics in Perinatology* 37: 29–47.

Institute of Medicine. 2004. *Facilitating Interdisciplinary Research*. Washington, DC: National Academies Press.

Jones, Ken and David Smith. 1975. The Fetal Alcohol Syndrome. *Teratology* 12(1): 1–10.

Kelly, Len, Joe Dooley, Helen Cromarty, Bryanne Minty, Alanna Morgan, Sharen Madden and Wilma Hopman. 2011. Narcotic Exposed Neonates in a First Nations Population in Northwestern Ontario: Incidence and Implications. *Canadian Family Physician* 57, no. 11: e441–7.

Kenner, Carol and McGrath, Jacqueline. 2010. Developmental Care of Newborns and Infants: A Guide for Health Professionals (2nd ed.). Chicago, IL: National Association of Neonatal Nurses.

Leap, Nicki. 2008. Woman-Centered or Women-Centered Care: Does it Matter? *British Journal of Midwifery* 17, no. 1: 12–16.

Lester, Barry, Lynne Andreozzi and Lindsey Appiah. 2004. Substance Use During Pregnancy: Time for Policy to Catch up with Research. *Harm Reduction Journal* I, no. 5: 1–44.

MacKean, Gail, Wilfreda Thurston and Catherine Scott. 2005. Bridging the Divide Between Families and Health Professionals' Perspectives on Family-Centred Care. *Health Expectations* 8, no.1: 74–85.

Marcellus, Lenora. (2000). The Safe Babies Project. *Canadian Nurse* 96, no. 10: 22–26.

Marcellus, Lenora. (2004). Developmental Evaluation of the Safe Babies Project: Application of the COECA model. *Issues in Comprehensive Pediatric Nursing* 27, no. 2: 107–119.

Marcellus, Lenora. (2007). Neonatal Abstinence Syndrome: Reconstructing the Evidence. *Neonatal Network* 26, no. 1: 33–40.

McGrath, Jacqueline, Haifa Samra and Carole Kenner. 2011. Family Centered Developmental Care Practices and Research: What Will the Next Century Bring? *Journal of Perinatal and Neonatal Nursing* 25, no. 2: 165–170.

McGuire, Denise, Mary Webb, Denise Passmore and Genieveve Cline. 2012. NICU Nurses' Lived Experience: Caring for Infants with Neonatal Abstinence Syndrome. *Advances in Neonatal Care* 12, no. 5: 281–285.

McPherson, Neil. 2008. The Role of Sociology in Nurse Education: A Call for Consistency. *Nurse Education Today* 28: 653–656.

Messing, Jill, Madelaine Adelman and Alesha Durfee. 2012. Gender Violence and Transdisciplinarity. *Violence Against Women* 18, no. 6: 641–652.

Michaels, Paula. 2014. *Lamaze: An International History*. Oxford: Oxford University Press.

Morrow, Raymond and David Brown. 1994. *Critical Theory and Methodology*. New York: Sage.

Murphy-Oikonen, Jodie, Keith Brownless, William Montelpare and Keri Gerlach. 2010. The Experiences of NICU Nurses in Caring for Infants with Neonatal Abstinence Syndrome. *Neonatal Network* 29, no. 5: 307–313.

Nathoo, Tasnim, Nancy Poole, Margaret Bryans, Lynda Dechief, Samantha Hardeman, Lenora Marcellus, Elizabeth Poag and Marliss Taylor. 2013. Voices From the Community: Developing Effective Community Programs to Support Pregnant and Early Parenting Women Who Use Alcohol and Other Substances. *First Peoples Child and Family Review* 8, no. 1: 93–106.

National Association of Neonatal Care. 2009. *Developmental Care of Newborns and Infants: A Guide for Health Professionals*. New York: Mosby.

Oakley, Ann. 1984. *The Captured Womb: A History of the Medical Care of Pregnant Women*. Oxford: Blackwell.

O'Donnell, Melissa, Natasha Nassar, Helen Leonard, Ronnie Hagan, Richard Mathews, Yvonne Patterson and Fiona Stanley. 2009. Increasing Prevalence of Neonatal Withdrawal Syndrome: Population Study of Maternal Factors and Child Protection Involvement. *Pediatrics* 123, no. 4: e614–21.

Patrick, Stephen, Robert Schumacher, Brian Benneyworth, Elizabeth Krans, Jennifer McAllister and Matthew Davis. 2012. Neonatal Abstinence Syndrome and Associated Health Care Expenditures, United States, 2000–2009. *Journal of the American Medical Association* 307, no. 18: 1934–1940.

Poole, Nancy and Barbara Isaac. 2001. *Apprehensions: Barriers to Treatment for Substance-Using Mothers.* Vancouver, BC: British Columbia Centre of Excellence for Women's Health.

Reynolds, Nedra. 2000. Who's Going to Cross This Border? Travel Metaphors, Material Conditions, and Contested Places. *Journal of Applied Communications* 20, no. 3: 541–564.

Rodkey, Elissa and Rebecca Pillai Riddell. 2013. The Infancy of Pain Research: The Experimental Origins of Infant Pain Denial. *Journal of Pain* 14, no. 4: 338–350.

Schellenberg, C. (2007). Knowing About Women, Children and Fetal Alcohol Syndrome: What Knowledge and Whose Caring Counts? In *With Child: Substance Use During Pregnancy: A Woman-Centered Approach*, edited by Susan Boyd and Lenora Marcellus, 124–136. Peterborough, ON: Fernwood Books.

Shields, Linda. 2010. Questioning Family-Centered Care. *Journal of Clinical Nursing* 19: 2629–2638.

Symington, Amanda and Janet Pinelli. 2009. Developmental Care for Promoting Development and Preventing Morbidity in Preterm Infants. *Cochrane Database of Systematic Reviews* 2, no. CD001814. DOI: 10.1002/14651858.CD001814.pub2

Vandenberg, Kathy. 2007. Individualized Developmental Care for High-Risk Newborns in the NICU: A Practice Guideline. *Early Human Development* 83, no. 7: 433–442.

Varcoe, Colleen and Gweneth Hartrick Doane. 2007. Mothering and Women's Health. In *Women's Health in Canada: Critical Perspectives on Theory and Policy*, edited by Marina Morrow, Olena Hankivsky and Colleen Varcoe, 297–323. Toronto: University of Toronto Press.

Young, Nancy, Sharon Boles and Cathleen Otero. 2007. Parental Substance Use Disorders and Child Maltreatment: Overlap, Gaps, and Opportunities. *Child Maltreatment* 12, no. 2: 137–149.

Suggestions for Further Reading

British Columbia Provincial Mental Health and Substance Use Planning Council. 2013. *Trauma Informed Practice (TIP) Guide.* Victoria, BC. Available on line at: www.health.gov.bc.ca/mhd/publications.html#Trauma

Marcellus, Lenora. 2014. Supporting Women With Substance Use Issues: Trauma Informed Care as a Foundation for Practice in the NICU. *Neonatal Network* 33 (6): 307–314.

Poole, Nancy and Lorraine Greaves. 2012. *Becoming Trauma Informed.* Toronto, ON: Centre for Addiction and Mental Health.

7
BRIDGING THE BIOLOGICAL AND THE SOCIAL IN NEUROSCIENCE

Gillian Einstein

Gillian Einstein is a Professor in the Department of Psychology and the Dalla Lana School of Public Health at the University of Toronto. She is founder and director of the Collaborative Graduate Program in Women's Health. Her current research spans memory, pain, sex/ gender representations in the nervous system, cultural practices, and the bridge between our scientific understanding of the nervous system and identity, self and feminism. In this interview with Lorraine Greaves and Nancy Poole, Einstein discusses transdisciplinarity in the context of her own border crossing between biological and social sciences and quantitative and qualitative methods, the opportunities and challenges for training new researchers and the parallels between arguing for sex and gender and transdisciplinarity in health research.

Q: What does transdisciplinarity mean to you?
A: To me, it means finding the methods to bring together the social with the biological. It means reaching across disciplines as diverse as the humanities and the biological sciences. I think it is broader than the way it is commonly used in the biomedical sciences—that is, if somebody uses molecular biology to study an immune system problem, or somebody uses anatomy to understand a molecular biology problem, that's considered transdisciplinary. But to me, those are still aspects of the same disciplinary approach. What I think is important to a full understanding of any scientific question is to actually reach across the human knowledge sciences to incorporate the humanities and the social sciences and the biological sciences together so that you really understand a problem from the full perspective of the organism.

Q: You first said 'finding the methods.' Is that how you would define transdisciplinarity?
A: I think finding the methods is a critical part of transdisciplinarity, because it's really hard to bridge the humanities and the biological sciences unless you

know how to link up the different kinds of methods and approaches that are used in each of those areas. So, I do think methodology has a lot to do with transdisciplinarity, actually.

Q: How would you describe what you do? Would you call it multidisciplinarity or transdisciplinarity?

A: I think what I do is both! To me, transdisciplinarity is really about reaching across disciplines for different ways of understanding the human condition. I think of multidisciplinarity as kind of how you organize your approaches—whether one person owns a whole range of disciplines or approaches or whether they bring in different people each to represent a different approach. I think of what I do as transdisciplinary in the sense that I try to incorporate the humanities and first-person approaches, but I think of it as multidisciplinary in the sense that I can't own all those approaches and I need to bring people with different expertise to collaborate with me. Does that make sense?

Q: Does the approach that you've just described lead to transdisciplinarity?

A: I think it certainly can. I think that's the pathway I've used to try to ensure that, if I'm doing a study that includes qualitative and quantitative research, for example, that somebody who's really a qualitative researcher, which I am not, could come to my data and think that it was really good qualitative data. And the same with somebody who is a neuroscientist, could come to my data and think, "Oh, this is really good neuroscience data," instead of subordinating one to the other. A lot of times, when you see mixed-methods papers, you see that the quantitative research might be subordinated to the qualitative, or vice versa. So, I think of multidisciplinarity as a way for each approach to stand on its own two feet and not be subordinated to the other. That was the approach that I took with the female genital cutting project or mutilation (FGM/C).

Q: Could describe how you set up that project? How did you conceive the questions, and assemble a team?

A: That particular project I had been thinking about for probably ten years. I had been studying sex differences in the nervous system and then I was reading the newspaper about immigration from Northern Africa to North America, and one of the things that kept coming up in the newspaper accounts was accounts of female genital cutting or mutilation (FGM/C). And, because I was studying sex differences, and there aren't that many sex differences in the nervous system of humans that are really clear-cut, as in rodents, and I began to wonder whether female genital cutting wasn't a way to actually exacerbate sex differences where sex differences hadn't existed before. So I kind of took this social problem that was being portrayed in a social way and I wonder, "What can neuroscience say about this?" So, I started thinking about it in terms of nerve and muscle, and developmental neuroscience, and the field of sex differences. Once I was able to actually do the project, and started interacting with women who actually had FGM, I realized that my methodologies were not giving proper due to the stories that the women wanted to tell me. So, I had to reach for other methodologies in order to give an honest account of what the women wanted to tell me. It just seemed like a very important thing to do with a practice that was a social practice as well as a biological practice. So, for me, it started off, in a way, as a thought experiment, and then the actual doing of that thought experiment pushed me to reach for other methods that I had never encountered or done before, myself. That was the progression of that study, as it ended up being both a qualitative study, with a full, qualitative interview, and then a study that tried to understand physiologically what pain responses in the women were.

Q: How did you enlarge your team when you came to that realization, that you needed to include other methods?

A: Right. I realized that I was not a qualitative interviewer and probably that wasn't my forte, and I knew colleagues, like Robin Mason (a scientist a Women's College Research Institute), who had interviewed immigrant women on the issue of intimate-partner violence. I told them about my project and asked if they would be willing to participate, and they said yes, and they turned out to be really fantastic collaborators in that respect, and they actually helped enormously on the qualitative interviewing guide and did some early pilot interviews. As I started wanting to understand pain more, I talked to people about pain, and a number of people suggested that I should do quantitative sensory testing. Not being an expert on quantitative sensory testing of the vulvar region, I turned to people who were, like Caroline Pukall (a researcher of human sexuality affiliated with Queen's University). I told her about my project and asked her if she would be interested, and she said yes. So she taught me how to do quantitative sensory testing and provided me with the equipment to do it. So I think it was kind of a journey of what's the next logical step. "Here's my question, how can I really answer it in a way that does justice to the question itself and the women I'm studying?" I just reached out to people.

Q: You said earlier that the qualitative aspect of your project was demanded by what you were hearing from the women and your goal of doing justice to their stories. What did they say that made you feel that?

A: Well, we had a community advisory group of three, sometimes four, women from the community who were part of a community health center. I discussed the research question and all the instruments with the community advisory group. When I asked them the semi-structured questions I wanted to get answers to, they didn't answer them. They started talking about their cutting: what it was like and their feelings about it. So, I realized that I couldn't get answers to my questions and, second of all, to try to get answers to my questions would be to force kind of round pegs into square holes. I felt I would be doing violence, in a way, to the women themselves, to make them answer these questions, and I didn't want to set up the conditions that would be required in order to do that, so that's when I realized I needed to basically ask open-ended questions that would let them tell the story they wanted to tell, and then see what came out of that.

Q: What did you get from the open-ended qualitative data? How do you think it was different than if you had asked them your original semi-structured questions?

A: I think the qualitative data in some ways are a lot more rich, for many reasons, but one of the reasons is that this is not a culture that I am from and so it allowed what was important to those women in that culture to say what they wanted to say. And it allowed me to understand the themes that were meaningful to them rather than the themes that I wanted to know about. One of the things that came out of that, that was so stunning to me, was an understanding or a misunderstanding of Western ideas of pain that actually have very broad ramifications for Somali women's use of the health-care system. Even if they've lived in the country for twenty years, their own understandings of what we consider disease and illness, and also of pain in general, I think have broad ramifications for their use of health care.

Q: How do you think the Somali women benefitted from you taking the broader transdisciplinary approach?

A: I think they felt that somebody would tell their story in a way that it hadn't been told before. So, not just a respectful version of what it means to be a Somali woman who had experienced FGM, living in Canada, but a story that took their whole body into account and not just their genitalia. The first thing I said to them was that I'm not interested in your genitalia, I'm interested in your brains. And that really meant something to them. So you can change the problem by how you approach it. To apply it to trauma and addiction, if you said to people, "I'm not really interested in the fact that you're addicted. I'm really interested in pain or I'm really interested in what your body feels like," it shifts the conversation and you might learn a lot about addiction. From this approach I think they became convinced that theirs is a story that would contribute experience and knowledge that would be a benefit to all women, such as issues around female sexuality. We can learn things about that from women who've had their clitorises excised. I think the Somali women really appreciated that by understanding something about them in particular, they could contribute to a more general knowledge for women. I think that meant a lot to them.

Q: Based on what you learned in the Somali women's project, you said that there are implications for the health system. Can you talk a bit more about that and apply that to addiction?

A: What struck me so much for the Somali women is that their conceptualization of pain was really different. For them, pain has to be really extreme before they think they're sick. In fact, pain and sickness or illness is the same word in Somali. Practically speaking, this means that they don't go to a doctor until they're in so much pain that they think they're sick. The implication is that they enter the health system much later than maybe you or I might. That's not to say that there aren't people who are born and raised in Canada and won't go to a doctor until they're in so much pain that they're already experiencing septicemia or the like. But it's rarer. In Canada, we're taught that pain is an indication of something being wrong. The first glimmer of pain and we need to go check it out. For Somali women, they don't get into the health-care system, even if it might be accessible to them. They don't get into it by their own volition or until it may be way down the line in terms of the progression of their own illness. And you see this, for example, with respect to problems with pregnancy and delivery. And that means that the outcome is often worse for them.

With respect to pain and addiction, I wonder if pain isn't conceptualized or experienced very differently in people who become addicted, who are experiencing addiction. This also means that their encounter in the health-care system is very different. They may not access the system for their pain or they may access it so much that their pain is no longer taken seriously and doesn't get treated. This has led me to wonder quite literally whether, not just mental trauma but actually tissue trauma and pain resulting from tissue trauma or even pain resulting in, or trauma resulting in neuropathic pain doesn't drive addiction in some way. From this perspective, addiction can be seen as a kind of self-treatment. So, rather than going into the health-care system, or if the health-care system is inadequate, people with addiction are people who are self-treating pain. Obviously, this is not a new idea but the pain is often thought of as a sociological or mental pain and not a pain in which brain circuits are activated—i.e., a pain that could be treated as pain rather than say, mental illness.

I would also think that addiction has its own culture and so, to understand the physiology of addiction along with the social aspects of addiction, one has to understand the culture of addiction and what people tell you about it. And obviously that culture changes depending on the culture or other aspects of culture that people come from. So, one of the things that shaped a project by one of my master's students, was that we would need to understand something about the women's own conceptualizations of their addictions and their misuse of opioids, which was her project, as well as what their physiological measurements of pain within a pain clinic told us.

Q: Gillian, you were talking earlier about one of the benefits of transdisciplinarity being an ability to see the health-system implications more widely. I think that's an interesting way to describe it because it means that transdisciplinarity can also allow you to do better knowledge translation (KT) in some ways.

A: I think that's true. When you start doing things in a transdisciplinary way, you start getting refractions that you wouldn't ordinarily have. One of those refractions is a much broader perspective. One of the things that I found is that any one of my projects could be described in about five or six different contexts, depending on the discipline to which I'm speaking. So, I think another real advantage of transdisciplinarity is getting out of the silos. Your work is no longer siloed as research as opposed to KT.

One important silo that affects KT is the silo of what's known in animal research as opposed to what's known in human research. For example, in a study on pain and addiction by one of my students, Samah Hassan, a literature review of the clinical literature revealed that what people know perfectly well in animal research—that there are sex differences in pain perception as well as interpretation, as well as sex differences in response to opioids—was not being applied in the human research at all. It took a literature review to reveal that these lines were not being crossed.

Another silo, working with IMPART really made us think about was the intersection of trauma with chronic pain and vice versa. And yet the literature on trauma qua trauma doesn't think much about any possible resulting neuropathic pain, and the opposite is certainly true about the literature on neuropathic pain. Yet, they're probably very closely related. For example, people with fibromyalgia—a type of neuropathic pain—will often have an early childhood experience of some kind of physical or emotional trauma, and yet people don't translate that trauma into *physiological* pain. But it's important to do that because acknowledging physiological pain is a link between the trauma and the self-treatment that leads to addiction. So, breaking down the silos can lead to important, new insights that might be a route to other types of discovery.

With respect to female genital cutting, I just submitted a paper that tries to bring together the anthropological literature with the biomedical literature and divides those findings by whether the findings are from the natal country or the country in diaspora because all of those locations are going to make a big difference to understanding how the social and the biological go together. One thing that just hasn't been done successfully in the literature on female genital cutting is to bring together the social with the biological. I think breaking down of the silos as well as considering the whole health-care system implications is really important. You might design approaches to the health-care system very differently. You might reach out to people very differently. A lot of times we talk about access to the health-care system and assume that is about whether or not the health-care system is open to people who need to use it. But the people needing to use it have to understand how to use it as well. That's an important part of access.

Q: Earlier you said that there are many different versions of the results of your female genital cutting study that you can give depending on the setting you're in. Is there a transdisciplinary version?

A: Yes, there is a transdisciplinary version, and that version is given to people who want to understand a problem in its entirety. But a lot of times one is not invited to give a talk by an organization that wants to understand a problem in its entirety. They just want to know how what you found relates to what they're doing.

Q: In terms of knowledge translation at large, do you ever move into describing the problem in its entirety as opposed to the siloed version? How do you navigate that?

A: I am trying to do that with female genital cutting work by doing the review that I did, and I've also written a chapter in a book. But I find that journals are extremely narrow, for the most part and there really aren't transdisciplinary journals. If you submit a transdisciplinary manuscript, the journal has a hard time finding reviewers, understanding which editorial section your paper belongs in and oftentimes they don't completely understand what you're trying to get at. I think that is a real struggle when you're doing transdisciplinary work. There is always the strategic issue of how you are going to organize your findings.

Q: What kinds of challenges do you experience due to working in a transdisciplinary way? You've mentioned publishing but what other challenges have you had? Colleagues, students, funders?

A: Funding is always a big challenge for the same kinds of reasons as publication. People think in their silos and they don't completely understand that, when you bring different disciplines together, or you translate across approaches, that actually the outcome is greater than the sum of the parts. Often reviewers look at the individual parts and try to decide whether they're good enough and then they wonder what the different parts are doing together. So funding is a real issue as are colleagues. It's very difficult. What I found interesting was that my public health colleagues understand better what I'm doing than my psychology colleagues, because psychology is such a discipline-bound field. They don't completely understand why would I be looking at hormones or why I would be recruiting a certain patient population. So, yes, colleagues can be a challenge but what you need are people with open minds who will say, "Oh, yeah, that's a really interesting idea. I want to participate in that." Sometimes I'm really lucky with it, and sometimes I'm not.

Q: What about students?

A: I have to some extent the same issues with students. For example, I have a doctoral student in psychology that I need to prepare to get a job in psychology. And even though she's exposed to a lab seminar that is quite broad with students from public health as well as students from medical sciences, people working on pain as well as people working on hormones as well as people working on global issues, that's not going to be her bread and butter. To some extent, to expect her to do that and want that for herself is not exactly going to be doing her a service. I also have another student who has struggled with her committee because they wanted her to prove to them that her experiment was necessary. She had a really good experiment that she proposed but couldn't actually just go do it because, first, she had to do a literature review and a chart review to convince her committee that the experiment was necessary. By the time that she was done proving it, she'd finished her degree. So I think that is a real challenge.

Q: What kind of solutions do you see to these different forms of resistance?

A: Well, it's not exactly a solution but I think the argument that often wins people over is the importance of transdisciplinarity to human health as opposed to the siloed approach, which only teaches you a little bit about a very little. In talking to and recruiting biological colleagues to my work, I will talk about a Nobel Prize winner who first conceptualized memory as a molecular event in a sea slug, but then expanded it the mouse and then took the human, which has taught us something very important about human memory. I approach them by saying, "Look, here's this guy who took a massive issue and—bearing in mind this massive human issue that requires multiple approaches—he just took one small approach but bore in mind and developed his research program to contain the enormity of it, if you will." I've been trying to build a gender medicine platform at a medical school in Sweden, Linköping, and I've recruited fourteen different investigators to the project. I've had to use my best translation skills—to apply some aspect of the entire project to their interests. Translation is very important; taking your ideas and translating them into the terms of the group that you're talking to and then slowly, if you bring them all together, they begin to see what the benefit to them really is.

Q: Do you think that trends, larger trends in universities and research are going against transdisciplinarity or do you think there are any trends that are going in favor of it?

A: I think universities are talking more and more about transdisciplinarity. In the sciences, they're couching it in terms of personalized medicine, stratified medicine and translational research. I don't know how it's being thought of in the humanities and the social sciences, but I wouldn't be surprised if it weren't also being approached. But the problem remains that universities are not giving any credit for it. So, you're stuck between a rock and a hard place with respect to the demands of your job as a faculty member. There is a lot of talk about it, but I still don't think people are being promoted or funded for it. I think team grants and consortia will get you into that realm and if you can convince people that that's the path to innovation, sometimes that helps. We just had kind of a success. I don't want to declare it a final success because it hasn't completely happened yet, but there's a Canadian Consortium on Neural Degeneration and Aging that a couple of colleagues and I got called about because there are partners funding sex and gender research. The PI of this consortium called up the usual suspects and asked, "What shall we do?" So we proposed a sex-and-gender core, or a platform that would go across all the teams and basically try to ensure that all the teams were thinking about sex and gender. You could imagine that model working for pain or working for addictions. But I can't say it's been a success yet. All I can say is that we've gotten the funds and that people have thought it was innovative. Now the really hard work begins.

Q: Do you think that there are any parallels between the challenges faced in arguing for including sex and gender in research and arguing for transdisciplinarity?
A: Yes. I do think that to do sex and gender right, you have to be transdisciplinary. You're trying to bring together the biological and the social and to do that, you have to have multiple approaches and many types of researchers. There might even be a deeper issue to this, which has to do with the philosophical convictions that lead one to advocate for sex and gender analysis or other kinds of transdisciplinarity. There might be something about transdisciplinarity that requires a different way of thinking about the science, which is more aligned with feminism. And in that might be people's resistance to it.

Q: In terms of breaking down silos or disciplines, we can also think about them as bastions of power. I wonder if that is part of the difficulty with bringing transdisciplinarity forward because it challenges nodes of power in ways that causes resistance. For example, one of the aims of transdisciplinarity is to derive more of a common language for things and that gets at the essence of some of those power nodes.
A: Yes, it certainly taps into people's insecurities and discomfort with not owning or owning something entirely.

Q: How would you say that taking a more integrated, transdisciplinary approach changed you?
A: I feel a lot freer because I can explore a question and not be bound by certain ways of answering it. This sounds kind of self-serving, but I feel that my moral compass is being served by the way in which I go about research. Not being bound by disciplines allows one the opportunity to try to do justice to what it is I'm studying rather than pounding out a study in the form of what it is I know is 'done.' I try to teach this approach to the students in my gender and health course, but it's difficult to get across—although, IMPART has done this very well. Research on humans and animals is always going to present ethical challenges. There are always going to be grey areas. You're using animals; you're using people. You, as researcher, are in a position of power. How you deal with that grey area, I think, is by doing justice to the question you're asking, to the best of your ability. And to acknowledge that you are in a moral grey area. Now, there are not very many people who are actually going to get the answer that would justify killing thirty cats or potentially risking a human being's health. But that's what we're doing, and I think there's arrogance in thinking that if you just use a particular transgenic animal and a particular method and then you ask questions about memory, that's going to give you the whole story.

I think that's very circumscribed. At the very least, we owe it to the animals and we owe it to the question to keep the context in mind. And it's really hard to keep the context in mind if you're not transdisciplinary. I think that if you're honest and true to the question, at least that's something. I think that it is really important to the ethics of research. By doing transdisciplinary research you have the opportunity to be as true as possible to the question you're asking, or at least knowing when you're rejecting a possibility. By the way, transdisciplinarity is also a source of creativity and innovation because it brings different perspectives to bear on the question. It's hard to get funded and you have to learn to walk the walk but that doesn't mean you can't have a lot of fun and learn incredible things while doing it.

8

MOVING TOWARDS TRANSDISCIPLINARITY IN RESEARCH WITH MARGINALIZED POPULATIONS

Iris Torchalla, Verena Strehlau, Erika Neilson and Michael Krausz

Our research team studies marginalized populations, including homeless people and individuals with chronic substance use. Research with these populations is inherently fraught with a number of challenges and requires consideration of the interplay of multiple psychosocial and environmental conditions and risk factors (rather than examining these factors in isolation). Such an understanding is fundamental to the ability to develop helpful, tailored interventions.

In this chapter, we reflect on a series of studies that we conducted to explore the effects of trauma, substance use, and mental health experienced by marginalized women from British Columbia. We describe theoretical and practical considerations encountered when exploring the intersections of mental health concerns, trauma, and gender in addictions research, reflect on our own perspectives as clinicians and researchers, and describe how—through our experience of researching these complex and intertwined conditions—we challenged ourselves to think beyond interdisciplinarity and acknowledge the importance of a transdisciplinary approach. We discuss how changes in our thinking from unidisciplinary to inter- and multidisciplinary and later towards transdisciplinary research have led us to apply frameworks and methods that have resulted in a more comprehensive understanding of addictions. We also describe our efforts and struggles of engaging in knowledge exchange and bridging gaps between research, practice, and the healthcare system to better address the complex concurrent conditions of these clients.

The Need to Understand the Intersections of Substance Use, Trauma, Mental Health, and Gender

Our team is located in Vancouver, British Columbia, Canada. Vancouver has one of the poorest neighborhoods in Canada: the Downtown Eastside (DTES), a small geographical area of about 17,000 people. Concentration of poverty in certain neighborhoods is often associated with social problems as well as negative health outcomes for their residents (Kawachi and Berkman 2003). Indeed, many community members in the DTES experience unemployment, precarious housing, violence and crime. Illicit drugs are readily available in this area, resulting in high usage of crack cocaine, crystal methamphetamine, and heroin. Many residents struggle with substance dependence, mental illness, and medical diseases such as HIV/AIDS and hepatitis, and some become involved in sex work and drug trafficking to survive and support their addiction (Campbell, Boyd, and Culbert 2009). The majority of the DTES population (about 62%) are men (City of Vancouver 2006) and there is also a dominantly male street culture. This creates a gendered risk environment in which women experience particular marginalization, exploitation, increased safety risks, and gender-based violence (Lazarus et al. 2011). For women residing in the DTES, trauma is a common experience, and yet the majority of research efforts and program planning in the DTES have focused on injection drug use and infectious diseases prevention. Mental health issues and trauma have often been neglected (Linden et al. 2013). Our goal was to complement existing work in the DTES by developing a research program that explores themes of trauma, violence, and mental health issues concurrent with the experience of addiction, through a gender-sensitive framework. We strongly value the need to bridge the gap between research and practice and foster a collaborative partnership with other disciplines and community services. In order to do so, we employed a stepwise process in which we conducted a series of studies to examine homeless women's issues using quantitative measures and information. The findings from these studies prompted the collection of more in-depth qualitative information about women's understanding of the role of trauma in their lives. It led to collaboration with a community-based harm-reduction service for pregnant women and new mothers with substance use problems and addiction. Seeking to build a collaborative research agenda, our team had met the consultant physician at our community partner's location on previous occasions and had invited him to speak at a trauma symposium in Vancouver. As the collaboration with our community partner evolved, we chose to center our qualitative study in our new partners' location, allowing us to interview their clients as well as hold regular meetings for knowledge exchange.

Starting with Unidisciplinary Studies of Mental Illness and Homelessness

In an initial project, the British Columbia Health of the Homeless Survey (BCHOHS), our team examined psychosocial and psychiatric issues in 500 homeless women and men. Participants were recruited from three cities in British Columbia: Vancouver/DTES, Victoria, and Prince George. Measurements included a socio-demographic questionnaire; a profile of current use of alcohol and illicit drugs as well as signs of psychological distress and somatic symptoms;

and an assessment of substance use disorders and mental disorders (based on the criteria of the *Diagnostic and Statistical Manual for Mental Disorders*, 4th edition; DSM-IV) as well as suicidality. Of the 500 participants in our study, 39% were women. On average, participants were 38 years old. Fifty-six percent self-identified as Caucasian and 40% as Aboriginal. Half of our sample lived on the street, and the other half stayed in shelters.

We conducted a series of three studies to provide an initial in-depth exploration of women's issues before extending the focus to include gender-specific patterns in the co-occurrence of posttraumatic stress disorder (PTSD) and substance use disorders (SUDs). At the beginning of the project, we employed a unidisciplinary approach. Our team consisted of clinical psychologists and psychiatrists who tend to conceptualize health issues as results of individual pathology and individual behaviors and pay less attention to social, environmental, or economic factors. Similarly, psychiatry or psychology training targets individuals, rather than the individual's environment or the health, social, legal, or political systems. The focus in this study series was on DSM-IV-based diagnostic categories, which typically do not reflect the language and concepts of many other health researchers and professionals.

The first sub-study aimed at describing substance use behaviors among the women (Torchalla et al. 2011). We found extraordinarily high rates of substance use and polysubstance use. Overall, 82% of our sample had at least one type of substance use disorder (SUD) diagnosis at the time of the assessment. We also found a high comorbidity of drug use disorders and alcohol use disorders, whereas recovery from SUDs was rare. Multivariate analyses showed that women who were of younger age, living on the street, engaging in sex work, and having ever attempted suicide were more likely to have a diagnosis of drug dependence. In a parallel study, we examined the women's mental health (Strehlau et al. 2012). The results indicated that 63% of the participants had at least one current mental disorder (not including SUDs) and that PTSD was the most prevalent current mental disorder. Eighty-five percent of those participants who had a current mental disorder had concurrent SUD. Furthermore, 50% of the women reported at least one suicide attempt in their life and 26% have had suicidal thoughts in the past year.

The most striking result from our perspective (focusing on individual and clinical issues) was the co-occurrence of multiple diagnoses and risk factors and the complexity of the study participants' health problems. Building on the findings of these two studies, we investigated gender-related patterns of SUD, PTSD, and their comorbidity in the entire sample of women and men (Torchalla et al. 2014). By this time, a researcher with a public health degree had joined the team, adding a perspective of community health and public policy to our work.

Unexpectedly, we found that women and men had almost identical SUD prevalence rates, and that of all mental disorders examined, PTSD was the only current diagnosis that showed significantly different prevalence rates between women and men (28% versus 16%). We then examined if SUD–PTSD comorbidity was associated with impaired psychosocial functioning (i.e., suicidality, psychological distress, somatic symptoms, incarceration history, and polysubstance use). We observed significant main effects of both PTSD and gender on clinical outcome variables among individuals who had current SUD: Individuals with PTSD reported greater suicide risk, psychological distress, and somatic symptoms than individuals without PTSD. In addition, women reported greater suicide risk and somatic symptoms than men. Analysis of interaction effects resulted in additional interesting findings, indicating that PTSD diagnosis was associated with a greater suicide risk only among women. That is, women with PTSD were more than seven times more likely to have an increased suicide risk than men without PTSD, whereas women without PTSD and men with and without PTSD did not differ from each other. And although analysis of main effects indicated that women experienced psychological distress similar to males, interaction analyses showed that this was only true for individuals without PTSD, whereas among participants with current PTSD psychological distress scores were substantially higher for women than for men. Overall, women with PTSD had the most severe pattern of psychosocial impairment in this study.

Thus, although homeless women and men appeared to be very similar when considering their DSM-IV-based diagnoses, differences in trauma experiences and other psychosocial dimensions relevant for recovery could be observed. These results suggest that men and women will have different treatment needs, which may be addressed by incorporating additional and gender-specific components (e.g., crisis intervention, emotional regulation techniques, and stress management training tailored for women) to the services. But still more research is needed to determine how these issues are best incorporated. We need to clarify if that should occur in the context of substance use treatment, PTSD or mental health treatment, or a combination of approaches. In addition, our team recognized that recovery from such complex concurrent conditions would be very difficult while living on the streets. As such we see the need for integrated trauma-informed approaches to housing interventions to support the stabilization and recovery of homeless women with substance use and trauma experiences. Such support requires structural interventions and interdisciplinary research, program planning, and care.

At this point, we recognized that other aspects of our participant's lives related to their physical health, built environment, interpersonal relationships, or cultural background had not been addressed. It was clear that addressing these complex concerns would be beyond the scope and resources of one or two disciplines. We were challenged by the limits of the medical model that appeared to simplify our study participant's complex realities and to ignore the social determinants of their health problems. A second researcher with a Public Health degree joined the team, thus extending the narrow focus on individuals and individual behaviors and risk factors, to include expertise in the social determinants of health. Upon introduction of the new team members, the number of meetings and discussions increased. This should be expected by any researcher moving away from a unidisciplinary focus. In order to communicate ideas, we could no longer depend on clinical terminology and clinical models that were specific to the psychology/psychiatry field, and found ourselves engaging in communication that was understood across disciplines.

Based on the conclusions derived from the three studies, we decided to conduct a qualitative study among women from the DTES to enrich our depth of understanding of the role of trauma in their lives. Such information would allow for enhanced complexity of the quantitative data by providing first-hand accounts of women's experiences and perceptions and issues they considered relevant. We were interested in understanding how the women made sense of their lives and how they conceptualized the intersections of trauma with addiction and mental health within the environment they lived. We interpreted the findings in the context of the 'risk environment' (Rhodes 2009), which comprises different types of environments—physical, social, economic, and policy—that interact on both the micro-level (e.g., locations of drug use and sex work, access to social housing, etc.) and the macro-level (e.g., gender inequalities, public health policy regarding harm reduction and addiction treatment, etc.) to produce drug-related harm. Obtaining this information from the women is important for the delivery of an empowering model of care where services and programs are grounded in respect for the clients and a full understanding of the challenges they face in their everyday lives.

Moving to Interdisciplinarity: Understanding the Links between Trauma and the Experience of Addiction for Pregnant Women and New Mothers

A study was conducted with women who struggled with substances during pregnancy and/or early motherhood. We recruited participants by collaborating with a drop-in center that offers prenatal and postnatal care, sexual health counseling, addiction counseling and methadone maintenance treatment, practical support, food and nutrition counseling, parenting classes, and First Nation–specific services for about 120–160 women. Some participants were also recruited from two of the drop-in center's partnering services, a transitional housing program for pregnant and parenting women who use substances, and a residential program at a Women's Hospital providing care for substance-using women and their newborns.

Thirty-one women were interviewed, using questions to explore the context of substance use, the context of trauma and violence, and the interplay of trauma and substance use. The women were on average 31.9 years old, and 16 identified as Aboriginal. Twenty-one women had a history of foster care. Thirteen women had one or two children, 18 had three or more children; 14 women reported they had a partner at the time of the interview. Key themes that emerged from the interviews highlighted the ubiquity of adversities and trauma—often in form of gender-based violence (e.g., sexual violence, violence in pregnancy, sexual slavery), beginning in early childhood and continuing to adulthood, and to their own families/relationships. Drug use and trauma followed complex patterns, where women experienced multiple early childhood adversities in form of both single traumatic events and chronic stressors; they experienced distress resulting from these adversities and used substances to self-medicate their distress. Once regular substance use was established, they entered a damaging cycle of engaging in high-risk behaviors and situations to secure drug supply, resulting in more trauma exposure and a lifestyle that was characterized by gendered risks, ongoing adversities, and violence in a variety of contexts (including experiences in the health-care system), and through a variety of offenders. All of the women reported experiences of homelessness or precarious housing at some point in their lives; and many of them at a young age. Life on the streets in combination with drug use often involved engagement in risky activities (e.g., street-based prostitution) and exposure to high risk and traumatic situations (e.g., sexual and physical assault) which typically deteriorated participants' health. All of these conditions mutually intensified and maintained each other and interfered with natural, healthy resolution of trauma/PTSD symptoms and substance use. Women also expressed concerns that trauma can be passed from one generation to the next (Torchalla et al. 2015).

We learned from the study that the reality tends to go beyond models that focus on individual factors to explain the long term sequelae of childhood adversities and trauma. The study participants named environmental and social constructs as factors that affected their ability to cope with trauma. For example, gender-based violence was organically raised by many participants in our interviews. Understanding gender-based violence in the context of drug dependency, shelter, and earning income through sex work further illustrates the need to consider the broader environmental and social context and for intervening on multiple levels including changes in policy, laws, and programs. The added public health lens on our team encouraged discussion of the social determinants of health, conceptualizing health inequities as developed in and maintained by complex psycho-socio-environmental conditions. The findings suggest that service providers in the DTES could integrate trauma-informed care into their program, but that it is also necessary to shift the focus from the individual to include socio-political and structural changes (e.g., safe housing for women, protection of sex workers), and from issues of drug use and reduction of drug-related harms to include issues of gendered vulnerabilities. We also became aware that the results of our studies called for improvement of clinical education, and advocacy for and with this population.

Towards Transdisciplinarity

Addressing Trauma and Other Determinants of Health in Interventions and Services

To advance trauma-informed interventions, one of our team members—a former IMPART trainee—conducted a meta-analysis together with other IMPART trainees to evaluate the effectiveness of integrated treatment programs for individuals with concurrent substance use problems and trauma/PTSD. The results indicated that integrated programs are promising interventions which effectively reduced trauma-related symptoms and substance use, although they produced similar results as non-integrated interventions (Torchalla et al. 2012). As discussed above, understanding gender-related patterns in PTSD-SUD comorbidity and psychosocial functioning may provide important information for further tailoring and improving the existing integrated interventions.

Our team recognizes the importance of advancements in addictions treatment, particularly with regards to harm reduction approaches. However, in our aforementioned study among individuals accessing the drop-in center for pregnant and postpartum women (Torchalla et al. 2015), our participants expressed hesitation, ambivalence, or often clear refusal when asked about their interest in receiving trauma-specific counseling, raising questions about how their experiences and needs can best be addressed. Others have advocated for adopting a trauma-informed approach in all facilities providing services for women (Poole et al. 2013; Poole and Greaves 2012). Trauma-informed approaches are distinct from trauma-specific interventions in that the care delivery practices take into account an understanding of the impact of trauma on an individual's life, development, and substance use; create safety and avoid retraumatization; but do not necessarily require disclosure of trauma or a focus on healing from trauma. In contrast, trauma-specific interventions address trauma experiences directly and facilitate trauma recovery through counseling and treatment. Thus, trauma-informed approaches can be offered to clients who do not wish to work on their trauma issues; and they may also pave the way for considering additional steps towards recovery from trauma. Women with trauma histories such as those accessing our collaborator's services may have other health, social and financial issues which they see as more pressing in the short term than trauma recovery. As such our study participants' responses suggest that trauma-informed approaches may be more appropriate than trauma-specific interventions in harm-reduction services for women in the DTES. Our wider lens on the intersections of trauma, gender, and other determinants of health with addiction and mental illness allowed us to see merits of the transdisciplinary practice of our collaborator's service providers, where staff from multiple disciplines all seek to begin relationships with women using trauma-informed, welcoming relational practices and deliver cross-disciplinary support, at a pace women can manage.

Learning Together and Addressing Trauma in Collaboration

In order to fully understand the situation of individuals with chronic substance use and complex concurrent conditions, researchers and clinicians from varied disciplines need to collaborate to produce, synthesize, and integrate knowledge that leads to a better understanding of the complexities of providing services for these individuals. As an example for moving towards a transdisciplinary approach we describe a project where—subsequent to the aforementioned study—our team has continued to collaborate with our community partner to develop a series of 2-hour workshops on a variety of topics that both clinicians and researchers found relevant for providing services for marginalized women in joint pre-workshop meetings.

Our community partner as an organization includes a variety of health-care professionals with different levels of training and experience, such as an alcohol and drug counselor, community health nurses, social workers, a nutritionist, infant development consultants, outreach workers, housing support workers, family physicians, a cook, a family support worker, and an Aboriginal community support worker. Through these staff members, our partner offers a range of social and medical services for the women, with the overall goals of: 1) supporting mothers in their capacity as parents; 2) promoting the health and development of their children; 3) supporting the women's self-determination, choices, and empowerment; and 4) linking the families to a network of health-related, social, emotional, cultural, and practical supports. Thus, our partners' philosophy itself is rooted in the idea of transdisciplinarity where individuals from different disciplines and backgrounds work towards the common goal of serving the complex needs of their population. With integrated and multidisciplinary practitioners in place, transdisciplinary, interdisciplinary, and unidisciplinary care are all possible, based on women's needs and readiness. The workshop was designed to support joint learning and knowledge exchange between a multidisciplinary group of researchers and clinicians, collaboratively expand the staff's knowledge and clinical skills for addressing trauma issues in the context of addiction, and increase the researchers understanding for the challenges clinicians face in their everyday work.

An important insight that we learned from this is that knowledge translation has to go in both directions between researchers and clinicians: frontline clinical care has to be informed by research so that community health services can offer interventions that have been shown to have successful outcomes. At the same time, research needs to be informed by frontline clinical care so that studies can be designed with an understanding about how treatment works in the "real world" in the context of clients' lives. The lack of communication and cooperation has often been attributed to their different philosophies, cultures, missions, and perceptions of the world and each other (Marinelli-Casey, Domier, and Rawson 2002). Researchers derive their knowledge by drawing cautious conclusions from their data; scientific knowledge is generally based on lengthy observations that are subject to constant revision or falsification, and the results do not reveal much about an individual client. Practitioners, on the other side, are often confronted with situations that need quick decisions; they may not have access to scientific evidence, and may rely on common sense, anecdotal evidence, and strategies that had worked for them in the past (Altman 1995). Substance use services in particular historically had been developed in isolation from the mainstream health-care services and have often been provided primarily by peers with personal histories of addiction and recovery, many of whom had no scientific knowledge. The theoretical scientific approach, apparently lacking practical relevance and empathy for the client's multiple challenges, may be frustrating for practitioners. Likewise, scientists may be frustrated by the practitioners "inaccurate" and "ideology-driven" approaches. However, since the 1990s, a shift towards evidence-based practice, and practice-based evidence has gained popularity (Kazdin 2008). This model is more conducive to transdisciplinarity.

During the interactive, practice-oriented workshop with our community partner, we discussed background information about concurrent substance use and trauma, including its epidemiology, possible pathways, clinical impact, and women's issues. Furthermore, clinical topics such as the assessment of traumatic experiences and the PTSD diagnosis, evidence-based treatment for PTSD, and treatment approaches for individuals with concurrent substance use and trauma were presented and debated. In addition, therapeutic strategies and techniques that clinicians can use to help clients cope with trauma symptoms (e.g., breathing, relaxation, grounding exercises) were introduced and practiced in small groups. The clinicians on their part informed the researchers about their work, discussed their own conceptualization of their client's problems, and compared how the scientific findings fit their own observations and experiences from the "real world."

It required considerable work to bridge our disciplinary perspectives. From the beginning there was a common understanding that the workshop was not unidirectional (from researchers to community health workers) using traditional teaching models, but a knowledge exchange project involving both parties in bi-directional exchange. However, our team encountered challenges related to the language, perspectives, and understanding of the client's problems despite the fact that both researchers (IT and VS) had a clinical education (as a clinical psychologist and a physician with psychiatry background) and previous clinical experience working with clients at addiction services and psychiatric university hospitals. For example, many participants from the drop-in center found our use of DSM diagnostic categories labeling and judgmental (although we emphasized the difference between labeling and diagnosing). In order to communicate ideas, we could no longer depend on clinical terminology and clinical models that were specific to the psychology/psychiatry field, and found ourselves working to engage in communication that was understood across disciplines. We started paying more attention to our use of technical terms and moved away from using diagnostic categories (such as "substance use disorder" and "posttraumatic stress disorder") to a more descriptive language. On the other hand, we sometimes felt that the language of the practitioners (e.g., their use of the term *trauma*) was imprecise and too general, and their approach to clients was guided by preconceptions (e.g., "Everyone has severe trauma histories") rather than a comprehensive assessment. Other problems related to our practice of using examples derived from our research interviews and research-related settings to illustrate certain topics, assuming that the practitioners could translate these examples into their own work. However, their feedback frequently indicated that this was not the case, and both practitioners and researchers were left with the impression that we did not move towards the joint goal of transcending our disciplines. We took measures to address this gap and facilitate deeper exchange; for example, we changed the procedures towards more flexible scheduling of topics to allow for even more time dedicated to general and case discussion, exchange and processing of experiences, and validating each other's work. We paid more attention to discussing scientific findings and evidence-based methods and interventions in the context of clinical and case examples brought by the practitioners and our own clinical experiences. We got in touch with the community partner coordinator between the sessions and tailored subsequent session based on their feedback and input from previous sessions. Over time, the relationship between our organization and theirs was strengthened, and we were able to overcome these boundaries of discipline.

As well as adapting the language and content of our educational exchange, we found it helpful to add more disciplinary diversity to our team. The engagement of an Addiction Knowledge Exchange Leader from BC Mental Health and Substance Use Services was a significant marker in our journey to transdisciplinary research. This individual has worked as a social worker in community-based services for women with substance use and mental health issues for over 15 years, and her Métis heritage and cultural competence as well as her social determinants of health perspective were appreciated at the community organization. Her involvement proved beneficial in making our research knowledge relevant for the service context and for facilitating communication between academic researchers and non-academic staff. In our final evaluation of the workshop, the interactive discussions and exchange of views and experiences were listed among the most positive and helpful aspects of the workshop.

Taken together, of this collaboration, we found the greatest value in the different disciplines' inspiration to adopt one another's perspectives, whilst valuing that both researchers and practitioners have significant though distinct expertise. Through our research studies on marginalized women, we have learned much about the complex needs of this population from a scientific point of view. The workshop was a unique opportunity for knowledge exchange of different perspectives and mutual learning experiences, which enabled us to see complexity and the continuum of care from a front-line point of view, and how in this subsequently transdisciplinary approach, researchers and practitioners can find a better way to move forward.

A Way Forward

Interventions to improve the health and well-being of women who use substances need to account for the complex, multifaceted needs of their clients and address individual vulnerabilities and characteristics as well as societal, cultural, and political deficiencies, and include issues of gendered vulnerabilities and human rights. Ultimately, we would like our approach to future research to be mindful of all

	Pros			Cons	
	for the team	for the clients		for the team	for the clients
Opportunities			Challenges		
Strengths			Threats		
Assets			Limitations		
Prospects			Restrictions		

categories of social determinants of health (Mikkonen and Raphael 2010). To date, our researchers have seen potential relationships between social determinants of health, such as gender, early childhood development, social status, housing, work conditions, and social exclusion. Specifically, the team has explored elements of gender-based violence, childhood trauma, the status of being homeless and a lack of familial support, and issues of sex work involvement, respectively. We are aware that many more factors play a role in the population of women we are studying. However, it is not enough to explore these factors in isolation and from isolated disciplinary perspectives; we should aspire to bring them together as a whole in a transdisciplinary research endeavor. By being open to new collaborations and perspectives that differ from their own, researchers and clinicians from many disciplinary traditions can stretch themselves beyond interdisciplinarity thinking and create space for transdisciplinary exchange that paves the way for shared theories, language, methods, frameworks, and perspectives. Ultimately, the benefits of transdisciplinary practice will help move forward our understanding of addiction and our approach to addiction research, treatment, services, teaching, and policy.

Discussion Questions

1. Thinking about your current team, what perspectives are you currently missing in your work, and why?
2. Thinking about your current team, what positive forces and potential problems would a transdisciplinary approach pose for both your clients and your team?
3. Your transdisciplinary team has identified a client with addiction, trauma, and nutritional challenges. However, the client only wants methadone maintenance treatment. How would your team support the client?

References

Altman, David G. 1995. "Sustaining Interventions in Community Systems: On the Relationship between Researchers and Communities." *Health Psychology* 14 (6): 526–36. doi:10.1037/0278-6133.14.6.526.
Campbell, Larry, Neil Boyd, and Lori Culbert. 2009. *A Thousand Dreams: Vancouver's Downtown Eastside and the Fight for Its Future*. Vancouver, BC: D&M.

City of Vancouver. 2006. *2005/2006 Downtown Eastside Community Monitoring Report, 10th Edition*. Vancouver, BC. www.vancouver.ca/commsvcs/planning/dtes/pdf/2006mr.pdf. Accessed: 5/01/2015.

Kawachi, Ichira, and Lisa F. Berkman, eds. 2003. *Neighborhoods and Health*. New York, NY: Oxford University Press.

Kazdin, Alan E. 2008. "Evidence-Based Treatment and Practice: New Opportunities to Bridge Clinical Research and Practice, Enhance the Knowledge Base, and Improve Patient Care." *American Psychologist* 63 (3): 146–59. doi:10.1037/0003-066X.63.3.146.

Lazarus, Lisa, Jill Chettiar, Kathleen Deering, Rose Nabess, and Kate Shannon. 2011. "Risky Health Environments: Women Sex Workers' Struggles to Find Safe, Secure and Non-Exploitative Housing in Canada's Poorest Postal Code." *Social Science & Medicine* 73 (11): 1600–1607. doi:10.1016/j.socscimed.2011.09.015.

Linden, I. A., Marissa Y. Mar, Gregory R. Werker, Kerry Jang, and Michael Krausz. 2013. "Research on a Vulnerable Neighborhood—the Vancouver Downtown Eastside from 2001 to 2011." *Journal of Urban Health* 90 (3): 559–73. doi:10.1007/s11524-012-9771-x. Accessed: 1/01/2015.

Marinelli-Casey, Patricia, Catherine P Domier, and Richard A. Rawson. 2002. "The Gap between Research and Practice in Substance Abuse Treatment." *Psychiatric Services* 53 (8): 984–87. doi:10.1176/appi.ps.53.8.984.

Mikkonen, Juha, and Dennis Raphael. 2010. *Social Determinants of Health: The Canadian Facts*. Toronto, ON: York University School of Health Policy and Management.

Poole, Nancy, and Lorraine Greaves, eds. 2012. *Becoming Trauma Informed*. Toronto, ON: Centre for Addiction and Mental Health,.

Poole, Nancy, Cristine Urquhart, Fran Jasiura, Diane Smylie, Rose A. Schmidt, Trauma Informed Practice Project Group, and Trauma Informed Practice Advisory Committee. 2013. *Trauma Informed Practice Guide*. Vancouver, BC: British Columbia Centre of Excellence for Women's Health, and British Columbia Ministry of Health. http://bccewh.bc.ca/publications-resources/documents/TIP-Guide-May2013.pdf.

Rhodes, Tim. 2009. "Risk Environments and Drug Harms: A Social Science for Harm Reduction Approach." *International Journal of Drug Policy* 20 (3): 193–201. doi:10.1016/j.drugpo.2008.10.003.

Strehlau, Verena, Iris Torchalla, Kathy Li, Christian Schuetz, and Michael Krausz. 2012. "Mental Health, Concurrent Disorders, and Health Care Utilization in Homeless Women." *Journal of Psychiatric Practice* 18 (5): 349–60. doi:10.1097/01.pra.0000419819.60505.dc.

Torchalla, Iris, Isabelle A. Linden, Verena Strehlau, Erika Neilson, and Michael Krausz. 2015. "'Like a Lots Happened with My Whole Childhood': Trauma and Addiction in Pregnant and Postpartum Women from Vancouver's Downtown Eastside." *Harm Reduction Journal* 12 (1): doi:10.1186/1477-7517-12-1.

Torchalla, Iris, Liz Nosen, Hajera Rostam, and Patrice Allen. 2012. "Integrated Treatment Programs for Individuals with Concurrent Substance Use Disorders and Trauma Experiences: A Systematic Review and Meta-Analysis." *Journal of Substance Abuse Treatment* 42 (1): 65–77. doi:10.1016/j.jsat.2011.09.001.

Torchalla, Iris, Verena Strehlau, Kathy Li, and Michael Krausz. 2011. "Substance Use and Predictors of Substance Dependence in Homeless Women." *Drug and Alcohol Dependence* 118 (2–3): 173–79. doi:10.1016/j.drugalcdep.2011.03.016.

Torchalla, Iris, Verena Strehlau, Kathy Li, Isabelle A. Linden, Francois Noel, and Michael Krausz. 2014. "Posttraumatic Stress Disorder and Substance Use Disorder Comorbidity in Homeless Adults: Prevalence, Correlates, and Sex Differences." *Psychology of Addictive Behaviors* 28 (2): 443–52. doi:10.1037/a0033674.

Suggestions for Further Reading

Back, Sudie E., Angela E. Waldrop, and Kathleen T. Brady. 2009. "Treatment Challenges Associated with Comorbid Substance Use and Posttraumatic Stress Disorder: Clinicians' Perspectives." *The American Journal on Addictions / American Academy of Psychiatrists in Alcoholism and Addictions* 18 (1): 15–20. doi:10.1080/10550490802545141.

Najavits, Lisa M. 2009. "Psychotherapies for Trauma and Substance Abuse in Women Review and Policy Implications." *Trauma, Violence, & Abuse* 10 (3): 290–98. doi: 10.1177/1524838009334455.

Ramadier, Thierry. 2004. "Transdisciplinarity and Its Challenges: The Case of Urban Studies." *Futures, Transdisciplinarity* 36 (4): 423–39. doi:10.1016/j.futures.2003.10.009.

9
USING REFLEXIVITY TO ACHIEVE TRANSDISCIPLINARITY IN NURSING AND SOCIAL WORK

Nancy Clark, Ingrid Handlovsky and Deborah Sinclair

This chapter illuminates reflexivity and intersectionality as possible heuristic tools for promoting transdisciplinarity approaches in addictions research. Through our academic and practitioner roles in the fields of nursing and social work, we have come to appreciate the need to move beyond interdisciplinary approaches to our clinical and scholarly practice. Increased attention is being paid to building capacity for trauma-informed care and practice with an emphasis on interdisciplinary collaboration to foster evidence-based practices and interventions that are client centered (Peck and Capyk 2012). Similarly, scholars in the field of addiction research have urged for a broader understanding of addiction, in which environments and social contexts intersect with individual determinants of health (Rhodes 2002, 2009; Maté 2009; Moolchan et al. 2007). The inclusion of broader social contexts and client-centered approaches calls for innovative approaches to research in addiction, in particular, transdisciplinarity. By transdisciplinarity we refer to the process in which collaboration blurs boundaries within and between disciplinary practice, ultimately bringing forth new conceptual and theoretical frameworks that better equip researchers in addressing the complexity of addiction. These frameworks include participatory approaches and shared learning amongst various citizens, including but not limited to academics, community, and intersectoral stakeholders, and those who are most affected by research outcomes and social policy on addiction. Transdisciplinary research thus concerns real-world problems in which the framing of research questions and practices extends beyond traditional disciplinary frameworks (Kessel and Rosenfield 2008; Larouche and Potvin 2013; Maasen and Lieven 2006). While many scholars have delineated what constitutes transdisciplinarity in research, including the challenges inherent in the integration of diverse fields of knowledge, few have discussed specific tools or pragmatic strategies that can facilitate empirical research within transdisciplinary projects.

In this chapter, we propose that critical reflexivity and intersectionality can assist scientific disciplines in developing transdisciplinary approaches to knowledge production, specifically those concerning health promotion in addiction research. Based on our own knowledge and practices within the disciplines of nursing and social work, we foreground critical reflexivity and intersectionality as useful theoretical and methodological approaches for promoting transdisciplinarity in the study of addiction in the lives of marginalized women. We argue that both critical reflexivity and intersectionality can facilitate dialogue among disciplines, offer the potential for building equitable relations, and what Maasen et al. (2006) refer to as scientifically and socially "sound science." As scholars embedded in critical theoretical approaches to knowledge production, we apply not only a self-reflexive stance in positioning ourselves in our work but also how our positioning contributes to the construction of knowledge between and across different academic communities (e.g. biomedical sciences and social sciences). In what follows we provide a brief description of critical reflexivity and intersectionality and then illustrate the utility of these approaches for understanding addiction in the lives of differently marginalized women specifically, through discussions of each of our respective areas of work: Handlovsky discusses her work with women living with severe mental illness and addiction in Vancouver, Canada's, Downtown Eastside (DTES) neighbourhood and Clark discusses community capacity in relation to resettlement strategies and the broader social, historical and political factors that shape the lives of refugee women during resettlement in Canada. Sinclair brings attention to resistance movements in her work with violence against women (VAW) in Canada and the need to redress traumas incurred through advocacy and political action. While each of us adopts a slightly different intersectional perspective, we collectively argue for a more contextual understanding of women's experiences and the broader intersecting forces that shape women's risk for negative consequences of addiction and mental health. These vignettes are followed by a discussion of the potential challenges and opportunities afforded by the use of reflexivity and intersectionality as practical tools for moving towards transdisciplinarity in addictions related research.

Critical Reflexivity and Intersectionality in Nursing and Social Work

Despite a long historical tradition in the pursuit of caring for the sick, nursing in particular has felt the need to carve out a distinct mandate and unique body of knowledge that goes beyond understandings of human physiology to include intuitive knowing (Benner 1984), knowledge of the person within the healthcare system (Purkis and Bjornstoddir 2006) and recognition of the greater sociopolitical milieu that influences health outcomes (Reimer Kirkham and Browne 2006). Social work had its early roots in the care of the poor and needy, situated philosophically within a "charity" model of voluntary assistance. As the profession evolved both in size and expertise, it became more associated with the provision of public services, shifting from a "charity" model to a "citizenship rights" model under the Canadian welfare state (Jennissen and Lundy 2011). In recent years, critical feminist scholars and activists within the social work profession have turned their attention to address the multiple forms of oppression and systems that interact to strengthen conditions of discrimination and social injustice (Alaggia et al. 2012; Sakamoto 2007).

Similarly, nursing scholarship has shifted toward not only the integration of various theoretical perspectives stemming from the fields of anthropology, sociology and philosophy but also toward various approaches that embrace reflexivity and include but are not limited to feminist, Marxist, poststructural, and postcolonial approaches to generating knowledge in the field of health (Reimer-Kirkham and Anderson 2002). According to Reimer-Kirkham and Anderson (2002), these new directions in nursing science prompted "a redefining of what nursing science should encompass-a more social and moral mandate to illuminate the experience of those marginalized within society and health care" (p. 2). Although there are historically overlapping similarities between nursing and social work, contemporary academic and clinical practices of these fields often reify them by drawing clear boundaries. It can be argued that both nursing and social work bring distinct bodies of knowledge to those whom we care for; however, the creation of distinct boundaries restricts potential for collaboration and bringing together the unique and shared philosophical underpinnings of knowledge that both of these disciplines bring to research and practice.

Critical Reflexivity

Reflexivity is the tool that has enabled us to gain insight into how historical, social and political aspects of knowledge production has positioned us in our academic and practitioner roles as well as how our opinions, potential biases and theoretical assumptions are implicated in our research. Maintaining a keen awareness of our position, thoughts, opinions and perspectives ensures that research and clinical work are conducted in such a way that benefits the health and well-being of the individuals, groups and populations to which we commit ourselves. Thus, reflexivity offers an ethics of accountability, which is in keeping with the aims of transdisciplinarity. As Maasen and Lieven (2006) have argued, "extended accountability of science is the result of both extended responsibilization of all actors involved and ubiquitous instances and institutions of audit in contemporary society" (p. 401). In other words, because transdisciplinarity involves multiple actors across disciplines and broader aspects of society, this mobilizes participant engagement but also shifts production of knowledge toward a social "politics of accountability."

Reflexivity has both an introspective and collective dimension, the "'collective' dimension [is] centered on assumptions of the field of health promotion and their influences on research practices. It also considers [how] the researcher's personal assumptions can influence the operational course and results of a specific research project" (Larouche and Potvin 2013, p.67). Both Larouche and Potvin (2013) and Orr and Bennett (2009) draw attention to the aims of reflexivity, which are to critique and problematize the taken-for-granted ideologies that produce knowledge, including social, political and historical processes. This more radical view of reflexivity moves beyond a benign introspection toward a methodological approach that brings together interdisciplinary scholars to develop a set of competencies for *real world* understandings and skills necessary for building professional and academic competency (Derry and Fischer 2005). Adopting a reflexive position may therefore challenge epistemological and ontological foundations of mainstream scientific research (Maasen et al. 2006). Reflexivity also allows for clinicians, researchers and advocates to gain a deeper understanding of how social positioning vis-à-vis broader structural policies and practices impact health disparities and outcomes for diverse groups of people.

In the context of promoting transdisciplinarity, reflexivity may challenge alliances across cultural boundaries of disciplines and confront dominant interests and values shaping addiction research. As explained by Maasen and Lieven (2006): "Integrating heterogeneous types of knowledge, values and interests are found to cause complexities that border on the irresolvable task of rendering incommensurabilities commensurate" (p. 402). While theoretical perspectives such as intersectionality may provide the theoretical framework in which to more comprehensively unpack and assess social inequities as situated within complex power relations, reflexivity provides the method by which researchers and clinicians can apply these tenets in day-to-day work. Often described within feminist discourse, reflexivity assumes that the constructed nature of the social world be embraced as opposed to dismissed (and thereby resists the objectivist neutrality of positivism). We suggest that reflexivity can be applied as a unifying practice amongst diverse groups of scholars and clinicians across divergent communities of practice. Reflexivity is not limited to a specific paradigm. In fact, feminist scholars such as Sandra Harding have argued that scientific claims were produced only through "dispassionate, disinterested, value-free, point-of-viewless objective inquiry procedures" (1986, p. 302) and that discovery of the most comprehensive account of "how things actually work" necessitates starting the process of inquiry from specific social locations, rather than removing social factors from knowledge production (as is the approach of the Western scientific method). Hence, reflexivity can and ought to play a foundational role in biomedical and clinical sciences in addition to social-science-based approaches to inquiry. Similarly, scholarship on transdisciplinarity suggests that transdisciplinarity initiatives involve *cognitive tasks* in order to "envision how various disciplines may overlap in constructive ways that could generate scientific breakthroughs and new understandings in a specific problem area" (Gray 2008, p. 3). Thus, reflexivity may promote both a critical awareness of the social processes underpinning knowledge production while examining potential conflicts rooted in historical, parochial differences (Gray 2008).

Intersectionality

In a similar fashion, intersectionality foregrounds different dimensions of social life to unpack the relational aspects of knowledge that produce social and structural inequities in relation to individuals and groups that may be marginalized by social practice and policy (Hankivsky et al. 2010). Drawing on Bimber (1996), Maasen and Lieven (2006) argue that both benefits and risks arise in a knowledge-based society, which may or may not lead to safe, just and sustainable ways of life. These authors conclude that "increased dependency on scientific knowledge and experts is accompanied by an increased mistrust in those experts whose knowledge can no longer be regarded as neutral and objective. . . [and therefore] both scientific knowledge and expertise are increasingly thought to contribute to producing rather than reducing risk" (p. 400). In keeping with transdisciplinary approaches which aim to 'democratize expertise' (Maasen and Lieven 2006), intersectionality specifically addresses issues of power, "in the process of knowledge uptake and knowledge translation" (Hankivsky et al. 2010, p. 5).

As a framework for addressing health inequities, intersectional perspectives draw attention to multiple, complex and interacting inequities that are produced by various categories of social disadvantage. Intersecting categories of difference do not themselves shape individual experiences; rather, social categories are fluid and historically and socially constructed in producing contexts of inequity (Cole 2009). In the context of addiction research, social constructs such as geographical location, migration, gender, race/ethnicity and class may intersect in unique ways to shape women's experiences of addiction, trauma and violence. The benefits of applying an intersectional lens is that it foregrounds complexity and contingency of social inequities and facilitates an analysis of what the interactions reveal about how power functions (Dhamoon and Hankivsky 2011; Sinclair 2012). Thus, intersectionality helps us to look upstream toward broader social structures that intersect with individual experiences. One of the challenges with applying an intersectional analysis is that intersecting categories of difference are not assumed *a priori*. Rather, each context will vary depending on wider social, economic, historical and political structures and how they are embedded within disciplinary practice. In the vein of looking upstream, intersectionality can be a tool for looking across disciplines to examine who is included and who is excluded in the knowledge production process (Maasen et al. 2006).

In our research and clinical practice, critical reflexivity and intersectional analysis have been instrumental in foregrounding the multiple levels in which power operates to directly impact the lives of marginalized women living with addiction and mental health risk. We now turn to discuss how various elements of intersectionality and reflexivity have shaped our disciplinary approaches to research and practices related to addiction, trauma and violence.

Vignettes of Reflexivity and Intersectionality: Addiction in the Lives of Marginalized Women
Handlovsky

The Downtown Eastside (DTES) of Vancouver, Canada, has been referred to as one of Canada's poorest neighbourhoods in which many women and men engage in open drug use and commercial sex trade as a means of survival. Unfortunately, this community is overrepresented by women from Aboriginal ancestry who have lived experience of violence and trauma (Maté 2009). This is further supported by research that draws attention to social determinants and structural conditions in which Aboriginal people experience increased risk of homelessness and mental health problems as a result of systemic, historical oppression (Boyd et al. 2008; Buxton 2007). While not all Aboriginal communities and groups live with addiction, research has linked broader systemic and social processes as risk factors for addiction amongst Aboriginal and other population groups (Maté 2009; Rhodes 2009). However as Maté argues:

> With the mass migration of Europeans to North America and the economic transformation of the continent came also the loss of freedom of mobility for Native peoples, the inexorable and still continuing despoliation and destruction of their homelands, the loss of their traditional livelihoods, the invalidation of their spiritual ways, persistent discrimination and abject poverty (p. 263).

By reflecting upon my own positioning as a Caucasian, middle-class, heterosexual, able-bodied woman, my research with women involved in crack cocaine use in the community of the DTES afforded me the opportunity to examine how broader social and environmental contexts shaped the lives of Aboriginal and other women, and to push back against biomedical individualism that pervaded public health approaches to addiction. As such, reflexivity has ultimately become a guiding principle in my work and further allowed me to examine disciplinary ideologies and how they play out in the day to day world of women's lives.

Despite the resource insufficiency as a major obstacle, the available resources (and, consequently, professional practices) have not fully integrated the multiple traumas many Aboriginal women experience due to various systemic forces; in particular, history of colonization.[1] Without critical reflexive practice clinicians and scholars may unwittingly reinforce the marginalization of Aboriginal women. Therefore there is a need for academic research practice to engage with real world contexts of women's lives to mitigate ongoing structural inequities and potential for harms. The implications of these findings have been disseminated to the local health authority with the political aim of spurring the production and development of much-needed, community-based, women-centered safer crack use initiatives. Reflexivity played a crucial role in this endeavor to ensure meaningful and effective resource development. As a researcher I occupied a different social location than the women involved in the study, reflexivity necessitated ongoing reflection on how my own biases and perspectives as well as biomedical ideologies of addiction impacted the lives of Aboriginal women living in the DTES.

Clark

An emerging body of evidence suggests that immigrant, refugee and other ethnocultural racialized groups (IRER) underutilize mainstream mental health and addiction services as a result of discrimination, dominance of biomedical individualism and lack of linguistic/language and cultural integration (Beiser 2009; Hansson et al. 2010). Without collaboration and reflexive attention to the expertise of multiple disciplines, the potential result is further marginalization and inequities in access to comprehensive health care, which is necessary for addressing trauma from different women's and men's experiences.

Community capacity requires reflexive positioning of various community actors to engage in praxis-oriented work aimed at mitigating health disparities and promoting health and well-being of vulnerable groups. Drawing on my research examining community capacity in the context of Karen women's resettlement in Canada, findings showed that community capacity required intersectoral collaboration across various levels of communities of practice, including government and non-governmental organizations (NGO's), health and social services in order to support the mental health and well-being of Karen women and their families.[2] Community capacity also required elements of social capital such as reciprocity, trust and mutual learning and support within and across institutions.

In the context of fiscally driven policy agendas embedded in neo-liberal policies, a systemic practice in settlement and health-care services in Canada resulted in service fragmentation, challenging the partnerships, reciprocal support and flexibility required to meet the cultural health and social needs of Karen women. Karen women were not able to access health-care services and settlement support as a result of intersecting social and structural inequities. Exclusionary health-care practices based on lack of knowledge and interpreter services resulted in forms of structural violence and discriminatory health-care practices. Violence does not end with refugee women's migration, rather "it is embedded in the structures of most receiving societies" (Kirmayer 2007, p. 377). Trauma, therefore, needs to be reconsidered as a structural determinant of health that includes an examination of dominant cultural practices constraining women's agency. Contemporary understandings of trauma suggest that trauma "is not simply a story of the march of scientific, medical, and psychiatric progress toward greater clarity about a concept with fixed meaning, but a matter of changing social constructions of experiences, in the context of particular clinical, cultural, and political ideologies" (Kirmayer 2007, p. 4). However, trauma is often defined as monolithic, linear event, with a beginning and an end (Lester 2013).

Intersectionality provided another level of analysis for the examination of Karen women's experiences of violence at both systemic and individual levels. Integrating shared knowledge through transdisciplinary approaches can enhance nursing practice and the critical thinking that is required to redress systemic barriers to health care for vulnerable groups. The social context of migrant women's experiences necessitates increased collaboration amongst diverse disciplines in order to understand the broader intersecting factors that shape immigrant and refugee women's mental health. Gender, health literacy, education, local geography and migration intersect to shape Karen women's experiences of vulnerability and dependency in the context of their resettlement. These findings are also substantiated by other studies in which migration and gender are thought to play a role in intimate partner violence (IPV) and alcohol and drug use (Kyriacou et al. 1999; Mason and Hyman 2008; Rhodes 2009).

The complexity of immigrant and refugee women's needs requires holistic response that cannot be addressed through a single discipline or perspective. In particular, refugee women's pre- and post-migration experience of violence and trauma has necessitated the need for transdisciplinarity, which brings together multiple perspectives, expertise and knowledge. Yet, institutional policies construct mental health and addiction in ways that give primacy to biological processes and individual behaviors without attention to broader systemic and even global factors that create conditions of health (Rhodes 2009). Frontline service agencies, such as the NGOs that provide the majority of services and supports to newcomer women in Canada, are often left out of the knowledge production process. Critical reflexivity that promotes transdisciplinary social policy for refugee groups in Canada has demonstrated enhanced community capacity (Sherrell et al. 2011).

Sinclair

Similar to my nursing colleagues, I have come to understand the world around me through a social justice lens, whether in my academic, clinical or everyday life. It was through privileging the voice of women, intersectional factors and the standpoint of women that my journey into developing a critical consciousness/reflexivity began. Through clinical reflexive practice I became acutely aware of the dangers women experience in relation to their social locations and risk of interpersonal and systemic violence. Intersectionality broadened my analysis of how a gender-only analysis does not fully embrace woman's multiple identities and differences (Anderson 2000; McCann and Kim 2003; Sinclair 2003). My early work with the Domestic Violence Project (DVP) in Toronto, Canada, challenged the dominant discourse of battered women and their abusive partners held by professionals, institutions and the community at large. As stakeholders committed to women's experiences as a starting point of knowledge production, the DVP team sought to create legitimate alternative knowledge claims to the dominant discourse by "using the radical research tool of believing women and what they say" as their beginning point (Cole 1995, p. 18). We developed a holistic community intervention model that provided a visual map of effective intervention aimed at *both* individual advocacy *and* systemic advocacy (Harris and Sinclair 1981). The philosophical and practice approach embodied in this document articulated a fundamental departure from the victim-blaming, pathology-oriented, "social worker as expert" understanding that was the prevailing view in the social work profession at that time (Sewpaul 2005).

There is a growing number of practitioners and scholars in both the nursing and social work profession who employ a critical social justice lens to make explicit the power dynamics that lay beneath the rising inequities that limit people's opportunities for health and wellness and their access to resources (Alaggia et al. 2012; Bhuyan 2008; Sakamoto and Pitner 2005; Sinclair 2012).

As a social worker in Ontario, Canada's, Violence Against Women (VAW) movement, I adopted a position of reflexivity to understand the ways in which my own theoretical and epistemic privilege as a fifth-generation European Canadian woman of Irish and Scottish heritage, might unknowingly, take part in dominant, often taken for granted cultural dominant practices, in working with women living with violence. It was not until I engaged in the study of critical feminist perspectives (particularly those scholars who problematized whiteness) during my doctoral work that I was able to fully grasp the complexities of intersecting and multiple identities (Frankenberg 1993; Hill-Jackson 2007; Pewewardy 2004). More importantly, these teachings helped me make explicit the macro- and micro-intersections that reproduce context of social disadvantage in the lives of women, and how certain groups of women have been excluded from the "culture of power" (Ng et al. 1995).

Feminist thinking has continually evolved to give credibility to other intersecting aspects of identity formation that may predispose women to violence and trauma. Historically, mainstream research had focused primarily on white women's and poor women's experience of IPV, leading to the erroneous conclusion that *all* women suffer equally from IPV, giving rise to the notion of the "universal woman" and perhaps a universal experience of violence. In fact, this has not been validated by research. Evidence suggests that other intersecting factors perpetuate risk of IPV, such as access to resources, level of education of the perpetrator of violence, immigration status and gender roles (Mason and Hyman 2008). If the goal is to prevent VAW and provide effective intervention, then an integrated collaboration amongst diverse stakeholders, activists and policy makers is required—one that calls for transdisciplinary approaches.

Through sharing our experiences, we have aimed to illustrate through our own positions and research that critical reflexivity can promote transdisciplinarity by raising critical consciousness of how knowledge is produced and embedded in historical, social and political processes. This reflexive stance aims to bridge the gap between real-world experiences and those that might be framed by institutions in positions of power. Thus, our engagement with reflexivity as a method not only pushed us to evaluate the social context that shape those whom we serve, but also pushed us to examine how our own positioning might be implicated in knowledge production. Reflexivity not only offers a method for addressing nuanced approaches for understanding complexity but also a bridge for enhancing transdisciplinary understandings of trauma, violence and addiction. In particular, our reflective analysis of our positioning suggests that training initiatives designed to bring together multiple actors engaged in knowledge production can enhance our understanding of how broader structural processes intersect with individual and/or group experiences to promote mental health and well-being of women, men, boys and girls. We now turn to discuss how researchers from similar disciplines have done research with reflexivity as a starting point of inquiry.

Handlovsky

Reflexivity was fundamental to producing knowledge to inform resource development for safer crack use amongst street-involved women. Initially, I approached the project with perspectives that were shaped by my social positioning, which meant predominantly neo-liberalist, individualist assumptions of health and well-being. I assumed that women would benefit from information and education, and that needs were guided by personal motivations and responsibility. However, in cultivating transparent and trusting relationships that identified women as expert informants, the contrary became evident. Women were very knowledgeable about the harms of crack use and the sharing of pipes but were motivated greatly by altruism: namely, a drive to look after one another which was a root determinant of pipe sharing. Therefore, there was a need for more pipes and a safe place for women to gather that became fundamental components for a resource designed to facilitate women's safer crack use.

Clark

In the context of Karen refugee women's resettlement in Canada, I employed critical reflexivity as a methodological approach to establish trust with Karen women and their families in a community context. Critical reflexivity allowed for a more introspective analysis of my own academic privilege and issues of power and cultural safety in conducting research with minority women. Being reflexive of my own position as an immigrant woman, nurse and researcher also assisted me to examine the macro-intersecting factors that promoted and/or challenged the mental health and well-being of Karen women, i.e. intersections of gender, geography, language and health literacy. Lastly, critical reflexivity promoted critical consciousness amongst community health and NGO's regarding the structural and social processes that produce cultural risk and structural violence for Karen women.

Sinclair

Critical reflexive practice made space and/or allowed for social workers, community activists and advocates to re-examine "essentialist" understandings of IPV and VAW so that differences between women based on their social location (i.e. class, race, culture, sexual orientation, ability) could be tailored into policies, programs and support services for women. In particular, the development of a specialized anti-racist feminist training program for police officers in Ontario challenged the criminal justice system (CJS) to respond to the needs of diverse groups of women. In one community study, women abuse survivors reported that they felt satisfied with CJS intervention when officers treated them with respect, took their concerns seriously, informed them about their rights, gave them helpful information about local resources and, most importantly, assured them they did the right thing by calling the police. By building critical reflexivity into the training program, police officers were more effective in engaging women from diverse backgrounds (Sinclair 2000).

Employing Reflexivity in Transdisciplinary Research

We have demonstrated through our own research endeavours concerning addiction, trauma and violence work with women that there is a need for more reflexive and intersectional approaches. While intersectionality has been used as a framework for the development of more complex understandings of addiction, reflexivity provides the methodology to achieve this. However, taking reflexivity as a starting point of research within transdisciplinarity brings both challenges and opportunities. Larouche and Potvin's (2013) review of innovative approaches to health promotion research argues that "research involves the adoption of a reflexive approach wherein consideration of context plays different roles. The reflexive process consists of questioning what is taken for granted in the conceptualization and operationalization of research" (p. 64). Reflexivity as a methodology of inquiry fits with transdisciplinary approaches to research that employ a wide range of procedures and methods in knowledge production and that involve co-operative practices and participation (Maasen, Lengwiler and Guggenheim 2006).

The inclusion of various actors in knowledge production such as those who conduct research with community organizations and non-academic citizens, or what Maasen et al. (2006) call "extra-scientific actors," necessarily challenges hierarchies of authority over knowledge production and evidence. As a way of increasing societal engagement in research with marginalized groups to address 'real world' problems in a social justice context, there are increased calls for conducting participatory research with Aboriginal communities (Varcoe et al. 2011). As Varcoe et al. point out,

> relationships [are] the core of research partnerships, are embedded in historical, social and material circumstances . . . thus relationships must be

developed with intention, authenticity, and transparency with attention to power dynamics, how power dynamics are shaped by wider circumstances, and the potential for harm. (p. 213)

In order to counter the pitfalls of colonizing practices and associated neo-liberal frameworks, employing critical reflexivity in transdisciplinary research projects is necessary. A study conducted by McPhail-Bell, Fredericks and Brough (2013) utilized critical reflection to conduct a discourse analysis of the Ottawa Charter on health promotion. Informed by a postcolonial framework, McPhail-Bell et al. used a reflexive approach to document and analyze relationships between various texts underpinning the Ottawa Charter. A discourse analysis showed two dominant narratives: the normalization of a Western view of health, and exclusionary tactics regarding non-Western views within discursive practices. Reflexivity in this research assisted the researchers to examine how personal histories, educational experiences and scholarly training shaped interpretations of the Charter and argue that "Eurocentric academics have a history of failing to inform learners of the complex history of ideas and events that shape human growth and development" (McPhail-Bell et al. 2013, p. 25). The implication of this research is that there is a danger in conducting health promotion practice (research and community engagement of different stakeholders) when exclusion of other models and worldviews are based on predominantly western individualistic, neo-liberal assumptions. This finding is akin to Maasen and Lieven's (2006) view of transdisciplinarity as offering a new mode of governing science in which there is an orientation toward the common good. A critical reflexive method can assist researchers in challenging universal approaches to knowledge and examine the historical, social and political contexts of research processes. As McPhail-Bell et al. (2013) have argued, "in order to work collaboratively and respectfully health promotion practitioners must turn their gaze from the 'other' onto themselves, to reflect critically on their own position of privilege . . . to examine power imbalances . . . and voices that are silenced" (p. 27). Similarly, Orr and Bennett (2009) argue that reflexivity in the co-production of academic-practitioner research must attend to who is left out of the conversation as this will enable us to tell a more sophisticated story and add legitimacy to our work. In this regard transdisciplinarity offers the potential for strengthening what is common knowledge, promotion of social justice and making space for multiple disciplines (e.g. nursing and social work) to engage with broader discourse and practices.

In this regard, Judd and Keleher (2013) conducted participatory action research (PAR) with multidisciplinary workforce of 66 employees (54 community health nurses, social workers, Aboriginal health workers, administrative staff and management) in a Community Health Setting (CHS) in the Northern Territory of Australia. The aims of their research were to build capacity to address real-world problems in relation to the social determinants of health, and address inequities and social justice issues experienced by Aboriginal and multicultural communities.

The researchers employed a series of reflective exercises with multiple participants to develop a conceptual model that could reorient health services from the ground up. Critical reflexive exercises structured the PAR process in which participants used diaries to document professional practice problems. This process involved six reflection and action cycles developed over a two-year period. The results of the workplace diary enabled practitioners to collect information, ask reflexive questions analyze documents and review actions (Judd and Keleher 2013). This study supports transdisciplinarity that encourages collaborative partnerships outside of academic institutions so that services are more in keeping with the needs of individuals and communities.

An important role of critical reflexivity in building these kinds of transdisciplinary relationships is to create safe space for team members to be open to different epistemological viewpoints, especially to those that have been historically subjugated. Thus, where participation is a major component of transdisciplinarity (Pohl 2010), openness to other's viewpoints requires understanding of one's own viewpoint as "relative in contrary to an absolute one amongst many others" (Pohl 2010, p. 77).

Conclusion

While many scholars promote transdisciplinarity as a way of integrating multiple paradigms and transcending of disciplinary boundaries, little attention has been given to describing potential tools or methods for actually applying this form of collaboration. In this chapter we have discussed critical reflexivity and intersectionality as effective tools for moving towards transdisciplinarity in addiction research. Through sharing examples from our own research, informed by diverse clinical contexts and research practices in the field of nursing and social work, we aimed to show how engaging with intersectionality and critical reflexivity challenged our thinking about addiction and the intersecting factors that shape the lives of marginalized women. Taken together, our vignettes provide examples of ways in which transdisciplinarity can be fostered through the examination of broader power structures that shape knowledge production, the need for developing relationship across disciplines and the need to bring in *real world* experiences to include multiple perspectives and better representation of individuals and groups most affected by addiction, trauma and violence.

Thus, intersectionality and critical reflexivity can move us towards the highest ideals of transdisciplinary by taking collaborators beyond the aim of simply integrating knowledge, but to integrate knowledge in ways that can recognize power and inequality embedded in hierarchies of knowledge and evidence. Reflexivity in particular, asserts that researchers must theorize as much as possible how their own social positioning impacts knowledge production in *all* disciplines. In this way, intersectionality and reflexivity add to the integrity and validity of transdisciplinary research because they bring into view *real world* contexts, the complexity of issues as well as address issues of power and authority over knowledge.

Employing intersectionality and critical reflexivity are important considerations in transdisciplinary research in order to reach for the highest ideals and most ethical responses to the complex issue of addition.

Discussion Questions

1. Transdisciplinarity brings potential challenges to disciplinary identity. How might reflexivity address these challenges in the context of research in addiction?
2. How can an intersectional analysis address issues of power in various levels of research contexts (community, institutional, global).
3. How can a reflexive methodology be integrated within a framework of transdisciplinarity in order to mitigate potential harms associated with neo-liberal policy decision making?

Notes

1 By colonization we refer to not only historical oppressive forces imposed by one culture or another but also the ongoing neocolonial practices that systemically reproduce oppressions amongst women in the minority.
2 Karen refugee women represented the largest government-assisted refugee women and families to be resettled in British Columbia, Canada, between the years 2005 and 2009. What was unique about these women is that they came to Canada with histories of pre-migration trauma, low literacy in their own language and complex medical conditions. Karen women were also primary caretakers for their families' health. Existing policies and practices at the community level, however, lacked infrastructure to support them. These factors posed significant challenges to support these women's mental health and well-being in the context of their resettlement.

References

Alaggia, Ramona, Cheryle Regehr, and Angelique Jenney. 2012. "Risky business: An ecological analysis of intimate partner violence disclosure." *Research on Social Work Practice* 22(3): 301–312. doi:0.1177/1049731511425503.
Anderson, Kim A. 2000. *A recognition of being: reconstructing native woman-hood.* Toronto: Second Story Press.
Beiser, Morton. 2009. "Resettling refugees and safeguarding their mental health: Lessons learned from the Canadian refugee resettlement project." *Transcultural Psychiatry* 46(536): 52–79. doi: 10.1177/1363461509351373.
Benner, Patricia. 1984. *From novice to expert.* Menlo Park: Addison-Wesley.
Bhuyan, Rupaleem. 2008. "The production of the 'battered immigrant' in public policy and domestic violence advocacy." *Journal of Interpersonal Violence* 23(2): 153–70. doi: 10.1177/0886260507308317.
Bimber, Bruce A. 1996. *The politics of expertise in congress: The rise and fall of the office of technology assessment.* Albany: State University of New York Press.
Boyd, Susan C., Joy L. Johnson and Barbara Moffat. 2008. "Opportunities to learn and barriers to change: Crack cocaine use in the Downtown Eastside of Vancouver." *Harm Reduction Journal* 5(34): 1–36. doi:10.1186/1477-7517-5-34.

Buxton, Jane A. 2007. Vancouver drug use epidemiology, Vancouver site report for the Canadian Community Epidemiology Network on Drug Use. Vancouver, BC, Canada: CCENDU. www.ccsa.ca/Resource%20Library/CCENDU-Bibliography-en.pdf. Accessed: August 22, 2014.

Cole, Elizabeth R. 2009. "Intersectionality and research in psychology." *American Psychologist* 64(3): 170–180. doi: 10.1037/a0014564.

Cole, Susan G. 1995. *Power surge: Sex, violence, and pornography*. Toronto: Second Story Press.

Derry, Sharon. J. and Gerhard Fischer. 2005. "Toward a model and theory for transdisciplinary graduate education." (Paper presented at 2005 AERA meeting as part of Symposium, "Sociotechnical Design for Lifelong Learning: A Crucial Role for Graduate Education." http://psyjournals.ru/authors/25163.shtml. Accessed: June, 14, 2014.

Dhamoon, Rita K. and Olena Hankivsky. 2011. "Why the theory and practice of intersectionality matter to health research and policy." In *Health Inequities in Canada: Intersectional Frameworks and Practices*, edited by Olena Hankivsky, 16–45. Vancouver: UBC Press.

Frankenberg, Ruth. 1993. *The social construction of whiteness: White women, race matters*. Minneapolis: University of Minnesota Press.

Gray, Barbara. 2008. "Enhancing transdisciplinary research through collaborative leadership." *American Journal of Preventative Medicine* 35 (2): S12–S132. doi: 10.1016/j.amepre.2008.03.037.

Hankivsky, Olena, Colleen Reid, Renee Cormier, Colleen Varcoe, Natalie Clark, Cecilia Benoit and Shari Brotman. 2010. "Exploring the promises of intersectionality for advancing women's health research." *International Journal for Equity in Health* 9(5): 1–15. doi:10.1186/1475-9276-9-5.

Hansson, Emily, Andrew Tuck, Steve Lurie and Kwame McKenzie, for the Task Group of the Services Systems Advisory Committee, Mental Health Commission of Canada. (2010). *Improving mental health services for immigrant, refugee, ethno-cultural and racialized groups: Issues and options for service improvement*. www.mentalhealthcommission.ca/SiteCollectionDocuments/Key_Documents/en/2010/Issues_Options_FINAL_English%2012Nov09.pdf. Accessed: July 1, 2013.

Harding, Sandra. 1986. *The science question in feminism*. New York: Cornell University Press.

Harris, Susan and Deborah Sinclair. 1981. *Domestic violence project: A comprehensive model for intervention into the issue of domestic violence*. Toronto: Family Service Association Metropolitan Toronto.

Hill-Jackson, Valerie. 2007. "Wrestling whiteness: Three stages of shifting multicultural perspectives among white pre-service teachers." *Multicultural Perspectives* 9(2): 29–35. doi: 10.1080/15210960701386285.

Jennissen, Therese and Colleen Lundy. 2011. *One hundred years of social work: A history of the profession in English Canada 1900–2000*. Waterloo: Wilfrid Laurier University Press.

Judd, Jenni and Helen Keleher. 2013. "Reorienting health services in the Northern Territory of Australia: A conceptual model for building health promotion capacity in the workforces." *Global Health Promotion* 20(53): 53–62. doi: 10.1177/1757975913486685.

Kessel, Frank and Patricia L. Rosenfield. 2008. "Toward transdisciplinary research: Historical and contemporary perspectives." *Journal of Planning and Education Research* 35(2S): S225–S234. doi: http://dx.doi.org/10.1016/j.amepre.2008.05.005.

Kirmayer, Laurence. 2007. "Failures of imagination: The refugee's predicament." In *Understanding trauma, integrating biological, clinical, and cultural perspectives*, edited by Laurence J. Kirmayer, Robert Lemelson and Mark Barad, 363–381. Cambridge: Cambridge University Press.

Kyriacou, Demetrios A., Deirdrie Anglin, Ellen Taliaferro, Susan Stone, Toni Tubb, Judith A. Linden, Robert Muelleman, Eric Barton and Jess F. Kraus. 1999. "Risk factors for injury to women from domestic violence." *The New England Journal of Medicine: 1892–1898.* doi:10.1056/NEJM199912163412505.

Larouche, Anne and Louise Potvin. 2013. "Stimulating innovative research in health promotion." *Global Health Promotion* 20: 64–69. doi: 10.1177/1757975913490428.

Lester, Rebecca. 2013. "Back from the edge of existence: A critical anthropology of trauma." *Transcultural Psychiatry* 50(5): 753–762. doi:10.1177/1363461513504520.

Maasen, Sabine, Martin M. Lengwiler and Michael Guggenheim. 2006. "Practices of transdisciplinary research: Close(r) encounters of science and society." *Science and Public Policy* 33(6): 394–398. doi:10.3152/147154306781778830.

Maasen, Sabine and Oliver Lieven. 2006. "Socially robust knowledge. Transdisciplinarity: A new mode of governing science?" *Science and Public Policy*, 33 (6): 399–410. doi:10.3152/147154306781778803.

Mason, Robin, and Ilene Hyman. 2008. "Intimate partner violence among immigrant and refugee women." In *Working with immigrant women,* edited by Sepali Guruge and Enid Collins, 279–300. Toronto: Centre for Addiction and Mental Health.

Maté, Gabor. 2009. *In the realm of hungry ghosts: Close encounters with addiction.* Toronto: Vintage Canada.

McCann, Carol R. and Seuong-Kyung Kim. 2003. *Feminist theory reader: Local and global perspectives.* London: Routledge.

McPhail-Bell, Karen, Bronwyn Fredericks and Mark Brough. 2013. "Beyond the accolades: A postcolonial critique of the foundations of the Ottawa Charter." *Global Health Promotion* 20(22): 22–29. doi:10.1177/175795913490427.

Moolchan, Eric T., Pebbles Fagan, Anita F. Ferander, Wayne F. Velicer, Mark Hayward, Gary King and Richard R. Clayton. 2007. "Addressing tobacco-related health disparities." *Addiction* 102 Suppl. 2: 30–42. doi:10.1111/j.1360-0443.2007.01953.x.

Ng, Roxana, Pat Staton and Joyce Scane. 1995. *Anti-racism, feminism and critical approaches to education.* Westport: Greenwood.

Orr, Kevin and Mike Bennet. 2009. "Reflexivity in the co-production of academic-practitioner research." *Qualitative Research in Organizations and Management: An International Journal* 4(1): 85–102. doi:10.1108/17465640910951462.

Peck, Barbara, K. and Stephanie R. Capyk. 2012. "Building community capacity for trauma-informed practice". In *Becoming trauma informed,* edited by Nancy Poole and Lorraine Greaves, 253–262. Toronto: CAMH.

Pewewardy, Nocona. 2004. "The political is personal." *Journal of Feminist Family Therapy* 16 (1): 53–67. doi:10.1300/J086v16n01_05.

Pohl, Christian. 2010. "From transdisciplinarity to transdisciplinary research." *Transdisciplinary Journal of Engineering & Science* 1(1): 74–83. www.tsama.org.za/index.php/documents/category/2-td-summer-school-jan?download=33:pohl-2010-from-td-to-tdr&start=20. Accessed August 23, 2014.

Purkis, Mary E. and Kristen Bjornsdottir. 2006. "Intelligent nursing: Accounting for knowledge as action in practice." *Nursing Philosophy* 7: 247–256. doi:10.1111/j.1466-769X.2006.00283.x. Accessed: August 22, 2014.

Reimer, Kirkham, Sheryl and Joan Anderson. 2002. "Postcolonial nursing scholarship: From epistemology to method." *Advances in Nursing Science* 25(1): 1–17.

Reimer, Kirkham, Sheryl and Annette J. Browne. 2006. "Toward a critical theoretical interpretation of social justice discourses in nursing." *Advances in Nursing Science* 29(4) 4: 324–339. pdfs.journals.lww.com/advancesinnursingscience/. . . /Toward_a_Critical_. Accessed: July 13, 2014.

Rhodes, Tim. 2002. "The 'risk environment': A framework for understanding and reducing drug-related harm." *International Journal of Drug Policy* 13: 85–94. doi: 10.1016/S0955-3959(02)00007-5.

Rhodes, Tim. 2009. "Risk environments and drug harms: A social science for harm reduction approach." *International Journal of Drug Policy* 20: 193–201. doi:http://dx.doi.org/10.1016/j.drugpo.2008.10.003.

Sakamoto, Izumi. 2007. "A critical examination of immigrant acculturation: Toward an anti-oppressive social work with immigrant adults in a pluralistic society." *British Journal of Social Work* 37(3): 515–35. doi:10.1093/bjsw/bcm024.

Sakamoto, Izumi and Ronald O. Pitner. 2005. "Use of critical consciousness in anti-oppressive social work practice: Disentangling power dynamics at personal and structural levels." *British Journal of Social Work* 35(4): 420–37. doi:10.1093/bjsw/bch190.

Sewpaul, Vishanthie. 2005. "Global standards: Promise and pitfalls for re-inscribing social work into civil society." *International Journal of Social Welfare* 14(3): 210–217. DOI: 10.1111/j.1468-2397.2005.00361.x.

Sherrell, Kathy, Chris Friesen, Jennifer Hyndman and Subrath Shrestha. 2011. "From 'One Nation, One People' to 'Operation Swaagatem': Bhutanese refugees in Coquitlam, BC." *Immigration Services Society of BC*, Metropolis British Columbia Centre of Excellence for Research Immigration and Diversity, Working Paper Series, 11(11): 3–50. www.issbc.org/system/cms/files/439/files/original/Operation_Swaagatem_Pre-Arrival_Planning_Process_-_May_2011Working_Paper_(2).pdf. Accessed: June 14, 2014.

Sinclair, Deborah. 2000. *In the center of the storm—Durham speaks out: A community response to custody and access issues affecting woman abuse survivors and their children.* Durham Region, ON: A Report Prepared for the Status of Women, Canada.

Sinclair, Deborah. 2003. "*Overcoming the backlash: Telling the truth about power, privilege, and oppression. Exploring gender-based analysis in the context of violence against women—a resource kit for community agencies.*" Durham Region, ON: The Violence Prevention Coordinating Council. Status of Women, Canada.

Sinclair, Deborah. 2012. "Voices of women from the margins: Re-examining violence against women." In *Cruel but not unusual: Violence in Canadian families*, edited by Ramona Alaggia and Cathy Vine, 13–41. Waterloo: Wilfrid Laurier University Press.

Varcoe, Colleen, Helen Brown, Betty Calam, Maria J. Buchanan and Vera Newman. 2011. "Capacity building is a two-way street: Learning from doing research with aboriginal communities." In *Feminist community research*, edited by Gillian Creese and Wendy Frisby, 210–231. Vancouver, Toronto: UBC press.

Suggestions for Further Reading

Kessel, Frank and Patricia L. Rosenfield. 2008. "Toward transdisciplinary research: Historical and contemporary perspectives." *Journal of Preventive Medicine* 35, no. 2S: S225–S234.

Moolchan, Eric T., Pebbles Fagan, Anita F. Ferander, Wayne F. Velicer, Mark Hayward, Gary King and Richard R. Clayton. 2007. "Addressing tobacco-related health disparities." *Addiction* 102 Suppl. 2: 30–42, accessed August 26, 2014. doi:10.1111/j.1360-0443.2007.01953.x.

Stokols, Daniel, Shalini Misra, Richard P. Moser, Kara L. Hall and Brandie K. Taylor. 2008. "The ecology of team science: Understanding contextual influences on transdisciplinary collaboration." *American Journal of Preventive Medicine* 35, no. 2S: S96–S114, accessed August 24, 2014. doi:10: 1016/j.amepre.2008.05.003.

10
TRAUMA AND TRANSDISCIPLINARITY IN WOMEN'S ADDICTION TREATMENT

Denise Bradshaw

Denise Bradshaw is a social worker and program director of Heartwood Centre for Women, a program of BC Mental Health & Substance Use Services (BCMHSUS), located at the British Columbia Women's Hospital & Health Centre in Vancouver. In this interview, with Nancy Poole and Lorraine Greaves, Bradshaw discusses Heartwood's unique interdisciplinary, relational, client-centered and client-driven approach to care. The conversation also touches on how trauma is experienced by the women and how addressing trauma becomes foundational to the ways in which the work at Heartwood goes beyond interdisciplinarity to transdisciplinarity.

Q: Can you tell us about Heartwood's approach to care? Is it interdisciplinary, multidisciplinary or both?

A: Heartwood Centre for Women has an interdisciplinary team of professionals. There are nurses, social workers, counsellors, dieticians, physicians, psychiatrists and recreational therapists, among others. It has multiple disciplines coming together to provide an integrated approach to the practice of providing treatment to women who have come to us as a result of significant substance dependence and mental health concerns. These are women who are fairly progressed with their use of substances. However, we're all clear that the substance use is likely a result of trauma histories. The data that we have on our women at Heartwood today reveal that 85 to 90 percent of the women have serious childhood trauma of sexual, physical or severe neglect, and then of that 85 to 90 percent, a further 80 percent of those women have had continuous trauma. Then, for aboriginal women, there is trauma from oppression as a result of colonization; either they have been in residential school or they are children of families that have been in residential school. So, we have a very complex mix of women that come to us as we try to find ways to support them with what they need at the time that they come to us. Our belief as a clinical team is that the best support that we can bring to them is through the foundation of trauma-informed care. In terms of interdisciplinary practice first and foremost, what we have done is to really help everyone to understand that regardless of what your discipline is and the expertise you bring, that respecting each other's strengths and bringing those strengths together, is the only way we're going to provide the patchwork quilt that the women need. Sometimes that means that the social worker needs to understand the nurse's role, the nurse needs to understand the recreational therapist's role, and we all need to understand each other's roles. It's not good enough to say, at any given time when a woman is seeking support from you, "You need to go talk to the social worker about that," because you are there in the moment. The first instinct maybe to push the concern away to a discipline that seems to align more closely without actually asking that probing question, "What's happening for you right now?" I think it's also about learning skills in terms of being trauma-informed that will drive your disciplinary practice, because if you have the foundation and understand that foundation of doing trauma-informed work, you will take that time to hear what the woman's real need is at that moment.

Q: How do you encourage your staff members to take this approach?

A: What we've used is really an open dialogue in an interdisciplinary way, including our physicians who have the least experience in interdisciplinary practice, as opposed to multidisciplinary. It is about really ensuring that we never think we are in the dialogue and work alone, and that the work is driven by an interdisciplinary team. No one person on our team carries any more power than anyone else in terms of interdisciplinary practice. I think this has been a remarkable experience for all of the other disciplines on the team, and it is a result of how, while we're in an organization that is driven by a medical model, we have said we need to be more than that. For example, while our medical doctor is the lead physician, she has been able to remove that hat and join in the team, bringing her strengths and scope of practice to enrich the team and care provided to the women. She really considers the rest of the team to be the experts in their domain, and she's an expert on addiction medicine. I think the ability to step back and say, "I don't need to be the expert here all of the time. We are all experts of our own domain," allows you to bring out the best in one another.

Q: How would you define transdisciplinarity in your context?

A: I think the first thing, in a context like Heartwood, is that you have to have a safe environment for transdisciplinarity to flourish. You have to have trust between your disciplines. We create a safe environment for the staff to work in, so that people understand that we all bring strengths, we all have scopes of practice that are legislated and each perspective matters. Yet, we also know that there is a huge area of intersectedness in the middle. If you look at our different areas or disciplines as spheres, then there is this area of intersectedness where in any discipline can involve themselves with the client. It should be the person whom the woman has indicated is the best person to support her, without "the shuffle approach." You're not allowed to shuffle anybody over to somebody else. You engage them where they're at. You do what you can, and you say "We've got others on the team who have more expertise." You ask for permission, "Can I share this with them?" Sometimes they say no, and we respect that, but most of the time, they say, "For sure. Can you tell Maureen? Because I'd really like to talk to her about that tomorrow." The women get such a sense of value from this type of engagement and dialogue.

Q: How do you talk about transdisciplinarity with your staff at the program?
A: We try to stay away from discipline and look at who can best support the woman. Who do they need to rely on from the disciplinary point of view, and who could provide them with the knowledge and information they may need? It is about being very open about who has the strongest relationships at any given time with any given woman, and going with the relationship as the woman defines it rather than how the system of care would like to define it. Another area that is really interesting from a transdisciplinary model is family work. I think a lot of disciplines have not had to consider family as part of who they are providing care for. They will see that patient or client in front of them and don't necessarily engage with the family or feel that they have the skills and abilities to do that, so it falls to the more traditional family-oriented disciplines. We really encourage all disciplines to engage with family, to help them learn, and we do knowledge exchange with those folks on the team who have more experience working with families. How can we shift healthcare from the individual disease model to something more inclusive if we can't have disciplines get very comfortable engaging, supporting and working with families, particularly in the area of addiction? With all the impacts that addiction has within families, and given the impact of trauma, how can we not do that work? It can't sit with one discipline.

Q: How is the Heartwood approach trauma-informed?
A: I speak about trauma-informed care as a universal approach. That's something that we do all of the time with all of our women, and every discipline has a responsibility to approach their work in a trauma-informed manner and to understand what that means. This understanding must extend beyond the relationship to clients and to that with colleagues, supervisors and organizations. We also use a patient-centered or client-driven approach that has the woman define what it is that she wants to achieve in her treatment experience. It's that evolution that occurs. They come and say, "All I want to do is be able to get visitation with my kids. I haven't been able to even visit with them in a non-supervised way, and I doubt I ever will." Then we have women who, by the time they are leaving, say, "You know what? I think I could actually get shared custody." There are expectations for them in the program, but one of the things that we aim for in a trauma-informed environment is how to meet the needs of the individual and still ensure the safety of the whole. For example, when there is a sense that one woman is not able to fit within the

broader community for a variety of reasons, maybe she has bought drugs on the site and has attempted to share them, what we really focus on, first and foremost, is how do we create safety for her, and how do we create safety for the community? We have a discussion with her about what this has meant. There is no shame and blame, but as soon as there is a sense of lack of safety for other women, we have to say, "Right now, this program is not the best for you." It is about the here and now: "Where do you need to be, and how are we going to help you get there?" It's not about discharging to the street. There is no discharging without a plan. We have never done that. For the women who have often come back a second time, they have said that having a plan for their transition was the most incredible thing that ever happened to them, because it wasn't from the perspective of shame and blame, it was from the perspective of: "This is the program, this is what we can do, and we are not meeting your needs right now, so we need to find something that will, and what is it that you think you need?"

Q: You have mentioned trauma as part of Heartwood's approach, but can you talk a bit more specifically about how trauma fits in as a core piece of your multi/interdisciplinary and women-centered approach to care?

A: The trauma-informed approach really is the core piece of it. I think that is something that within addiction, if we could make that happen, if we could have all programs evolve from trauma-informed care as a foundation, I think we would have phenomenal shifts in terms of reducing stigma and improving treatment outcomes. It would take away shame; it would take away blame, stemming from that moralistic approach to addiction. All of those other models would begin to fragment and disappear. I think that when you actually understand the trauma foundation, the trauma-informed care and the elements of that, you can't help but build in the spiritual component for healing. When we analyze the feedback from clients at different stages in their stay, what we see is that as women progress through the program, they start to talk more about the spiritual healing that they have experienced from the trauma and how they can now name that. I think it's really amazing that through Seeking Safety,[1] women constantly say, "Nobody has really ever helped me join these dots together before. I didn't really understand the connection between my trauma and my subsequent substance use." It is the first time that they have really pulled those pieces together in any kind of coherent way. Women talk about how freeing it is for them to understand that. This is what Norma Finkelstein has said reflecting on the Women Co-occurring Disorders and Violence Study[2] that often women said, "I made that connection with trauma, mental health, and substance use, and I see myself with an integrated identity of all three."

Q: Do the women draw in other issues?

A: Absolutely they do. It's really interesting to watch them starting to draw connections that we hadn't even thought about. One example is tobacco and self-harm. It's really interesting to hear the women talk about their history with self-harm through adolescence and into young adulthood, and then as older women, begin a process of understanding self-harm within the broader context of trauma. We apply the same kind of approaches, including the skills that you can develop to manage the anxiety and the physical, emotional, psychological pain, but we don't focus very much on the behavior.

Q: Does this approach allow women to use the word *healing* as opposed to *recovering*?

A: I avoid using the word *recovery* if I can, because recovery assumes that you can eradicate it, like pneumonia. It is not about eradication, it's about understanding: "How am I going to live with the addiction and underlying trauma and live as well as I can?" With recovery, people think that somehow addiction and substance use is going to be gone forever and is not going to resurface. We are very clear about the fact that there is no panacea in this work and the use of substances may occur. But you are going to be very real about it, and you are going to understand what is happening, and we hope that we have begun to provide a foundation for developing the skills to manage the feelings associated with trauma. We are very focused on developing skills, whether they are mindfulness or dialectical behavior therapy. There are a number of approaches that we use, and we sit with the woman and show her how to use them when she is triggered in her environment. We'll ask, "What is it that I can do right now, and what can you do right now? Let's talk about that." Often they'll say, "You could take me into a quiet place where I can practice my mindfulness, visit the gym or go for a walk," or whatever it happens to be for that woman at the moment. The challenge that the women talk about, is when they have to go back to their home communities, they don't always have the next piece to help them continue to practice those skills; they don't have safe places for women to go where they can talk about how they're feeling in the moment with people who are like-minded. That is what we're hearing is really hard for them. I think that trauma-informed care is really going to help with that. If we can make that happen, it will be much better for everyone.

Q: How do you think transdisciplinary research needs to be carried out in order to benefit a context like yours? What do you feel is necessary to support what you do and what you're trying to do?

A: What would help would be articulating frameworks where people can feel that they can explore within it how to develop programs from that trauma-informed perspective; how to bring people into transdisciplinary practice on a trauma-informed foundation. What would that look like from an orientation and education perspective? I think that articulating the development pieces would help. It would be great to better understand how trauma can drive a transdisciplinary approach in a practice context. What does that look like for team meetings? For case consultation? How does transdisciplinary practice shift communication between team members? What are the models? How does it look? On the one hand, it is important to focus on the process, but on the other hand, we need to know what the structure is that will sustain transdisciplinary practice going forward. So, I think one of the most important contributions from research would be articulating what a framework for transdisciplinary practice looks like within complex teams, and how this model relates to trauma-informed practice.

Notes

1 Aspects of the Seeking Safety approach are integrated into the Heartwood program. See www.seekingsafety.org.
2 See Chapter 3.

11
EXPANDING SYSTEMATIC REVIEWS USING TRANSDISCIPLINARITY

Natalie Hemsing, Lorraine Greaves and Nancy Poole

In this chapter we demonstrate how applying a lens of transdisciplinarity to systematic reviews can produce more complex cartographies of health problems and their potential solutions that could be helpful in informing health practice and policy. Public health interventions need to be based on a broad range of research evidence, but also informed by the experiences and challenges encountered in practice, in order to make them useful and scalable (Shelton 2014). Systematic reviews are often seen as a gold standard in assessing evidence, as they provide an important means for summarizing, critiquing and presenting current published evidence on health topics. However, to fully inform practice and policy, there is a need to assess other forms of evidence, such as grey literature, testimonials, reports and evaluation documents. In addition, there is a need to understand how evidence can be taken up in the real world of health care or public health and made practicable, taking into account feasibility issues, plausibility, costs, cultures and politics (Shelton 2014).

Reliance solely on the evidence identified in systematic reviews is often insufficient when addressing complex health problems such as addiction among women. Evidence from some effective programs, such as community-based approaches may not be published, especially those that emerge from experience and engagement with women (Petticrew 2003); certain types of evidence may be prioritized, particularly experimental studies with large sample sizes (Petticrew 2003; MacLure 2005; Clegg 2005); and the context of findings may be ignored or understated (Clegg 2005).

Adhering to the hierarchies of evidence used within systematic reviews has some limitations when aiming to inform policy and practice. One potential issue is that the evidence base derived from systematic reviews is often inconclusive. For example, a Cochrane review of relapse prevention interventions for people who smoke concludes that there is insufficient evidence to recommend the use of behavioral interventions, including for pregnant women (Hajek et al. 2009). They note issues with the studies evaluated that hinders the development of evidence-based recommendations such as the heterogenous approaches of the interventions reviewed, and the lack of experimental and rigorous studies (Hajek et al. 2009). Due to the strict and often limiting parameters placed on what constitutes evidence, critics of systematic reviews note that a lack of sufficient or strong evidence should not preclude inaction (Petticrew 2003).

Conversely, prioritizing certain types of studies, through the use of assessment tools and methods that favor large, double blind, and scientifically rigorous studies, can also lead to the development of strong conclusions based on a small set of studies that may not be anchored in, or translatable to practice (MacLure 2005; Clegg 2005). While systematic reviews are a practical format for collecting and summarizing the literature within a given field, supplementing these methods with practice-based observations and wider contextualizations and reflections strengthens guidance on useful and promising approaches to address health issues.

Such supplementation also raises questions about what constitutes 'evidence.' Transdisciplinary approaches draw from and integrate diverse, disciplinary and cross-sectoral methods, evidence and approaches, to create more holistic and complex understandings of multi-factoral health issues (Kessel and Rosenfield 2008). To demonstrate the practice and benefits of a transdisciplinary approach to evidence reviews, we detail our approach to two systematic reviews, one a two-stage review on pregnancy and smoking reduction and cessation (Greaves et al. 2003; Greaves et al. 2011) and one on brief interventions to address alcohol use during pregnancy (Parkes et al. 2008). We describe how we blended a better practices methodology (CTCRI, 2006) with a systematic review methodology (NICE 2006). In each case we found insufficient evidence on the efficacy of interventions using systematic review methods only. We expanded the review process by applying better practice methods, integrating some contextual literature, and a mix of feedback from stakeholders or resource and program mapping. This allowed for the examination of the full dimensions of women's smoking and alcohol use during pregnancy, and the effects of intervening.

By taking a transdisciplinary approach, we are able to identify gaps in current evidence and ineffectiveness of interventions aimed narrowly at addressing smoking and alcohol during pregnancy. We share the recommendations and better practices developed out of our reviews to demonstrate how a transdisciplinary and multi-method approach enables reflection on, and extension beyond the identified evidence to more fully analyze the plausibility and feasibility of approaches. To support the work of others in applying a transdisciplinary approach to systematic reviews we share practical explanations and examples of how we applied methods and integrated information from a range of disciplines and stakeholders. Overall, we show how transdisciplinarity enhances our understanding of these complex health issues, invites integrated methods in systematic reviews, calls up better practices model (BPM) (Miller et al. 2001; Moyer et al. 2002). The BPM is a framework for assessing and synthesizing evidence from both research and practice, bringing together knowledge from published and unpublished literature and from practitioners working in the field (Moyer et al. 2002). In this way, BPM is a transdisciplinary approach, facilitating the inclusion of multiple forms of evidence from both researchers and providers. Going further, the 2011 update to *Expecting to Quit* and the 2008 alcohol and pregnancy review, *Double Exposure*, both blended systematic review methods developed by the National Institute for Health and Clinical Excellence (NICE 2006) with the BPM model. The NICE model involves rating individual studies by two independent reviewers to assess the studies for methodological rigor and quality using critical appraisal checklists. The NICE model also engages a wide range of stakeholders, users and practitioners to comment on review findings.

Studies were categorized by type, and different assessment tools were used for quantitative, qualitative and mixed methods studies. Quantitative studies examined criteria such as use of suitable control groups, outcomes, statistical analyses, attrition and other sources of potential bias. Qualitative studies were assessed for the consistency and quality of findings and applicability of evidence to the research questions. Based on fulfillment of assessment criteria, evidence was graded as "strong evidence of positive impact," "sufficient evidence of positive impact" or "insufficient evidence."

While this method is similar to traditional systematic review methods such as those used by the Cochrane Collaboration, we intentionally broadened the purview beyond that of traditional systematic reviews to support a transdisciplinary approach. First, to locate a wide range of evidence, we developed a search protocol that was inclusive of multiple forms and sources of evidence, rather than prioritizing randomized control trials and solely academic peer-reviewed journals. Hierarchical approaches which favor some forms of evidence (such as randomized control trials) and marginalize others (e.g. qualitative studies or unpublished evaluation materials) may lack "external validity," and not meaningfully reflect or inform practice (Victora, Habicht, and Bryce 2004; Shelton 2014; Lambert 2013). The NICE method includes a separate assessment tool for qualitative studies, which we used. We also conducted in-depth grey literature searches to locate evaluations of programs and research outside of the academic literature. These include methods and materials that may not have evaluation data. If programs did include evaluation data, these were reviewed and graded similar to academic literature. If programs did not have evaluation data, we examined the materials to identify and assess the individual intervention components used and related content.

Additionally, in keeping with the BPM, we conducted a plausibility assessment to situate findings within the community and practice context. Assessing studies for plausibility can provide a better picture of the capacity for interventions to be efficiently implemented in practice rather than strictly relying on

The narrow focus of interventions to address smoking and alcohol use during pregnancy is in part reflective of the historical focus in each of these fields on fetal health. For example, early tobacco control initiatives aimed at women, beginning in the 1970s, focused on the time of pregnancy and largely addressed preventing and reducing harm to the fetus rather than women's health (Greaves and Barr 2000; Greaves 1996; Jacobson 1986). Additionally, approaches to women's smoking during pregnancy have typically been fetus-centric and focused on individual behavior change, rather than understanding and addressing the context of women's smoking (Greaves et al. 2003; Greaves et al. 2011). This has translated into low rates of effectiveness and high rates of postpartum relapse (Greaves et al. 2011).

Similarly, interventions to address alcohol use during pregnancy have been narrow in scope and largely ineffective in addressing the needs of pregnant women at various levels of risk (Parkes et al. 2008). The review on alcohol and pregnancy identified three categories of intervention research: screening interventions aimed at identifying alcohol use, brief interventions and more intensive interventions. Similar to the tobacco literature, alcohol interventions tend to be focussed on early pregnancy, and frame pregnancy as a key time to address alcohol use and prevent fetal health effects. Likewise, studies typically do not acknowledge co-occurring influences on alcohol use such as violence or mental health concerns (particularly for screening interventions) and the potential for child apprehension associated with divulging alcohol use that prevents many women from seeking support (Parkes et al. 2008). Addressing social factors connected to smoking and alcohol use such as income, education, and housing are typically deemed as too complex or outside of the realm of tobacco or alcohol reduction health interventions. Finally, there is often a limited focus on cessation or abstinence in these fields, which contributes to a lack of knowledge of how harm reduction measures may improve women and fetal health.

Based on the gaps we noted in the intervention literatures, in both of our reviews we sought to consolidate evidence on the contextual factors associated with women's alcohol or tobacco use during pregnancy, as well as the potential practice implications associated with intervening with diverse women. In our view, developing a more complex and nuanced approach to interventions requires a transdisciplinary approach: gathering information from a variety of disciplines and sectors, using multiple methods for data collection and evidence assessment, applying a sex and gender analysis and engaging with a range of stakeholders to synthesize what is known and to reflect on the responses offered by multiple experts and professions across a range of settings.

Integrated Review Methods

The first review (2003) on smoking and pregnancy, *Expecting to Quit*, used an adaptation of the Canadian Tobacco Control Research Initiative (CTCRI)

Smoking and alcohol consumption during pregnancy are also high among Indigenous women. A study with Inuit women in Arctic Quebec found that 92% of women smoked and 61% consumed alcohol during pregnancy, of which 62% reported binge drinking; women who experienced violence, depression and who used illicit substances were at the greatest risk of alcohol use (Muckle et al. 2011). Violence and trauma is closely linked to alcohol use during pregnancy. A systematic review examining predictors of alcohol use during pregnancy found that the most prevalent predictors were pre-pregnancy alcohol use and history of abuse or exposure to violence (Skagerstróm, Chang, and Nilsen 2011). They found that unemployment, education and marital status were frequently studied, but infrequently predictive of alcohol use during pregnancy.

However, alcohol use during pregnancy is not restricted to women who are experiencing hardship. Recent data suggest that women who are older, White, and with higher socio-economic status are also at increased risk for alcohol use during pregnancy, although their rates of riskier binge drinking are generally low. Survey data from the USA reveals that 7.6% of women report consuming alcohol during pregnancy, with rates somewhat higher among women who were 35–44 years old (14.3%), college graduates (10%), White (8.3%) and employed (9.6%) (Centers for Disease Control and Prevention 2012).

Typical Approaches to Smoking and Alcohol Use During Pregnancy

The prevalence data suggest that smoking and alcohol use during pregnancy are clearly influenced by social and economic contexts such as income, education, experiences of violence and trauma, prior substance use and race/ethnicity. Hence, approaches to treating tobacco dependence ought to be sensitive to a range of structural issues and life experiences that influence use during pregnancy. We conducted two reviews, to examine the effectiveness of intervention research in these topic areas and to offer recommendations for proven and promising approaches (Greaves et al. 2011; Greaves et al. 2003; Parkes et al. 2008).

We found limited evidence for effective interventions to respond to both women's smoking and alcohol use during pregnancy. Furthermore, investigating the context of women's smoking and alcohol use during pregnancy is often lacking in intervention research. Generally, intervention efforts during pregnancy have been aimed at the general population of pregnant women to achieve broad-based prevention and cessation, or abstinence outcomes. Yet, interventions that do not acknowledge and address social and structural factors that shape women's tobacco and alcohol use prior to, during and beyond pregnancy are likely to be inadequate. Similarly, a recent scoping review of alcohol and tobacco use during pregnancy among adolescent girls reveals a limited focus in the literature on descriptive studies, and a lack of gender-informed interventions that address the context of substance use among girls (Bottorff et al. 2014).

questions of diversity and gender, and ultimately provides more nuanced evidence for informing treatment and policy.

Background on Alcohol and Tobacco Use in Pregnancy

Both smoking and alcohol use during pregnancy are key women's health issues and critical public health issues. Tobacco and alcohol use have serious health impacts for women and during pregnancy can result in a wide range of negative outcomes for the woman, her pregnancy and fetal health. In addition to these biological aspects of the issue, there is a range of broad determinants of health linked to women's use of tobacco and alcohol both in general and in pregnancy. These influences are often not adequately understood or factored into prevention, harm reduction, cessation and treatment interventions, or integrated into intervention studies.

Smoking during pregnancy among women in high income countries (including: USA, Finland, Germany, France and the UK) is approximately 14% to 28% (Schneider et al. 2010; Mohsin, Bauman, and Forero 2011). Yet smoking rates, and level of intensity, are even higher among some sub-groups of women. Data from British Columbia reveal that women who are single mothers, using drugs or alcohol, and who have not graduated high school are most likely to be heavy smokers during pregnancy (smoking 10 or more cigarettes per day; Erickson and Arbour 2012). In general, in high-income countries, women who are young, living on a low income and using alcohol or illicit substances are also more likely to smoke (Al-Sahab et al. 2010; Burns, Mattick, and Wallace 2008; Delpisheh et al. 2006; Kennare, Heard, and Chan 2005). Furthermore, Canadian data reveal that almost half of women who quit smoking during pregnancy report relapsing by fourteen months postpartum (Heaman, Lindsay, and Kaczorowski 2009). Relapse statistics in Canada also indicate a higher risk of relapse for women living in the Territories (Yukon, Northwest Territories and Nunavut), likely due to the high proportion of Inuit women living in these regions (Gilbert, Nelson, and Greaves accepted August 2014). National USA data measuring smoking trends between 2000 and 2005 reveal that the prevalence of smoking before pregnancy has not changed significantly (22.3% vs. 21.5%), although there have been relatively small decreases in smoking during pregnancy (15.2% to 13.8%) and smoking after delivery (18.1% vs. 16.4%) in this time (Tong et al. 2009). Together these data suggest that further work is needed to address smoking among diverse groups of women before, during and after pregnancy.

Alcohol use among women during pregnancy is also a significant issue. Canadian survey data reveal that 10.8% of women report consuming alcohol during pregnancy, and that women who smoke and have a partner are more likely to consume alcohol during pregnancy (Walker et al. 2011). In addition, women who report indifference or unhappiness with their pregnancies are 1.89 and 2.5 times more likely to consume alcohol during pregnancy, respectively (Walker et al. 2011).

the reported outcomes and grading of available evidence. Effective interventions may not be generalizable across all settings, populations and time. Plausibility criteria adapted from the BPM included assessment for time sensitivity (is the intervention current and reliable?); replicability (is there adequate information regarding how to effectively replicate and implement the intervention?); generalizability (is the intervention appropriate for the population or sub-populations); and cost benefit (is the benefit of the intervention worth the cost of implementation?) (CTCRI, 2006). A key tenet of the BPM is that what constitutes "best" or "better practices" is context-specific, subjective, and dynamic (Moyer et al. 2002).

Under the BPM, recommended interventions were classified as "best practices" if they showed strong evidence of effectiveness and achieved all of the plausibility criteria. Interventions with sufficient evidence of effectiveness and that met all plausibility criteria were classified as "better practices." Finally, interventions that demonstrated a significant effect but that were rated as insufficient strength of evidence were classified as "showing promise." Programs that utilized components that met plausibility criteria and were backed by evidence based on other studies, were also classified as "showing promise."

In the process of developing the final report of findings, preliminary recommendations that emerged from the best practices analysis were further examined within the context of the broader literature on women's health and smoking or alcohol use. Sources of literature that were examined to finalize the better practice approaches include women-centered care, women's health and substance use among girls and women and addictions research. Final better practice recommendations therefore accounted for evidence from the academic literature, feedback from stakeholders, program materials found in the grey literature and theoretical and contextual literature. Based on this mix of systematic review evidence and contextual literature, we developed better practice recommendations. A total of seven better practice recommendations were developed from the better practices review of interventions to address smoking during pregnancy or postpartum and four better practice recommendations were developed for the review of interventions to address alcohol use during pregnancy.

In the review of smoking reduction and cessation during pregnancy, *Expecting to Quit*, the following seven better practice approaches to intervening with women were recommended:

1. Tailoring
2. Woman-centered Care
3. Reducing Stigma
4. Relapse Prevention
5. Harm Reduction
6. Partner/Social Support
7. Integrating Social Issues

In the review of alcohol use during pregnancy, *Double Exposure*, the four better practice approaches were:

1. Integrating research and practice wisdom on women-centered care;
2. Integrating knowledge about the interconnections between women's substance use and other health, financial and social concerns;
3. Addressing diversity by tailoring interventions to the needs of different sub-groups of women;
4. Applying harm-reduction philosophy and practice.

The recommended approaches are similar across the reviews on the two topics, reflective of the common gaps observed in each field, as well as the wider need for approaches that acknowledge the social determinants of health and need for women-centered approaches to treating addictions. In both reviews, these better practice approaches guided the development of a contextualized set of recommendations for practice, research, knowledge translation and policy. These better practice approaches all rely on transdisciplinarity, involving multiple forms of evidence, a range of disciplines and practice-based perspectives. These different sources of knowledge were formed into an integrated whole to frame the recommendations. We argue that applying a transdisciplinary approach facilitates the use of methods and practices for conducting evidence reviews that are more accordant with both the context of women's use of alcohol and tobacco during pregnancy, and the treatment context. Resulting recommendations are therefore more likely to be meaningful to both women and providers. We provide some examples from each review to demonstrate how different forms of evidence were considered to develop these recommendations and how this enhanced our ability to guide practice.

The Additive Value of Transdisciplinarity to Systematic Reviews

For the Tobacco and Pregnancy Reviews

Based on the gaps in the evidence that we observed both within and between the two reviews on smoking reduction and cessation, we prepared an addendum for the 2011 publication to contextualize the complex social issues linked with smoking and challenges in reducing or quitting among three especially vulnerable sub-groups: young women, low-income women and women with other issues such as alcohol use, violence or past or current trauma. In the systematic review search, evidence on these sub-populations was extremely limited or lacking completely.

As a result of our added steps, we were able to determine the gaps, and develop some recommendations for filling them. Rather than simply noting the dearth of evidence in the published intervention literature, we engaged with the wide range of related literatures to explore the potential for applying the seven recommended better practice recommendations with these sub-groups of women. These literatures included innovative approaches in related fields, including alcohol treatment for women, trauma-informed programming, young women's health and violence prevention and treatment services. This process of engaging with supplementary evidence allowed us to further explore the potential application and meaning of some of the better practice recommendations for vulnerable sub-groups of women.

If this complexity is addressed along with multi-faceted interventions with these three sub-groups, reducing smoking during and beyond pregnancy could be more comprehensively addressed. Developing such interventions would not only require engagement with multiple disciplines and a range of community, academic and clinically based stakeholders but also reaching to develop a transdisciplinary, overarching understanding of the real-life situations facing women who smoke. Overlapping issues such as violence, trauma, mental health issues and other substance use, which strongly influence smoking during pregnancy among girls and women, would need to be integrated into interventions (Velez et al. 2006; Bailey and Daugherty 2007).

For girls and young women, there are some promising approaches that address substance use issues, childhood abuse, exposure to violence and dating violence, partner smoking and substance use, self-esteem and body image, depression and other forms mental ill health, and focus on girls' empowerment (Poole et al. 2012). For those with co-occurring substance use during pregnancy, it is helpful to integrate health education from preconception to postpartum, and address links with trauma, violence and the social determinants of health (Bialystok, Poole, and Greaves 2013). Finally, trauma-informed approaches are required that would entail providers becoming aware of the links between trauma and smoking, ensuring that interventions are non-judgmental and non-confrontational, actively reduce stigma and avoid triggering trauma (Poole and Lyon 2012). Addressing other relevant social issues is also crucial, as women who have experienced violence and trauma can also be experiencing other challenges, such as limited income and inadequate housing. Indeed, addressing smoking among those most vulnerable to tobacco use cannot be limited to the typical parameters of tobacco control but demands a truly transdisciplinary approach.

A narrow focus on smoking cessation during the relatively short time of pregnancy and an emphasis on the goal of cessation were evident in the outcome measures identified in our review. Measures of the following outcomes were often inconsistent of absent: relapse rates during pregnancy and postpartum, indicators of women's health status, structural factors such as income and education and harm reduction or decreased consumption. There is some evidence that harm reduction may be a useful approach for women; for example, among Canadian adults who have quit smoking, women are more likely than men to use gradual reduction as a strategy for cessation (Ismailov and Leatherdale 2010). One harm-reduction strategy that has been used to support low-income mothers who are experiencing disadvantage is *Start Thinking About Reducing Second-hand Smoke* (STARSS), developed by Action on Women's Addictions Research and Education

(AWARE) in Ontario, Canada. This program includes worksheets and tips to support low-income mothers in managing their tobacco use. The intention is not for women necessarily to quit smoking but instead to support women in making progress towards the management of second-hand smoke in the home, using a non-judgmental harm-reduction approach. Many researchers and practitioners working in tobacco control are hesitant to design, evaluate or implement interventions that focus on reducing smoking, arguing that health benefits are negligible (Lund 2009). However, working with women to increase motivation and identify barriers to and opportunities for change may help to build their confidence and ultimately improve their chances of achieving smoking reduction or cessation goals (Urquhart et al. 2012). Applying transdisciplinarity enhanced our capacity to make recommendations that are suited to the needs and experiences of women. The recommendations we developed for intervening with pregnant women who smoke relied in part on these various literatures (e.g. harm reduction, women-centered care, trauma-informed practice) that often fall well outside of the realm of tobacco control.

For the Alcohol and Pregnancy Review

This review presented similar challenges. Following the development of preliminary better practice recommendations (based on the systematic review and plausibility analysis), the research team examined the findings against broad practice-based and theoretical knowledge. These steps supported the understanding of transdisciplinary and women-centered approaches that reduce barriers to accessing help from health-care providers, and were tailored to the needs of specific sub-groups of women.

Similar to the overall findings in the smoking review, most studies did not situate alcohol use and pregnancy within the larger literatures related to women's health, women-centered care and women's substance use. The review identified a small number of relevant published studies that were narrowly focused on a medical model approach to substance use by pregnant women. Hence, the findings from the evidence review were contextualized within knowledge on approaches to women's substance use overall, not only in pregnancy. Contextualizations of each of the three sections of findings (screening/identification; brief interventions; and intensive interventions) were presented as "snapshots" on the key issues and gaps in the field.

For example, within the screening literature, important practice implications and knowledge gaps were identified. While some screening approaches or tools may be effective in identifying alcohol use, these may not always further the goal of improving women's health. Screening approaches have the potential to exacerbate the stigmatizing and blaming of women who use alcohol in pregnancy and may dissuade women from revealing alcohol use and seeking help for fear of the consequences such as apprehension of their children. This is particularly true for women who already experience disadvantages, such as women living on a low income or who have experienced violence and trauma. Yet, the potential for some of these approaches to further stigmatize women and impact the results of screening interventions is not addressed in the literature. Furthermore, screening interventions are often not followed up with supports and referrals due to lack of staff capacity or knowledge of appropriate services.

Women-centered approaches depend heavily on transdisciplinarity and the integration of various types of evidence. They are required in order to account for the broader issues affecting women's health, such as gender differences in substance use and addiction, the potential for stigma and discrimination and social and economic factors harming health and reducing access to care. Respectful, non-judgmental approaches are needed that seek to reduce stigma as well as harm-reduction approaches that may improve women's access to care. Approaches are required that value women's health holistically, rather than focusing solely on the identification and treatment of alcohol use. This may include assisting women with housing, education, childcare, prenatal health care, violence and trauma as well as substance use (Poole 2000; Finkelstein and Markoff 2005). Hence, both intervention research and the development and application of interventions to address alcohol use in pregnancy have the potential to benefit from a transdisciplinary approach.

Prevalence data reveal that there is a wide range of risk factors for alcohol use, and that vulnerability cannot be assumed based on income, race/ethnicity or education. Yet, there is a lack of research and development of alcohol interventions to address diversity among women who consume alcohol during pregnancy. Women who are older, White with moderate to high incomes and college education are at high risk of consuming alcohol during pregnancy, yet there is a lack of interventions examining the effectiveness of interventions among this sub-group. A study by Chang et al. (1999) found that older women were more likely to choose reduction rather than abstinence as an intervention goal. Even when interventions were primarily conducted with sub-populations of pregnant women such as American Indian, African American and low-income women, they were not tailored to the needs of these sub-groups, and the studies typically failed to examine differences based on ethnicity or income level. Taken together, this suggests that further development and evaluation of interventions is required to tailor to a range of sub-populations, including a range of tailored outcome goals.

Conclusion

Transdisciplinarity and integration of a range of evidence is key for improving interventions for women who use tobacco or consume alcohol during pregnancy. In conducting evidence reviews, we discovered that the available research that emerges using systematic review methods often does not address the full scope of the problem. Indeed, relying solely on such limited evidence may not improve access to care, identification or health status of women. Therefore, augmenting review methodologies with other forms of evidence is critical to expanding the knowledge base and utility in real-life application.

The process of developing better practice recommendations is intended to address issues of real-life application, taking into account plausibility and feasibility. In this chapter we have argued that a transdisciplinary approach can enhance evidence collection, application to practice and evaluation. An explicit transdisciplinary approach is also needed in intervention development and implementation. Health-care providers and other professionals who intervene with pregnant women who use substances need access to evidence that supports them in developing and applying more complex interventions that address sex and gender differences in alcohol and tobacco use, trauma-informed practice, women-centered interventions and the social determinants of health as they affect pregnant women.

Discussion Questions

1. Discuss how transdisciplinarity could be applied to intervention development, implementation and evaluation for other health issues. What do you expect the strengths and challenges would be in doing so?
2. Consider how a transdisciplinary approach could be used to enhance other research methodologies.
3. Discuss other limitations of systematic reviews and possible solutions.

References

Al-Sahab, Ban, Masarat Saqib, Gabriel Hauser, and Hala Tamim. 2010. Prevalence of smoking during pregnancy and associated risk factors among Canadian women: A national survey. *BMC Pregnancy and Childbirth* 10:24–32.

Bailey, Beth A., and Ruth Ann Daugherty. 2007. Intimate partner violence during pregnancy: Incidence and associated health behaviors in a rural population. *Maternal and Child Health Journal* 11 (5):495–503.

Bialystok, Lauren, Nancy Poole, and Lorraine Greaves. 2013. Preconception care: A call for Canadian guidelines. *Canadian Family Physician* 59 (10):1037–1039.

Bottorff, Joan L., Nancy Poole, Mary T. Kelly, Lorraine Greaves, Lenora Marcellus, and Mary Jung. 2014. Tobacco and alcohol use in the context of adolescent pregnancy and postpartum: A scoping review of the literature. *Health & Social Care in the Community*. Available from http://onlinelibrary.wiley.com/doi/10.1111/hsc.12091/pdf.

Burns, Lucy, Richard P. Mattick, and Cate Wallace. 2008. Smoking patterns and outcomes in a population of pregnant women with other substance use disorders. *Nicotine and Tobacco Research* 10 (6):969–974.

Canadian Tobacco Control Research Initiative (CTCRI). 2006. *Better solutions for complex problems: Description of a model to support better practices for health*. Toronto, ON: CTCRI.

Centers for Disease Control and Prevention. 2012. Alcohol use and binge drinking among women of childbearing age—United States, 2006–2010. *MMWR. Morbidity and Mortality Weekly Report* 61 (28):534.

Chang, Grace, Louise Wilkins Haug, Susan Berman, and Margaret Ann Goetz. 1999. Brief intervention for alcohol use in pregnancy: a randomized trial. *Addiction* 94 (10):1499–1508.

Clegg, Sue. 2005. Evidence-based practice in educational research: A critical realist critique of systematic review. *British Journal of Sociology of Education* 26 (3):415–428.

Delpisheh, Ali, Eman Attia, Sandra Drammond, and Bernard J. Brabin. 2006. Adolescent smoking in pregnancy and birth outcomes. *The European Journal of Public Health* 16 (2):168–172.

Erickson, Anders, and Laura Arbour. 2012. Heavy smoking during pregnancy as a marker for other risk factors of adverse birth outcomes: A population-based study in British Columbia, Canada. *BMC Public Health* 12 (1):102.

Finkelstein, Norma, and Laurie S. Markoff. 2005. The women embracing life and living (WELL) project: Using the relational model to develop integrated systems of care for women with alcohol/drug use and mental health disorders with histories of violence. *Alcoholism Treatment Quarterly* 22 (3–4):63–80.

Gilbert, Nicolas, C. Nelson, and Lorraine Greaves. 2014, accepted August. Smoking cessation during pregnancy and relapse after childbirth in Canada. *Journal of Obstetrics and Gynecology Canada*.

Greaves, Lorraine. 1996. *Smoke screen: Women's smoking and social control*. Halifax, NS: Fernwood.

Greaves, Lorraine, and Victoria Barr. 2000. *Filtered policy: Women and tobacco in Canada*. Vancouver, BC: Women's Health Bureau: Health Canada.

Greaves, Lorraine, Renée Cormier, Karen Devries, Joan Bottorff, Joy Johnson, Susan Kirkland, and David Aboussafy. 2003. *Expecting to quit: A best practices review of smoking cessation interventions for pregnant and postpartum girls and women*. Vancouver: British Columbia Centre of Excellence for Women's Health.

Greaves, Lorraine, Nancy Poole, Chizimuzo Okoli, Natalie Hemsing, Annie Qu, Lauren Bialystok, and Renée O'Leary. 2011. *Expecting to quit: A best practices review of smoking cessation interventions for pregnant and postpartum girls and women*. Vancouver: British Columbia Centre of Excellence for Women's Health.

Hajek, Peter, Lindsay F. Stead, Robert West, Martin Jarvis, and Tim Lancaster. 2009. Relapse prevention interventions for smoking cessation. *Cochrane Database Syst Rev* 1 (1). DOI: 10.1002/14651858.CD003999.pub3.

Heaman, Maureen, Joan Lindsay, and Janusz Kaczorowski. 2009. Chapter 10: Smoking. In *What mothers say: The Canadian Maternity Experiences Survey*, edited by Public Health Agency of Canada. Ottawa: Public Health Agency of Canada.

Ismailov, Rovshan M., and Scott T. Leatherdale. 2010. Smoking cessation aids and strategies among former smokers in Canada. *Addictive Behaviors* 35 (3):282–5.

Jacobson, Bobbie. 1986. *Beating the ladykillers: Women and smoking*. London, UK: Pluto Press.

Kennare, Robyn, Adrian Heard, and Annabelle Chan. 2005. Substance use during pregnancy: Risk factors and obstetric and perinatal outcomes in South Australia. *Australian and New Zealand Journal of Obstetrics and Gynaecology* 45 (3):220–225.

Kessel, Frank, and Patricia L. Rosenfield. 2008. Toward transdisciplinary research: Historical and contemporary perspectives. *American Journal of Preventive Medicine* 35 (2, Supplement):S225–S234.

Lambert, Helen. 2013. Plural forms of evidence in public health: tolerating epistemological and methodological diversity. *Evidence & Policy: A Journal of Research, Debate and Practice* 9 (1):43–48.

Lund, Karl Erik. 2009. A tobacco-free society or tobacco harm reduction. *Which objective is best for the remaining smokers in Scandinavia*. SIRUS-Report no. 6/2009. Oslo: Norwegian Institute for Alcohol and Drug Research.

MacLure, Maggie. 2005. "Clarity bordering on stupidity": Where's the quality in systematic review? *Journal of Education Policy* 20 (4):393–416.

Miller, Steve, Stephen Manske, Marie Rose Phaneuf, and Cheryl Moyer. 2001. *Identifying best practices for group smoking cessation: Comparing CCS Fresh Start to best practices*. Waterloo, ON: Centre for Behavioural Research and Program Evaluation, University of Waterloo.

Mohsin, Mohammed, Adrian E. Bauman, and Roberto Forero. 2011. Socioeconomic correlates and trends in smoking in pregnancy in New South Wales, Australia. *Journal of Epidemiology and Community Health* 65 (8):727–732.

Moyer, Cheryl, Judith Garcia, Roy Cameron, and Catherine Maule. 2002. *Identifying promising solutions for complex health problems: Model for a better practices process*. Unpublished work.

Muckle, Gina, Dominique Laflamme, Jocelyne Gagnon, Olivier Boucher, Joseph L. Jacobson, and Sandra W. Jacobson. 2011. Alcohol, smoking, and drug use among Inuit women of childbearing age during pregnancy and the risk to children. *Alcoholism: Clinical and Experimental Research* 35 (6):1081–1091.

NICE. 2006. *Methods for development of NICE public health guidance*. London, UK: National Institute for Health and Clinical Excellence.

Parkes, Tessa, Nancy Poole, Amy Salmon, Lorraine Greaves, and Cristine Urquhart. 2008. *Double exposure: A better practices review on alcohol interventions during pregnancy*. Vancouver: British Columbia Centre of Excellence for Women's Health.

Petticrew, Mark. 2003. Why certain systematic reviews reach uncertain conclusions. *Bmj* 326 (7392):756–758.

Poole, Nancy. 2000. *Evaluation report of the Sheway Project for high-risk pregnant and parenting women*. Vancouver, BC: BC Centre of Excellence for Women's Health.

Poole, Nancy, and Judy Lyon. 2012. Integrating treatment of tobacco and other substances in a trauma-informed way. In *Becoming Trauma Informed*, edited by Nancy Poole and Lorraine Greaves. Toronto, ON: Centre for Addiction and Mental Health

Poole, Nancy, Christina Talbot, Tatiana Fraser, Jennifer Bernier, Cheryl van Dalen-Smith, Bilkis Vissandjee, Margaret Haworth Brockman, Natalie Hemsing, Saman Ahsan, Barbara Clow, Mara Fridell, Jonathan Kuntz, Fabienne Pierre-Jacques, and Shvata Thakur. 2012. *"I love it because you could just be yourself": A study of girls' perspectives on girls' groups and healthy living*. Vancouver: British Columbia Centre of Excellence for Women's Health. http://promotinghealthinwomen.ca/wordpress/wp-content/uploads/2012/08/I-love-it-because-you-could-just-be-yourself-Full-Report.pdf.

Schneider, Sven, Christina Huy, Jessica Schutz, and Katharina Diehl. 2010. Smoking cessation during pregnancy: A systematic literature review. *Drug and Alcohol Review* 29 (1):81–90.

Shelton, James D. 2014. Evidence-based public health: not only whether it works, but how it can be made to work practicably at scale. *Global Health: Science and Practice* 2 (3):253–258.

Skagerstróm, Janna, Grace Chang, and Per Nilsen. 2011. Predictors of drinking during pregnancy: A systematic review. *Journal of Women's Health* 20 (6):901–913.

Tong, Van T., Jaime R. Jones, Patricia M. Dietz, Denise D'Angelo, and Jennifer M. Bombard. 2009. *Trends in smoking before, during, and after pregnancy: Pregnancy Risk Assessment*

Monitoring System (PRAMS), United States, 31 sites, 2000–2005. Washington, DC: Department of Health and Human Services, Centers for Disease Control and Prevention.

Urquhart, Cristine, Frances Jasiura, Nancy Poole, Tasnim Nathoo, and Lorraine Greaves. 2012. *Liberation! Helping women quit smoking: A brief tobacco intervention guide*. Vancouver, BC: British Columbia Centre of Excellence for Women's Health.

Velez, Martha L., Ivan D. Montoya, Lauren M. Jansson, Vickie Walters, Dace Svikis, Hendree E. Jones, Howard Chilcoat, and Jacquelyn Campbell. 2006. Exposure to violence among substance-dependent pregnant women and their children. *Journal of Substance Abuse Treatment* 30 (1):31–38.

Victora, Cesar G., Jean-Pierre Habicht, and Jennifer Bryce. 2004. Public health matters. Evidence-based public health: moving beyond randomized trials. *American Journal of Public Health* 94 (3):400–405.

Walker, Meghan, Ban Al-Sahab, Farah Islam, and Hala Tamim. 2011. The epidemiology of alcohol utilization during pregnancy: An analysis of the Canadian Maternity Experiences Survey (MES). *BMC Pregnancy and Childbirth* 11 (1):52.

Suggestions for Further Reading

Families Controlling and Eliminating Tobacco. http://facet.ubc.ca/

Greaves, Lorraine, Nancy Poole, Chizimuzo Okoli, Natalie Hemsing, Annie Qu, Lauren Bialystok, and Renée O'Leary. 2011. *Expecting to quit: A best practices review of smoking cessation interventions for pregnant and postpartum girls and women.* www.expectingtoquit.ca/

Oaks, Laury. 2001. *Smoking and pregnancy: The politics of fetal protection.* New Brunswick, NJ: Rutgers University Press.

Parkes, Tessa, Nancy Poole, Amy Salmon, Lorraine Greaves, and Cristine Urquhart. 2008. *Double exposure: A better practices review on alcohol interventions during pregnancy.* Vancouver: British Columbia Centre of Excellence for Women's Health.

Poole, Nancy, and Greaves, Lorraine. 2009. Mother and child reunion: Achieving balance in policies affecting substance-using mothers & their children. *Women's Health and Urban Life* 8 (1), 54–66.

PART 3

What is the Future of Transdisciplinarity?

This section focuses on the future of transdisciplinarity in addiction research and practice. The addictions field has embraced many different philosophies perspectives and explanatory models over the centuries. At present, these perspectives still compete and sometimes conflict. The chapters in this section discuss how transdisciplinarity, integration of co-occurring issues and the addition of sex and gender hold promise for unifying the field. While these shifts will not solve addiction, they may offer some needed hope for a more unified and functional approach, melding disciplines and sectors, aiming for better science and programming by attending to sex and gender and merging sectors and issues that link to addiction such as mental health, trauma and violence.

Will this new, combined approach lead to solving and responding to addiction in a more complete, successful, humane manner? The contributors to this section think so. Selby, in an interview with the editors, suggests that transdisciplinarity is the new Renaissance for science, and for addictions treatment and research in particular. He explains how his own personal voyage and experiences set him up for understanding this approach and speculates that more and more demographic diversity will aid future generations in adopting transdisciplinary thinking. Sotskova and colleagues illustrate how consciously choosing a theory to share and work with can operate in bringing together a transdisciplinary team. They offer the example of Meaning Management Theory (MMT) and explore its links to existential givens as an aid to understanding addiction.

Greaves considers how the essence of transdisciplinary thinking can be transposed to policy making and program design. She likens this to the process of generating intersectoral "health in all policies" and argues for a trans-sectoral approach to policy, using the contentious example of substance use during pregnancy as an illustration. Finally, Poole ponders how transdisciplinarity not only requires more advance-knowledge translation, but how knowledge translation can be expanded in its approach. She discusses mechanisms of facilitation, context recognition and broad views of evidence as key principles in generating knowledge translation that reflects transdisciplinarity, sex and gender and an integrated approach to addiction.

Finally, the editors conclude with a discussion of some of the barriers and facilitators to engaging more fully with transdisciplinarity in addiction research, treatment, practice and policy. They speculate that some of the institutional, structural and professional boundaries and barriers that currently impede sharing and merging may be positively shifted by new social and political trends in communication, research funding, health literacy and public engagement.

12
MIGRATING TOWARD TRANSDISCIPLINARITY IN ADDICTION TREATMENT

Peter Selby

Peter Selby, MD, Professor, Departments of Family and Community Medicine and Psychiatry and the Dalla Lana School of Public Health, is the chief and clinician scientist, Addictions Division, at the Centre for Addiction and Mental Health (CAMH). His research and clinical work includes smoking cessation, especially in pregnant women, smokers with co-morbid conditions and web-based interventions. As a principal investigator of the STOP program, his investigations include the effectiveness of NRT and medications in different types of intervention settings. He helped start the program for pregnant substance-using women at St. Joseph's Health Centre, providing both addiction medicine and obstetric care. He continues his clinical research on tobacco addiction and is the principal investigator of a knowledge translation program (PREGNETS) to increase the adoption of evidence-based interventions with pregnant smokers. In this conversation with Lorraine Greaves and Nancy Poole, Selby discusses his unique understanding of transdisciplinarity, his challenges for fostering it in clinical practice and training and the future of transdisciplinarity as a renaissance concept for health care and research.

Q: How does your understanding of transdisciplinarity shape how you approach your research?

A: After being introduced to transdisciplinarity, I opened up to the multiple and often more effective ways of addressing an issue. It made me focus more on the 'in-between-ness' rather than focusing on just my little in-the-box approach to problems. In tobacco control, for example, we know it's not just about the clinical management of the addiction that is going to lead to people quitting and living longer. When we have lawyers, policy makers, advocates and scholars from several health, and other, disciplines—we have the whole range of people who might share a common goal to address this complex problem. When I started to collaborate in this way, it helped me realize that all of us have a perspective that we need to bring together, because each one will come to the problem from our own perspective. If we can speak a common language and co-construct a better picture of the whole, we can align our efforts to move forward. Adopting transdisciplinarity opens up my understanding and helps me situate my work in a multi-level model. It further drives me to thinking systems. If I use a systems approach, I cannot simply study the person and the addictiveness of their cigarettes alone. My research then uses mixed methods and complex analyses to tease out the effects of moderators and mediators in treating addictive disorders.

Q: What happens when you try to merge issues, like, say, tobacco and trauma? How do you think transdisciplinarity applies there?
A: Transdisciplinary thinking helps break down the silos in our minds and fosters integrative rather than reductionist thinking. This is extremely freeing for me as a clinician who works with people presenting with complex or multiple problems. We have to reflect on and explore the commonalities and interrelationship between the issues bothering the patient. Rather than simply focusing on low motivation or the severity of the addiction that keeps the person smoking, it assists me in considering other hidden determinants of the behavior. For example, one can keep muddling around with all the medications, in the hopes that she will quit with just the right biological treatment. However, if one doesn't get to those deeper issues about trauma or attachment and what it means to the woman who is smoking, both the patient and the provider feel frustrated. Also, clinicians who specifically assist people address their trauma can similarly explore how the woman is using cigarettes to silence her voice or bury her negative emotions. Therefore, it fosters a more holistic approach to the woman rather than seeing them through a narrow disciplinary lens. Transdisciplinary thinking fosters creativity and the ingenuity because of the ability to consider all perspectives. By having combined competencies in the same practitioner for these seemingly disparate yet highly clustered problems, the client benefits tremendously. To be transdisciplinary, one has to develop comfort with the dual identity of being a specialist and generalist concurrently rather than view them as mutually exclusive professional identities. We have to learn to see them as complementary to each other. But the problem is deep rooted. Our years of training and socialization as specialists perpetuate the silos that exist within disciplines and explain why somebody says, "Well, that's not my job. You do that piece, I'll do this piece." This fracturing of care leads to inadequate care for patients who get bounced from one provider to the next. I'm not saying that one person has to do everything, but that you can at least have an appreciation of more than one perspective and pass that on to somebody else. In an ideal situation, working in a team can address some of these problems. As an example, in my training program for the treatment of tobacco addiction (the TEACH project) tailored for non-physician health professionals, we emphasize a holistic understanding and approach to the person. Therefore, there is a substantive section on neurobiology and pharmacotherapy. Many of our staff and faculty

made the assumption that the learners would not find these sections helpful given their non-medical background. However, the contrary is true. Moreover, in our clinic, by the time the physician sees the patient, they've already had counseling by the social worker and the pharmacist about the need for comprehensive treatment. So, the patient is coming in much more informed and the whole team is on the same page. We don't have the patient confused by one clinician pitting "medicine versus behavioral therapy" or the physician saying, "Oh, forget about therapy." Transdisciplinary thinking is inclusive of multidisciplinary and interdisciplinary clinical approaches to care but more than just those approaches to care.

Q: It seems then that you are giving the women themselves the opportunity to think through and be their own transdisciplinary case managers in some ways.
A: Yes. If we truly buy into the idea that in this day and age there is a democratization of knowledge, the "us/them" divide needs to be broken down. For some who don't accept that reality, it's akin to the story of the emperor having no clothes. It is still easy to operate on the assumption that people who are coming into care are these backward, mindless, non-thinking people. To me, this is kind of odd, especially in a country where you've got one of the highest literacy rates, you've got high Internet access, you have access to information and you've got great sophisticated ways of thinking, even though we may say overall health literacy is low. I think the traditional idea that doctors, or scholars or only the learned should be the keepers of knowledge needs to die. One way we change the status quo is to hear the voices of the person who is at the table and has a vested interest in the issue. This includes other members of the health-care team, the woman herself and whoever she chooses to include from her social support network. Each of them is going to contribute information and possible solutions to make a difference. If we can become more receptive to learning from others in the health-care system rather than always being the experts, we can potentially assist people with complex problems such as addictions. I'm not saying that we don't need specialists, we do, but for many issues that compound the person's problems, we need to engage others. As experts, we need to be facilitating and engaging everyone who can be of help valuing everyone's contributions, including those of the woman struggling to change. We develop pragmatism when we recognize that others may have ideas that we've never thought about. This approach can be very empowering for the woman.

Q: You link your own interest in and skill in transdisciplinarity to your personal journey, which is about migration and being an outsider in some senses. I think that's very interesting, and it makes me think about how do others who might not have had those experiences come to transdisciplinarity? Have you had any experience through your students, for example, in getting them to attach themselves to transdisciplinarity, even if they haven't had experiences like the ones you've had in your life?

A: Yes, life experiences really shape your thinking. I came to this country with a certain plan, and then I had to adapt because it didn't work out as planned, and so I ended up being a member of multiple "tribes," so to speak. As we know, medicine is an extremely tribal profession with its various specialties. Even the training for each specialty is very much geared towards a certain way of thinking. So I had to adapt and it really built my confidence that I could adapt. Many people who are immigrants or grew up on a farm are more likely to have dealt with adversity. To survive one has to learn to make do, recognize the value of collaboration and learn to multi-task. These experiences in my formative years made it that much easier to embrace transdisciplinarity. If one grows up in privilege, protected from struggles and the vicissitudes or life, without expectations of collaboration, then it is hard to integrate in this complex work space where there are multiple points of views and competing demands. For my students, some people will have that cognitive understanding of adversity, but no real-world experience or empathy for others with less fortunate circumstances. They often need to be immersed in the experience to appreciate the value of transdisciplinarity. In other words, they need to discover the skills on the job.

Q: What are your main challenges for fostering transdisciplinarity among your colleagues, students and in your practice?

A: For transdisciplinarity to work, each member of the team first needs to be secure in his or her own "tribe." Otherwise, everything goes against them. For example, if they're writing papers collaboratively, they may not get credit at their university department that doesn't value this kind of collaborative effort. It's hard, but that's how our academic reinforcing structures of grant applications, tenure and promotion come in the way of incentivizing people to work in transdisciplinary ways. For example, we may be at the same university, but if you come to it from anthropology, it's a single-author publication. If you come to it from medicine, it's multi-author publication. If it's in medicine and you're the senior author, you're last and your student goes first, whereas in public health that order may reflect the least contribution. So, there are all these different influences that are minimizing the recognition of this very important work. Therefore, learners find themselves wondering if and how they should do it. I notice that many do the least amount of transdisciplinary work because it negatively affects their careers. A good metaphor for young researchers, that a very senior "nontribal" researcher once told me, is that young researchers have to have focus on one thing, establish themselves and then branch out as quickly possible. The result of doing it that way is that the researchers become like trees with strong trunks. But if they are focusing on too many areas by branching out too early, they will be more like a fern that won't grow as high, and they won't have as much of an impact. I think it's interesting because ferns do serve a purpose, as does a tree. Not that one is better than the other, but it's just that in our current academic system you get more recognition if you are a tree.

Q: Yes, and I think the down side is that by focusing on being a tree, some people might miss the opportunity to do transdisciplinary work.
A: Exactly, because everything is fostering the trunk and nothing is more stable than a tree. Then you have to take a look at it in terms of, "What will make people do this?" I would say that once academics have got tenure, then they have the ability to do that because they are secure and can take that risk and be creative. But it is more challenging for the students who don't necessarily see themselves this way. I think it is happening and we should start young, but those people are trying to get their identity as doctors, nurses, pharmacists, etc.—they are still negotiating that identity themselves, and then, to have this deferred, makes it very difficult to do both well.

Q: You account for both sex and gender in your research. Could you talk a little bit about how you do that?
A: I have to go back to my family of origin to explain it. I have seen very strong women in my family. The women have always enjoyed a very high status in terms of never being denied education, in fact promoting education, autonomy and independence. I'm the youngest of my cousins, mostly women, some of whom were born in the late forties, and the there are many chose not to marry and ended up with very interesting careers. At the same time, I grew up in India, a very male-dominated society, and I was exposed to women with all levels of empowerment and roles. I think it all shaped how I think. In my medical school in the 1980s there was a real shift in the leadership—my dean was a woman, as were many heads of departments. When I came to Canada in the early 1990s, I was surprised to see that most of the leadership in medicine was still male. My wife is a physician, and I saw how she didn't have any gender barriers in her upbringing and medical school. The contrasting gender roles in medicine in Canada and India started me thinking about "what is the cause of these differences?" In my non-professional life, as I adapted to this country, I began to get a close-up of people's lives in terms of their roles, identity and position in society. By just scratching below the surface in many ways you start to see similarities between women here and women in India, and for me it was, like, "Wait a minute. There's supposed to have been a lot of emancipation, but not as much I had expected or read about." Then, when I started working with women who used substances whilst pregnant, all these experiences got me interested in understanding the nuances of sex and gender. It really forced me to step out of the expert role and just listen. As an example, when we were developing the first database for women who had substance use problems and pregnancy, the traditional database had "woman's name" and "husband's or partner's name," but there was only one field. Yet, the women coming in had the "baby daddy," some other guy and possibly a boyfriend or husband. Many women told me that these men played different roles in their lives, and not all were abusive or exploitative. I asked our database developer, how do we capture this? It started me thinking that we've got to think this through slightly differently and how do we not just become the "other group" that's

taking over this woman? It got me really focusing on that piece that if we are able to create a secure attached relationship with this woman in the context of care then there will be growth for her. In the pregnancy clinic, we worked from a principle of honesty right up front, including the legality of having to report so there are surprises and you're building the trust right away. You have to build that context of safety, engagement and empowerment from the work that you do but discharge it responsibility. That way, if the woman feels secure enough, that she that has a secure attachment, that we're not going to abandon, threaten or bully her, all the things that she's used to, she can see a different way of being. With that then comes the ability for the woman to find her voice and say, "You know what? I do want to be a good mother, I do want to be a good person and I do want to have all the sort of things in life that everybody else wants. I happen to have a drug problem, but that doesn't mean I have to be a certain way or act a certain way because now I'm getting respect, I'm getting responsibility." They need to know that you're not just pulling a fast one but that you are paying attention to that history of trauma, that history of being beaten down.

Q: Listening to all of the challenges you've had in moving towards transdisciplinarity, it leads me to think that the future of transdisciplinarity may very well be in the future. Perhaps transdisciplinarity will become more popular or more eagerly assumed by people as our population diversifies and gets more complex in so many ways.

A: That's right. I am excited that places of higher learning allow for greater flexibility and blurring of science and art. Students can choose classes from both faculties. I am interested in knowing if a science graduate who's taken a philosophy class does better in their approach to complex problems compared to a student who hasn't. Or, for somebody who's taken art appreciation and chooses medicine, how do they do compared to the students doing biochemistry and who are not seeing the bigger picture? I tend to think about transdisciplinarity as the next Renaissance. If you think about it, the old masters and artists who blurred science, philosophy and art were actually transdisciplinary, right? So, I think transdisciplinarity is a Renaissance idea that is coming back, and the main issues will be how to nurture it in a new generation and to what extent we will be able to shape the institutions in which they work, to foster it.

13
BUILDING A THEORETICAL BRIDGE FOR TRANSDISCIPLINARY EXCHANGE

Alina Sotskova, Cecilia Benoit, Lauren Casey, Bernadette Pauly and Barna Konkolÿ Thege

In the study and treatment of substance use and addiction, it is essential for researchers and clinicians to consider the complex forces that position people differently within historical, political, social, and cultural contexts and that shape health and substance use policies and professional practices. Current isolated disciplinary-bound explanations and understandings of problematic substance use often fail to adequately consider these complexities.

Substance use ranges from non-problematic to problematic or addictive, and encompasses the use and misuse of alcohol, tobacco, and illicit drugs. The occurrence of problematic substance use in societies around the world is widespread, with escalating levels in the use and misuse of psychoactive substances (World Health Organization 2004). The rates of prescription drug misuse in Canada and other countries are also of considerable health concern and an identified area for action (Davison and Perron 2013). Documenting the prevalence and patterns of use provides important information about these trends but does not illuminate the complex intersections and impacts of substance use in relation to gender, sex, class, ethnicity, mental health, and trauma. For example, people who use illicit drugs, especially if they are poor, are often subject to negative and stigmatizing stereotypes, such as being labeled as manipulative, drug seeking, or criminals (Lloyd 2010, Room 2005). Such labeling impacts mental health and shapes access to health-care services (Pauly 2008). Complicating matters are prevailing and intransigent assumptions that any type of substance use for certain populations, such as pregnant women, is immoral and always problematic (Chasnoff, Landress, and Barrett 1990, Lester, Andreozzi, and Appiah 2004, Benoit, McCarthy, and Jansson in press). When we explore the intersection of substance use with gender, sex, ethnicity, mental health, and trauma, the need for new approaches that transcend disciplinary boundaries is apparent. As noted above, disadvantaged women, especially those who are pregnant or in the early stages of parenting, may be subject to harsh judgments and censures related to their ability to mother (Boyd 2004). Aboriginal peoples in Canada are also especially subject to stigmatization (Tang and Browne 2008). What is not acknowledged is how substance use, for women and Aboriginal people, for example, occurs within a complex web of policies, societal attitudes, historical legacies, and economic realities (Loppie Reading and Wein 2009, Bungay et al. 2010).

In this chapter, we propose transdisciplinarity as an ideal approach to creating 'bridges' that can contribute to improving research, policy, and practice in addressing problematic substance use. In particular, we present Meaning Management Theory (MMT) as one promising theoretical framework for promoting transdisciplinary collaboration on problematic substance use among researchers, clinicians, and policy makers. We outline three specific challenges for transdisciplinary collaboration and describe strategies from MMT as a way to surmount these challenges. Specifically, we focus on the concept of "existential givens" in MMT (Wong 2010) and how themes related to existential givens can serve as starting points for transdisciplinary exchange. Existential givens are common life events/circumstances that are part of the human condition. These include life vs. death, self-control vs. helplessness, and self-direction vs. conformity. These conditions of human existence, posited on a continuum are something that most persons have to adapt to in life. Since people are drawn to creating meanings or, in cognitive-behavioral terms, to making sense of their environment, people create different answers, stories, and responses to the existential givens (Wong 2010). This chapter illustrates how researchers and clinicians from different disciplines can use the idea of the existential givens to foster greater understanding of meaning creation with respect to problematic substance use, sex, gender, mental health, and trauma and how these intersect to shape experiences and outcomes of addictions in the contexts of people's lives. Throughout the chapter, we provide examples that highlight these intersections and illustrate the applicability of the suggested approach to the complex reality of these phenomena.

Transdisciplinarity

Transdisciplinarity refers to "the transcendence of disciplines for addressing meta-questions, the intersection of two or more disciplines and the combination of methods/techniques/theories from several disciplines in the framing or testing of a hypothesis" (Krimsky 2000, p. 111). The main principles that underlie transdisciplinary research and practice are diversity, teamwork, and collaboration, occurring across a variety of academic disciplines and/or involving clinicians, non-academic community stakeholders, and policy makers (Kirst, Altenberg, and Balian 2011). Such diverse groups work together in information-exchanging activities, the sharing of resources, the altering of discipline-specific approaches, and synthesizing across disciplines in order to achieve a common goal.

It is important to note that collaboration does not necessarily involve agreement among disciplines; rather, it involves each discipline and sector bringing their perspectives to the collective enterprise to accelerate new knowledge about the interplay of individual, social, and environmental factors in addressing problematic substance use and its consequences. This approach is critical to further development of effective strategies to reduce harms of substance use. There are many benefits to engaging in a transdisciplinary approach, including (1) providing a higher level of explanatory power compared to reductionist orientations based on unidisciplinary perspectives; (2) enabling researchers to attain higher levels of validity in their studies through the combination of more diverse methodologies from different disciplines; (3) facilitating the development of public policies that are investigated from more aspects prior to implementation, thus minimizing unanticipated undesirable effects; and (4) generating a more innovative climate for researchers, clinicians, and policy makers, inspiring the creativity of both individuals and teams (Fuqua et al. 2004). As an example, an in-patient hospital clinical team that consists of psychiatry, neurology, psychology, and social work would bring four different perspectives that, together, can cover the psychobiology, individual pathology and strength/resilience, social circumstances and systemic obstacles, and biology. The multiple ways of understanding substance misuse would be more informative in directing triage and treatment decisions than any one perspective on its own.

Transdisciplinarity and Problematic Substance Use

The phenomenon of problematic substance use is complex and relevant to the domains of the individual (e.g., biological, psychological, or spiritual factors), the interpersonal (e.g., family functioning, peer influence, or working organizations), and the larger societal level (e.g., cultural norms, social policies, or criminal law; Sussman et al. 2004). Given the complexity of this phenomenon and the need for integration of disciplinary knowledge, transdisciplinary collaboration is an important and viable approach to the study of problematic substance use.

Problematic substance use is fraught with controversial conceptions and misconceptions that contribute to stigma and stereotypes associated with both licit and illicit substance use. Movement toward transdisciplinarity can involve a truly collaborative team approach where members share knowledge, skills, and responsibilities across many disciplines (Fuqua et al. 2004); facilitate openness to disciplinary integration as the norm; and recognize the complexity of the issue under study. Thus, such an approach would encourage thoughtful consideration of the many layers of *meanings* in problematic substance use and help unpack preconceived notions and theoretical differences in understanding it. For example, clinicians and researchers need to consider what meanings are ascribed to problematic substance use within their work sphere (e.g., is it construed as a disease? A maladaptive habit? A brain dysfunction?) and how such meanings influence the procedures of research and delivery of clinical services. This approach can be helpful in identifying biases and assumptions at both the level of the individual and the discipline (Benoit et al. 2014, Room 2005).

Three Challenges for Transdisciplinarity

The three challenges of transdisciplinary collaboration that we focus on here are (1) coming to a consensus on common language and defining themes in problematic substance use; (2) achieving a shared understanding of comprehensive models of problematic substance use and how they can be applied in practice; and (3) entrenchment in a single model and subsequent lack of communication between disciplines or sub-disciplines.

Coming to a Consensus on Common Language and Defining Themes

One of the most difficult aspects of transdisciplinary work is creating a productive dialogue among researchers and clinicians who understand the subject in different ways and use different terms to describe it. To extend the previous example, there are multiple descriptors of problematic substance use, including *addiction, substance misuse, substance dependence, chemical dependency*, and so on (Todd et al. 2004). In turn, each of these terms has specific connotations and implications and some of them may carry a moral judgment or be perceived by substance users as such. Further, each discipline tends to focus on one or two themes that they posit as the "main problem" about problematic substance use (Thompson 2012). For example, sociologists may focus on social inequality, discrimination, and stigma as the main determinants of the harms of problematic substance use (Benoit et al. 2014), while physicians may focus on the biological determinants and transmission of diseases (Thompson 2012). While the diversity of definitions and theoretical perspectives draws attention to different aspects and problems, it also makes dialogue between and across disciplines sometimes difficult.

Achieving a Shared Understanding of Comprehensive Models

There is a multitude of causal models of problematic substance use within and across different disciplines. For instance, within clinical psychology there are dozens of variations on the cognitive-behavioral model alone. A transdisciplinary approach encourages a more holistic process of model-building. An example of a comprehensive, transdisciplinary model outside of the problematic substance use field is the General Aggression Model (GAM; DeWall, Anderson, and Bushman 2011). The authors of GAM have integrated a number of evidence-supported theories of interpersonal aggression. As such, the GAM includes components that reflect the findings from the fields of genetics and biological science, sociological and social interactionist theories, and theories of psychological vulnerability and cognitive appraisal. There are many advantages of GAM-like model: (a) it is understandable to many disciplines because it thoughtfully combines information from different fields and uses non-technical language to describe their integration; (b) it paves the way for researchers from different fields to use the same model in their research and thus have some common language; and (c) it encourages an understanding of a construct as a complex, multi-determined phenomenon (Woodin, Sotskova, and O'Leary 2013). Comprehensive models that use non-technical language are also more likely to resonate with and be accessible to policy makers and clinicians, and thus help promote the uptake of research knowledge. While such models are lacking in the problematic substance use literature, there is a plethora of theories and evidence that has the potential to be thoughtfully integrated.

Entrenchment in Single Models and Lack of Communication

This third challenge concerns how researchers and clinicians relate to their own causal models of problematic substance use. Academic researchers are typically trained in specific disciplinary models upon which they build their programs of research. The result is that they may become narrowly focused on one model due to their disciplinary norms. For example, clinical psychology tends to focus on individuals and less so on broader social conditions, while disciplines like sociology and public health are concerned with social conditions and how inequalities are produced and reproduced (Maddi 1998). While it is expected for researchers and clinicians to subscribe to particular theories, the scientific ideal calls us to continue to critically assess and improve such theories (Harris and Lebowitz 1997). In this chapter, we approach entrenchment in disciplinary silos as a potential obstacle to transdisciplinarity because it promotes narrow, dichotomous thinking/attitude that counters collaborative goals.

Meaning Management Theory as a Framework for Transdisciplinary Collaboration on Problematic Substance Use

We propose that aspects of Meaning Management Theory (Wong 2010) may be helpful in beginning to address the three challenges to transdisciplinary collaborations described above. MMT is a result of a synthesis between an existentialism-based psychotherapy (called "logotherapy") developed by Viktor Frankl (1963) and cognitive-behavioral theories of human motivation, information processing, and behavior (Wong 2010). We focus on the "existential givens" aspect of MMT here. Existential givens are dialectically positioned conditions of human existence; they are posited on a spectrum such as the continuum between freedom and determinedness. The basis for our approach is to examine how each research discipline responds to and constructs meaning and knowledge related to existential givens that are particularly salient to substance use and its intersections with gender, trauma, and mental health.

With respect to phenomena like problematic substance use, the manner in which humans construct meaning of substance use will be different, but nevertheless patterned (Thompson 2012). For example, when considering how researchers construct hierarchical meanings systems of substance use, they may organize their models around the existential given of freedom vs. determinedness, a dichotomy that prompts questions such as "How much control do individuals have over their substance use?" Researchers in different disciplines tend to argue for completely different interpretations of this existential given. Biological researchers may argue that once a pattern of chemical dependence is established in people's brains, they will lose all control over their behaviors (Caplan 2008). A researcher coming from an existential tradition is likely to disagree and contend that even if a person appears or perceives to have no control over his or her substance use, he or she still retains the capacity to exert some control over behavior and makes choices, even though some choices may be very difficult to make (Schaler 2000). Other disciplines, such as nursing and sociology, tend to take a more structural perspective and focus on the broader contextual factors that shape substance use and choices over the life course that are often beyond individual control (Benoit, McCarthy, and Jansson in press).

MMT holds that all phenomena are multidimensional and need to be approached as such. That is, researchers and clinicians should strive to understand how various aspects of behavior or experience interact (Wong 2010). MMT suggests that when approaching the study of any phenomenon, whether one is working with a client in individual therapy or pursuing a research agenda in understanding the causes of problematic substance, the most effective approach involves the integration of information across different theories and disciplines, together with a general attitude of openness to new ideas and both confirmatory *and* disconfirmatory evidence of one's hypotheses (Wong 2010). Thus, the MMT approach aligns well with the transdisciplinary approach to the study of problematic substance, as it assumes a collaborative team of researchers from different disciplines collectively pondering upon shared concepts, appropriate methods, and common research strategies. Furthermore, MMT involves special attention to psychological processes involved in constructing meaning (Wong 2008). For example, MMT examines the role of cognitive processes of attribution (Wong and Weiner 1981) and executive decision-making (Maddi 1998). Based on research on these processes, MMT can provide fertile ground for applied methods and strategies that can foster transdisciplinary collaboration. Further, MMT operates on a dialectic principle: the idea that truth and knowledge are relative states and, as such, contradictory phenomena may co-exist and contradictory statements may each have validity to them (Wong 2010). With the previous example of contradictory stances on personal control in individuals with problematic substance use, MMT might posit that it is possible that the perspective on both sides of the dichotomy (no control vs. control) can be true simultaneously. This observation can be very helpful in transdisciplinary discussions and meetings.

Addressing the Three Challenges by Considering Existential Givens

We suggest that researchers consider focusing on existential givens to address the three challenges of transdisciplinarity touched upon above. The suggested strategies below can be applied to as many *levels of meaning* as possible: personal/individual meaning; small-group or team meaning; organizational meaning (e.g., workplace); system meaning (e.g., academia); disciplinary meaning (e.g., psychiatry); and, of course, transdisciplinary meaning (among and between disciplines, groups, and communities). Thus, the way one may apply the suggestions below will differ based on what level of meaning, or what level(s) are being targeted.

To address the three challenges, we suggest using MMT to focus on the existential givens as a way to provide some commonality in language and facilitate transdisciplinary dialogue. The applicable methods include group discussion, personal reflection, modeling in a team setting, and explicit goal setting in a transdisciplinary research or clinical team. We will focus on existential givens that have been previously documented in the research literature on problematic substance use and its intersections, including meaning vs. meaninglessness, freedom vs. determinedness, motivation vs. apathy, and authenticity vs. conformity (Alexander 2000, Chen 2010, DeMarinis, Scheffel-Birath, and Hansagi 2009, Haines 1997, Harlow et al. 1999, Noblejas de la Flor 1997, Paul and Lucas 2005, Ronel 1997, Thompson 2012, To et al. 2007, Wiklund 2008a, 2008b, Williams 2004). However, this is not an exhaustive list, and there are other existential givens that researchers and clinicians are likely to find relevant and helpful to consider/discuss.

We propose that researchers and clinicians using our approach cultivate a more *descriptive* focus on the existential givens. That is, we suggest that existential givens be viewed as core dialectical *themes* that emerge in the various aspects of substance use. For instance, rather than debating which discipline may have the most accurate response to the theme of freedom vs. determinedness (which inevitably poses the question, "Do people who engage in problematic substance use have control over their behavior?"), we invite researchers to temporarily detach themselves from the goal of answering this question and rather focus on *how* they would like to approach answering this question. A clinical team might consider the culture of their work setting: How does the culture in general relate to clients with problematic substance use? For instance, does the culture assume autonomy and protect integrity/personal choice? Or assume autonomy and apportion blame? Should the assumptions of the culture be reconsidered?

Also, a focus on descriptive themes of existential givens can provide a *non-argumentative space* for multidisciplinary teams to engage in a new type of dialogue about problematic substance use and its intersections. If debates between and within disciplines do emerge (as is likely to happen), a descriptive focus on existential givens can shape such a discussion into a constructive process that results in mutual learning rather than a defensive process that results in mutual stereotyping. Essentially, we encourage researchers to apply the MMT principles to engage in meta-reflection of their methods and models. In clinical work, this type of reflection is utilized to avoid polarized thinking, e.g., of substance users as completely autonomous and "just resistant" or completely helpless. It can also be applied to increasing awareness of 'black and white' thinking and growing self-reflection of one's own motivations in non-clinical situations, such as the inter-professional realm. It is important to note that we do not necessarily seek to promote consensus among disciplines, as disagreement during discussion can bring forth important issues that were previously not considered. The rich theoretical and methodological diversity in the field of problematic substance use studies can be used to advantage. Instead, we hope that our suggested framework can unite transdisciplinary conversations around common existential themes and decrease communication barriers.

Freedom vs. Determinedness

It is difficult to deny that this dialectic is relevant to problematic substance use and its intersections. The types of questions it elicits include: What is the extent of autonomy exercised by individuals who engage in problematic substance use? Are their actions determined by genetic factors, a spiritual vacuum, learning principles, traumatic experiences, or environmental conditions? See Figure 13.1 for examples of possible responses to this existential given, as well as a potential situation to which the dialectic of freedom vs. determinedness is relevant. A transdisciplinary question relevant to many disciplines that study the intersection of sex, gender, and substance use may be, "If men, compared with women, receive greater positive social support for seeing themselves as autonomous, how do men's and women's perceptions of autonomy relate to their patterns of use (relevant to disciplines such as sociology, psychology, public health)? Can differences in perceptions be detected at the neural systems level (neuroscience, medical science)? Are there implications for one's social economic position and risks of harm? (nursing, public health, sociology)." In this context, it is important to pay attention to how evidence from a divergent view be understood (e.g., making sense of evidence of spontaneous recovery from substance use and evidence of neural correlates of compulsive behavioral activity (Buchman and Russell 2009).

Meaningfulness vs. Meaninglessness

MMT conceptualizes humans in general as striving to create meaning and make sense of their environment and personal experiences (Wong 2010). Finding meaning in one's life has been connected to general mental health and well-being

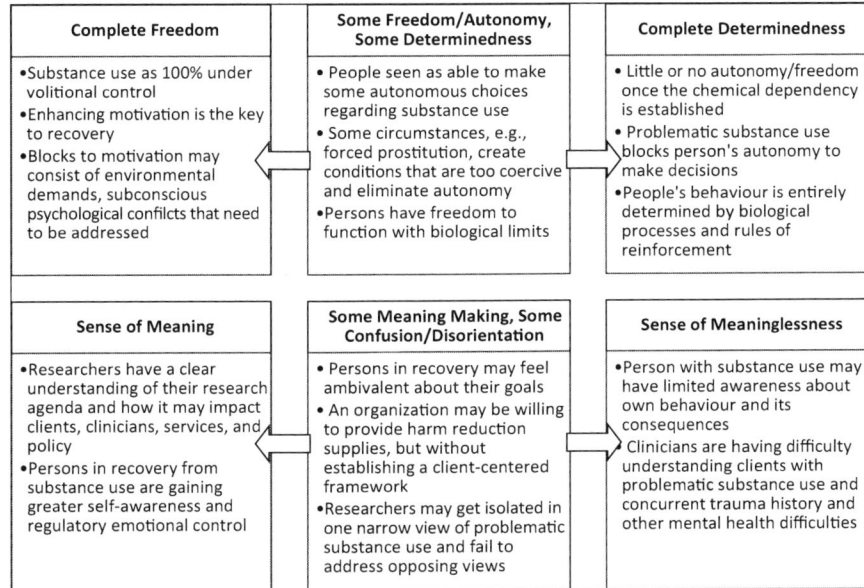

FIGURE 13.1 Continuum of Existential Givens: Examples of Beliefs Related to Freedom vs. Determinedness and Meaning vs. Meaninglessness

(Steger and Kashdan 2013) and to a decreased likelihood of problematic substance use (Konkolÿ Thege, Urbán, and Kopp 2013, Marsh et al. 2003, Rahman 2001). On the other hand, individuals who engage in problematic substance use, particularly towards the heavy use end of the spectrum, often report that such use tends to erode other sources of pleasure, coping, and meaning; substance use becomes the activity that seems most meaningful (e.g., Williams 2004). Illustrated in Figure 13.1 are some scenarios and beliefs that are relevant to this existential given. These can constitute important foci for further exploration within a team, organization, or research discipline.

A transdisciplinary discussion might focus on how one's research paradigm or theoretical orientation construes substance use and problematic substance use. A focus on *meaning construction* can invite individuals and teams to reflect on what significance their research participants create with respect to their substance use, research programs, or clinical services that are offered to them. For example, persons with concurrent history of trauma often report that their traumatic experiences seem meaningless, and the sense of meaninglessness elicits anxiety (Najavits et al. 2004). Substance use can relieve their anxiety in the short term. A transdisciplinary discussion point here is, How do various disciplines construe meaning vs. meaninglessness in the treatment of trauma and substance use? How does sex/gender influence these conceptualizations? How might men experience and relate to such anxiety, and are men more likely to be overwhelmed by a flooding of anxiety, as some authors have theorized (Gottman 1994)?

Here is an example about how some of these considerations have been helpful to the authors. One of the authors had the opportunity to work together with an organization that provides services for substance misuse recovery with the goal of conducting a study of that organization and providing training to individuals who facilitate group meetings. The organization consisted of trained and untrained volunteers and staff, as well as representatives from community mental health, persons in recovery from substance misuse, and professionals that study and work with the issue of problematic substance use, such as social work. There were disagreements among different levels of staff as to what the research study implied about the organization, staff, and volunteers. To help consider and process some of the members' apprehension about training and organizational changes, the researchers facilitated continuous meetings with various levels of members present to ensure that an open and validating forum was available for their concerns. A particular goal for the researchers was to understand how individuals and subgroups within the peer support organization constructed meaning of the organizational changes that were upcoming, the purpose of the research study, and the possible beneficial or harmful consequences of the study. The researchers focused on understanding the goals of all organization members and strove to facilitate discussions that can help to align goals within the staff team and so that the team could construct a more unified set of meanings about the on-going changes, while also conducting the research study in a way that provides benefit for the organization, not just for the researchers. In such discussions, the researchers also applied a trauma-informed framework to make sure a safe atmosphere was created during the discussions, so as to minimize tense interactions that can be particularly challenging for individuals with concurrent substance use and trauma history. The discussions continually touched on subjects relevant to existential givens, such as concepts of freedom and autonomy for particular staff vs. experiencing pressure (determinedness) from an organization. While there were challenges during this process, the training and study completed successfully and, in fact, the organization requested the process to be done again with a new group of staff one year later, suggesting that they also felt they benefitted from the process. We believe that an approach that emphasized listening to different disciplines, different community representatives, and creating a safe environment were key to this success.

Authenticity vs. Conformity

Authenticity can be defined as being aware of and able to behave in accordance with one's values, goals, and actions, with minimal distorting of the latter (e.g., Gillath et al. 2010). MMT proposes that when values and actions are mismatched, people will experience distress; but if individuals do not compromise their own goals and always go against social expectations, the outcome is social alienation (Wong 2008).

The authenticity vs. conformity dichotomy is concerned with questions such as: What capacity do individuals with problematic substance use have to pursue intrinsic goals? To what extent is their motivation for substance use determined by the desire for conformity and belonging? What is the meaning of authenticity to individuals with problematic substance use and how do they imagine moving towards authenticity? Do they perceive treatment and research as supporting or undermining authenticity? Different research disciplines may be working on different parts of the answers to the questions. For example, women in Alcoholics Anonymous sometimes report that the first step, surrendering to a Higher Power (often referred to as a male Christian deity), does not fit with their own values and recovery goals (Bogart and Pearce 2003, Covington 1994). In some studies, women have reported that they feel the pressure to conform to what they perceive as a patriarchal belief system and do not see opportunity for an authentic expression and, consequently, feel less satisfied with the group experience and report poorer mental health (Bogart and Pearce 2003). For researchers who study peer support groups for problematic substance use, one important consideration to discuss is: How can peer support programs offer an environment that matches women's needs and beliefs, and encourages authentic expression, while supporting their goals of recovery and mental wellness?

A transdisciplinary approach might seek to involve multiple disciplines in understanding what other factors are related to women's sense of authenticity in peer support settings. For example, a social science researcher may examine how social determinants of health, including access to health care, may predict women's capacity for experiencing a match between their own beliefs and the AA philosophy. On the other hand, researchers from any number of disciplines that may utilize a feminist framework would examine how the systems of patriarchy and organized religion influence the structure and process of AA, as well as the experience of the women who attend it (Covington 1994). Even further, researchers in neuroscience may focus on the neural correlates of the rewards associated with groups belonging vs. isolation. By discussing different aspects of the issue, scientific study may move towards a more nuanced understanding of women's experience in AA in general.

Motivation vs. Apathy

An important transdisciplinary discussion might focus on what factors contribute to decisions to engage in problematic substance use. A transdisciplinary approach might highlight more than one factor to be the key cause or motivation, and a discussion that elicits a variety of disciplinary perspectives can contribute to building a more comprehensive model of motivation in problematic substance use. For instance, corporate media often casts the motivation of pregnant women who use substances in a stigmatizing and negative light, assuming that their motivations are to cause harm to their fetus (Lester, Andreozzi, and Appiah 2004). However, research reveals a more complex picture and a variety of influences and motivational factors. Psychological factors might include lack of self-efficacy (DeMarinis, Scheffel-Birath, and Hansagi 2009); sociological factors may include lack of access to supportive social organizations (Benoit, McCarthy, and Jansson in press) and vulnerability to partner violence and controlling influences (Astley, Bailey, Talbot, and Clarren 2000); neuropsychological factors might include a dysregulation of the dopamine system (Caplan 2008). Considering these factors simultaneously in the service of model building would be one example of transdisciplinary collaboration on this existential given, addressing challenges #2 and #3. An improved model of motivation may also help reduce stigmatizing stereotypes that clinicians or researchers may hold subconsciously, due to a lack of understanding of the many complex facets related to psychological motivation, role of stressors, opportunities, and influences related to engagement in substance use. Finally, acknowledging motivation as an important theme in problematic substance use can also help to remind researchers and clinicians to practice awareness and reflexivity of their own motivation to pursue a particular line of research, hypothesis, or direction in therapy.

In summary, focusing a transdisciplinary discussion on existential givens provides a space for cross disciplinary dialogue that prompts clinicians and researchers to discuss issues relevant to problematic substance use, thus addressing the three challenges. By paying special attention to how gender, sex, trauma, and mental health difficulties can change one's perspective on an existential given, researchers as well as clinicians can also move towards greater complexity and comprehensiveness of their models, as well as more informed discussions about the role of sex and gender in problematic substance use.

Distilling Core MMT-based Strategies as Building Blocks in a Transdisciplinary Bridge

In this final section we distill additional MMT-based strategies and suggestions with greater specificity. We believe they will be useful to researchers, clinicians, and others (e.g., community service organizations) wishing to undertake transdisciplinary work. The following list is not exhaustive but rather illustrative of strategies that can be derived from MMT. These strategies can be applied at different levels of meaning and can be used in group, individual, and educational formats to promote discussion, self-reflection, effective communication, and learning among disciplines. We encourage readers to think about applying them to multiple meaning levels: a personal meaning level, a dyadic interpersonal meaning level. or macro-interpersonal level.

- From the planning stages of the research study/program evaluation to the dissemination of results, continue to engage with the following questions: What existential givens are relevant to this project? How can reflexivity be encouraged for all members of the research project? The attitude of reflexivity must stem from the team and/or principal investigators in order to be experienced by others as authentic.
- Once relevant existential given(s) are identified (e.g., autonomy vs. determinism), continue to engage with the following questions: Where are the conceptual gaps between my theory and other theories on the team? What angle or

disconfirming evidence that we may be ignoring? For example, in a team setting, an exercise based on these questions may encourage team members to answer these questions on paper and then share what they noticed with the team. This type of process can help facilitate learning about perspectives from other disciplines in a way that reduces individual, discipline-specific biases.
- When engaging in transdisciplinary collaboration, it may be particularly helpful to adopt an exploratory attitude and to temporarily bracket the model(s) of problematic substance use that one typically relies on. An attitude of *scientific curiosity* specifically about evidence and perspectives that are *different* from one's own may be helpful. For instance, in a mentoring relationship, the mentor can continuously engage the mentee in reflecting on his/her own challenges with bracketing and openly listening to other models.
- *Reflexivity* refers to cultivating awareness of one's assumptions and relationships of power in the research process. Useful reflection points in a research team or with students and clients include: Am I or someone else in the dialogue engaging in black-and-white thinking or cognitive distortions? Is there a power struggle developing within the discussion? How can we step out of this struggle? In such cases, consultation with individuals who *do not* share one's theoretical orientation is often most helpful because they are less likely to simply confirm one's point of view and more likely to offer a fresh perspective. Even if not all agree on new ideas/perspectives, just the process of considering them may create pathways to more open learning and discussion.

Conclusion

Meaning Management Theory (Wong 2010) provides a useful framework for how one might approach transdisciplinary research, clinical work, or community work in the field of problematic substance use. MMT emphasizes the process of meaning construction (Thompson 2012, Wong 2008), which can be a helpful vehicle for cultivating thoughtful engagement with researchers who are outside one's discipline or who hold different views of problematic substance use and its intersections with gender, trauma, and mental health. MMT also outlines the dual dialectical principle (Wong 2010), which illustrates that contradictory theories or research results can actually reflect how contradictory states exist in reality. A stance that acknowledges this can be helpful to individuals and teams from academic disciplines, clinical practices, and community organizations when engaging in transdisciplinary work to enhance the understanding of their own research and practice goals, assumptions that underlie these goals, blind spots, and areas for improvement in program evaluation questions.

Furthermore, MMT invites researchers to consider existential givens and descriptive dialectical themes that researchers inevitably encounter in their work with problematic substance use. The invitation is to consider these themes descriptively, not causally, and to engage groups of individuals from different disciplines in an authentic conversation that can help identify how researchers perceive these givens and how their work may attempt to answer the typical questions posed by them. This type of discussion can be helpful to transdisciplinary collaboration by fostering an atmosphere that supports a diversity of opinions and respectful communication about differences of opinions and theoretical orientations, and promotes correction of assumptions of each other's work. The suggested strategies outlined in this chapter begin at the level of the individual, but they can also be adopted by teams either by implicit modeling and open consideration of contradictory information and/or by explicit discussion/norm setting that encourages persons within a team or system to consider how perspectives from diverging disciplines can actually be helpful to one another, despite theoretical and methodological differences. Furthermore, reflections and strategies outlined in this chapter can be used pedagogically, for educating new generations of researchers and clinicians in the application of transdisciplinarity.

Discussion Questions

1. What aspects of the concept of "existential givens" are most accessible to your team/discipline/work setting? What factors contribute to this accessibility?
2. What aspects of the concept of "existential givens" are least accessible/least applicable to your team/discipline/work setting? What may be some challenges or blocks to this accessibility?
3. When considering other professions or disciplines, is there a profession or discipline whose view on problematic substance use you understand the least?

References

Alexander, Bruce K. 2000. "The globalization of addiction." *Addiction Research & Theory* no. 8 (6):501–526. doi: 10.3109/16066350008998987.

Astley, Susan J., Diane Bailey, Christina Talbot, and Sterling K. Clarren. 2000. "Fetal Alcohol Syndrome (FAS) Primary Prevention through FASD Diagnosis II: A comprehensive profile of 80 birth mothers of children with FAS." *Alcohol and Alcoholism* no. 35 (5):509–519.

Benoit, Cecilia, Bill McCarthy, and Mikael Jansson. in press. "Stigma, service work, and substance use: A two-city, two-country comparative analysis." *Sociology of Health & Illness*.

Benoit, Cecilia, Camille Stengel, Lenora Marcellus, Helga Hallgrimsdottir, John Anderson, Karen MacKinnon, Rachel Phillips, Pilar Zazueta, and Sinead Charbonneau. 2014. "Providers' constructions of pregnant and early parenting women who use substances." *Sociology of Health & Illness* no. 36 (2):252–263. doi: 10.1111/1467-9566.12106.

Bogart, Cathy J., and Carol E. Pearce. 2003. "'13th-stepping': Why Alcoholics Anonymous is not always a safe place for women." *Journal of Addictions Nursing* no. 14 (1):43–47. doi: 10.1080/10884600305373.

Boyd, Susan C. 2004. *From witches to crack moms: Women, drug law, and policy*. Durham: Carolina Academic Press.

Buchman, Daniel Z., and Barbara J. Russell. 2009. "Addictions, autonomy and so much more: A reply to Caplan." *Addiction* no. 104 (6):1053–1054. doi: 10.1111/j.1360-0443.2009.02569.x.

Bungay, Vicky, Joy L. Jonson, Colleen Varcoe, and Susan Boyd. 2010. "Women's health and use of crack cocaine in context: Structural and 'everyday' violence." *International Journal of Drug Policy* no. 21:321–329.

Caplan, Arthur. 2008. "Denying autonomy in order to create it: the paradox of forcing treatment upon addicts." *Addiction* no. 103 (12):1919–1921. doi: 10.1111/j.1360-0443.2008.02369.x.

Chasnoff, Ira J, Harvey J. Landress, and Mark E. Barrett. 1990. "The prevalence of illicit-drug or alcohol use during pregnancy and discrepancies in mandatory reporting in Pinellas County, Florida." *The New England Journal of Medicine* no. 322 (17):1202–1206. doi: 10.1056/NEJM199004263221706.

Chen, Gila. 2010. "The meaning of suffering in drug addiction and recovery from the perspective of existentialism, Buddhism and the 12-step program." *Journal of Psychoactive Drugs* no. 42 (3):363–375. doi: 10.1080/02791072.2010.10400699.

Covington, Stephanie S. 1994. *A woman's way through the twelve steps*. Centre City, MN: Hazelden Educational Materials.

Davison, Carolyn, and Michel Perron. 2013. *First do no harm: Responding to Canada's prescription drug crisis*. Ottawa: Canadian Centre on Substance Abuse.

DeMarinis, Valerie, Christina Scheffel-Birath, and Helen Hansagi. 2009. "Cultural analysis as a perspective for gender-informed alcohol treatment research in a Swedish context." *Alcohol and Alcoholism* no. 44 (6):615–619. doi: 10.1093/alcalc/agn092.

DeWall, C. Nathan, Craig A. Anderson, and Brad J. Bushman. 2011. "The general aggression model." *Psychology of Violence* no. 1 (3):245–258. doi: 10.1037/a0023842.

Frankl, Viktor E. 1963. *Man's search for meaning. An introduction to logotherapy*. New York: Washington Square Press.

Fuqua, Juliana, Daniel Stokols, Jennifer Gress, Kimari Phillips, and Richard Harvey. 2004. "Transdisciplinary collaboration as a basis for enhancing the science and prevention of substance use and 'abuse'." *Substance Use & Misuse* no. 39 (10–12):1457–1514. doi: 10.1081/JA-200033200.

Gillath, Omri, Amanda K. Sesko, Phillip R. Shaver, and David S. Chun. 2010. "Attachment, authenticity, and honesty: Dispositional and experimentally induced security can reduce self- and other-deception." *Journal of Personality and Social Psychology* no. 98 (5):841–855. doi: 10.1037/a0019206.

Gottman, John M. 1994. "An agenda for marital therapy." In *The heart of the matter: Perspectives on emotion in marital therapy*, edited by S. M. Johnson and L. S. Greenberg, 256–293. New York: Brunner/Mazel.

Haines, Patricia E. 1997. "Addiction recovery: Transcending the existential root of relapse." *International Forum for Logotherapy* no. 20 (1):37–45.

Harlow, Lisa L., Kimberly J. Mitchell, Sherri N. Fitts, and Susan E. Saxon. 1999. "Psycho-existential distress and problem behaviors: Gender, subsample, and longitudinal tests." *Journal of Applied Biobehavioral Research* no. 4 (2):111–138. doi: 10.1111/j.1751-9861.1999.tb00059.x.

Harris, Herbert W., and Barry D. Lebowitz. 1997. "Clinically oriented basic science: Emerging opportunities for research in late-life mental disorders." *The American Journal of Geriatric Psychiatry* no. 5 (4):284–286.

Kirst, Maritt, Jason Altenberg, and Raffi Balian. 2011. "In search of empowering health research for marginalized populations in urban settings: The value of a transdisciplinary approach." In *Converging disciplines*, edited by Maritt Kirst, Nicole Schaefer-McDaniel, Stephen Hwang, and Patricia O'Campo, 23–37. New York: Springer.

Konkolÿ Thege, Barna, Róbert Urbán, and Mária S. Kopp. 2013. "Four-year prospective evaluation of the relationship between meaning in life and smoking status." *Substance Abuse Treatment, Prevention, and Policy* no. 8 (1):8. doi: 10.1186/1747-597X-8-8.

Krimsky, Sheldon. 2000. "Transdisciplinarity for problems at the interstices of disciplines." In *Transdisciplinarity: reCreating Integrated Knowledge*, edited by Margaret A. Somerville and David J. Rapport, 109–114. Paris: EOLSS.

Lester, Barry, Lynne Andreozzi, and Lindsey Appiah. 2004. "Substance use during pregnancy: Time for policy to catch up with research." *Harm Reduction Journal* no. 1 (1). doi: 10.1186/1477-7517-1-5.

Lloyd, Charlie. 2010. *Sinning and sinned against: The stigmatization of problem drug users*. London: The UK Drug Policy Commission.

Loppie Reading, Charlotte, and Fred Wein. 2009. *Health inequities and social determinants of aboriginal peoples' health*. Prince George, BC: National Collaborating Centre for Aboriginal Health.

Maddi, Salvatore R. 1998. "Creating meaning through making decisions." In *The human quest for meaning: A handbook of psychological research and clinical applications*, edited by Paul T. P. Wong and Prem S. Fry, 3–26. Mahwah, NJ: Lawrence Erlbaum.

Marsh, Ali, Leigh Smith, Jan Piek, and Bill Saunders. 2003. "The Purpose in Life Scale: Psychometric properties for social drinkers and drinkers in alcohol treatment." *Educational and Psychological Measurement* no. 63 (5):859–871. doi: 10.1177/0013164403251040.

Najavits, Lisa M., Johanna Sonn, Marybeth Walsh, and Roger D. Weiss. 2004. "Domestic violence in women with PTSD and substance abuse." *Addictive Behaviors* no. 29 (4):707–715. doi: 10.1016/j.addbeh.2004.01.003.

Noblejas de la Flor, M. Angeles. 1997. "Meaning levels and drug-abuse therapy: An empirical study." *International Forum for Logotherapy* no. 20 (1):46–51.

Paul, Natalie C., and Marijo N. Lucas. 2005. "Reconceptualizing treatment for tobacco abuse: Exploring subjectivity and intentionality." *The Humanistic Psychologist* no. 33 (1):45–57. doi: 10.1207/s15473333thp3301_5.

Pauly, Bernadette. 2008. "Shifting moral values to enhance access to health care: Harm reduction as a context for ethical nursing practice." *International Journal on Drug Policy* no. 19 (3):195–204. doi: 10.1016/j.drugpo.2008.02.009.

Rahman, Tania. 2001. "Mental health and purpose in life of drug addicts in Bangladesh." *International Forum for Logotherapy* no. 24 (2):83–87.

Ronel, Natti. 1997. "The universality of a self-help program of American origin: Narcotics Anonymous in Israel." *Social Work in Health Care* no. 25 (3):87–101. doi: 10.1300/J010v25n03_08.

Room, Robin. 2005. "Stigma, social inequality and alcohol and drug use." *Drug and Alcohol Review* no. 24 (2):143–155. doi: 10.1080/09595230500102434.

Schaler, Jeffrey A. 2000. *Addiction is a choice*. Chicago: Open Court.

Steger, Michael F., and Todd B. Kashdan. 2013. "The unbearable lightness of meaning: Well-being and unstable meaning in life." *The Journal of Positive Psychology* no. 8 (2):103–115. doi: 10.1080/17439760.2013.771208.

Sussman, Steve, Alan W. Stacy, C. Anderson Johnson, Mary Ann Pentz, and Elizabeth Robertson. 2004. "A transdisciplinary focus on drug abuse prevention: An introduction." *Substance Use & Misuse* no. 39 (10–12):1441–1456. doi: 10.1081/JA-200033194.

Tang, Sannie Y., and Annette J. Browne. 2008. "'Race' matters: Racialization and egalitarian discourses involving aboriginal people in the Canadian health care context." *Ethnicity & Health* no. 13 (2):109–127. doi: 10.1080/13557850701830307.

Thompson, Geoff. 2012. "A meaning-centered therapy for addictions." *International Journal of Mental Health and Addiction* no. 10 (3):428–440. doi: 10.1007/s11469-011-9367-9.

To, Siu-ming, Steven Sek-yum Ngai, Ngan-pun Ngai, and Chau-kiu Cheung. 2007. "Young people's existential concerns and club drug abuse." *International Journal of Adolescence and Youth* no. 13 (4):327–341. doi: 10.1080/02673843.2007.9747983.

Todd, Jennie, Gill Green, Martin Harrison, Benson AdebowaleIkuesan, Catherine Self, Alex Baldacchino, and Sarah Sherwood. 2004. "Defining dual diagnosis of mental illness and substance misuse: Some methodological issues." *Journal of Psychiatric and Mental Health Nursing* no. 11 (1):48–54. doi: 10.1111/j.1365-2850.2004.00683.x.

Wiklund, Lena. 2008a. "Existential aspects of living with addiction—Part I: meeting challenges." *Journal of Clinical Nursing* no. 17 (18):2426–2434. doi: 10.1111/j.1365-2702.2008.02356.x.

Wiklund, Lena. 2008b. "Existential aspects of living with addiction—Part II: Caring needs. A hermeneutic expansion of qualitative findings." *Journal of Clinical Nursing* no. 17 (18):2435–2443. doi: 10.1111/j.1365-2702.2008.02357.x.

Williams, Beverly Rosa. 2004. "Dying young, dying poor: A sociological examination of existential suffering among low-socioeconomic status patients." *Journal of Palliative Medicine* no. 7 (1):27–37. doi: 10.1089/109662104322737223.

Wong, Paul T. P. 2008. "Meaning management theory and death acceptance." In *Existential & spiritual issues in death attitudes*, edited by A. Tomer, E. Grafton and P.T.P. Wong, 65–88. Mahwah, NJ: Lawrence Erlbaum.

Wong, Paul T. P. 2010. "Meaning therapy: An integrative and positive existential psychotherapy." *Journal of Contemporary Psychotherapy* no. 40 (2):85–93. doi: 10.1007/s10879-009-9132-6.

Wong, Paul T. P., and Bernard Weiner. 1981. "When people ask 'why' questions, and the heuristics of attributional search." *Journal of Personality and Social Psychology* no. 40 (4):650–663. doi: 10.1037/0022-3514.40.4.650.

Woodin, Erika M., Alina Sotskova, and K. Daniel O'Leary. 2013. "Intimate partner violence assessment in a historical context: Divergent approaches and opportunities for progress." *Sex Roles* no. 69 (3–4):120–130. doi: 10.1007/s11199-013-0294-z.

World Health Organization. 2004. *Global status report on alcohol* 2004 [cited March 21, 2014. Available from www.who.int/substance_abuse/publications/globalstatusreport alcohol2004_introduction.pdf.

Suggestions for Further Reading

The human quest for meaning. A handbook of psychological research and clinical applications, edited by Paul T. P. Wong and Prem S. Fry. 2010. Mahwah, NJ: Lawrence Erlbaum.

Schneider, Kirk J. 2008. *Existential-integrative psychotherapy: Guideposts to the core of practice*. New York, NY: Routledge/Taylor & Francis Group.

Wong, Paul T. P. 2010. "Meaning therapy: An integrative and positive existential psychotherapy." *Journal of Contemporary Psychotherapy* no. 40 (2):85–93. doi: 10.1007/s10879-009-9132-6.

14
THE CHALLENGE OF TRANS-SECTORAL POLICY IN PREGNANCY AND ADDICTION

Lorraine Greaves

The complexity of addiction issues often confronts society with difficult choices and challenges. In keeping with the multiple perspectives on addiction, we respond to issues of addiction with a range of instruments and services: social policy, law, regulatory schemes, criminal justice decisions, social services, treatment and health care, among others. Similar to quests to improve programming, research and practice, it is just as important to ask how policy making could adopt features of transdisciplinarity.

Policy making is a political process, dependent upon both formal and informal political attitudes and contexts, as well as the gender politics among those designing policy (Schofield and Goodwin 2005). Ultimately, our political systems determine the policy context through setting priorities and direction, and then set policy resulting from the work of both bureaucrats and politicians. Sometimes, but not always, the public or key experts are involved in these processes. Policies get created at many levels: international, national, provincial/state and local. They also govern activities in institutions (hospitals, school, prisons) and organizations (social services, child welfare agencies, treatment centers). Sometime, one level supersedes another (such as being a signatory to an international treaty, which will affect national policy options, or provincial/state laws that regulate activity). In turn, policy affects programming, by assigning priorities, setting funding guidelines, or endorsing, limiting or prohibiting particular approaches to an issue.

While bureaucrats may research, draft, consult on and design policy, politicians are responsible for initiating and enacting it (or not). In this context, both ideology and evidence mix together, and, in the case of addiction and its effects, moral judgments can also come into play. Some in the addictions field maintain that evidence is less often the basis for policy than it ought to be (Miller and Carroll 2006), and that historically, much addiction policy (e.g., alcohol prohibition, safe injection sites, syringe exchange, harm reduction) becomes the site of ideological, rather than evidence-based debate.

Even in this complicated environment, there are options for making policy more equitable, gender sensitive and integrated in ways that could assist in creating better responses to addiction issues. Specifically, this chapter asks: Can policies responding to addiction be designed to reflect merged multiple viewpoints, a common understanding and language and an integrated, gendered and equitable response? Can even the most demanding and conflict ridden issues in addiction, such as substance use during pregnancy, one of the most highly contested areas in addiction and social and political debate, receive more progressive and enhanced responses by taking elements of transdisciplinarity into the policy-making process?

This chapter addresses these difficult and challenging questions by delving into the issues of tobacco use and alcohol use during pregnancy as two case examples. Substance use by women during pregnancy is a key issue of concern among governments, women's health providers as well as wider society, evoking strong reactions among many sectors. Historically, societal responses have typically focused on fetal health and child welfare, as opposed to women's health. Indeed, substance use during pregnancy has often garnered much more concern than the use of substances by women at any other life stage. In addition, substance use during pregnancy (and indeed by mothers of young children) has evoked much blame and shame, and ultimately punitive responses over the years (Schroedel and Fiber 2001). Not surprisingly, substance use during pregnancy has been a tricky area for policy and program development.

Much of the policy and program response to date has been tainted by stigma, prejudice and fetus-centricity (a central or sole focus on fetal health and welfare). The undertone of these responses has been the primary perception of women's value as a reproductive vessel, which has, not surprisingly, often been critiqued as sexist (Jacobson 1981, 1986; Greaves 1996; Oaks 2001). Public opinion and the voices of media have often supported these perspectives. The challenge of developing policy and program responses that are more humane, women-centered and effective is explored here. It is suggested that integrating transdisciplinarity, gender and equity concerns and an organized intersectoral response to women who use substances during pregnancy are options for improving policy in this area.

Within the women's substance use field, there has arguably been no subject more studied than substance use during pregnancy. The high intensity focus on pregnant women who use alcohol, drugs or tobacco during pregnancy illustrates a conflux of sexism, objectification, stigma and social control (Greaves 1996; Jacobson 1981, 1986; Oaks 2001; Greaves and Poole 2004; Boyd 1999, 2004; Campbell 2000a, 2000b). Likewise, responding to the issues raised by pregnant women who use substances, and particularly those who may be unable to stop because of addiction, serves to illustrate some of the challenges to policy and programming in this field. In some jurisdictions, the vilification of women who use drugs or alcohol during pregnancy extends to criminal proceedings, imprisonment and ultimately apprehension of infants and children (Paltrow and Flavin 2013). Indeed, this response is one that configures consumption of drugs, tobacco or alcohol during pregnancy variously as child abuse, endangering the life of a fetus or similar crimes. These attempts to criminalize reflect a legal model of addiction that has been variously used to try to apply mandatory treatment to women, involuntarily commit or incarcerate women, apprehend infants and other children in the woman's care, and lay criminal charges of various kinds (Lester, Andreozzi, and Appiah 2004; Schroedel and Fiber 2001; Mohapatra 2011; Fentiman 2008b).

For those who consider addiction during pregnancy a health issue, there is a legitimate focus on fetal health, the effects of drugs, alcohol and tobacco use on fetal development and residual negative effects affecting children as they grow or, in some cases, for life. Unfortunately, this concern has often been either limited to the fetus, or primarily focused on the fetus, rendering it fetus-centric. This perspective inevitably renders the pregnant woman lesser. There has been a long tradition of fetus-centricity in tobacco control (Greaves and Barr 2000; Jacobson 1986; Oaks 2000) and in drug and alcohol use and FASD prevention efforts (Marcellus 2003; Fentiman 2008a). This approach, while seeing addiction and its consequences on the fetus or child as a key health issue, has often overlooked women's health. This, too, reflects a sexist approach where women's health is somehow less relevant and important than fetal health. It is also ironic in that this approach fails to realize that women's health is key to fetal health, and ignoring women or simply excoriating women is counter productive.

But modern-day moralistic overtones seep in to create considerable blaming and shaming of pregnant women who use drugs or alcohol or tobacco (Rutman et al. 2000), that are often mixed in with legalistic responses or even health responses. This moralism conveys attitudes that many pregnant women want to avoid, and can create situations where pregnant women with addiction issues who want treatment are afraid to seek it (Mohapatra 2011; Roberts and Pies 2011), or, if they do, mask the details of their substance use. This approach also masks the effects of social structural factors that affect women's use of substances during pregnancy as well, obfuscating the victimizing effects of abuse, poverty and early trauma on women's behavior. Hence, it seems that pregnant women with addiction issues, particularly ingestion addiction issues, are often the most vilified in the context of health policy and treatment regimes (Greaves and Poole 2004).

This attitude is not limited to health care providers, child welfare authorities, or judges. Rather, the general public and the media also hold views that embody negative attitudes about how they perceive pregnant women who use substances. One content analysis of Canadian news media on these issues compared pregnant women and mothers with mental health issues and those experiencing domestic violence with women using substances, and the ranking of the latter was most negative (Greaves et al. 2002). Stories pertaining to women using substances evoked negative language and blame, with the feeling that this was the women's fault, whereas women with mental health issues who were mothering were considered as blameless, and women with domestic violence experiences somewhere in the middle (Greaves et al. 2002; Greaves et al. 2004). This reveals the depth of animosity and negativity aimed at pregnant women with addiction issues.

Because so many policy, media and programmatic responses have focused on the fetus and its health (often positioned as in opposition to women's health), and combined with the potential for legal intervention or child welfare apprehension, many women have been deterred from engaging with health authorities, or seeking treatment for reducing alcohol, drug or tobacco use during pregnancy. One study investigating why women with addictions issues did not seek treatment during pregnancy revealed that they felt fear, shame and guilt (Poole and Isaac 2001). Fear related to child apprehension, and shame and guilt created by absorption of the medical, legal and social attitudes about their situation and behaviors.

Two Examples: Alcohol and Tobacco

Both alcohol use and tobacco use during pregnancy have negative effects on the developing fetus. In both instances fetal health issues often appear to supersede those related to women's health in the eyes of observers. As a result, both alcohol and tobacco use during pregnancy, (as well as the use of several illegal drugs) have long been condemned and stigmatized, and efforts to prevent these practices have long been established (Oaks 2001; Wilsnack and Wilsnack 2013).

Tobacco Use

Smoking during pregnancy has a range of deleterious effects on the fetus including an increased risk of preterm delivery and stillbirth (Baba et al. 2014; Dietz et al. 2010), low birth-weight (Juárez and Merlo 2013) and obstetric complications such as: preterm rupture of the membrane, incompetent cervix, threatened premature delivery, placental abruption and pregnancy-induced hypertension (Hayashi et al. 2011). Some researchers have suggested that there may be lifelong effects on infants and children such as attention deficit, hyperactivity and behavioral conduct issues (Gaysina et al. 2013; Keyes, Davey Smith, and Susser 2014), congenital heart defects (Lee and Lupo 2013), and obesity and other cardiac health risk factors (Dior et al. 2014).

Tobacco use by women has escalated considerably over the past 50 years as manufactured cigarettes and their associated marketing and advertising evolved to cater to and target women (Prasad, Prasad, and Baker 2014; Amos and Haglund 2000; Berridge and Loughlin 2005). After an initial silence, when little was known about the effects of tobacco use, attention turned to men who had typically taken up cigarette smoking before women and hence showed the health effects first. But after more women took up smoking in the 1950s and 1960s attention began to focus on the harms associated with smoking during pregnancy. Since the 1970s, tobacco use by pregnant women and girls has been a key target for prevention and intervention by public health and medical researchers. Any focus on harms to women's health was overlooked during these decades, supporting the view that the key health issue in 'women and smoking' was pregnancy and smoking (Jacobson 1981; Jacobson 1986; Greaves 1996).

The key element in responding to women's smoking during pregnancy has been to generate health information and education that will convince or impel pregnant women to avoid tobacco. By the late 20th century, the rates of smoking among women during pregnancy were diminishing, although secular changes in smoking rates among the general population of women were also a factor in this reduction. The focus of campaigns was typically fetus-centric: exhorting women to quit often using shame and blame or guilt inducing messages. Examples of such campaigns include a print campaign in 1973 by the Health Education Council (HEC) in Britain which featured a naked pregnant woman smoking and the caption, "Is it fair to force your baby to smoke cigarettes?" (Berridge and Loughlin 2005). Similarly, campaigns from the American Cancer Society and American Lung Association used imagery of "smoke filled wombs," and equated quitting with maternal love (urging women to quit "because you love your baby…"), and continuing to smoke with a lack of caring (Oaks 2000)

These campaigns and messages had a few characteristics: they were focused on the pregnancy period, they were aimed at enhancing fetal or infant health, and they exhorted women to protect their fetus or infant by quitting completely and immediately. Pregnancy was widely understood as a "window of opportunity" for making changes in women's behavior and the fetus an incentive or motivator for change. A two-stage review of program interventions aimed at tobacco cessation during pregnancy from 1990–2010 revealed that there were some that were effective at reducing smoking during pregnancy, but overall, few, if any, had any effect on postpartum relapse (Greaves et al. 2003; Greaves et al. 2011). In other words, if measured by the effect on women's smoking, their effectiveness was limited to the pregnancy period and was a failure at preventing or reducing women's smoking overall. In this context cessation during pregnancy was deemed by some as "temporary abstinence" (Stotts et al. 2000) and not cessation.

Over the last two decades of the 20th century, the smoking rates among women during pregnancy decreased in countries such as the USA and Canada from about 29%–37% to 12%–18% (Martin 2002; Government of Canada 2003; US Department of Health Human Services 1990). While this has represented progress, these reductions were not uniformly experienced across the population of pregnant women. When the prevalence rates are age-disaggregated, it is clear that young pregnant women are most likely to smoke during pregnancy, according to Canadian and American statistics (CDC 2008; PHAC 2009). In addition, women who have had trauma histories, women on low income, with low education, or Aboriginal women also have higher rates of smoking during pregnancy. These groups were not generally catered to in intervention design, or in research.

The cessation rates among these groups also differ from the average, as do the relapse rates postpartum (Gilbert, Nelson, and Greaves 2015). The groups left out of the gaze of interveners included young women, those who had experienced trauma and violence, and Aboriginal women (Greaves et al. 2011). In all of these groups, there is heightened concern and higher rates of smoking during pregnancy, as well as lower rates of cessation and relapse rates postpartum (Blalock et al. 2013; Bottorff et al. 2014; Cui et al. 2014).

In short, the history of responding to tobacco use during pregnancy has been fetus-centric, limited to the pregnancy period, ignoring of multi-substance use or social factors affecting use, and often blaming and shaming. These approaches ignore preconception and postpartum periods, women's health in its own right, the social determinants of health and the effects of stigma. More specifically, they ignore trauma experiences, the effects of gender on smoking and pregnancy and the role of policy in determining responses to women. Overarching program and campaign responses to smoking during pregnancy are tobacco control policies regarding issues such as smoking locations, sales to minors, price and tax, advertising and marketing, health warnings on packaging and related issues. But these policies have typically been generic, not responding to either gender issues, social determinants of health or health inequity (Amos et al. 2011). Furthermore, they are not constructed with considerations of multi-substance use or experiences of multiple issues in women, such as concurrent mental health, violence, trauma or poverty. All of these aspects affect women who smoke during pregnancy, but are not positively shifted by existing policy.

Alcohol Use

Similarly, alcohol use during pregnancy has been a source of intense public scrutiny, and stigmatizing responses. Alcohol is the substance most commonly used by women and girls. Among pregnant women in Canada the rate of drinking alcohol is approximately 11%, according to self-reported retrospective surveys (Public Health Agency of Canada 2009). However, getting accurate data may be difficult, due to the perceived risks associated with reporting alcohol use during pregnancy to medical or child welfare personnel as well as a social desirability bias. In Canada, the use of any alcohol during pregnancy is considered unsafe, and policy and program initiatives reflect this. This advice has been established in Canada since 2009 (Carson et al. 2010), but advice in other countries ranges from moderate use to no use (McBride 2014; Lowe and Lee 2010).

The effects of alcohol use on fetal development during pregnancy include Fetal Alcohol Syndrome (FAS), Alcohol-Related Neurodevelopmental Disorder (ARND) and Alcohol-Related Birth Defects, all of which result in lifelong disabilities. Together these conditions are termed Fetal Alcohol Spectrum Disorder (FASD). In the case of alcohol use, damage to fetal health has been documented to include abnormal facial features, growth problems and central nervous system

(CNS) problems. Prenatal alcohol exposure affects every area of the brain, causing a constellation of disabilities related to affect regulation, motor skills, coordination and balance, attention, speech and language, executive function, learning, memory and cognition as well as adaptive skills. People with a FASD are likely to have problems in school and throughout life related to difficulties with math, memory, attention, judgment and impulse control.

As with tobacco, women's alcohol use most often gains attention when it intersects with pregnancy and with concerns about preventable fetal health effects (Drabble et al. 2011). The attention to women's alcohol use in the context of pregnancy is complicated by the fact that alcohol's teratogenic effects vary in relation to different levels of exposure, differences in genetic backgrounds, and larger determinants of health such as nutrition (Barry et al. 2009; May et al. 2005). FASD risk is greatest in the context of heavy drinking during pregnancy, but varying outcomes have been found related to light drinking, and thus no generic safe level of alcohol use in pregnancy can be offered (Swedish National Institute of Public Health 2009; Testa, Quigley, and Das Eiden 2003; Henderson, Gray, and Brocklehurst 2007). The social construction of alcohol-related risks and how risks are communicated play an important role in the development of policy, programs and public discourse related to women's alcohol use and FASD. Often, risk is framed in moral or legal terms (not nuanced as to level of alcohol use) and linked to prevailing beliefs about motherhood, addiction and the status of the fetus (Armstrong 1998; Golden 2000, 2005; Armstrong 2003; Waterson 2000; Knupfer 1991).

A recent examination of policies on alcohol use during pregnancy in English-speaking countries found considerable variation in policy statements between countries as well as differences in recommendations between different government and health organizations (O'Leary et al. 2007). A survey of state responses to alcohol and pregnancy in the USA (Drabble et al. 2014) has illuminated a number of areas where alcohol policies could be improved in a way that support women's and fetal health—for example, priority treatment for pregnant women and changes to mandatory reporting of alcohol use to child welfare authorities (which serves to drive women away from health care for fear of losing custody or having civil or legal action taken against them). This study analyzed data from the Alcohol Policy Information System (APIS), which provides federal and state statutory and regulatory data in the USA for 33 alcohol policy topics,[1] including those related to alcohol use during pregnancy, and found that 19 of 50 states had primarily supportive policies, 12 primarily punitive, 12 with a mixed approach and 8 with no policies (Drabble et al. 2014). Thus, beyond shaming educational campaigns (of which there are many) and lack of attention to gendered and structural influences on women's drinking, there are concerns about harmful policies and interventions that directly target pregnant women and mothers. As a result, women with alcohol problems are not being encouraged and referred to treatment, and less than 22% of children being diagnosed with FASD in clinics attending with their birth mother (Astley 2010).

As in tobacco control, there are overarching alcohol policies in most jurisdictions that legislate or regulate issues such as availability and pricing, marketing and advertising, drinking and driving and age and location restrictions on consumption (Babor et al. 2010). Again, these policy responses have typically been generic, not responding to or tailoring for gender, health inequity or the social determinants of health. Hence, women who drink alcohol during pregnancy have suffered from a limited but strong focus on fetal health and fetal damage, and little focus on women's health, harm reduction or destigmatization. As a result, women are deterred from entering or accessing treatment programming, and unlikely to encounter friendly and welcoming health and social service providers who may be supportive to them. As in tobacco policy, alcohol policy is rarely, if ever, tailored and unlikely to account for multiple substance use or co-occurring issues such as violence, trauma, poverty and gendered effects on alcohol use for women.

Critical Policy Responses

What can we learn from decades of experience of the policy response to women and tobacco and women and alcohol? In the case of tobacco, comprehensive policy responses to tobacco are widely recommended (WHO 2013), consisting of: monitoring of tobacco use and prevention policies; protection from secondhand smoke; offering cessation support; warning about dangers of tobacco use; enforcement of bans on tobacco advertising, promotions and sponsors and raising of taxes on tobacco. These approaches have been found to be effective, and have been formalized in an international public health treaty, the WHO-Framework Convention on Tobacco Control (FCTC; WHO 2003), created in 2004 and ratified by over 170 countries worldwide. In the case of alcohol, the World Health Organization (WHO) has more recently developed a global strategy on alcohol (WHO 2010), a less robust initiative. Its features include 10 areas for action ranging from community action to addressing the availability and marketing of alcohol, pricing and improving the health system's response to alcohol use.

But critiques have arisen, as vulnerable populations of women who smoke and drink alcohol (and other sub-populations) have not responded equivalently to the general population (Greaves 2014; Bottorff et al. 2014; Wilsnack and Wilsnack 2013). Additionally, broad policy measures have been identified as having inequitable effects (Hemsing et al. 2012; Greaves and Hemsing 2009; Greaves and Jategaonkar 2006; McLellan and Kaufman 2006; Graham et al. 2006; Greaves, Vallone, and Velicer 2006; Burgess, Fu, and van Ryn 2009). Critics have questioned the mainstream and generic approaches inherent in tobacco control (Greaves and Jategaonkar 2006; Graham et al. 2006; Poland et al. 2006), with their focus on population-level interventions, lack of tailoring and focus on individual behavioral change. Similarly, critics have questioned broad alcohol policies as ineffective when not linked to interlocking levels of prevention—such as awareness campaigns, brief interventions by health professionals with all women and holistic treatment and support interventions with women with alcohol problems—tailored to various levels of risk (Thomas et al. 2014).

There have been calls for making tobacco control policies more equitable to adapt them to various subpopulations (Greaves and Jategaonkar 2006; Amos et al. 2011; Hemsing and Greaves 2014), including women who smoke during pregnancy (Bottorff et al. 2014; Greaves et al. 2011). In line with this, recent critical suggestions for reforming interventions suggest shifting the gaze from individual-level change to the social structural factors affecting smoking during pregnancy, and from fetal health to women's health to respond to the failure of interventions to date (Greaves, Hemsing, Poole, Bialystok and O'Leary 2014). Similarly, there are calls for improving alcohol policy as it pertains to women (WHO 2014), and pregnant women in particular. For example, the Women Want to Know project has been developed by the Foundation for Alcohol Research and Education (FARE), in collaboration with leading health professional bodies across Australia, and funded from the Australian Government Department of Health. The Women Want to Know project promotes a national policy approach that promotes routine discussion of alcohol and pregnancy by all health professionals (see www.alcohol.gov.au).

There are also unintended consequences of policy that are often as important as the intended goals of policy. For example, tobacco control has pursued denormalization policies in some jurisdictions that determine increasingly stringent smoking location restrictions, and result in less visible smoking, in an effort to make non-smoking the norm. However, remaining smokers, especially low-income and more marginalized smokers who have less access to private spaces, have become more visible and stigmatized (Thompson, Pearce, and Barnett 2007). Visibly pregnant women who smoke in public spaces are increasingly subject to negative social reaction and unwanted intrusive commentary (Hemsing et al. 2012; Wigginton and Lee 2013). Similar dynamics arise in the context of alcohol consumption, with visibly pregnant women who find themselves subject to public scrutiny, judgment, loss of custody of children and even civil commitment (Rutman et al. 2005; Greaves and Poole 2004; Paltrow and Flavin 2013; Drabble et al. 2014) Indeed, the stigma attached to smoking or drinking alcohol during pregnancy is considerable, and serves as a barrier to women seeking treatment (Wigginton and Lee 2013; Roberts and Pies 2011).

Transdisciplinary Policy Responses

The two case studies in this chapter demonstrate that ingesting substances during pregnancy remains a key public health issue, where both women's and fetal health are degraded. However, the general program and policy responses to both of these substances has fallen short by failing to address structural factors and psychosocial factors affecting pregnant women's smoking and drinking alcohol. These responses have also failed to address root causes and factors that affect substance use during pregnancy, such as trauma, violence, facing sole motherhood, stress or poverty. Furthermore, despite their focus on women, they often fail to consider gender in their design and are rarely women-positive.

A transdisciplinary approach to policy making could assist in remedying some of the criticisms of policy responses to women who use substances like alcohol or tobacco (or other drugs) during pregnancy. It would aim for integrated responses, multi-discipline engagement and gender equity in determining policy. In so doing, consensus building and generation of common policy goals, values and language would be key to success.

In creating an integrated response, it may help to focus on the health and welfare of the *mother–child unit*, as opposed to just the fetus or just the woman, in order to render more progressive thinking and more creative and humane initiatives. As both the physical and psychological health of the fetus is dependent upon the health of the mother, both pre- and post-birth, this viewpoint may seem both obvious and overdue. But currently much policy, programming and legislation is premised on the separation of the mother and child, and can create punitive responses to women that alienate them from treatment, help or support, or their own offspring.

There are innovative approaches that attempt to take this integrated stance by taking a women-centered approach in responding to this tricky issue. For example, addressing women as the center of a response means that treatment and programming as well as policy takes her context and wishes into account (Cory 2007). Addressing both the mother and child as a unit (Greaves et al. 2002), with a view to keeping them both healthy, pre- and post-birth, is a paradigm shift that leads to some very different policies and programs. Proposals for doing this lean on generating more comprehensive risk assessments, embrace harm reduction and use strengths-based approaches to improve the health of mothers and children, or pregnant women and fetuses. Risk assessment might include measures of how women are dealing with their substance use but also keeping their fetus or child safe. Harm reduction is often part of this approach, accepting that cessation or abstinence may not be achieved but reduction of substance use may, and ought to be encouraged. Using supportive techniques such as motivational interviewing can work to build respect and generate change. Policies, regulations or legislation in related areas such as child welfare, addiction treatment or health care can reflect these principles and support this integrated approach.

Similarly, trauma-informed approaches in services and systems for addiction treatment reflect an integrated approach: taking into account potential co-occurring issues, rendering an environment more welcoming and avoiding re-victimization (Poole and Greaves 2012). Overt recognition of multiple substance use and multiple issues, along with recognition of the social determinants of health, all pave the way for integration of services, policies and programs.

Improving Gender Equity

Designing gendered policy that improves women's health *and* equity, as well as improving the health of the fetus or infant, is a challenge, but one that, if taken, could assist in responding more effectively to the issues of substance use during pregnancy. Although calls for including gender in health promotion and programming have long been ignored (Gelb, Pederson, and Greaves 2012), a recent call for gender transformation in health could be applied to this issue (Greaves, Pederson, and Poole 2014).

Designing policy, health promotion and public health campaigns that seek to improve health and gender equity *at the same time* could better support women's, fetal and infant health. It is not enough to be gender specific, making the obvious recognition that women need special consideration regarding substance use during pregnancy, but rather it is critical to acknowledge the importance of the many gendered and inequitable contexts in which they may be using substances during pregnancy.

Taking a gender-transformative approach to policy and programming in response to pregnancy and substance use would provide an integrated response (taking into account more than immediate health issues, and accounting for other social structural factors affecting substance use) and a gendered response (taking into account both women's sex-specific reproductive role and the gendered factors affecting women and substance use during pregnancy, such as domestic violence, low income and caregiving burdens). Most importantly, it would aim toward and measure outcomes that improve equity for women as well. Such advances would undoubtedly advance the health of their children as well.

Transdisciplinary Responses

Multiple disciplines are also required to consider how to best respond to substance-using women during pregnancy. This could mean a team composed of health-care providers, social workers and psychotherapists coming together to create programs or treatment, but it could be interpreted more broadly, as well. For example, bringing together representatives from health, social services, child welfare, addiction treatment, criminal justice and education departments or organizations could assist in refining an integrated policy response that would base its work on common values and goals. Such processes and consortia encourage cross training, common language development and mutual learning, often resulting in more realistic and useful approaches. They also offer the opportunity for various sectors to see the effects of their policies, and judge how compromises or adaptations might assist in reaching goals.

At the highest levels, governments can overtly orchestrate merging interests by engaging in intersectoral actions, sometimes known as "health in all policies" (HIAP) and ideally measured by "health equity impact assessments" (HEIA). In policy making, multiple departments or ministries in all levels of governments would set aside their narrow interests in favor of assessing how health can be improved in the design and implementation of *all* policies. Interministerial or interdepartmental coordinating committees are one mechanism for addressing complex issues, such as violence against women or addiction.

Questions can be asked in these contexts that are crosscutting. For example, how does child welfare policy affect the health of substance using pregnant women and their fetuses? If the answer is that it deters women from accessing treatment or being able to mother, then it needs to be redesigned in the interests of health and equity, perhaps by engaging child-welfare and substance-use treatment advocates and professionals in a collaborative approach. How do housing policy or social welfare benefit rates affect the health of women and fetuses or infants? If the answer is that they prevent women who face violence from leaving unsafe relationships or supporting themselves and their children, adjustments in housing and social welfare policy could solve these problems. How does tax policy affect women who use substances during pregnancy? If the answer is that consuming tobacco or alcohol is increasingly expensive and reducing a woman's food and housing budget, there may be ways to provide free cessation aids, treatment or alternatives to them in the interests of improving their health.

Such questions are best asked and answered in a HIAP framework that aims to reach common goals around an issue as complex as substance use during pregnancy. Once answered, remedies can be proposed that reach wider health and equity goals. While many governments have adopted intersectoral action, HIAP or HEIA related principles (Shankardass et al. 2012), few have succeeded in breaking down silos of decision making to effect real action and change (Greaves and Bialystok 2011). Nonetheless, the nascent goal of doing "trans-sectoral" (Greaves and Bialystok 2011, p. 408) policy making is still very real.

Different experts, research and practice disciplines and communities are needed to work together to create a holistic response to women who use substances during pregnancy. These include at the treatment level: at least, physicians, nurses, social workers, substance use workers, pediatricians, neonatologists, psychiatrists and obstetricians. At the research level, social scientists, clinical scientists and a range of biomedical researchers, working in concert with health-system designers. At the community level, politicians, professionals, community leaders, women and the public are needed to coalesce on how best to respond to women who use substances during pregnancy. Such a coherent response has a set of features: addressing more than one substance at once, if necessary; offering mental health care, if necessary; taking a harm reduction approach; offering women-centered care and trauma-informed practices; and recognizing structural factors such as poverty and domestic violence, as implicated in substance use during pregnancy.

In current mothering policies that affect both pregnant women and mothers, there is little trans-sectoral effort in play at the moment (Greaves et al. 2002;

Greaves et al. 2004). Transdisciplinarity in policy would explicitly aim to lift women up, and improve women's and fetal health, while encouraging reduction in substance use during pregnancy. A transdisciplinary approach requires a range of sectors and disciplines to form a coherent policy and program response to the issue of addiction and substance use during pregnancy. This area is ripe for broader commitment, innovation and risk taking.

Discussion Questions

1. Why do you think governments often fail to develop policy in a trans-sectoral manner?
2. How might meso-level institutional policies, such as those in schools, hospitals or prisons, better reflect a transdisciplinary approach?
3. How do you think "health in all policies" approaches might be sold to the general public in a more effective manner?

Note

1 The six policies were (a) mandatory signs posted in establishments that sell or serve alcohol to warn patrons of the impact of alcohol use during pregnancy, (b) priority treatment for pregnant women with alcohol dependence, (c) prohibitions against criminal prosecution of women who have exposed a fetus to alcohol, (d) mandatory reporting by health-care providers and related personnel of indicators of fetal exposure to alcohol, (e) use of indicators of alcohol use or abuse during pregnancy as evidence of child abuse or child neglect and (f) civil commitment of pregnant women who use or abuse alcohol.

References

Amos, Amanda, Lorraine Greaves, Mimi Nichter, and Michelle Bloch. 2011. Women and tobacco: A call for including gender in tobacco control research, policy and practice. *Tobacco Control* 21:236–243.

Amos, Amanda, and Margaretha Haglund. 2000. From social taboo to "torch of freedom": The marketing of cigarettes to women. *Tobacco Control* 9 (1):3–8.

Armstrong, Elizabeth M. 1998. Diagnosing moral disorder: The discovery and evolution of fetal alcohol syntrome. *Social Science in Medicine* 47 (12):2025–2042.

Armstrong, Elizabeth M. 2003. *Conceiving risk, bearing responsibility: Fetal alcohol syndrome & the diagnosis of moral disorder*. Baltimore: Johns Hopkins University Press.

Astley, Susan. 2010. Profile of the first 1,400 patients receiving diagnostic evaluations for Fetal Acohol Spectrum Disorder at the Washington State FAS Diagnostic & Prevention Network. *Canadian Journal of Clinical Pharmacology* 17 (1):e132–e164.

Baba, Sachiko, Anna-Karin Wikström, Olof Stephansson, and Sven Cnattingius. 2014. Influence of snuff and smoking habits in early pregnancy on risks for stillbirth and early neonatal mortality. *Nicotine & Tobacco Research* 16 (1):78–83.

Babor, Thomas F., Raul Caetano, Sally Casswell, Griffith Edwards, Norman Giesbrecht, Kathryn Graham, Joel W. Grube, Linda Hill, Harold Holder, Ross Homel, Michael Livingston, Esa

Österberg, Jurgen Rehm, Robin Room, and Ingeborg Rossow. 2010. *Alcohol: No ordinary commodity—Research and public policy*. 2nd ed. New York: Oxford University Press.

Barry, Kristen L., Raul Caetano, Grace Chang, Mary C. DeJoseph, Lisa A. Miller, Mary J. O'Connor, Heather Carmichael Olsen, R. Louise Floyd, Mary Kate Weber, Frank DeStefano, Suzanne Dolina, and Kimberly Leeks. 2009. *Reducing alcohol-exposed pregnancies: A report of the National Task Force on Fetal Alcohol Syndrome and Fetal Alcohol Effect*. Atlanta, GA: Centers for Disease Control and Prevention.

Berridge, Virginia, and Kelly Loughlin. 2005. Smoking and the new health education in Britain. *American Journal of Public Health* 95 (6):956–964.

Blalock, Janice A., Jennifer A. Minnix, Amanda R. Mathew, David W. Wetter, James P. McCullough Jr., and Paul M. Cinciripini. 2013. Relationship of childhood trauma to depression and smoking outcomes in pregnant smokers. *Journal of Consulting and Clinical Psychology* 81 (5):821.

Bottorff, Joan L., Nancy Poole, Mary T. Kelly, Lorraine Greaves, Lenora Marcellus, and Mary Jung. 2014. Tobacco and alcohol use in the context of adolescent pregnancy and postpartum: A scoping review of the literature. *Health & Social Care in the Community* 22 (6):561–574.

Boyd, Susan C. 1999. *Mothers and illicit drugs: Transcending the myths*. Toronto: University of Toronto Press.

Boyd, Susan C. 2004. *From Witches to Crack Moms: Women, Drug Law, and Policy*. Durham, NC: Carolina Academic Press.

Burgess, Diana J., Steven S. Fu, and Michelle van Ryn. 2009. Potential unintended consequences of tobacco-control policies on mothers who smoke: A review of the literature. *American Journal of Preventive Medicine* 37 (2):S151–S158.

Campbell, Nancy. 2000a. Mother fixations. In *Using women: Gender, drug policy, and social justice*, edited by N. Campbell. New York: Routledge.

Campbell, Nancy. 2000b. *Using women: Gender, drug policy, and social justice*. New York: Routledge.

Carson, George, Lori Vitale Cox, Joan Crane, Pascal Croteau, Lisa Graves, Sandra Kluka, Gideon Koren, Marie-Jocelyne Martel, Irena Nulman, Nancy Poole, Vyta Senikas, and Rebecca Wood. 2010, August. Alcohol use and pregnancy: Consensus clinical guidelines *Journal of Obstetrics and Gynaecology Canada* 32 (8 Supplement 3):S1–S32.

CDC. 2008. *Pregnancy Risk Assessment Monitoring System (PRAMS) and smoking*. Atlanta, GA: Centers for Disease Control and Prevention.

Cory, Jill. 2007. *Women-centred care: A curriculum for health care providers*. Vancouver, BC: BC Women's Hospital & Health Centre.

Cui, Yang, Shahin Shooshtari, Evelyn L. Forget, Ian Clara, and Kwong F. Cheung. 2014. Smoking during pregnancy: Findings from the 2009–2010 Canadian Community Health Survey. *PloS one* 9 (1):e84640.

Dietz, Patricia M., Lucinda J. England, Carrie K. Shapiro-Mendoza, Van T. Tong, Sherry L. Farr, and William M. Callaghan. 2010. Infant morbidity and mortality attributable to prenatal smoking in the U.S. *American Journal of Preventive Medicine* 39 (1):45–52.

Dior, Uri P., Gabriella M. Lawrence, Colleen Sitlani, Daniel Enquobahrie, Orly Manor, David S. Siscovick, Yechiel Friedlander, and Hagit Hochner. 2014. Parental smoking during pregnancy and offspring cardio-metabolic risk factors at ages 17 and 32. *Atherosclerosis* 235 (2):430–437.

Drabble, Laurie, Nancy Poole, Raquel Magri, Nazarius Mbona Tumwesigye, Qing Li, and Moira Plant. 2011. Conceiving risk, divergent responses: Perspectives on the construction of risk of FASD in six countries. *Substance Use & Misuse* 46 (8):943–958.

Drabble, Lauri. A., Sue Thomas, Lisa O'Connor, and Sarah C.M. Roberts. 2014. State responses to alcohol use and pregnancy: Findings from the Alcohol Policy Information System. *Journal of Social Work Practice in the Addictions* 14 (2):191–206.

Fentiman, Linda C. 2008a. The "fetal protection" wars: Why America has made the wrong choice in addressing maternal substance abuse—A comparative legal analysis. *Pace Law Faculty Publications* 479.

Fentiman, Linda C. 2008b. Pursuing the perfect Mother: Why America's Criminalization of Maternal Substance Abuse is Not the Answer—A Comparative Legal Analysis. *Michigan Journal of Gender & Law* 15:389.

Gaysina, Dary, David M. Fergusson, Leslie D. Leve, et al. 2013. Maternal smoking during pregnancy and offspring conduct problems: Evidence from 3 independent genetically sensitive research designs. *JAMA Psychiatry* 70 (9):956–963.

Gelb, Karen, Ann Pederson, and Lorraine Greaves. 2012. How have health promotion frameworks considered gender? *Health Promotion International* 27 (4):445–452.

Gilbert, Nicolas, Chantal Nelson, and Lorraine Greaves. 2015. Smoking cessation during pregnancy and relapse after childbirth in Canada. *Journal of Obstetrics and Gynecology Canada*.

Gilbert N, Nelson C and Greaves L. Smoking Cessation during Pregnancy and Relapse after Childbirth in Canada. Journal of Obstetrics and Gynecology Canada, 2015;37(1): 32–39. http://www.jogc.ca/abstracts/201501_Obstetrics_3.pdf.

Golden, Janet. 2000. "A tempest in a cocktail glass": Mothers, alcohol, and television, 1977–1996. *Journal of Health Politics, Policy and Law* 25 (3):473–498.

Golden, Janet. 2005. *Message in a bottle: The making of fetal alcohol syndrome*. Cambridge, MA: Harvard University Press.

Government of Canada. 2003. *The well-being of Canada's young children: Government of Canada report*. Ottawa: Human Resources and Social Development Canada.

Graham, Hilary, Hazel M. Inskip, Brian Francis, and Juliet Harman. 2006. Pathways of disadvantage and smoking careers: Evidence and policy implications. *Journal of Epidemiology and Community Health* 60 (Supplement 2):ii7–ii12.

Greaves, Lorraine. 1996. *Smoke screen: Women's smoking and social control*. Halifax, NS: Fernwood.

Greaves, Lorraine. 2014. Can tobacco control be transformative? Reducing gender inequity and tobacco use among vulnerable populations. *International Journal of Environmental Research and Public Health* 11 (1):792–803.

Greaves, Lorraine, and Victoria Barr. 2000. *Filtered policy: Women and tobacco in Canada*. Vancouver, BC: Women's Health Bureau: Health Canada.

Greaves, Lorraine, and Lauren Bialystok. 2011. Health in all policies: All talk and little action? *Canadian Journal of Public Health* 102 (6):407–409.

Greaves, Lorraine, Renée Cormier, Karen Devries, Joan Bottorff, Joy Johnson, Susan Kirkland, and David Aboussafy. 2003. *Expecting to quit: A best practices review of smoking cessation interventions for pregnant and postpartum girls and women*. Vancouver, BC: British Columbia Centre of Excellence for Women's Health.

Greaves, Lorraine, and Natalie Hemsing. 2009. Sex, gender, diversity and second-hand smoke policies: Implications for disadvantaged women. *American Journal of Preventive Medicine* 37 (2 Supplement):S131–137.

Greaves, Lorraine, Natalie Hemsing, Nancy Poole, Lauren Bialystok, and Renée O'Leary. 2014. From fetal health to women's health: Expanding the gaze on intervening on smoking during pregnancy. *Critical Public Health*.

Greaves, L., Hemsing, N., Poole, N., Bialystok, L., O'Leary, R. From fetal health to women's health: expanding the gaze on intervening on smoking during pregnancy. *Critical Public Health*. 2014 http://dx.doi.org/10.1080/09581596.2014.968527.

Greaves, Lorraine, and Natasha Jategaonkar. 2006. Tobacco policies and vulnerable girls and women: Toward a framework for gender sensitive policy development. *Journal of Epidemiology and Community Health* 60 (Supplement 2):ii57–ii65.

Greaves, Lorraine, Ann Pederson, and Nancy Poole, eds. 2014. *Making it better: Gender transformative health promotion*. Toronto, ON: Canadian Scholars' Press.

Greaves, Lorraine, Ann Pederson, Colleen Varcoe, Nancy Poole, Marina Morrow, Joy Johnson, and Lori Irwin. 2004. Mothering under duress: Women caught in a web of discourses. *Journal of the Motherhood Initiative for Research and Community Involvement* 6 (1).

Greaves, Lorraine, and Nancy Poole. 2004. Victimized or validated? Responses to substance-using pregnant women. *Canadian Woman Studies* 24 (1):87–92.

Greaves, Lorraine, Nancy Poole, Chizimuzo T.C. Okoli, Natalie Hemsing, Annie Qu, Lauren Bialystock, and Renée O'Leary. 2011. *Expecting to quit: A best-practices review of smoking cessation interventions for pregnant and post-partum women*. 2nd ed. Vancouver, BC: British Columbia Centre of Excellence for Women's Health.

Greaves, Lorraine, Donna Vallone, and Wayne Velicer. 2006. Special effects: Tobacco policies and low socioeconomic status girls and women. *Journal of Epidemiology and Community Health* 60 (Supplement 2):ii1–ii2.

Greaves, Lorraine, Colleen Varcoe, Nancy Poole, Marina Morrow, Joy Johnson, Ann Pederson, and Lori Irwin. 2002. *A motherhood issue: Discourses on mothering under duress*. State College, PA: CiteSeer.

Hayashi, Kunihiko, Yoshio Matsuda, Yayoi Kawamichi, Arihiro Shiozaki, and Shigeru Saito. 2011. Smoking during pregnancy increases risks of various obstetric complications: A case-cohort study of the Japan Perinatal Registry Network Database. *Journal of Epidemiology* 21 (1):61–66.

Hemsing, Natalie, and Lorraine Greaves. 2014. Igniting global tobacco control. In *Making it better: Gender-transformative health promotion*, edited by L. Greaves, A. Pederson, and N. Poole. Toronto, ON: Canadian Scholars' Press.

Hemsing, Natalie, Lorraine Greaves, Nancy Poole, and Joan Bottorff. 2012. Reshuffling and relocating: The gendered and income-related differential effects of restricting smoking locations. *Journal of Environmental and Public Health*. Article ID 907832. http://dx.doi.org/10.1155/2012/907832.

Henderson, Jane, Ron Gray, and Peter Brocklehurst. 2007. Systematic review of effects of low-moderate prenatal alcohol exposure on pregnancy outcome. *BJOG: An International Journal of Obstetrics and Gynaecology* (114):243–252.

Jacobson, B. 1981. *The ladykillers: Why smoking is a feminist issue*. London: Pluto Press.

Jacobson, B. 1986. *Beating the ladykillers: Women and smoking*. London: Pluto Press.

Juárez, Sol Pía, and Juan Merlo. 2013. Revisiting the effect of maternal smoking during pregnancy on offspring birthweight: a quasi-experimental sibling analysis in Sweden. *PloS one* 8 (4):e61734.

Keyes, Katherine M., George Davey Smith, and Ezra Susser. 2014. Associations of prenatal maternal smoking with offspring hyperactivity: causal or confounded? *Psychological Medicine* 44 (04):857–867.

Knupfer, Genevieve. 1991. Abstaining for foetal health: The fiction that even light drinking is dangerous. *British Journal of Addiction* 86:1063–1073.

Lee, Laura J., and Philip J. Lupo. 2013. Maternal smoking during pregnancy and the risk of congenital heart defects in offspring: A systematic review and metaanalysis. *Pediatric Cardiology* 34 (2):398–407.

Lester, Barry, Lynne Andreozzi, and Lindsey Appiah. 2004. Substance use during pregnancy: Time for policy to catch up with research. *Harm Reduction Journal* 1 (1):5.

Lowe, Pam K., and Ellie J. Lee. 2010. Advocating alcohol abstinence to pregnant women: Some observations about British policy. *Health, Risk & Society* 12 (4):301–311.

Marcellus, Lenora. 2003. Critical social and medical constructions of perinatal substance misuse: Truth in the making. *Journal of Family Nursing* 9 (4):438–452.

Martin, Joyce A. 2002. *Births: Final data for 2001.* Washington, DC: US Department of Health and Human Services, Centers for Disease Control and Prevention, National Center for Health Statistics.

May, Philip A., J. Phillip Gossage, Lesley E. Brooke, Cudore L. Snell, Anna-Susan Marais, Loretta S. Hendricks, Julie A. Croxford, and Denis L. Viljoen. 2005. Maternal risk factors for fetal alcohol syndrome in the Western Cape Province of South Africa: A population-based study. *American Journal of Public Health* 95 (7):1190–1199.

McBride, Nyanda. 2014. Alcohol use during pregnancy: Considerations for Australian policy. *Social Work in Public Health* 29 (6):540–548.

McLellan, Deborah L., and Nancy J. Kaufman. 2006. Examining the effects of tobacco control policy on low socioeconomic status women and girls: An initiative of the Tobacco Research Network on Disparities (TReND). *Journal of Epidemiology and Community Health* 60 (Supplement 2):ii5–ii6.

Miller, William R., and Kathleen M. Carroll. 2006. *Rethinking substance abuse: What the science shows, and what we should do about it.* New York: Guildford Press.

Mohapatra, Seema. 2011. Unshackling addiction: A public health approach to drug use during pregnancy. *Wisconsin Journal of Law, Gender & Society* 26:241.

O'Leary, Colleen M., Louise Heuzenroeder, Elizabeth J. Elliott, and Carol Bower. 2007. A review of policies on alcohol use during pregnancy in Australia and other English-speaking countries, 2006. *Medical Journal of Australia* 186 (9):466–471.

Oaks, Laury. 2000. Smoke-filled wombs and fragile fetuses: The social politics of fetal representation. *Signs* 26 (1):63–108.

Oaks, Laury. 2001. *Smoking and pregnancy: The politics of fetal protection.* New Brunswick, NJ: Rutgers University Press.

Paltrow, Lynn M., and Jeanne Flavin. 2013. Arrests of and forced interventions on pregnant women in the United States, 1973–2005: Implications for women's legal status and public health. *Journal of Health Politics, Policy and Law* 38 (2):299–343.

PHAC. 2009. *What mothers say: The Canadian Maternity Experiences Survey.* Ottawa: Public Health Agency of Canada.

Poland, Blake, Katherine Frohlich, Rebecca J. Haines, Eric Mykhalovskiy, Melanie Rock, and Robert Sparks. 2006. The social context of smoking: the next frontier in tobacco control? *Tobacco Control* 15 (1):59–63.

Poole, Nancy, and Lorraine Greaves, eds. 2012. *Becoming trauma informed.* Toronto, ON: Centre for Addiction and Mental Health.

Poole, Nancy, and Barbara Isaac. 2001. *Apprehensions: Barriers to treatment for substance-using mothers.* Vancouver, BC: British Columbia Centre of Excellence for Women's Health.

Prasad, Pushkala, Anshuman Prasad, and Kelly Baker. 2014. Smoke and mirrors: Institutional entrepreneurship and gender identities in the US tobacco industry, 1920–1945. *Organization.* doi: 10.1177/1350508414547148.

Public Health Agency of Canada. 2009. *What mothers aay: The Canadian Maternity Experiences Survey.* Ottawa, ON: Author.

Roberts, Sarah C. M., and Cheri Pies. 2011. Complex Calculations: How drug use during pregnancy becomes a barrier to prenatal care. *Maternal and Child Health Journal* 15 (3):333–341.

Rutman, Deborah, Marilyn Callahan, Audrey Lundquist, Suzanne Jackson, and Barbara Field. 2000. *Substance use and pregnancy: conceiving women in the policy-making process.* Vol. 112. Ottawa: Status of Women Canada.

Rutman, Deborah, Barbara Field, Suzanne Jackson, Audrey Lundquist, and Marilyn Callahan. 2005. Perspectives of substance-using women and human service practitioners: Reflections from the margins. In *Unbecoming mothers: The social production of maternal absence,* edited by D.L. Gustafson. Binghamton, NY: Haworth Clinical Practice Press.

Schofield, Toni, and Susan Goodwin. 2005. Gender politics and public policy making: Prospects for advancing gender equality. *Policy and Society* 24 (4):25–44.

Schroedel, Jean Reith, and Pamela Fiber. 2001. Punitive versus public health oriented responses to drug use by pregnant women. *HeinOnline* 1(Spring): 217–235.

Shankardass, Ketan, Orielle Solar, Kelly Murphy, Lorraine Greaves, and Patricia O'Campo. 2012. A scoping review of intersectoral action for health equity involving governments. *International Journal of Public Health* 57 (1):25–33.

Stotts, Angela L., Carlo C. DiClemente, Joseph P. Carbonari, and Patricia D. Mullen. 2000. Postpartum return to smoking: Staging a" suspended" behavior. *Health Psychology* 19 (4):324.

Swedish National Institute of Public Health. 2009. *Low dose alcohol exposure during pregancy—does it harm? A systematic literature review.* Stockholm: The Swedish National Institute of Public Health. www.fhi.se/en/Search/?quicksearchquery=alcohol+exposure+during+pregnancy.

Testa, Maria, Brian M. Quigley, and Rina Das Eiden. 2003. The effects of prenatal alcohol exposure on infant mental development: A meta-analytical review. *Alcohol & Alcoholism* 38 (4):295–304.

Thomas, Gerald, Ginny Gonneau, Nancy Poole, and Jocelynn Cook. 2014. The effectiveness of alcohol warning labels for reducing drinking in pregnancy: A brief review *International Journal of Alcohol and Drug Research (IJADR), Second Special Issue on FASD* 3 (1):91–103.

Thompson, Lee, Jamie Pearce, and J. Ross Barnett. 2007. Moralising geographies: Stigma, smoking islands and responsible subjects. *Area* 39 (4):508–517.

US Department of Health Human Services. 1990. Healthy people 2000: National health promotion and disease prevention objectives—Nutrition priority area. *Nutrition Today* 25 (6):29–39.

Waterson, Jan. 2000. *Women and alcohol in social context: Mother's ruin revisited.* New York: Palgrave.

WHO. 2003. WHO Framework Convention on Tobacco Control. Geneva: World Health Organization.

WHO. 2010. *Global strategy to reduce the harmful use of alcohol.* Geneva: World Health Organization.

WHO. 2013. *WHO report on the global tobacco epidemic.* Geneva: World Health Organization.

WHO. 2014. *Global status report on alcohol and health.* Geneva: World Health Organization.

Wigginton, Britta, and Christina Lee. 2013. Stigma and hostility towards pregnant smokers: Does individuating information reduce the effect? *Psychology & Health* 28 (8):862–873.

Wilsnack, Richard W., and Sharon C. Wilsnack. 2013. Gender and alcohol: consumption and consequences. *Alcohol: Science, Policy and Public Health*:153–160.

Suggestions for Further Reading

Boyd, Susan C. 2004. *From witches to crack moms: Women, drug law, and policy*. Durham, NC: Carolina Academic Press.

Oaks, Laury. 2001. *Smoking and pregnancy: The politics of fetal protection*. New Brunswick, NJ: Rutgers University Press.

Ståhl, Timo, Matthias Wismar, Eeva Ollila, Eero Lahtinen, and Kimmo Leppo, eds. 2006. Health in all policies: Prospects and potentials. *European Observatory on Health Systems and Policies and Ministry of Social Affairs and Health, Finland*. Available from asiakas-palvelu@stakes.fi

15
ENLARGING KNOWLEDGE TRANSLATION TO REFLECT TRANSDISCIPLINARITY

Nancy Poole and Lorraine Greaves

Addiction, and its research and treatment activities, is a complex and challenging field. Not only is it essential to understand a range of perspectives and disciplines to unravel the problem, it is equally important to consider how to transmit knowledge and evidence about addiction to as wide an audience as possible. Knowledge translation is always challenging. It has to consider both content and process in determining its best approaches, and engage with a range of audiences and modes of learning and sharing to be effective in affecting outcomes, whether in research, treatment, policy or program arena. Amid calls for transdisciplinarity in research and treatment, this challenge is even more complex and yet more necessary to meet. On one hand, the content being shared is more developed, reflecting multiple disciplinary inputs. At the same time, the processes of knowledge translation must address multiple audiences, respecting each perspective, but representing transdisciplinarity in its messages. This chapter addresses these challenges.

Knowledge translation has been defined as the "synthesis, dissemination, exchange and ethically-sound application of knowledge" (Straus, Tetroe, and Graham 2009, 4). Mechanisms for knowledge translation that include synthesis are particularly needed in the addictions arena, where multiple health issues, such as trauma, substance use and mental health concerns are often involved, and where multiple disciplines need to apply findings to practice and policy in a systematic way. Indeed, recent conceptions of knowledge translation identify the importance of connecting researchers, practitioners and policy makers in ways that support all these sectors in the consideration of contextually relevant application to practice and policy. The need to engage these multiple disciplines and sectors on the complexities of addiction and sex/gender could benefit from new approaches to knowledge translation.

Challenges remain about how to design knowledge translation strategies that involve multiple holders of different kinds of knowledge in multidirectional collaborative learning and consensus-building processes. A wide range of new approaches is being developed, including networks and communities of practice, non-linear exchange processes and change management and integrative and interactive processes. All of these are being proposed and applied as mechanisms and approaches that address who needs to be involved in knowledge translation, and how to address context-specific barriers to their involvement.

The PARiHS (Promoting Action on Research Implementation in Health Services) framework researchers suggest that knowledge translation is a function of three factors: the nature of the evidence to be shared and applied, the qualities of the context of implementation, and the approach to facilitation of the involvement of knowledge users (Kitson, Harvey, and McCormack 1998; Kitson et al. 2008; Rycroft-Malone, Harvey, et al. 2004; Helfrich et al. 2010). This PARiHS framework "has proved to be a useful practical and conceptual heuristic for many researchers and practitioners in framing their research or knowledge translation endeavours" (Kitson et al. 2008, 2). In this chapter, these three elements of the PARiHS framework—evidence, context and facilitation—frame the discussion of knowledge translation in the substance use field and the consideration of gender in knowledge translation efforts. A fine balance of multiple forms of evidence, capacity to meaningfully factor in multiple contexts for application to practice and policy, and skilled facilitation of wide, multi-sector engagement is necessary for effective knowledge translation of transdisciplinary content in addiction.

Evidence, Transdisciplinarity and Knowledge Translation

Different disciplines value different forms of evidence. A major challenge in surfacing and examining research from multiple disciplines and to create a form of knowledge translation that is truly transdisciplinary is to not only include multiple forms of research but also to blend research evidence with other sources of evidence. In addictions, this includes knowledge from clinical practice, personal knowledge and experience of patients, and data from the local context. Kitson reflects on this issue in an editorial in the *International Journal of Evidence Based Health Care*:

> Our problem is that we still tend to see evidence as a product, a commodity, a thing that can be put into a system. Indeed evidence is a complex construction of facts, propositions, experiences, biographies and histories and ultimately an exercise of judgement bounded by time and context. (Kitson 2008, 1)

Indeed if we see the practice of transdisciplinarity to be about the exchange and interpretation of knowledge from multiple disciplines brought together in order to see new possibilities for solving problems, then the need for fora where people can draw on many sources of knowledge and can "question their own pre-existing knowledge hierarchies" (Ward et al. 2012, 302) becomes important. The need for sharing perspectives and identifying a range of sources of evidence is highly relevant, especially where there is polarization of how an issue is problematized and prioritized (Contandriopoulos 2011), as is the case in the context of the addiction field in general.

When applying evidence in real life processes such as policy making, researchers studying public health decision making in the UK have noted the tension between an evidence-*informed* approach and people's deeply held desire for concrete data and concepts that help simplify (rather than capture) messy realities (Smith and Joyce 2012, 73). In the policy context, as well as the health-care delivery context, there is acknowledgement of how advances can be evidence-*informed* as opposed to evidence-*based*, and how other influences on policy and practice need acknowledgement. Others have suggested that when informing policy makers, it may be useful to work backwards to research evidence, that is, to start the preparation of evidence briefs by supporting deliberation on the characteristics and influences related to the policy issue (Moat, Lavis, and Abelson 2013). Ultimately, the challenge is to find ways to engage practitioners, policy makers and health-system planners in exploring not only evidence for what works, but also what is the nature of the problem, why it occurs and how it might be addressed in specific contexts, an assessment often referred to as "fitness of purpose" (Nutley, Walter, and Davies 2007, 13).

Finally, there are different ways to use research evidence in decision making and policy development. Nutley and colleagues (2007, 37) identify both the direct use of research to make decisions as well as indirect or conceptual use of research. In the latter case, research is used to reshape thinking around policy and practice problems or play "a more 'consciousness-raising role'" (p. 2). In conceptual research use, the focus is not only to convey research findings, but also to promote the assimilation of research ideas, theories and concepts into discourse and debates. This conceptual use of research is highly relevant to bringing sex- and gender-based analysis and action to addiction, substance-use policy and practice. Successfully blending sex and gender into research and treatment and policy making requires the incorporation of a critical analysis, integrated into the assessment of research evidence, sources of evidence and the audiences.

Context, Transdisciplinarity and Knowledge Translation

Equally important is the consideration of the context of knowledge translation. Not surprisingly, there has often been a focus on the needs of individual practitioners and professional groups as recipients and implementers of evidence and the barriers to implementation with these audiences, such as knowledge user time, professional affiliation, agency interests and ideological environment (Legare 2009; Thompson et al. 2008). However, in a study within the National Health

Services in the UK, Checkland and colleagues found that the barriers reported by practitioners as preventing implementation were *less* important than the context and the underlying social relations that give rise to the barriers (Checkland, Harrison, and Marshall 2007). They spoke of the importance of supporting collective 'sensemaking,' using intermediary forums of exchange. Kitson speaks of collective sensemaking in relation to health guideline implementation:

> Successful knowledge translation therefore becomes more reliant on processes that create 'shared meaning' and on mechanisms, such as the establishment of cross functional teams, co-location and the use of various shared methodologies, such as nominal group technique or consensus building. In addition, processes, such as communities of practice and learning collaboratives enable diverse, heterogeneous groups to be able to share their different perspectives in order to come to a mutually acceptable view of what works and what matters for each group. (Kitson 2009a, 136)

Researchers are just beginning to implement and study these and other mechanisms for knowledge translation that include discussion and synthesis of context for application of evidence. Complexity and feminist theorists have identified the importance of transdisciplinary involvement (Bammer 2005; Kirby, Greaves, and Reid 2006). Bammer explains:

> Limited interaction and communication across different areas of application mean that, for example, researchers in the environment are not exposed to developments in public health or business or security. Thus, there have been only low levels of intellectual cross-fertilization and learning, and limited exploitation of the significant synergies between approaches—This will involve bringing together and providing a clear identity and accepted place for a large "college" of peers, who can be both supportive and critical of each other's work—need systems thinking, participatory methods. (Bammer 2005, 1)

Transdisciplinary engagement can address these problems of context in a range of ways. It can generate opportunities related to traversing disciplinary boundaries and paradigms and identify the challenges in doing so. On the one hand, adherents of different paradigms may talk past each other lacking common ground for productive dialogue (Dopson 2007, S73). On the other hand, transdisciplinary involvement may also lead to the development of a new common language. Hulme and colleagues (2009) in describing the achievement of 'integrated' or 'trans-professional' knowledge in a collaboration process with multi-professional practitioners and health-system planners in the UK found that new ways of working could be found in 'undecided' reflective spaces. They discuss theories of 'third space' and 'hybridity' as foundations for the broader application of transdisciplinary collaborations. In such processes the users are synthesizing, not only exchanging information; and the researcher is decentered in the multidimensional and multi-directional co-construction of knowledge (McWilliam, Kothari, Ward-Griffin, Forbes, Leipert, et al. 2009). In such circumstances, a broader conceptualization of knowledge is embraced and the involvement of community members, practitioners, policy makers and researchers is acknowledged. For this to happen, "scientists must humbly engage people from diverse sectors in the research process so that knowledge systems can converge and be synthesized" (Hobin et al. 2012, 107). These concerns with professional and sectoral boundaries between various users and generators of knowledge impel the development of new mechanisms for collective work such as networks, communities of practice or inquiry, epistemic communities, and strategic research training programs organized around cluster-based learning. The IMPART program, which forms the impetus and context for this book, is one such cluster.

As described in Chapter 1, a range of views of substance use and addiction continue to operate, which can affect openness to use of evidence, collaborative examination of evidence and sex- and gender-based analysis. While newer views of addiction have been advanced, such as a public health approach, the moral view of addiction and the disease models remain very present. Hence, views of addiction as disease, as a mental health disorder, as a brain disorder and as a public health issue, coexist. This is the broader context that significantly affects knowledge translation in the substance use field. In the public health view of addiction, recently put forth by some governments, there is, perhaps, the most potential for transdisciplinary knowledge building. In the public health view, attention is brought to the how determinants of health such as gender, violence, income, genetics, social support and health services all combine to affect the health and substance use of individuals and communities.

Clearly, to incorporate context, to improve research-to-policymaking and practice, translation opportunities need to be created for people from multiple contexts to bring together and synthesize wider sources of knowledge; to discuss contextual issues affecting the application of this evidence; and to consider the possibilities for individual, organizational and health system level action. In such contexts, we abandon the view of knowledge as something that can be managed in a logical and staged process and instead see the health care system "as a complex, interactive, organic entity where experimentation, experiential learning and reflection are central to creating a culture of innovation, improvement and consequently effectiveness" (Kitson 2009b, 218).

Facilitation, Transdisciplinarity and Knowledge Translation

In addition to addressing the nature of evidence, and discerning the context(s) for knowledge translation, facilitation is a critical process. Facilitation is required to engage fully with evidence and to the understanding of context (Kitson 2009a;

Harvey et al. 2002). In fact, Clavier and colleagues recently described knowledge translation as "the skilled crafting of cognitive, strategic and logistic practices that interweave the values, interests and ideas of each partner so as to contribute to new problematizations of participatory research and the research issue under scrutiny" (Clavier et al. 2012, 802).

A number of researchers have described the levels or stages of knowledge exchange, requiring management or facilitation. For example, Landry et al. (2001) describes a ladder of stages from transmission to application. Glasziou and Haynes (2005) frame the process of research use by practitioners as following a seven-stage pipeline model: Palmer and Kramlich (2011) describe the stages as reflective inquiry, knowledge seeking/generation, integration, implementation, evaluation, mentoring, and additional reflective inquiry (33). Best and colleagues (2004) see the need to understand system antecedents for innovation, and system readiness for innovation, as well as linkages between researchers and community. However the process is conceptualized, there is a need for attending to and improving collaborative processes, including "ensuring that appropriate researchers and sectoral representatives are included, that their world-views are made explicit, that their interests are accommodated, that different strengths are harnessed, that communication mechanisms are strong, and that conflicts are appropriately mediated" (Bammer 2005, 2).

In order to accomplish this, knowledge translation processes require infrastructure that supports interactivity and facilitators of interactivity. Working in the area of health promotion as complexity theorists, Best and colleagues proposed "investing in networks that promote, support, and sustain ongoing dialogue and sharing of experience; finding common ground in an approach to community partnering; and gaining consensus on the proposed integrating framework" (Best et al. 2003, 168) as a way of closing the gap between health promotion research and practice.

Dopson and Fitzgerald (2005) have proposed that local communities of practice can play a critical social role in the diffusion of evidence and innovation, and that the boundaries between these communities affect the way evidence and knowledge are perceived and interpreted. With technological advances, the practice of transnational communities of practice related to health policy have also been studied as mechanisms for enhancing "exchange and co-production of knowledge" (Bertone et al. 2013, 5) across borders. Wenger has described communities of practice as "groups of people who share a concern, a set of problems, or a passion about a topic, and who deepen their knowledge and expertise in this area by interacting on an ongoing basis" (Wenger, McDermott, and Snyder 2002, 4). Communities of practice are viewed as a pragmatic or conceptual framework, useful for a knowledge translation model (Hart and Wolff 2006; Cox 2005), particularly for examining social learning and the situated social construction of meaning (Baek and Barab 2005, 163).

Communities of practice value both tacit and explicit forms of knowledge. They recognize the need to complement individuals' intuitions, perceptions and vernacular knowledge with the more explicit concepts of an evidence-based paradigm. Communities of practice are social learning structures: they are open venues of exploration, "where it is safe to speak the truth and ask hard questions" (37) and where members "develop the habit of consulting each other for help" (84). As such, the community of practice model can be used as a location where facilitation of learning can take place with diverse participants on complex, gendered health issues, in a context with moral as well as scientific discourses in play. They can engage participants with appreciation of or expertise in different forms of knowledge; support collective examination of knowledge in ways that break down isolation and promote dialogic deliberation; and help with the consideration of "how activism succeeds, and how action is and can be influenced by evidence" (Bammer 2005, 2).

Participatory action research (PAR) has been advanced as a useful approach to underpin knowledge translation processes, in a rural community context (Campbell 2010) for examining nursing practice (Corbett, Francis, and Chapman 2007) in/with indigenous communities (Smylie, Kaplan-Myrth, and McShane 2009; Fornssler et al. 2013) in primary-care groups (Thomas et al. 2005) and in health policy development (Themba and Minkler 2003). The focus on supporting interactivity has extended even to the micro level to the role of conversation—conversation that supports co-learning and collective sensemaking in health-care settings and at kitchen tables in Aboriginal communities (Hopkins 2012; Jordan et al. 2009).

All of these forums—networks, communities of practice, participatory action research, engaged conversations—support the processes of dialogue, synthesis, co-construction of knowledge, co-learning, reflection, integration and collaboration (Ebener et al. 2006; Landry et al. 2006; Lavis et al. 2006; Ginsburg and Gorostiaga 2006). They involve a dialogical learning approach which draws on the work of Friere in adult education (Friere 2006), and Habermas's concept of egalitarian dialogue and communicative action (Goode 2005; Morrow and Torres 2002) as well as dialogic feminism (Merrill 2005; Bickford 1996).

All of these collective fora for knowledge exchange and knowledge synthesis such as communities of practice need facilitators or leaders who manage the integrated, interactive process (Chunharas 2006; Flood 2010; Cherney et al. 2013; Sinfield et al. 2012).

> Roles, such as knowledge brokers (roles positioned between producers and users of knowledge in order to ease the spread of the new innovations) and boundary spanners (roles which can network effectively in order to understand the culture of an organisation), can be used to enable the flow of knowledge between different groups. These roles are recommended when it is clear that multiple interpretations are required before a shared understanding of the impact of the new knowledge (guideline) can be assessed against the old (current) knowledge. (Kitson 2009a, 136)

Green and colleagues compare the brokers, boundary leaders and linking agents advocated in the knowledge translation field to Gladwell's description in *The Tipping Point* of connectors, mavens[1] and salesmen (Green et al. 2009, 163). Nutley and her UK colleagues (2007) pick up and expand upon the idea of the researcher as spanner and interpreter of context, to discuss how researchers can take a stance outside the prevailing paradigm, "using their work to problematize established frameworks and ways of thinking" (12). Further, others have said that such boundary spanners need to be "fluent in both activist and scholarly cultures" (Sudbury and Okazawa-Rey 2009, 8) with the potential to see teaching in learning communities as concerned with fostering oppositional work. Van de Ven and Johnson (2006) use the term "engaged scholarship." They see the need for "collaborative inquiry in which academics and practitioners leverage their different perspectives and competencies to coproduce knowledge about a complex problem or phenomenon that exists under conditions of uncertainty" (Van de Ven and Johnson 2006, 803).

Conclusion

Over the past two decades, the literature on knowledge translation has documented multiple shifts in knowledge translation's scope: from a one way process of bringing evidence into practice and policy, to multidirectional processes, involving multi-holders of multi-forms of knowledge. Much of the early literature focused on only one form of knowledge, research evidence, as a commodity to be to be applied directly to practice and policy. We are now wrestling with transdisciplinarity and knowledge translation, and coming to new methods, processes and considerations that reflect emergent common languages, theories and projects. But over time, many complexities have emerged related to this research-to-action trajectory. The conceptual as well instrumental use of research, the sociopolitical context of the application of evidence, the emergent nature of knowledge(s) through interactivity, and the triaging influence of prior knowledge and assumptions have all been identified as confounders to a narrow and linear evidence-to-practice or evidence-to-policy path. Indeed, many of these confounders can be seen to be in play in the substance use field, as it slowly shifts from ideologically driven approaches to prevention, harm reduction and treatment, to more evidence-informed and evidence-based ones. This need to bring in various forms of evidence to the substance use field, along with the challenge of integrating sex and gender in this work, drive creation of knowledge translation mechanisms that support reflexive processes where multiple, and possibly even transdisciplinary forms of knowledge can be considered and interpreted.

Expanding our notions of the users of evidence and of their contexts has been another important trend in knowledge translation practice. The move from a bi-directional exchange between researchers and health-care practitioners to the involvement of multiple knowledge users including researchers, practitioners, policy analysts, decision makers, community advocates and the people with the health concerns is a huge and challenging shift. Equally challenging is moving further to include transdisciplinarity, taking in diverse disciplines, contexts, perspectives and opportunities and where researchers are often decentered and no one research discipline privileged. The organizational and sociopolitical contexts of all these players, disciplines and contexts, not only their individual learning needs, are now key elements to be weighed and addressed. Transdisciplinary research, exchange and action not only challenges typical knowledge translation but also may facilitate and accommodate these complexities. By overtly reaching for a common purpose and language in understanding addiction, transdisciplinarity flourishes and forms an equally transdisciplinary approach to knowledge translation.

The call for a focus on facilitation of interactivity in knowledge exchange highlights the need to find processes that engage knowledge users in learning about, synthesizing and applying the evidence to their specific context in a way that is linked to system wide efforts. Communities of practice have been described in the knowledge translation literature as offering an ideal context for integration, interactivity, synthesis and action on knowledge. Given that knowledge users have diverse agendas, time frames, cultures and sources of knowledge they consider legitimate, the need for facilitating intersectoral or interdisciplinary processes becomes critical. Beyond countering isolation or managing differences, the facilitation role becomes one of promoting participation, preventing oversimplification, and supporting whole systems view, employing a range of strategic and critically reflective practices. Feminist participatory action research processes, with their focus on inclusion, participation, action, change and reflexivity, have the potential to offer much to such processes, by integrating evidence making with knowledge exchange and translation.

Clearly, to tackle addiction, researchers must collaborate and integrate across traditional boundaries. They must bring together academic disciplines, develop new research skills and become more involved in the implementation of research in policy, product and action (Bammer 2005, 1). Transdisciplinarity, with its focus on new thinking and the melding or meeting of many forms of knowledge, not only fulfills a key need in addictions research and treatment, but it also demands equally advanced approaches to knowledge translation.

Discussion Questions

1. What opportunities are there for bringing a more ecological approach to knowledge translation, one that takes various levels of context into account?
2. What mechanisms do we have for facilitating collaborative and coordinated processes that involve multidisciplinary and multisectoral participants in all stages of the research process (including knowledge translation)?
3. What challenges are created for knowledge translation practice by multi-method studies that bring forth transdisciplinary findings?

Note

1 *Maven* is a term used by Gladwell to mean an expert who likes to pass on knowledge, and which Green discusses as relevant to the concept of early adopter.

References

Baek, Eun-Ok, and Sasha A. Barab. 2005. "A study of dynamic design dualities in a web-supported community of practice for teachers." *Educational Technology & Society* no. 8 (4):161–177.

Bammer, Gabriele. 2005. "Integration and implementation sciences: Building a new specialization." *Ecology & Society* no. 10 (2):78–103.

Bertone, Maria Paola, Bruno Meessen, Guy Clarysse, David Hercot, Allison Kelley, Yamba Kafando, Isabelle Lange, Jérôme Pfaffmann, Valéry Ridde, Isidore Sieleunou, and Sophie Witter. 2013. "Assessing communities of practice in health policy: A conceptual framework as a first step towards empirical research." *Health Research Policy & Systems* no. 11 (1):1–28. doi: 10.1186/1478-4505-11-39.

Best, Allan, Gregg Moor, Bev Holmes, Snjezana Kralj, Kim Thomas, and Tim Huerta. 2004. *How do we make knowledge exchange work? Using systems and network theory to improve strategy*. Vancouver, BC: Community for Health Systems Study (CHeSS) and the Vancouver Coastal Health Research Institute.

Best, Allan, Daniel Stokols, Lawrence Green, Scott Leischow, Bev Holmes, and Kaye Buchholz. 2003. "An integrative framework for community partnering to translate theory into effective health promotion strategy." *American Journal of Health Promotion* no. 18 (2):168–176. doi: 10.4278/0890-1171-18.2.168.

Best, Allan, Jennifer L. Tempstra, and Gregg Moor. 2004. *Improving knowledge to action: Models partners and tools*. Powerpoint presentation.

Bickford, Susan. 1996. *The dissonance of democracy: Listening, conflict and citizenship*. Ithaca, NY: Cornell University Press.

Campbell, Barbara. 2010. "Applying knowledge to generate action: A community-based knowledge translation framework." *Journal of Continuing Education in the Health Professions* no. 30 (1):65–71. doi: 10.1002/chp.20058.

Checkland, K., S. Harrison, and M. Marshall. 2007. "Is the metaphor of 'barriers to change' useful in understanding implementation? Evidence from general medicine practice." *Journal of Health Services Research and Policy* no. 12 (2):95–100.

Cherney, Adrian, Brian Head, Paul Boreham, Jenny Povey, and Michele Ferguson. 2013. "Research utilization in the social sciences: A comparison of five academic disciplines in Australia." *Science Communication* no. 35 (6):780–809. doi: 10.1177/1075547013491398.

Chunharas, Somsak. 2006. "An interactive integrative approach to translating knowledge and building a 'learning organization' in health services management." *Bulletin of the World Health Organization* no. 84 (8):652–657.

Clavier, Carole, Yan Sénéchal, Stéphane Vibert, and Louise Potvin. 2012. "A theory-based model of translation practices in public health participatory research." *Sociology of Health & Illness* no. 34 (5):791–805. doi: 10.1111/j.1467-9566.2011.01408.x.

Contandriopoulos, Damien. 2011. "On the nature and strategies of organized interests in health care policy making." *Administration & Society* no. 43 (1):45–65. doi: 10.1177/0095399710390641.

Corbett, Andrea M, Karen Francis, and Ysanne Chapman. 2007. "Feminist-informed participatory action research: A methodology of choice for examining critical nursing issues." *International Journal of Nursing Practice* no. 13:81–88.

Cox, Andrew. 2005. "What are communities of practice? A comparative review of four seminal works." *Journal of Information Science* no. 31 (6):527–540.
Dopson, Sue. 2007. "A view from organizational studies." *Nursing Research* no. 56 (4 Suppl):S72–7. doi: 10.1097/01.NNR.0000280635.71278.e9.
Dopson, Sue, and Louise Fitzgerald. 2005. *Knowledge to Action? Evidence-based health care in context*. New York: Oxford University Press.
Ebener, S., A. Khan, R. Shademani, L. Compernolle, M. Beltran, M. A. Lansang, and M. Lippmana. 2006. "Knowledge mapping as a technique to support knowledge translation." *Bulletin of the World Health Organization* no. 84 (8):636–642.
Flood, Robert Louis. 2010. "The relationship of 'systems thinking' to action research." *Systemic Practice & Action Research* no. 23 (4):269–284. doi: 10.1007/s11213-010-9169-1.
Fornssler, Barbara, Holly A. McKenzie, Colleen Anne Dell, Larry Laliberte, and Carol Hopkins. 2013. "'I got to know them in a new way": Rela(y/t)ing rhizomes and community-based knowledge (brokers') transformation of western and Indigenous knowledge." *Cultural Studies Critical Methodologies* doi: 10.1177/1532708613516428.
Friere, Paulo. 2006. *Pedagogy of the oppressed*. 30th anniversary ed. New York: Continuum.
Ginsburg, Mark, and Gorostiaga, Jorge M. 2006. "Relationships between theorists/researchers and policy makers/practitioners: Rethinking the two cultures thesis and the possibility of dialogue." *Comparative Education Review* no. 45 (2):173–196.
Glasziou, Paul, and Brian Haynes. 2005. "The paths from research to improved health outcomes." *ACP Journal Club* 142 (2):A8–A10.
Goode, Luke. 2005. *Jurgen Habermas: Democracy and the public sphere*. Ann Arbor, MI: Pluto.
Green, Lawrence W., Judith M. Ottoson, César García, and Robert A. Hiatt. 2009. "Diffusion theory and knowledge dissemination, utilization, and integration in public health." *Annual Review of Public Health* no. 30 (1):151–174. doi: 10.1146/annurev.publhealth.031308.100049.
Hart, Angie, and David Wolff. 2006. "Developing local 'communities of practice' through local community—university partnerships." *Planning Practice & Research* no. 21 (1):121–138. doi: 10.1080/02697450600901616.
Harvey, G., A. Loftus-Hills, J Rycroft-Malone, A. Titchen, Alison L. Kitson, and B. McCormack. 2002. "Getting evidence into practice: The role and function of facilitation." *Journal of Advanced Nursing* no. 37 (6):577–588.
Helfrich, Christian D., Laura J. Damschroder, Hildi J. Hagedorn, Ginger S. Daggett, Anju Sahay, Mona Ritchie, Teresa Damush, Marylou Guihan, Philip M. Ullrich, and Cheryl B. Stetler. 2010. "A critical synthesis of literature on the promoting action on research implementation in health services (PARIHS) framework." *Implementation Science* no. 5:82. doi: 10.1186/1748-5908-5-82.
Hobin, Erin P., Sarah Hayward, Barbara Riley, Erica Di Ruggiero, and Judy Birdsell. 2012. "Maximising the use of evidence: Exploring the intersection between population health intervention research and knowledge translation from a Canadian perspective." *Evidence & Policy: A Journal of Research, Debate and Practice* no. 8 (1):97–115. doi: 10.1332/174426412x620155.
Hopkins, Susan. 2012. "The TŁĮCHQ Community Action Research Team: Place-based conversation starters." *Pimatisiwin: A Journal of Aboriginal & Indigenous Community Health* no. 10 (2):191–205.
Hulme, Rob, David Cracknell, and Allan Owens. 2009. "Learning in third spaces: Developing trans-professional understanding through practitioner enquiry." *Educational Action Research* no. 17 (4):537–550. doi: 10.1080/09650790903309391.

Jordan, Michelle, Holly Lanham, Benjamin Crabtree, Paul Nutting, William Miller, Kurt Stange, and Reuben McDaniel. 2009. "The role of conversation in health care interventions: Enabling sensemaking and learning." *Implementation Science* no. 4 (1):15.

Kirby, Sandra L., Lorraine Greaves, and Colleen Reid. 2006. *Experience research social change: Methods beyond the mainstream*. 2nd ed. Peterborough, ON: Broadview Press.

Kitson, Alison L. 2008. "The uncertainty and incongruity of evidence-based healthcare " *International Journal of Evidence-Based Healthcare* no. 6 (1):1–2.

———. 2009a. "Knowledge translation and guidelines: A transfer, translation or transformation process?" *International Journal of Evidence-Based Healthcare* no. 7 (2):124–139.

———. 2009b. "The need for systems change: Reflections on knowledge translation and organizational change." *Journal of Advanced Nursing* no. 65 (1):217–228. doi: 10.1111/j.1365-2648.2008.04864.x.

Kitson, Alison L., J. Harvey, and Brendan. McCormack. 1998. "Enabling the implementation of evidence-based practice: A conceptual framework." *Quality in Health Care* no. 7:149–158.

Kitson, Alison L., J. Rycroft-Malone, Gill Harvey, Brendan McCormack, Kate Seers, and Angie Titchen. 2008. "Evaluating the successful implementation of evidence into practice using the PARiHS framework: Theoretical and practical challenges." *Implementation Science* no. 3 (1). doi: doi:10.1186/1748-5908-3-1.

Landry, Réjean, Nabil Amara, and Moktar Lamari. 2001. "Climbing the ladder of research utilization." *Science Communication* no. 22 (4):396–422.

Landry, Réjean, Nabil Amara, Ariel Pablos-Mendes, Ramesh Shademani, and Irving Gold. 2006. "The knowledge-value chain: A conceptual framework for knowledge translation in health." *Bulletin of the World Health Organization* no. 84 (8):597–602.

Lavis, John N., Jonathan Lomas, Maimunah Hamid, and Nelson K Sewankambod. 2006. "Assessing country-level efforts to link research to action." *Bulletin of the World Health Organization* no. 84 (8):620–628.

Legare, France. 2009. "Assessing barriers and facilitators to knowledge use." In *Knowledge translation in health care: Moving from evidence to practice*, edited by Sharon E. Straus, Jacqueline Tetroe, and Ian D. Graham, 83–93. Chichester, UK: Blackwell-Wiley

McWilliam, Carol L., Anita Kothari, Catherine Ward-Griffin, Dorothy Forbes, Beverly Leipert, and Collaboration South West Community Care Access Centre Home Care. 2009. "Evolving the theory and praxis of knowledge translation through social interaction: A social phenomenological study." *Implementation Science* no. 4 (1):26.

Merrill, Barbara. 2005. "Dialogical feminism: Other women and the challenge of adult education." *International Journal of Lifelong Education* no. 24 (1):41–52.

Moat, Kaelan A., John N. Lavis, and Julia Abelson. 2013. "How contexts and issues influence the use of policy-relevant research syntheses: A critical interpretive synthesis." *Milbank Quarterly* no. 91 (3):604–648. doi: 10.1111/1468-0009.12026.

Morrow, Raymond A., and Carlos Alberto Torres. 2002. *Reading Freire and Habermas: Critical pedagogy and transformative social change*. New York: Teachers College Press.

Nutley, Sandra M., Isabel Walter, and Huw T. O. Davies. 2007. *Using Evidence: how research can inform public derivces*. Bristol, UK: The Policy Press.

Palmer, Debra, and Debra Kramlich. 2011. "An introduction to the multisystem model of knowledge integration and translation." *Advances in Nursing Science* no. 34 (1):29–38.

Rycroft-Malone, J., Gill Harvey, Kate Seers, Alison L. Kitson, Brendan McCormack, and Angie Titchen. 2004. "An exploration of the factors that influence the implementation of evidence into practice." *Journal of Clinical Nursing* no. 13 (8):913–924.

Sinfield, Paul, Kim Donoghue, Adele Horobin, and Elizabeth S. Anderson. 2012. "Placing interprofessional learning at the heart of improving practice: The activities and achievements of CLAHRC in Leicestershire, Northamptonshire and Rutland." *Quality in Primary Care* no. 20 (3):191–198.

Smith, Katherine E., and Kerry E. Joyce. 2012. "Capturing complex realities: Understanding efforts to achieve evidence-based policy and practice in public health." *Evidence & Policy: A Journal of Research, Debate and Practice* no. 8 (1):57–78. doi: 10.1332/174426412x6201371.

Smylie, Janet, Nili Kaplan-Myrth, and Kelly McShane. 2009. "Indigenous knowledge translation: Baseline findings in a qualitative study of the pathways of health knowledge in three indigenous communities in Canada." *Health Promotion Practice* no. 10 (3):436–446. doi: 10.1177/1524839907307993.

Straus, Sharon E., Jacqueline Tetroe, and Ian D. Graham. 2009. *Knowledge translation in health care: Moving from evidence to practice*. Chichester, UK: Blackwell-Wiley

Sudbury, Julia, and Margo Okazawa-Rey. 2009. "Introduction: Activist scholarship and the neoliberal university after 9/11." In *Activist Scholarship: Antiracism, feminism, and social change*, edited by Julia Sudbury and Margo Okazawa-Rey, 1–14. Boulder, CO: Paradigm.

Themba, Makani N., and Meredith Minkler. 2003. "Influencing policy through community based participatory research." In *Community-based participatory research for health*, edited by Meredith Minkler and Nina Wallerstein, 349–370. San Francisco, CA: Jossey-Bass.

Thomas, Paul, Juliet McDonnell, Janette McCulloch, Alison While, Nick Bosanquet, and Ewan Ferlie. 2005. "Increasing capacity for innovation in bureaucratic primary care organizations: A whole system participatory action research project." *Annals of Family Medicine* no. 3 (4):312–317. doi: 10.1370/afm.309.

Thompson, David S., Kathy O'Leary, Eva Jensen, Shannon Scott-Findlay, Linda O'Brien-Pallas, and Carole A. Estabrooks. 2008. "The relationship between busyness and research utilization: It is about time." *Journal of Clinical Nursing* no. 17 (4):539–548.

Van De Ven, Andrew H., and Paul E. Johnson. 2006. "Knowledge for theory and practice." *Academy of Management Review* no. 31 (4):802–821.

Ward, Vicky, Simon Smith, Allan House, and Susan Hamer. 2012. "Exploring knowledge exchange: A useful framework for practice and policy." *Social Science & Medicine* no. 74 (3):297–304. doi: 10.1016/j.socscimed.2011.09.021.

Wenger, Etienne, Richard McDermott, and William C. Snyder. 2002. *cultivating communities of practice: A guide to managing knowledge*. Boston, MA: Harvard Business School.

Suggestions for Further Reading

Bammer, Gabriele. 2005. "Integration and implementation sciences: Building a new specialization." *Ecology & Society* no. 10 (2):78–103.

Greenhalgh, Trisha, Glenn Robert, Fraser Macfarlane, Paul Bate, and Olivia Kyriakidou. 2004. "Diffusion of innovations in service organizations: Systematic review and recommendations." *Milbank Quarterly* no. 82 (4):581–629.

McWilliam, Carol L., Anita Kothari, Catherine Ward-Griffin, Dorothy Forbes, Beverly Leipert, and South West Community Care Access Centre Home Care Collaboration. 2009. "Evolving the theory and praxis of knowledge translation through social interaction: A social phenomenological study." *Implementation Science* no. 4 (1):26.

Nutley, Sandra M., Isabel Walter, and Huw T. O. Davies. 2007. *Using evidence: How research can inform public services*. Bristol, UK: The Policy Press.

16
THE FUTURE OF TRANSDISCIPLINARITY IN ADDICTION

Lorraine Greaves, Nancy Poole and Ellexis Boyle

Addiction is clearly a complex problem that requires equally complex analyses and solutions. Contemporary thinkers have provided some provocative ways to think about addiction that go beyond the limitations of illness or disease models, moralistic or legal responses. This book underscores this and suggests that to achieve real progress on this often intractable individual or social problem, we need to go much further. This book has argued that to generate innovation and a refreshed approach we need to respect the complexities of addiction by transforming our approach. Our contribution has been to demonstrate a range of tools, methods and strategies for taking a transdisciplinary, gendered, trauma-informed approach. We have identified three key actions for enhancing our understanding of addiction: 1) Forming transdisciplinary collaborations that work across disciplinary, sectoral and personal boundaries; 2) including sex- and gender-related concepts and factors in research, treatment, program and policy and 3) integrating issues that are linked to addiction, particularly trauma, into our responses. Taking these three actions will elevate the addiction field to better meet the needs of individuals, groups and communities struggling with addiction.

Ideally, all of these actions can be taken to form a contemporary approach. Integration of issues that link with addiction requires an understanding of the various and intersecting factors such as poverty, violence, racism, trauma and mental health as elements that shape the context of people's lives. It also requires an understanding and willingness for multisectors and agencies to work together in remedying such issues. Including sex and gender is the essential glue for joining social and biological factors together, and for understanding important differences and inequalities between and among all genders and sub-populations. They are also the building blocks for taking a transdisciplinary approach to research and treatment. Indeed, in order to integrate issues and factors related to addiction and to fully include sex and gender, one must breach many disciplinary boundaries and enthusiastically reach for other perspectives, methods, theories, frameworks and experiences in order to begin to fully grapple with addiction.

Like addiction, doing the work of transdisciplinarity is not easy, either in its methods and approaches or in finding the space in our roles or institutions to do it. Many of the authors in this book reflect on the challenges that accompany transdisciplinary efforts. These include entrenchment in disciplinary and hierarchical forms of knowledge, evidence and processes, or lack of communication and investment in multifaceted knowledge translation among employers, colleagues, funders or journals. Nor, because of discipline-based education and training, along with entrenched professional identities, does transdisciplinary work come naturally to all researchers or students, practitioners or policy makers. Only after experiencing the joys, challenges and benefits in traversing sectors, disciplines and territories do professional and personal benefits become clearer. As we have seen, these experiences can shift identities, understandings and work goals. Yet, none of this takes place on an unfettered, straight road. In this chapter we discuss some of the challenges and facilitators that could either impede or progress the uptake of transdisciplinarity, integration and the inclusion of sex and gender in future addiction research and treatment design. Finally, we address some contemporary social and political trends that might help to generate this change.

Challenges to and Facilitators of Transdisciplinarity in Addiction

Institutional Structures

A discipline-bound world where institutions of research, education and health care, and their processes of tenure and promotion, publishing, organization and rules of belonging, can present barriers to truly transformative work. Indeed, the business of university-based education and hospital-based clinical training is often to replicate these rigidities in professional training of students. Licensing bodies and associations harden these professional groups, by creating self-replicating networks, associations, regulations and codes of behavior. Few institutions of higher learning directly aim to create either inter- or transdisciplinary departments, teams or training programs. It is often after practicing in real world situations, or with seemingly intractable and complicated issues such as addiction, that individuals begin to appreciate the worth of taking a multi-pronged approach, recognizing the features of thinking and planning that integrate a range of view points, skills and perspectives. Some individuals choose to hone these skills, and some do not, likely feeling more comfortable in a discipline bound, clearly defined role.

Not surprisingly, funders of academic research reflect these disciplinary boundaries in their core funding programs. In recent years, however, strategic funding in some major research funding organizations has successfully funded partnership models, multi- or transdisciplinary teams, centers of excellence, knowledge translation and other innovations such as inclusion of non-academic, community or policy-based partners in research. These added innovations are welcome buttresses for incubating transdisciplinarity. These efforts bode well for increasing integration, more real-world engagement in research and innovation in thinking and creating evidence.

Equally rigid in structure are policy making enterprises, especially in governments. Typical organizations include departments, divisions or Ministries that are accountable for a singular area, such as housing, health or employment. These sections of government do not often work together, except at the highest levels of Cabinet or executive offices, where Ministers or Department Heads account to each other and to their Prime Ministers or Presidents. But this is not usually a location of detailed cross-cutting thinking and planning on complicated issues. In some instances, interministerial initiatives are generated, especially on multifaceted social issues, such as violence or the status of women, but this is not the rule. The result of this rigidity and silo-type structure is often a lack of unified vision or integration of policies and initiatives on a problem such as addiction. In some settings, there have been recent moves to connect addiction and mental health services, but this is not enough to fully respond to the range of determinants and issues embedded in the addiction problem.

Some innovations in the policy arena that show some hope are the "Health in all Policies" (HIAP) (Shankardass et al. 2011; Freiler et al. 2013) approach and Health Equity Impact Assessments (HEIA) (Orenstein and Rondeau 2009; Povall et al. 2013) of policies. Both of these trends reflect the view that intersectoral policy making and measuring its impact are critically important for improving health, and both could be adopted for moving the addiction issue forward. However, even these positive ideas have floundered (Greaves and Bialystok 2011), as they too run into barriers and do not address the potential of trans-sectoral policy making, which would generate a shared, new understanding of a policy area, and innovations that reflect this.

In academia, professional training and policy making, jargon and language can serve as barriers to amalgamated change making. Jargon, professional short forms and insular language can be formidable barriers to working on transdisciplinary solutions. Only in identified, focused transdisciplinary teams can this be addressed in a positive manner, where new, shared language is deliberately developed for bettering communication between team members and underpinning a new approach. Unfortunately, there are few examples of this to date.

Technology and Communication

One of the key shifts in contemporary society is an increased ease of communication, increased access to information and a democratization of engagement in defining and engaging with societal issues. Sharing and communicating what we know through mechanisms such as websites, networks, wikis, communities of inquiry and other forms of collective learning provide spaces where we can not only find additional perspectives on complicated and every changing realities but also exchange, discuss, generate, take stock and take inspiration from each other's work (Wenger, White, and Smith 2009; Lewis et al. 2011). In addition, the average person with Internet access can read information (not always accurate) about addiction and other health issues, generate online groups and fora and inform themselves of new findings and thinking on the issue.

This increased communication is critically important to transdisciplinarity, as it creates a more level playing field to accessing previously protected information, thinking and work. It also offers a window for communities of people to engage with professionals, researchers and treatment providers, free of barriers (Kothari and Armstrong 2011). It also provides a platform for the public to make demands of professionals and researchers, and to bring them to a more real-world level, both creating, translating and explaining evidence (Coleman and Gotze 2001; de Zúñiga, Jung, and Valenzuela 2012; de Zúñiga and Valenzuela 2011; Sæbø, Rose, and Skiftenes Flak 2008). Ongoing openness and access to information will facilitate efforts to achieve transdisciplinarity.

Higher Standards in Research

In recent years, scientific advocacy has accelerated the inclusion and awareness of sex and gender in health research, particularly in the United States and Canada (Grant and Ballem 2000; Greaves et al. 1999; Johnson, Greaves, and Repta 2007). This push has been steady and consistent: claiming that such inclusion will render better science, a key and compelling argument for health research funding agencies. After initiatives that began in the women's health movement, this push has broadened to include men's health and gender and health (Greaves 2008) and, more recently, transgender health and has consistently pushed for a broader understanding of how sex and gender play out in disease, health and treatment.

After 30 years of advocacy, paradigm shifts have finally begun. There are new requirements from health research funders to not only justify exclusions of women and minorities (NIH 1993; http://orwh.od.nih.gov/about/pdf/NIH-Revitalization-Act-1993.pdf), but more important to include women and minorities in clinical trials (NIH 2014; www.nih.gov/news/health/sep2014/od-23.htm) and account for sex and gender in all research proposals (CIHR 2014; www.cihr-irsc.gc.ca/e/32019.html). These initiatives signal a sea change in how health research is designed and conducted, and push researchers into thinking more thoroughly about the sex of their cell lines, animals or human subjects. More and more theorizing about how sex and gender matter to health is emerging, and concomitant research designs are flourishing (Oliffe and Greaves 2011).

Social Trends

There are numerous trends and pressures that may, in the future, facilitate a more transdisciplinary and integrated approach. The general public may play a key part in this. The public is increasingly health literate and informed as a result of an increased availability to and ease of accessing information. There is also an element of direct personal and family experience of addiction that can get transformed into action, change and political pressure (Johnston 2013; Boyd, MacPherson, and Osborn 2009). The intractability of addiction is a considerable pressure on families and communities of all income levels, and one that is attracting increasing social action, and translating into demands on policy makers and politicians. Communities are interested in solving overt addiction issues, and families and communities are highly invested in resolving the pain of addiction for their members.

In concert with access to increased scientific knowledge about addiction, and personal experiences, there is more information about individualized diagnosis, care and treatment. The public is primed to demand more and more personalized medicine in many areas of disease, as promising findings in genetics, epigenetics and clinical medicine make this more and more likely. At the program and policy level, this translates into a tailoring of approaches to meet growing concerns and publicity about inequities and inequalities among various social groups.

In personalized medicine and tailored programming, a growing awareness and concern about the absence of sex and gender in clinical, biomedical and other health research, and the costs of this pattern, particularly for women's health will also be felt. More widespread dismay with the toll and delay in righting this inequity is inevitable, as three decades of scientific advocacy is finally bearing fruit in the form of higher standards for research funding. All of these pressures will confront levels of government from municipal to federal, and will also affect regulations and standards for funding, conducting (NIH 2014), and publishing research (Gendered Innovations 2014). The frustrations and pain associated with intractable problems such as addiction invite multisectoral responses and those responses necessarily include the general public.

Other social trends matter. If alienation and loneliness are key elements in the development of addiction, as several authors have proposed, including Gabor Maté (Maté 2010) and Bruce Alexander (Alexander 2008), then there will be demands to address these root causes. Cities such as Vancouver, Canada, are already addressing this issue among an increasing proportion of residents who live alone, and who complain about limited social networks and resulting isolation (Vancouver Foundation 2012). Strengthening social networks and safety nets for individuals and families who may experience dislocation is a critical arena for building community, and may be seen as a way to combat or reduce addiction and other mental health concerns.

In addition, an increased public familiarity with trauma, and post-traumatic stress disorder (PTSD) has emerged in the last decade, in part through veterans returning home with such conditions, and in part through more public discourse on the prevalence and effects of sexual violence, domestic violence, child abuse, colonization, dislocation, refugee experiences and conflict. Such social problems were often not discussed freely or fully in the past, but now are, resulting in a greater understanding of how they contribute to ongoing mental and physical health issues, including addiction and suicide. These links will also converge with public opinion and knowledge to impel advocates, legislators and health-care providers to take a more compassionate and broader view of trauma. Trauma-informed practice will grow in popularity as a response (Poole and Greaves 2012).

Inequity and inequality is also more on the public mind. The social divide represented by inequality of income and power is also more widely debated, due to the 99% vs. 1% income divide popularized by the Occupy movement (Wikipedia 2014). The despair associated with lack of mobility in capitalist-based societies and the shortage of opportunities for young people, migrants and minorities will contribute to frustration and demands for action. As Schaef (1987) suggests, our systems can also be addicted to things such as profit or ambition, high expectations and rigid roles, all negatively affecting individuals. These social and economic structures leave people out or damage some groups, and may need to be shifted to release pressures on society. Responding to these shifts in public opinion, public engagement and discourse will implicate all of us engaged in addiction research and treatment. Furthermore, it will challenge us to create more engaged, transdisciplinary and open efforts to design policy, program and treatment.

Linked to this awareness is the growing strength of Indigenous ways of knowing. The pressure and clarity of indigenous populations, world wide, who experience addiction disproportionately, is aimed at engaging all of us in a wider, more holistic view of addiction and health (Jeffries 2006). This wider view is based on medicine wheels, "Two-Eyed Seeing," spirituality, legends and elder wisdom, and invites the mainstream addiction treatment circle to engage in a truly transdisciplinary manner (Rowan et al. 2014). Indigenous political movements, not only in North America but worldwide, are engaged in claiming this space and proposing these perspectives, much to the benefit of all populations (Howard-Bobiwash and Krouse 2009; White 2009; Evans et al. 2012; Coyhis and White 2002).

In science and evidence circles, there will have to be an endorsement of ambiguity, of not knowing, or of partial knowing, in order to fully embrace transdisciplinarity. This is perhaps one of the most difficult transitions yet to be made. The idea that all evidence is not discrete, firm and provable is anathema to some disciplines and some individuals. But knowledge translation and integrated solutions will require multiple views and types of evidence and will threaten the notion that positivist concrete answers are always available to answer such difficult questions as what causes addiction, and how it can be solved. When accounting for addiction's multifaceted elements, there will be aspects that elude science and experiments, and attract philosophical and spiritual theorizing or simple human solutions, not complex pharmaceuticals or intricate treatment programs.

While the contributors to this book do not purport to have all of the answers or address every facet of addiction research and treatment—a large field—they all offer an additional piece of strategy, method, advice, approach, insight, response or idea that will assist in moving toward the transformation that the addiction field so needs. Openness to these myriad thoughts is required for transdisciplinarity to take root. From these offerings, it is hoped that readers develop their own ideas and are inspired to take the risks and creative solutions to invigorate and innovate in the interests of improving the countless lives and communities who experience addiction.

Moving Forward

The chapters in this book have demonstrated that integrated approaches, including sex and gender, and doing transdisciplinary research, education, practice and policies are necessary and possible. The chapters have covered research, education, practice and policy and have demonstrated the utility and breadth of these approaches. While some people may be more open to transdisciplinarity based on their own prior work and life experiences, learning to embrace complexity and innovation is a journey that anyone can take. We can move beyond the deeply entrenched, rigid stances taken towards addiction that create negativity and stigma, impede recovery or degrade public opinion. Indeed, flexibility and iterative policy and practice development are critical aspects of a new overall response to substance use and addiction.

The rewards of this work are transformation, both public and private. Each chapter demonstrates, in some way, the transformative potential of working in transdisciplinary ways and through integrating multiple factors and issues including addiction, trauma, mental ill health, sex and gender. This transformation can occur at a personal, disciplinary, project or policy level through individuals being able to recognize both the strengths and limitations of their own knowledge, discipline, methods and world views. As the contributors demonstrate this has occurred for both students and mentors, researchers, clinicians and program developers who, through being open to migrating across borders and being open to listening to the perspectives and needs of clients and communities, have fundamentally changed the way in which they do research or practice.

In 2015, transdisciplinarity remains a nascent approach, but one that represents a Renaissance in addiction research, treatment and policy. Its full potential may be in the future. As populations diversify, and social and political trends indicate the need for change in our collective response to addiction, institutions that guard knowledge and notions of disciplinarity will also be forced to relax, shift and change. As health care systems are pressured and restructured, new generations of researchers, clinicians and policy makers will reach for improved and integrated ways to address addiction and its related issues. The boundaries of what we now know and how we currently practice can thus be seen not as outer edges of the field, but as the permeable beginnings of new collaborations and approaches. The spaces between disciplines and sectors are not empty, but rather territories ripe for transformation.

References

Alexander, Bruce K. 2008. *The globalisation of addiction: A study in poverty of the spirit*. New York: Oxford University Press.
Boyd, Susan C., Donald MacPherson, and Bud Osborn. 2009. *Raise shit!: Social action saving Lives*. Halifax, NS: Fernwood.
CIHR. 2014. *Gender, sex and health research guide: A tool for CIHR applicants*. Ottawa ON, Canadian Institutes for Health Research
Coleman, Stephen, and John Gotze. 2001. *Bowling together: Online public engagement in policy deliberation*. London: Hansard Society.
Coyhis, Don, and W. White. 2002. Addiction and recovery in Native America: Lost history, enduring lessons. *Counselor* 3 (5):16–20.
de Zúñiga, Homero Gil, Nakwon Jung, and Sebastián Valenzuela. 2012. Social media use for news and individuals' social capital, civic engagement and political participation. *Journal of Computer-Mediated Communication* 17 (3):319–336.
de Zúñiga, Homero Gil, and Sebastián Valenzuela. 2011. The mediating path to a stronger citizenship: Online and offline networks, weak ties, and civic engagement. *Communication Research* 38 (3):397–421.
Evans, Arthur C., Ijeoma Achara-Abrahams, Roland Lamb, and William L. White. 2012. Ethnic-specific support systems as a method for sustaining long-term addiction recovery. *Journal of Groups in Addiction & Recovery* 7 (2–4):171–188.
Freiler, Alix, Carles Muntaner, Ketan Shankardass, Catherine L. Mah, Agnes Molnar, Emilie Renahy, and Patricia O'Campo. 2013. Glossary for the implementation of Health in All Policies (HiAP). *Journal of Epidemiology and Community Health* 67 (12):1068–1072.
Gendered Innovations. 2014. *Sex and gender analysis policies of peer-reviewed journals* [cited September 28, 2014]. Available from http://genderedinnovations.stanford.edu/sex-and-gender-analysis-policies-peer-reviewed-journals.html.
Grant, Karen, and Penny Ballem. 2000. *A women's health research institute in the Canadian Institutes for Health Research*. Vancouver: BC Centre of Excellence for Women's Health.
Greaves, Lorraine. 2008. Women, gender and health research. In *Women's health: Intersections of policy, research, and practice*, edited by P. Armstrong and J. Deadman. Toronto, ON: Canadian Scholars' Press.
Greaves, Lorraine J., and Lauren R. Bialystok. 2011. Health in All Policies–All talk and little action? *Canadian Journal of Public Health / Revue Canadienne de Sante'e Publique*:407–409.
Greaves, Lorraine, Olena Hankivsky, Carol Amaratunga, Penny Ballem, Donna Chow, Maria De Koninck, Karen Grant, Abby Lippman, Heather Maclean, Janet Maher, Karen Messing, and Bilkis Vissandjee. 1999. *CIHR 2000: Sex, gender and women's health*. Vancouver, BC: BC Centre of Excellence for Women's Health.
Howard-Bobiwash, Heather, and Susan Applegate Krouse. 2009. *Keeping the campfires going: Native women's activism in urban communities*. Lincoln: U of Nebraska Press.
Jeffries, Rod. 2006. Healing our spirit worldwide: The fifth gathering. *Pimatziwin* 1 (2):173–177.
Johnson, Joy L., Lorraine Greaves, and Robin Repta. 2007. *Better science with sex and gender: A primer for health research*. Vancouver, BC: Women's Health Research Network.

Johnston, Ann Dowsett. 2013. *Drink: The intimate relationship between women and alcohol*. New York: HarperCollins.

Kothari, Anita, and Rebecca Armstrong. 2011. Community-based knowledge translation: Unexplored opportunities. *Implementation Science* 6 (1):59–64.

Lewis, Laura A., Zoe Koston, Marjorie Quartley, and Jason Adsit. 2011. Virtual communities of practice: Bridging research and practice using Web 2.0. *Journal of Educational Technology Systems* 39 (2):155–161.

Maté, Gabor. 2010. *In the realm of hungry ghosts: Close encounters with addiction*. Berkeley, CA: North Atlantic Books.

NIH. 1993. NIH Revitalization Act: Subtitle B, Part 1. *Sec* 131:103–143.

NIH. 2014. *New supplemental awards apply sex and gender lens to NIH-funded research*. Bethesda, MD: National Institutes of Health.

Oliffe, John L., and Lorraine Greaves. 2011. *Designing and conducting gender, sex, and health research*. Thousand Oaks, CA: SAGE.

Orenstein, Marla, and Krista Rondeau. 2009. *Scan of health equity impact assessment tools*. Calgary: Habitat Health Impact Consulting.

Poole, Nancy, and Lorraine Greaves, eds. 2012. *Becoming trauma informed*. Toronto, ON: Centre for Addiction and Mental Health.

Povall, Susan L., Fiona A. Haigh, Debbie Abrahams, and Alex Scott-Samuel. 2013. Health equity impact assessment. *Health Promotion International* 29 (4):621–633.

Rowan, Margo, Nancy Poole, Beverley Shea, Joseph Jone, P. David Myota, Marwa Fang, Carol Hopkins, Laura Hall, Christopher Mushquash, and Colleen Dell. 2014. Cultural interventions to treat addictions in Indigenous populations: Findings from a scoping study. *Substance Abuse Treatment, Prevention, and Policy* 9 (34).

Sæbø, Øystein, Jeremy Rose, and Leif Skiftenes Flak. 2008. The shape of eParticipation: Characterizing an emerging research area. *Government Information Quarterly* 25 (3):400–428.

Schaef, Anne Wilson 1987. *When society becomes an addict*. San Francisco: Harper and Row.

Shankardass, K., O. Solar, K. Murphy, A. Freiler, S. Bobbili, A. Bayoumi, and P. O'Campo. 2011, February. *Getting started with Health in All Policies: A resource pack*. Toronto, ON: Centre for Research on Inner City Health (CRICH), St. Michael's Hospital.

Vancouver Foundation. June 2012. *Connections and engagement. A survey of metro Vancouver*. www.vancouverfoundation.ca/sites/default/files/documents/VanFdn-SurveyResults-Report.pdf.

Wenger, Etienne, Nancy White, and John D. Smith. 2009. *Digital habitats: Stewarding technology for communities*. Portland, OR: CPSquare.

White, William L. 2009. The mobilization of community resources to support long-term addiction recovery. *Journal of Substance Abuse Treatment* 36 (2):146–158.

Wikipedia. *We are the 99%* 2014 [cited September 28, 2014]. Available from http://en.wikipedia.org/wiki/We_are_the_99%25.

INDEX

Aboriginal communities and populations 125, 130, 131; community support workers 114; indigenous knowledge 2, 44, 221; Indigenous Knowledge Framework 74; Indigenous political movements 221; interactivity with 209
Aboriginal people 168; Alaskan Natives 43; American Indian or Alaskan Natives (AI/AN) 43; First Nation–specific services 111; Iroquois knowledge 75; Mi'kmaq tribe 44; response to historical trauma by 40; social work and trauma treatment 43–4; stigmatization of 168; with substance use problems 44
abuse: and alcohol use during pregnancy 146; domestic 221; victimizing effects of 186; *see also* child abuse; trauma; violence
Action on Women's Addictions Research and Education (AWARE) 151–2
addiction: alienation and 220; and attachment 162; biological factors of 20, 26, 216; biology of 5, 38; causes of 220–1; coexisting views of 207; co-morbidities to 21; contemporary thinking re 7–10; costs of 3; culture of 101; defined 5; explanations for 3; factors affecting 124; geographical location as factor in 124; historical understandings of 6–7; as illness/disease 6–8, 11, 207; integrated approach 10; intersection with trauma and gender 11–13, 16, 37–40, 129, 132; key terms 26–7; legal frameworks for 6, 10–11; loneliness and 220; moral framework of 6, 11; neurobiology of 51–6; and pain 101; during pregnancy 186; policy-making in response to 184–96; positive vs. negative reinforcement aspects of 56; as a problem of learning and memory 51; public health views of 207; responses to 3–4, 184; science 89; as self-medication 9, 112; social class and 124, 167; substance, relational and process 8; system 8; transdisciplinary approaches to 4–5, 13–16, 117; treatment in Indigenous populations 69–75; various interpretations of 26–7; and violence against women 42; and women 40–2; *see also* alcohol, addiction to; gambling addiction; substance use/abuse/dependence
addiction treatment 111, 113, 194; folding cultural/spiritual practices into 44; integrated approach to 42, 112; transdisciplinary 137–42, 161–6; for women 77, 137–42
adrenocorticotropic hormone (ACTH) 54–5
adversity: childhood 4, 111, 112; early life 60; neurobiological effects of 55; *see also* abuse; child abuse; violence
Alaskan Natives *see* Aboriginal people

alcohol: addiction to 5–6; alcohol disorders 109; Alcoholics Anonymous 6, 177; alcoholism 9, 56; Alcohol Policy Information System (APIS) 190; Alcohol-Related Birth Defects 189; Alcohol-Related Neurodevelopmental Disorder (ARND) 189; binge drinking 146; binge stage 56; birth defects (alcohol-related) 189 and FASD 57; gendered effects of 191; *in utero* exposure to 59; regulation and control of 10; research on addiction to 21; teratogenic effects of 56–8, 190; *see also* alcohol use and abuse; alcohol use during pregnancy; prenatal alcohol exposure (PAE)

alcohol use and abuse 7–8, 38, 108; gender gap in 39; and neural changes 53; risk factors for 153; *see also* alcohol use during pregnancy

alcohol use during pregnancy 144–6, 185, 189–91; harmful effects of 189–90; interventions for 146–7; lack of research and interventions for 153–4; response to 190–1; social and economic contexts influencing 146; transdisciplinarity and systematic reviews 152–3; transdisciplinary responses to 192–6; typical approaches to 146–7

Alexander, Bruce 5, 8–9, 220
Als, Heidilise 85
American Indian or Alaskan Natives (AI/AN) *see* Aboriginal people
amphetamine sensitization paradigm 59
animal models: in addiction and mental health studies 62; of the effects of PAE and stress/trauma 61; for the teratogenic effects of alcohol 57–8
Anishinaabe *see* Aboriginal people
antenatal care *see* prenatal health care
anthropology 8, 122
anxiety 55; and FASD 57–8
assault, sexual and physical 112; *see also* trauma; violence

Bammer, Gabriele 206
BC Women's Hospital 90
Best, Allan 208
best practice recommendations 82, 149
better practices model (BPM) 144, 148–9, 150, 154
Bickel, Warren K. 7

biology 10; and substance use disorders 50, 54; *see also* addiction
biomedical health research 195, 220; cellular medicine 89; cellular sciences 21; physiological sciences 21
biopsychosocial model 10; bio-psycho-social-spiritual approach 44; *see also* Fetal Alcohol Spectrum Disorder; Fetal Alcohol Syndrome
Bowlby, John 83
boys: adolescent 54; gendered health issues of 16, 31; mental health and well-being of 129; results of "still face" procedure 59; substance use by 54
brain physiology 77; dysregulation of dopamine systems 51–2
Breaking the Cycle 90
British Columbia Health of the Homeless Survey (BCHOHS) 108
British Columbia Ministry for Children and Family Development 88
British Columbia Reproductive Care Program 88

Canadian Consortium on Neural Degeneration and Aging 104
Canadian Institutes of Health Research (CIHR) 12–13, 20
Canadian Tobacco Control Research Committee (CTCRI) 147
cardiovascular disease 21, 57
Carlson, Robert G. 7–8
central nervous system (CNS) problems 189–90
Centre for Addiction and Mental Health (CAMH) 72
Checkland, K. 206
child abuse 221; substance use during pregnancy as 186
child welfare services 89, 194
children: effect of early trauma on 186; of women with substance abuse disorders and mental health issues 40
cigarettes *see* tobacco
Clavier, Carole 206
cocaine use 53, 56; *see also* crack cocaine
Cochrane Collaboration 148
Cochrane systematic review 85
cognition: cognitive appraisal 171; cognitive-behavioral model 170, 171; cognitive control center 51–2; cognitive tasks 123; and substance use disorders 50

Cole, Donald 15
collaboration: interdisciplinary 120; intersectoral 126; vs. transdisciplinarity 169; transdisciplinary 180, 216; in addressing trauma 113–16
colonization 43, 73, 125, 131, 137, 221
community: communities of practice, transnational 208; Community Health Setting (CHS) 131; community health workers 114–15; community partner organizations 115; community support, erosion of 79
complexity theory 206
corticotropin-releasing hormone (CRH) 55–6
cortisol 54–5, 59
counseling: grief and bereavement 79; sexual health 111; for trauma-related experiences 113
counsellors 137; alcohol and drug 114; peer parent 81
crack cocaine 21, 108, 129; *see also* cocaine use
crime, and poverty 108
criminal justice 130, 184, 194
critical reflexivity 122–3, 124, 127–33
cross-cultural work 43
crystal methamphetamine 108
C/S/R (*consumers* of mental health system services, *survivors* of violence and trauma, and/or in *recovery* from substance use problems) 40–2
culture(s): of addiction 101; cultural issues 92, 110; diversity in 45, 114, 130, 211; dominant 83; indigenous 44, 69–75, influence on public health and policies 143; loss of 43; of power 128; and psychoactive drug use 7, 10; and substance use disorders 50; of work setting 173; *see also* Honoring Our Strengths Project
custody issues 41, 139, 190, 192

decolonization 36, 43–5, 70, 73, 75
Deleary, Mary 70
Dell, Colleen 71
depression 41, 55; and FASD 57–8
developmental care, in NICU 85–6
Developmental Origins of Health and Disease (DOHaD) 57, 62
diabetes 21, 57
dialectical behavior therapy 141

Dick-Reed, Grantley 86
dislocation 8–9, 220–1
Domestic Violence Project (DVP) 127; *see also* abuse, domestic; violence, domestic
dopamine 51–3; dopaminergic cell bodies 51–2; and FASD 57; interaction with stress 56; and prenatal stress and alcohol exposure 61; and stress dysregulation 54
dopamine systems 53, 55–6; dysregulation of 53–4, 58, 178; and prenatal alcohol exposure 58–9
Dopson, Sue 208
Double Exposure 148, 150
drug abuse *see* drug use and misuse
drug use and misuse 9, 38, 108, 111; by adolescents 54; disorders 109; during pregnancy 185; gender differences in 11–13; pipe sharing 129; *see also* alcohol use; alcohol use during pregnancy; substance use
drugs: addiction to 5–6; availability of 8–9; hallucinogenic 7; illicit 108; prenatal exposure to 60; psychoactive 7; regulation and control of 10–11; trafficking 108; *see also* crack cocaine; cocaine use; heroin use; opioids
Dumont, Jim 69–70, 74

early childhood development 89, 117
early life experience, as vulnerability factor 50
early trauma, effects of 186; *see also* trauma
eating disorders 5, 89
economic factors 20; *see also* poverty
Elk Ridge 72
environmental factors 54, 62, 92, 107
estradiol 53; *see also* sex (gonadal) hormones
estrous cycle 60
ethanol, and PAE 60
ethics 28, 89, 106, 122
ethnicity, and substance use 124, 146, 153, 167
Ettorre, Elizabeth 12
Eurocentricity 131
evidence: evidence-based practice 62, 115–16, 120, 161, 185, 205, 209–10; multiple forms of 150, 153, 204–5; in systematic reviews 143–4; and transdisciplinarity 221; wide range of 148
existentialism 8, 168, 171, 172
Expecting to Quit 147–8, 149

families: and addiction 220; Families in Recovery (FIR) Square 90, 91; and support workers 114; lack of support from 117; support for 114; *see also* parents
family-centered care (FCC) 87, 139; in NICU 83–5
Fassel, Diane 6
female genital cutting (FGC, FGM) 77, 98–100, 102–3
feminism 12, 86, 105, 122–3, 130, 177, 206, 209, 211; critical 12, 88, 122, 128; dialogic 209
feminist theory 206; critical feminism 128; *see also* feminism
Fetal Alcohol Spectrum Disorder (FASD) 1, 39–40, 51, 57–8, 189–90
Fetal Alcohol Syndrome (FAS) 189; research on 88
fetus-centricity 185–6, 189
Finnegan, Loretta 88
First Nations *see* Aboriginal people
Fitzgerald, Louise 208
Fornssler, Barb 74, 75
foster care 60, 88, 90, 111
Foundation for Alcohol Research and Education (FARE) 192
Framework Convention on Tobacco Control (FCTC) 191
Frankl, Viktor 171
Friere, Paulo 209

gambling addiction 5–6, 11; research on 21
gender: constructs 62; equity 194; as factor in research and treatment 216; and health 89–90, 216, 219; in health and addiction research 105, 107, 216, 219, 220; and identity 4; intersection with trauma and addiction 4–5, 20, 37–40, 78, 111, 113, 124, 216–17, 222; and mental health 111; politics 184; and PTSD 110; relations 4; roles and expectations 54; studies 89; and substance use 12–13, 16, 50, 167, 172; terminology related to 27; *see also* sex-related factors
gender differences 54; in mental health issues 61; in effect of stress and PAE 59–61
General Aggression Model (GAM) 170–1
genetics 170; and substance use disorders 50, 54; variability in 62

Gift-Economy Network 75
girls: addiction in 21; adolescent 54, 146; alcohol use by 189; empowerment of 151; results of "still face" procedure 59; social determinants of health for 36, 38; substance use by 54, 146, 149; tobacco use by 146, 151, 188; treatment for 11, 16; *see also* women
Gladwell, Malcolm 210
Glasziou, Paul 208
globalization, and drug availability 8–9
glucocorticoid hormones 54
gonadal (sex) hormones 38, 53, 60
Green, Lawrence W. 210
grey literature 143, 148, 149

Habermas, Jürgen 209
Hall, Kara 14
hallucinogens 7; *see also* drugs
Harding, Sandra 123
harm reduction movement 87, 88, 108, 111, 113, 149–50, 195
Hassan, Samah 102
Haudenosaunee knowledge 75; *see also* Aboriginal communities and populations
Haynes, Brian 208
health: equity 89, 189; and health-system designers 195; literacy 127; pillars 45; social determinants of 89, 117, 131, 154, 189, 191, 193
health care: access to 102; family-centered 83–5, 87, 139; prenatal 86, 111, 153; primary 42; trauma-informed 39–42, 45, 78, 90–1, 110, 112–13, 120, 139–40; women-centered 86–7, 195
Health Education Council (HEC; Britain) 188
Health Equity Impact Assessments (HEIA) 194–5, 218
Health in All Policies (HIAP) 159, 194–5, 218
Heartwood Centre for Women 137–42
hepatitis 108
heroin use 53, 82, 108
HerWay Home 90
Highs and Lows: Canadian Perspectives on Women and Substance Use (Poole and Greaves) 11
HIV/AIDS 108
homelessness 77, 107, 108, 110, 112, 117; *see also* housing issues

Honouring Our Strengths: Indigenous Culture as Intervention in Addiction Treatment 44, 69–70
Hopkins, Carol 70, 71
hormones: in the HPA axis 54; in the hypothalamus 54; sex 38, 53, 60; stress 38
housing issues 108, 110–12, 153, 195; see also homelessness
Hulme, Rob 206
hypothalamic-pituitary-adrenal (HPA) axis 36, 54–6; disruption of 54–6; dysregulation of 62; and FASD 57; hyperresponsiveness of 59–60; and later-life outcomes 61; and prenatal alcohol exposure 59–60; and the stress-diathesis hypothesis 60–2; vulnerability to programming 57

immigrant, refugee and other ethnocultural racialized groups (IRER), underutilization of mental health and addiction services by 126
immigration 126–7, 129, 133n2; see also migration
IMPART program 20–1, 31; challenge of maintaining communication in 24; cluster-based learning in 207; educational value of 81, 93; flipped classroom approach in 28–9; influence of 89; research on addiction and mental health 50, 62; use of technology in 23–4; transdisciplinary approach of 105
Indigenous peoples see Aboriginal communities and populations
inequities and inequality: gender 194, 220; health 83, 112, 124, 126, 128, 131, 189, 191; social 111, 123, 124, 170, 221; structural 11, 124, 125, 126
infants: with alcohol-related birth defects 189; with congenital conditions 79; cues and behaviors of 85; low birth weight 79–80; perinatal health 89; with physiological conditions 79; premature 79–80; postnatal care 111
Institute of Gender and Health (IGH) 12–13
Institute of Medicine (IOM) 91
Integrated Mentor Program in Addictions Research Training (IMPART) see IMPART program
interdisciplinary: approach 137–8; studies 21
interpersonal violence (IPV) 128

intersectionality 120–1, 122, 124, 127, 133
Intersections of Mental Health Perspectives in Addictions Research Training (IMPART) see IMPART program
interventions: for alcohol and tobacco use during pregnancy 153–4; behavioral 144; crisis 41; cultural 44; for domestic violence 128; evidence-based 120; housing 110; integrated vs. non-integrated 113; public health 143; for smoking reduction 146–7, 152; timing of 41; trauma-specific 112, 113; women-centered 154; for women with substance issues 116

Jellinek, Elvin M. 6
Johnson, Paul E. 210
Jones, Ken 88

Karen women 126–7, 129, 133n2
Kessel, Frank 13
Kitson, Alison L. 204, 206
knowledge: brokers 209–10; democratization of 163; Haudenosaunee 75; Indigenous 44, 69–75, 221; indigenous vs. Western 2; Iroquois 75; keepers 70, 72; from non-medical disciplines 91; production of 123, 128–30; relational aspects of 124; scientific 114–15; shared 127; synthesis of 209; transfer of 5; uptake 124; vernacular 209; Western 2, 44, 71–3
knowledge translation (KT) 101–3, 114, 124, 160, 161, 217, 221; challenges in 204; context of 205–6; defined 203, 208; evidence and 204–5; facilitation of 207–10; levels/stages of 208; translation of ideas 104
Kramlich, Debra 208

Lamaze, Fernand 86
Landry, Réjean 208
Lau, Evelyn 9–10
Linklater, Renee 44
logotherapy 171
Longboat, Dan 73

Mann, Barbara Alice 75
marginalization 8, 13, 87, 91–2, 107, 122, 124, 130; of smokers 192; see also women, marginalized
marijuana 11, 21

Marshall, Albert 44
Marshall, Murdena 44
Marxism 75, 122
Mason, Robin 99
Maté, Gabor 9, 220
maternal and child health 42
maternity care, integrated 90, 193
Maxxine Wright Community Health Centre 90
Meaning Management Theory (MMT) 159, 168, 171–3; as building blocks for transdisciplinarity 178–9; meaningfulness vs. meaninglessness 174–6; applied to transdisciplinarity 173–8
men: health issues of 219; with PTSD 110
menstrual cycle 53
mental health: and addiction 4, 21, 216; in addiction research 107; of marginalized women 107; of refugee women 127; and substance use 167, 172
mental health disorders 5; in FASD populations 61–2; and homelessness 109; substance use 50
mental health issues 5, 31, 36, 41, 77, 89; gender differences in 53; stress-related 57; and tobacco use during pregnancy 189; and violence against women 42; vulnerability to 53–4; of women 186
mental health treatment 42, 195; for women 40–4
mental illness 6–7; and addiction 20, 21; and poverty 108; understanding of 42
mentors and mentoring 22–3, 31, 179
methadone clinics 91
midwives 86
migration 124, 126, 127, 163; *see also* immigration
mindfulness 141
moralism: and addiction 3, 6, 8, 11, 140, 170, 207, 209; and substance use by pregnant women 80, 82–3, 87, 167, 186, 190; in public policy 184
morphine, and PAE 60
multidisciplinarity 98

National Association of Neonatal Nurses 85
National Health Services (UK) 206
National Institute for Health and Clinical Excellence (NICE) 148
National Institutes of Health (NIH) 11, 12
neo-Freudianism 8
neo-liberalism 131

neonatal: neonatal abstinence scoring system 88; neonatal withdrawal 80, 87, 92; neonatologists and neonatology 81, 89, 195; neonatology 89
Neonatal Abstinence Syndrome (NAS) 81, 88; as medical diagnosis 82–3; clinical case 89–91
neonatal intensive care units (NICUs) 77, 78; developmental care 85–6; factors affecting infant admission to 79; family-centered care in 83–5; transdisciplinarity in 81; and the Vermont Oxford Network 90; woman-centered care in 86–7
nervous system, sex differences in 98
neurobehavioural abnormalities 57
neurobiology 42–3, 62, 162; dysregulation of dopamine systems 51–2; neurodecolonization 43–4, 45; neurodevelopmental abnormalities 57; neuroendocrine function 62; neuromodulatory system 51; neuroplasticity 43; neuroscience 45, 50, 97–8; of substance use disorders and addiction 50–6
Nicolescu, Basarab 14
nicotine *see* tobacco
non-governmental organizations (NGOs) 126
nurses 137, 138, 195; community health 114; education and training of 80, 87, 92–3; *see also* nursing
nursing 172; scholarship in 122; *see also* nurses
Nutley, Sandra M. 205, 210
nutrition 54, 62; nutritionists 114; prenatal 56

obstetricians and obstetrics 86, 89, 195
occupational therapists 81
opioids: effects on infant outcomes 88; historical use of 82; legal status of 82; sex differences in response to 102; as teratogens 82; use and misuse of 80
orbitofrontal cortex 51–3
Orozco, Fadya 15
Ottawa Charter 131

pain: and addiction 101; and the brain-body link 77; cultural perceptions of 100–1; and FGM 99; sex differences in perception of 102
Palmer, Debra 208
parents: involvement in developmental care 86; involvement in family-centered

care 83–5; parenting skills and classes 41, 111; *see also* families
participatory action research (PAR) 131–2, 209
pedagogy, innovative approaches to 28–9
pediatric intensive care 82
pediatricians and pediatrics 89, 195
Peele, Stanton 6–7
peer parent counselors 81
perinatal health 89
pharmacists 163; pharmacotherapy 162
philosophy 8, 89, 122
physical assault 112; *see also* violence
physical health 110; and historical trauma 43
physical therapists 81
physicians 137, 195; pediatricians 195; obstetricians 86, 195; neonatologists 81, 195
policy-making: and alcohol use during pregnancy 189–91; application of evidence to 205; critical responses 191–2; effect on programming 184; factors influencing 185–7; improving gender equity in 194; iterative 222; options for 185; rigidity in 218; and tobacco use during pregnancy 187–9; transdisciplinary policy responses 192–6
polysubstance use 109, 110; *see also* substance use/abuse/dependence
Poole, Nancy 13
postcolonialism 122, 131
postnatal care 111
poststructuralism 122
post-traumatic stress disorder (PTSD) 38, 220–1; comorbidity with SUD 109–10, 113; diagnosis of 115; evidence-based treatment for 115; gender-specific patterns of 109; among homeless women and women in poverty 112; and psychosocial impairment 110; women with 116
Potenza, Mark N. 7
poverty: and addiction 216; and cognitive development 83; and infant health issues 79; and negative health outcomes 108; and social problems 107–8; and substance use during pregnancy 186, 189, 191, 193, 195; victimizing effects of 186
power: culture of 128; relations 123; structures 4
pregnancy *see* alcohol use during pregnancy; perinatal health care; smoking during pregnancy; substance use during pregnancy
PREGNETS 161
prenatal alcohol exposure (PAE) 57; and amphetamine sensitization 59; and the dopamine system 58–9; effects of stress 61; HPA axis 59–60; maternal/paternal 58; *see also* fetal alcohol spectrum disorder (FASD)
prenatal: health care 86, 111, 153; nutrition 56; substance exposure 80, 88
primary health care 42
progesterone 53; *see also* sex (gonadal) hormones
Promoting Action on Research Implementation in Health Services (PARiHS) framework 204
prostitution 112; *see also* sex work and workers
psychiatry and psychiatrists 8, 42, 109, 137, 156, 195
psychology and psychologists 6, 8, 10, 42, 72, 89, 109, 115, 171
psychosocial factors 20, 107; in substance use disorders 53
psychotherapy and psychotherapists 194; existentialism-based 171
public health 89, 91, 111, 171; views of addiction 207
Public Health Revitalization Act (US, 1993) 12
publication, transdisciplinary issues in 103
Pukall, Caroline 99

qualitative: data 98, 100; studies 148
quantitative studies 148

race/ethnicity, substance use 124, 146, 153, 167
racism 43; and addiction 216; and infant health issues 79
Rankin, Pauline 72
reflexivity 77, 120–1, 122, 125–6, 179; critical 122–3, 124, 127–31; critical reflection 131; in transdisciplinary research 130–2
refugees 121, 221
Reid, Stephen 10
research: on addiction 21, 107, 120–1; on alcohol addiction 21; biomedical 195; on brain structure, activity and neuroplasticity 43; education 21; and existential givens 179–80; on FAS and

FASD 62, 88; feminist participatory action 211; on Indigenous addiction 69–75; from non-medical disciplines 91; funding for 103, 104–5, 106, 160, 217–18; higher standards in 219; innovative training for 20–1; interdisciplinary 91–3; on marijuana addiction 21; neurobiology 43; on perinatal substance use outcomes 83; pillars of 23, 32, 39; qualitative vs. quantitative studies 148; sex and gender in 105, 219, 220; transdisciplinary 21, 130–2, 176, 211, 222; and Two-Eyed Seeing 74; use of in decision-making 205
residential schools 137
resilience, and vulnerability 61–2
risk environment: gendered 108; poverty as 111
risk factors: co-occurrence of 109; gendered 112; in marginalized populations 107
Robertson, James 83
Rosenfield, Patricia 13

Schaef, Anne Wilson 5, 6, 8, 221
sciences: addiction 89; biological 97, 170, 172; biology 10, 50, 54; biomedical 121, 123; cellular 21; clinical 123, 195; neurobiology 42, 50–6, 62, 162; neuroscience 45, 50, 62, 162; physiological 21; social 97, 121, 195; sociology 8, 10, 42, 89, 92, 122, 170–1, 172
secondary disabilities 57
second-hand smoke issues 151–2
Seeking Safety 42
self-efficacy 177
self-esteem 42, 151
self-harm 141
self-medication 9, 112
services: First Nation–specific 111; mental health 41; peer-run 41; responses to trauma and addiction 39; social 194; substance use 41; trauma-specific 41
sex (gonadal) hormones 38, 53, 60; regulation of 60
sexism 185
sex-related factors: and addiction 4–5, 216–17, 222; differences in response to opioids 102; as factor in health research and treatment 89, 90, 105, 216, 219, 220; impact of PAE 62; a nervous system differences 98; and substance use 12–13,
16, 50, 167; terminology related to 27; *see also* gender
sex work and workers 108, 109, 111, 112, 117
sexual assault 112; *see also* violence
sexual health counseling 111
sexual slavery 111
Sheridan, Joe 73
Sheway 90, 91
Smith, David 88
smoking during pregnancy *see* tobacco use during pregnancy
Snow, Mary E. 14
social: construction 82–3; environment, and substance use disorders 50, 54; issues 92; justice/injustice 89, 122, 127, 128, 131; sciences and scientists 97, 121, 195; support 38, 79, 220; trends, and transdisciplinarity 220–2; *see also* sociology
social work 8, 21, 42, 89, 121–2; and trauma treatment of Indigenous people 43–4
social workers 81, 114, 128, 137, 138, 163, 194, 195
sociologists 72, 170
sociology 8, 10, 42, 89, 92, 122, 170–1, 172; *see also* social sciences and scientists
spiritual health, and historical trauma 43
Start Thinking About Reducing Second-Hand Smoke 151
stigma: and substance use 185–7, 189, 190, 192; and use of tobacco during pregnancy 189
STOP program 161
stress: hypersensitivity to 60; and infant health issues 79; interaction with dopamine 56; maternal 56; neurobiological effects of 55; prenatal exposure to 60; responsivity 37–8, 54; stress-diathesis hypothesis 60; stressors, HPA axis response to 54; and substance use disorders 50; and substance use during pregnancy 193; system, dysregulation of 58
Substance Abuse and Mental Health Services Administration (SAMHSA) 40
substance use/abuse/dependence: among adolescent girls 146; associations with trauma, violence, and mental health issues 31; causal models of 170–1; criminalization of 11, 87, 185–6; and discrimination 170; effects of 107; hierarchical meanings systems of 172;

individual factors 169; interpersonal factors 169; and mental health 172; multi-substance use 4; and neonatal care 87; personality and 50; polysubstance use 109, 110; and poverty 108; and prejudice 185–7; problematic 27, 90, 167, 169–70; sex- and gender-based factors in 12, 16, 31, 172; and social class 124, 167; social context of 114–15, 169; stereotyping of 167; stigma attached to 170, 185–7, 189, 190, 192; terminology of 27; and trauma 36, 137, 172; understanding of 42; *see also* addiction

substance use disorders (SUDs): comorbidity with PTSD 109–10, 113; complexity of 50; etiology of 62; and FASD 57; gender differences in 53; gender-specific patterns of 109; and homelessness 109; neurobiology of 51–6; and sex- and gender-related variables 50; as stress response 55–6; transdisciplinary perspective 50–1; vulnerability to 51–3, 54, 59

substance use during pregnancy 78, 92, 111, 151, 153, 165–6, 185–7; as child abuse 186; legal response to 186

substance use workers 195

substantia nigra 51–2

suicidality 109, 110

sympathetic nervous system activation 36

systematic reviews 78; on alcohol use and pregnancy 152–3; on tobacco use and pregnancy 150–2; using transdisciplinarity 143–54

Tarnier, Stéphane 81

tax policy, and women's health 195

TEACH project 162

technology: in the IMPART program 23; and transdisciplinarity 218–19

testosterone 53, 60; *see also* sex (gonadal) hormones

Tipping Point 210

tobacco: addiction to 5–6; cessation programs 188, 195; control policies 10, 161, 189, 191–2; neural changes caused by 53; research on addiction to 21; teratogenic effects of 56

tobacco abuse and use 9, 38; by Inuit women 145

tobacco use during pregnancy 59, 144–6, 185, 187–9; by Aboriginal women 188–9; harmful effects of 187; interventions for 146–7; response to 188–9; social and economic contexts influencing 146; stigma associated with 189; transdisciplinary responses to 192–6; transdisciplinarity and systematic reviews 150–2; typical approaches to 146–7

Tobias, Virgil 70

training 5; for innovative research 20–1; for nurses 80

transdisciplinarity 13–16, 21, 29, 32–3; in academic studies 72; and addiction 117; in addiction treatment and research 120–1, 161–6; additive value for systematic reviews 150–3; advantages of 169; challenges of 173–8; defined 168; and FASD research 62; future of 159–60, 216–23; in higher research standards 219; in institutional structures 217–18; in knowledge translation 203–11; methodology of 97–8; need for common language 170; need for shared understanding of comprehensive models 170–1; in neonatal care 80; in neuroscience 97; practical application of 77–8; and problematic substance use 169–70; reflexivity and 123; and refugee services 127, 129; in social trends 220–2; and substance use disorders 50–1, 54; in systematic reviews 143–54; in technology and communication 218–19; three challenges for 170–1; Transdisciplinary Definitions of Addiction 26; *Transdisciplinary Public Health: Research, Education, and Practice* (Haire-Joshu and McBride) 15; Transdisciplinary Thesaurus of Addiction 27; and Two-Eyed Seeing 72–3; in universities 104; in the WCDVS study 40–2; *see also* transdisciplinary communities; transdisciplinary training benefits

transdisciplinary communities: innovative approaches to pedagogy 28–9; key factors for building 22–4; knowledge translation and transdisciplinary communication 25–8; need for communication in 25; supporting move towards collaboration and exchange 24–5

transdisciplinary training benefits 29; disciplinary and personal transformation 30–31; enhanced responsiveness to the complexities of addiction and its intersections 31–2

trauma: and Aboriginal women 125; and addiction 4, 5, 20, 21, 36–40, 45, 124, 129, 132, 162, 216; in addiction research 107; assessment of 115; as a bridge between neuroscience, clinical, population health and health services approaches 44–5; childhood 38, 112, 117, 137; discipline-based interpretations of 1; effects of 107; gendered 9, 37–40, 110, 113; as health factor 90; historical 43–4; history of 113; integration of into addiction responses 216; and poverty 108, 111; psychological 37; public familiarity with 220–1; recovery from 42; and the refugee experience 126–7; response to 36; and substance use 31, 137, 140, 167, 172; and substance use during pregnancy 189, 191, 193; understanding of 42; various perceptions of 27; and women's health 77, 153; *see also* post-traumatic stress disorder
trauma treatment 43–4
trauma-informed practices 42, 78, 195
treatment *see* addiction treatment; trauma treatment
Tupper, Kenneth W. 7
Two-Eyed Seeing approach 2, 44, 69–75, 221; gender issues in 73

unemployment 11, 108, 146
United States: obstetrical trends in 79; percent of women smoking during pregnancy 188

Van de Ven, Andrew H. 210
ventral striatum 52–3
ventral tegmental area (VTA) 51–2
Vermont Oxford Network (VON) 90
violence 5, 9, 41; and addiction 4, 5, 20, 21, 124, 129, 132, 216; and alcohol use during pregnancy 146; domestic 186, 194, 195; domestic partner 178; gender-based 9, 36, 108, 111, 112; in the health-care system 112; as health factor 90; and infant health issues 79; interpersonal 38–9, 127; intimate-partner 99; and poverty 108; in pregnancy 111; sexual 111, 221; structural 129; and substance use 31; and substance use during pregnancy 189, 191, 193; systemic 127; and women's health 153; *see also* violence against women
violence against women (VAW) 40, 42, 89, 99, 121, 127, 186–7

Violence Against Women (VAW) movement 128
vulnerability/vulnerabilities 92; gendered 112; psychological 171; and resilience 61–2

welfare benefits, and women's health 195
Wellness Framework 74
Wenger, Etienne 208
Western knowledge 2, 44, 71–3
Wilson, Sheri-D 10
withdrawal 56; in infants 88
woman-centered care 153; history of 86, 88; in NICU 86–7
Women Co-occurring Disorders and Violence Study (WCDVS) 39–42, 140
Women Want to Know project 192
women: and the AA experience 177; aboriginal 125, 137, 168, 188–9; and addiction 40–2, 77–8, 124; agency of 42; with alcohol disorders 40; with complex social challenges 84; C/S/R (*consumers* of mental health system services, *survivors* of violence and trauma, and/or in *recovery* from substance use problems) 40–2; disadvantaged 167–8; empowerment of 42, 86, 114, 165–6; exploitation of 108; fears of losing custody by 41; health issues of 117, 192; homeless 108–11; immigrant 126–7, 129, 133n2; Karen 126–7, 129, 133n2; marginalized 80, 92, 107, 108, 114, 116, 121, 125–30, 132; and mental health treatment 40–2, 186; post-partum 113; pregnant 39–40, 111–13, 146–7, 165–8; psychosocial health of 77; with PTSD 110; refugee 121, 126–7, 129, 133n2; safe housing for 112; self-determination of 86, 114; with severe mental illness 121; smoking during pregnancy by 145–7; Somali 100–1; and stress 56, 77; sub-groups of 151, 153; and substance use 31, 40, 109, 111, 116; support for 114; with trauma histories 113; value of as individuals 86; violence against 40, 42, 89, 99, 121, 127, 186–7; *see also* girls
women's health movement 86, 219
women's programs 91
women-centered care 86–7, 195
work conditions, and health issues 118
workplace diary 132
World Health Organization (WHO) 13, 191

Yellow Bird, Michael 43